J.S. BACH: THE VOCAL TEXTS IN ENGLISH TRANSLATION WITH COMMENTARY

J.S. BACH: THE VOCAL TEXTS IN ENGLISH TRANSLATION WITH COMMENTARY

Volume 1: *BWV 1-200*

Z. Philip Ambrose

Library of Congress Number:		2005902862
ISBN 10:	Hardcover	1-4134-4895-X
	Softcover	1-4134-4894-1
ISBN 13:	Hardcover	978-1-4134-4895-5
	Softcover	978-1-4134-4894-8

This book was printed in the United States of America.

To order additional copies of this book, contact:
Xlibris Corporation
1-888-795-4274
www.Xlibris.com
Orders@Xlibris.com
19976

CONTENTS

PREFACE

My translations of Bach's vocal works have been in circulation in various forms since the appearance of *The Texts to Johann Sebastian Bach's Church Cantatas* (Neuhausen-Stuttgart: Hänssler-Verlag, 1984. In 1997 *J.S. Bach: Texts of the Complete Vocal Works of Johann Sebastian Bach* were put online at ttp://www.uvm.edu/~classics/faculty/bach. Instead of merely referring to the "Vocal Texts," a more accurate title for the present publication might have been *J. S. Bach: The Extant Vocal Texts in English Translation with Commentary* respecting the fact that so much of Bach's works have disappeared and that Bach scholars continue to recover those losses. This version of my translations, however, should continue to be used in tandem with the online version, which itself will continue to be updated and will be the most convenient way to download texts and translations for program notes and the like. Because there are search engines at my online site (both to my translations and commentary and, through a link to the site of Walter F. Bischof, to the original texts), there is really no need to add an index here. Given the nature of my translation as explained in the *Introduction* (written in 1984), it would have been ideal to have the original German, Latin, or Italian texts set to the left of the English, but happily the original texts are now increasingly available.

It is a pleasure to thank those many users of the online site who have corresponded with me to convey their suggestions, queries, and encouragement. It would be impossible for me to thank adequately my daughter Julia Ambrose Viazmenski and her husband Alexei Viazmenski for their design and curatorship of the website during the past several years. Julia, *instar pietatis*, has now made all the many editorial adjustments required for the present publication.

Z. Philip Ambrose
Christmas 2003

INTRODUCTION

The present translation is offered to listeners, interpreters, and performers as a guide to the vocal works of Johann Sebastian Bach. Virtually the complete extant corpus, it includes the texts of lost compositions, but does not include untexted chorales. In not being intended primarily for singing, it differs from the two best known translations: Charles S. Terry, *J. S. Bach, Cantata Texts* (London, 1926; reprint, 1964) and Henry S. Drinker, *Texts of the Vocal Works of J. S. Bach* (New York, 1942-1943).

Two lessons from antiquity have influenced my approach to the translation of the works of Bach. The first has to do with the reliability of translation; the second, with the value and purpose of translation. One of the greatest concerted efforts of literary translation in antiquity was the Greek translation of the Hebrew Scriptures, the so-called Septuagint. Its value today rests partly on the fact that the sources it translates are older than any extant Hebrew versions. But the Septuagint had a certain negative result in the Greek-speaking Jewish and early Christian communities: Naive confidence in its reliabitly tended to suppress knowledge of the Hebrew (or Aramaic) original. Legends grew up about the veritably divine inspiration and miraculous agreement of the 72 (or 70) scholars thought to have been summoned to the island of Pharos near Alexandria by Ptolemy II Philadelphus (308-246 B.C.) for the task of translating the Jewish Law. Even though I have attempted to adhere closely to the word-order, metaphorical language, and sense of Bach's original texts, I would not tout the literalness of my translations. For my intention is not to leave readers content with the English version but to encourage them to consider the original.

The second example, from somewhat later antiquity, suggests to me the efficiency of translation as philology, by which I mean literary interpretation in the broadest sense. Lucius Apuleius, born c. 123 A.D. in North Africa in a Greek-speaking family, explaining in his introduction to the *Metamorphoses* that he first studied in Athens and then went to Rome to learn Latin, continues: "Behold I first crave and beg pardon lest I should happen to displease or offend any of you by the rude and rustic utterance of this strange and foreign language. Indeed this very change of language corresponds to the inconstant (i.e. changing) subject matter we undertake with our pen: we begin here a Grecian tale; reader attend; you will be delighted." In 1566 Apuleius' translator William Adlington writes: "But as Lucius Apuleius was changed into his human shape by a rose, the companions of Ulysses by great intercession, and Nebuchadnezzar by the continual prayers of Daniel, whereby they knew themselves and lived after a good and virtuous life: so can we never be restored to the right figure of ourselves, except we taste and eat the sweet rose of reason and virtue."[1] The transformation of Lucius from human to ass was for the purpose of enlightening the human. Apuleius implies that this movement through change to self-enlightenment is akin to his treatment of a Greek tale: its movement from Greek through the "rude and rustic utterance" of Latin for the purpose of illuminating the Greek mind of the author. To parody Adlington, a foreign language is the "sweet rose of reason" which returns Apuleius to his original form. Thus with this translation of the vocal texts of Bach the purpose is not to supplant, certainly not to upstage or obscure, but to enhance the original. And therewith let it be hoped that these translations of Bach's works may offer some service not only to the American or English or Japanese but even to the German listener, interpreter, or performer.

Several general problems posed by Bach's texts deserve special

---

[1] Reprinted in Apuleius, *The Golden Ass, being the Metamorphoses of Lucius Apuleius*, revised by S. Gaselee (Cambridge, U. S. A., and London: The Loeb Classical Library, 1915), p. xvii.

attention. First, their stylistic and formal variety: not only do they spring from over a dozen known and probably as many unknown poets, they also have the internal variety of their Biblical texts, chorales, recitatives, and arias. Second, many of the texts themselves, such as the hymns of Luther and Biblical passages, are translations from works which are known to English-speakers in other versions. A related difficulty is posed by the fact that at every moment Bach is himself translating these texts. Bach's music helps the translator understand the text, but in attempting to translate both the text and Bach's own musical translation of it I have been persuaded to depart sometimes from the most idiomatic English in order to maintain Bach's treatment of key words, the original meter, accent, and word- and phrase-breaks. I have thought the observance of these features more essential than the preservation of the rhyme-scheme, except in some of the secular cantatas. In the Evangelist's narrative in the Passions and the Christmas Oratorio exact syllabic equivalence with the original is impossible without doing violence to the familiar English form of the Biblical text. In the Latin texts of the Masses, without attempting syllabic equivalence with the original, I follow the style of the *American Book of Common Prayer* (1928), but translate directly from Bach's text since it differs occasionally from the *Missale Romanum*.

The spelling throughout is modern American (e.g., Savior, not Saviour). The vocabulary is contemporary but the style affects Handelian English. German *Du* and *Ihr* and related forms are translated throughout with the appropriate forms of *Thou* and *Ye*, but verbal morphology varies between such forms as "*giveth*" and "*gives*," depending upon metrical requirements. Punctuation frequently departs from that of the original without changing its meaning.

The translations are primarily based upon W. Neumann, *Sämtliche von Johann Sebastian Bach vertonte Texte* (Leipzig, 1974). They are numbered and ordered according to the catalogue of Schmieder (BWV) or, in the case of works for which the music is lost, according

to Neumann's Roman numerals. For historical and critical
information on each work I have consulted both Neumann's edition
of the texts and his *Handbuch der Kantaten Johann Sebastian Bachs*
(Leipzig, 1971); also Alfred Dürr's invaluable *Die Kantaten von Johann
Sebastian Bach* (Kassel, 1971) and the *Critical Commentaries* (*Kritischer
Bericht*) of the NBA. The original texts are reproduced from the
Kritischer Bericht. But when the *Kritischer Bericht* supplies no
transcription from the printed texts of lost works, I give one in the
original orthography (with corrections of obvious typographical
errors, mostly of punctuation). These transcriptions will provide, I
hope, an interesting contrast between original and modernized styles
of German spelling.

In the introductory material to each work, the following information
is given: 1. Occasion; 2. Author, if known, printed source, if any,
and facsimile, if available; 3. Biblical texts, hymn texts (with modern
printed source); 4. Date and place of first performance and of
revised versions, when known; parody relationships; 5. BG and
NBA editions. A Table of Occasions lists the Epistle and Gospel
lections for each sacred occasion and all works performed on each
occasion. The translation occasionally includes such subtitles as
Drama in Music, Dialogue, or Serenata. It also gives any Dramatis
Personae, with Bach's vocal assignments in parentheses. In chorale
cantatas the number of the verse of the hymn used verbatim is
given in square brackets (e.g. [Verse 7]). Biblical texts that establish a
principal theme for a cantata are indicated, as they frequently were
in the original printed editions, with the Latin word *Dictum* in square
brackets, preceded by Bach's musical treatment of the text and
followed in parentheses by Bach's vocal assignments as follows: 1.
Chorus [Dictum] (S, A, T, B) or 3. Aria [Dictum] (B). The assignment
of character, when known, is given as well: 2. Aria (S, B) Soul,
Jesus.

While the translation itself is intended to constitute a commentary on
the original, I explain in footnotes many proper and place names,
historical allusions to persons and events. Mere enthusiasm for the

texts has inspired me frequently to note subtle intentions of the poets, rhetorical figures, or parallel passages both from within Bach's corpus and from without, especially from such classical authors as Vergil, Horace, and Ovid.

The inspiration for this whole undertaking came from Professor Christoph Wolff. Since first suggesting the project in the late summer of 1979, he has helped me generously in both broad design and many details. I hope that others will yet find solutions to those passages in which I have not been up to the philological ideal he represents. Finally, I must confess that I would not have accepted Professor Wolff's challenge to wander awhile from the mainstream of classical studies without the encouragement of my companion in music, Professor Jane Ambrose. To her I dedicate this book.

The University of Vermont
Whitsuntide 1984
Burlington, Vermont

ABBREVIATIONS AND SIGNS

A = Alto

Anh. = Anhang (Supplement)

B = Bass

BG = *Bach-Gesamtausgabe*, published by the Bachgesellschaft, 1851-1899.

BJ = *Bach-Jahrbuch*, published by the Neue Bachgesellschaft (Leipzig, 1904ff.)

BWV = Wolfgang Schmieder, *Thematisch-systematisches Verzeichnis der Werke Joh. Seb. Bachs* (Leipzig, 1950)

[Dictum] = A Biblical text which provides a principal theme or idea of a cantata. This indication is not used for the Evangelist's Biblical narrative in the Passions or in such works as the Christmas Oratorio.

Dürr = Alfred Dürr, *Die Kantaten von Johann Sebastian Bach* (Kassel, 1971)

Facs = Facsimile

Fischer-Tümpel = Albert Fischer and W. Tümpel, *Das deutsche evangelische Kirchenlied des 17. Jahrhunderts* (Gütersloh, 1904-1916; reprint, Hildesheim: Georg Olms, 1960), Vols. I-VI

Krit. Bericht = *Kritischer Bericht* (see NBA)

NBA = Johann Sebastian Bach, *Neue Ausgabe sämtlicher Werke*, published by the Johann-Sebastian-Bach-Institut Göttigen and by the Bach-Archiv Leipzig (Kassel and Leipzig, 1954ff.)

NBG = Publications of the Neue Bachgesellschaft

Neumann Hb= Werner Neumann, *Handbuch der Kantaten Johann Sebastian Bachs*, 4th rev. ed. (Leipzig, 1971)

Neumann T = Werner Neumann, *Sämtliche von Johann Sebastian Bach vertonte Texte* (Leipzig, 1974)

OP = Originalpartitur (Original Score)

OSt = Originalstimmen (Original Parts)

PT = Printed Text

S = Soprano

Spitta = Philipp Spitta, *Johann Sebastian Bach* (Leipzig, 1873 and 1880); translated by Clara Bell and J. A. Fuller-Maitland (London, 1899; reprint New York: Dover, 1951).

T = Tenor

[Verse] = Movement in a chorale cantata based upon more than one movement of the same hymn. The number of the verse will be indicated, e.g. [Verse 6].

Wackernagel = Carl Eduard Philipp Wackernagel, *Das Deutsche Kirchenlied* (Leipzig, 1862-1877; reprint, Hildesheim: Georg Olms, 1964), Vols. I-IV.

→ = Parody from . . . to

← = Parody to . . . from

BIBLICAL ABBREVIATIONS

Acts = Acts

Am. = Amos

1 Chr. = 1 Chronicles

2 Chr. = 2 Chronicles

Col. = Colossians

1 Cor. = 1 Corinthians

Dan. = Daniel

Dt. = Deuteronomy

Ec. = Ecclesiastes

Ecclus. = Ecclesiasticus

Eph. = Ephesians

Est. = Esther

Ex. = Exodus

Ezek. = Ezekiel

Ezra = Ezra

Gal. = Galatians

Gen. = Genesis

Hab. = Habakkuk

Hag. = Haggai
Heb. = Hebrews
Hos. = Hosea
Is. = Isaiah
Jas. = James
Jer. = Jeremiah
Jg. = Judges
Jl. = Joel
Jn. = John
1 Jn. = 1 John
2 Jn. = 2 John
3 Jn. = 3 John
Job = Job
Jon. = Jonah
Jos. = Joshua
Jude = Jude
1 Kg. = 1 Kings
2 Kg. = 2 Kings
Lam. = Lamentations
Lev. = Leviticus
Lk. = Luke
Mal. = Malachi
Mic. = Micah
Mk. = Mark
Mt. = Matthew
Nah. = Nahum
Neh. = Nehemiah
Num. = Numbers
Ob. = Obadiah
1 Pet. = 1 Peter
2 Pet. = 2 Peter
Phil. = Philippians
Philem. = Philemon
Pr. = Proverbs
Ps. = Psalms
Rev. = Revelation

Rom. = *Romans*
Ru. = *Ruth*
1 Sam. = *1 Samuel*
2 Sam. = *2 Samuel*
S. of S. = *Song of Solomon*
1 Th. = *1 Thessalonians*
2 Th. = *2 Thessalonians*
1 Tim. = *1 Timothy*
2 Tim. = *2 Timothy*
Tit. = *Titus*
Zech. = *Zechariah*
Zeph. = *Zephaniah*

A TABLE OF OCCASIONS
FOR THE SACRED WORKS

This table gives with a brief summary the Epistle and Gospel for each Sunday and festival for which Bach composed a vocal work. The works performed appear in relative chronological order after each occasion.

SUNDAYS AND MAJOR HOLY DAYS

First Sunday in Advent: BWV 61, 62, 36.

    Rom. 13:11-14: Our Salvation is near.

    Mt. 21:1-9: Entrance into Jerusalem.

Second Sunday in Advent: BWV 70a.

    Rom. 15:4-13: The Ministry to the Gentiles.

    Lk. 21:25-36: The Second Coming of Christ.

Third Sunday in Advent: BWV 186a.

    1 *Cor.* 4:1-5: The Stewardship of the Apostles.

    Mt. 11:2-10: John in Prison.

Fourth Sunday in Advent: BWV 132, 147a.

    Phil. 4:4-7: Joy in the Lord.

    Jn. 1:19-28: The Testimony of John the Baptist.

Christmas Day (25 December): BWV 63, 91, 110, 197a, 248I, 191, (Vesper Service: 243).

    Tit. 2:11-14: The Grace of God is manifest.

    Or: *Is.* 9:2-7: To us a Child is born.

    Lk. 2:1-14: The Birth of Christ.

Second Day of Christmas (St. Stephen, Deacon and Martyr, 26 December): BWV 40, 121, 57, 248II.

Tit. 3:4-7: The Washing of Regeneration.

Or: *Acts* 6:8ff. and 7:54-59: The Martyrdom of Stephen.

Lk. 2:15-20: The Shepherds at the Manger.

Or: *Mt.* 23:34-39: The Slaying of the Prophets.

Third Day of Christmas (St. John, Apostle and Evangelist, 27 December): BWV 64, 133, 151, 248III.

Heb. 1:1-14: Christ is higher than the angels.

Jn. 1:1-14: In the beginning was the Word.

Sunday after Christmas Day (Last Sunday of the Civil Year, not present in every year): BWV 152, 122, 28.

Gal. 4:1-7: Christ frees us from the Law.

Lk. 2:33-40: Simeon and Anna's Words to Mary.

New Year's Day (Feast of the Circumcision and Naming of Christ, 1 January): BWV 190, 41, 16, 171, 248IV, 143, XVIII.

Gal. 3:23-29: By Faith we are children of God.

Lk. 2:21: The Circumcision and Naming of Christ.

Sunday after New Year's Day (not present in every year): BWV 153, 58, 248V.

1 *Pet.* 4:12-19: The Sufferings of Christ.

Mt. 2:13-23: The Flight into Egypt.

Epiphany (6 January): BWV 65, 123, 248VI.

Is. 60:1-6: The Conversion of the Gentiles.

Mt. 2:1-12: The Wise Men from the East.

First Sunday after Epiphany: BWV 154, 124, 32.

Rom. 12:1-6: The Christian Rules of Life.

Lk. 2:41-52: The Twelve-year-old Jesus in the Temple. Second Sunday after *Epiphany*: BWV 153, 3, 13.

Rom. 12:6-16: The Christian Rules of Life.

Jn. 2:1-11: The Marriage Feast at Cana.

Third Sunday after Epiphany (not present in every year): BWV 73, 111, 72, 156.

Rom. 12:17-21: The Christian Rules of Life.

Mt. 8:1-13: The Healing of a Leper and a Man with Palsy.

Fourth Sunday after Epiphany (not present in every year): BWV
81, 14.

> *Rom.* 13:8-10: Love is the Fulfilment of the Law.
>
> *Mt.* 8:23-27: Jesus calms the storm.

Septuagesima Sunday: BWV 144, 92, 84.

> > 1 *Cor.* 9:24-10:5: Preparation for the Footrace; The
> > Baptism of Moses in the Red Sea.
> >
> > *Mt.* 20:1-6: The Parable of the Workers in the
> > Vineyard.

Sexagesima Sunday: BWV 18, 181, 126.

> > 2 *Cor.* 11:19-12:9: The Perfection of God's Power in
> > Weakness.
> >
> > *Lk.* 8:4-15: The Parable of the Sower.

Estomihi (Quinquagesima, or the Sunday before Lent): BWV
22, 23, 127, 159.

> > 1 *Cor.* 13:1-13: The Praise of Charity.
> >
> > *Lk.* 18:31-43: The Journey to Jerusalem and Healing
> > of a Blind Man.

Oculi (Third Sunday in Lent): BWV 54, 80a.

> > *Eph.* 5:1-9: Exhortation to a Pure Life; the Children
> > of Light.
> >
> > *Lk.* 11:14-28: The Casting Out of a Devil. Palmarum
> > (Palm Sunday): BWV 182.
> >
> > *Phil.* 2:5-11: Be of one mind with Jesus.
> >
> > Or: 1 *Cor.* 11:23-32: The Last Supper.
> >
> > *Mt.* 21:1-9: Entrance into Jerusalem.

Good Friday: BWV 244, 245, 247.

The Passion of Christ

Easter Sunday: BWV 4, 31, 249.

> > 1 *Cor.* 5:6-8: Christ, our Paschal Lamb.
> >
> > *Mk.* 16:1-8: The Resurrection of Christ.

Second Day of Easter (Easter Monday): BWV 66, 6, VI.

> > *Acts* 10:34-43: Peter's Sermon to the Centurion
> > Cornelius on Christ's Resurrection.

Lk. 24:13-35: The Journey of the Disciples to Emmaus.

Third Day of Easter (Easter Tuesday): BWV 134, 145, 158.

Acts 13:26-33: Paul's Sermon in Antioch.

Lk. 24:36-47: Jesus appears to the Disciples in Jerusalem.

Quasimodogeniti (First Sunday after Easter): BWV 67, 42.

1 *Jn.* 5:4-10: Faith overcomes the World.

Jn. 20:19-31: Jesus appears to the Disciples and Doubting Thomas.

Misericordias Domini (Second Sunday after Easter or Good Shepherd Sunday): BWV 104, 85, 112.

1 *Pet.* 2:21-25: Jesus, the Shepherd of the Lost Sheep.

Jn. 10:12-16: The Good Shepherd.

Jubilate (Third Sunday after Easter): BWV 12, 103, 146.

1 *Pet.* 2:11-20: The Duties of God's Servants to God and to Human Ordinance.

Jn. 16:16-23: Your Sorrow shall be turned into Joy.

Cantate (Fourth Sunday after Easter): BWV 166, 108.

Jas. 1:17-21: All perfect Gifts come from above.

Jn. 16:5-15: Jesus departeth, the Comforter cometh.

Rogate (Fifth Sunday after Easter or Rogation Sunday): BWV 86, 87.

Jas. 1:22-27: Be not Hearers, but Doers of the Word.

Jn. 16:23-30: On Prayer in Jesus' Name.

Ascension Day (sometimes called Holy Thursday): BWV 37, 128, 43, 11.

Acts 1:1-11: The Final Commission and Ascension of Jesus.

Mk. 16:14-20: The Commandment to Baptize and the Ascension.

Exaudi (The Sunday after Ascension Day): BWV 44, 183.

1 *Pet.* 4:8-11: On Christian Service in Good Works.

Jn. 15:26-16:4: The Prediction of the Persecution of the Disciples.

First Day of Pentecost (Whitsunday): BWV 172, 59, 74, 34.

> *Acts* 2:1-13: The Descent and Appearance of the Holy Ghost.

> *Jn.* 14:23-31: If ye love me, keep my commandments.

Second Day of Pentecost (Monday in Whitsun Week): BWV 173, 68, 174.

> *Acts* 10:42-48: The End of Peter's Sermon to Cornelius and the Baptism of the Gentiles.

> *Jn.* 3:16-21: God so loved the world, that he gave his only-begotten Son.

Third Day of Pentecost (Tuesday in Whitsun Week): BWV 184, 175.

> *Acts* 8:14-17: The Reception of the Holy Ghost in Samaria.

> *Jn.* 10:1-11: The Good Shepherd.

Trinity Sunday: BWV 165, 194, 176, 129.

> *Rom.* 11:33-36: God's Wisdom.

> *Jn.* 3:1-5: Jesus's Conversation with Nicodemus.

First Sunday after Trinity: BWV 54 (also Oculi), 75, 20, 39.

> 1 *Jn.* 4:16-21: God is Love.

> *Lk.* 16:19-31: Dives and Lazarus.

Second Sunday after Trinity: BWV 76, 2.

> 1 *Jn.* 3:13-18: On Brotherly Love.

> *Lk.* 14:16-24: The Parable of the Great Supper.

Third Sunday after Trinity: BWV 21, 135, 177 (also Fourth Sunday after Trinity).

> 1 *Pet.* 5:6-11: Cast your care upon God.

> *Lk.* 15:1-10: The Parables of the Lost Sheep and the Lost Coin.

Fourth Sunday after Trinity: BWV 185, 24, 177.

> *Rom.* 8:18-23: Salvation through the Hope of the Holy Spirit.

> *Lk.* 6:36-42: Be merciful; Judge not, and ye shall not be judged.

Fifth Sunday after Trinity: BWV 93, Neumeister's *Der Segen des Herrn machet reich ohne Mühe*, 88.

1 *Pet.* 3:8-15: Patience in Suffering.

Lk. 5:1-11: Peter's Miraculous Draught of Fishes.

Sixth Sunday after Trinity: Neumeister's *Wer sich rächet, an dem wird sich der Herr wieder rächen*, BWV 170, 9.

    Rom. 6:3-11: Deliverance from Sin through Christ's Death.

    Mt. 5:20-26: Christ's Reinterpretation of the Law.

Seventh Sunday after Trinity: BWV 54 (Oculi), 186, 107, 187, XVII.

    Rom. 6:19-23: The Fruits of the Service of God.

    Mk. 8:1-9: The Feeding of the Four Thousand.

Eighth Sunday after Trinity: BWV 136, 178, 45.

    Rom. 8:12-17: Those led by the Spirit of God are the sons of God.

    Mt. 7:15-23: The Warning against False Prophets.

Ninth Sunday after Trinity: BWV 105, 94, 168.

    1 *Cor.* 10:6-13: Warning against Idolatry and Smugness.

    Lk. 16:1-9: The Parable of the Unjust Steward.

Tenth Sunday after Trinity: BWV 46, 101, 102.

    1 *Cor.* 12:1-11: Concerning Spiritual Gifts.

    Lk. 41-48: The Prophecy of the Destruction of Jerusalem; the Driving-out of the Merchants from the Temple.

Eleventh Sunday after Trinity: BWV 199, 179, 113.

    1 *Cor.* 15:1-10: The Resurrection of Christ and the Apostolic Mission of Paul.

    Lk. 18:9-14: The Parable of the Pharisee and the Publican.

Twelfth Sunday after Trinity: BWV 69a, 137, 35, 69.

    2 *Cor.* 3:4-11: The Letter killeth, but the Spirit giveth life.

    Mk. 7: 31-37: The Healing of the Deafmute.

Thirteenth Sunday after Trinity: BWV 77, 33, 164.

    Gal. 3:15-22: The Promise to Abraham and the Law.

    Lk. 10:23-37: The Good Samaritan.

Fourteenth Sunday after Trinity: BWV 25, 78, 17.

> *Gal.* 5:16-24: The Works of the Flesh and the Fruits of the Spirit.

> *Lk.* 17:11-19: The Healing of Ten Lepers.

Fifteenth Sunday after Trinity: BWV 138, 99, 51.

> *Gal.* 5:25-6:10: Exhortation to Gentleness and Goodness.

> *Mt.* 6:24-34: Be not anxious for the morrow.

Sixteenth Sunday after Trinity: BWV 161, 8, 27.

> *Eph.* 3:13-21: Paul prays for the strengthening of the faith of the Ephesians.

> *Lk.* 7:11-17: The Young Man of Nain Brought Back to Life.

Seventeenth Sunday after Trinity: BWV 148, 114, 47.

> *Eph.* 4:1-6: Exhortation to Unity of the Spirit in the Bond of Peace.

> *Lk.* 14:1-11: The Healing of the Man with the Dropsy.

Eighteenth Sunday after Trinity: BWV 96, 169.

> 1 *Cor.* 1:4-9: Paul's Thanksgiving for the Grace of God Given to the Corinthians.

> *Mt.* 22:34-46: The First and Great Commandment; David's "Son" and David's "Lord."

Nineteenth Sunday after Trinity: BWV 48, 5, 56.

> *Eph.* 4:22-28: The Renewal in the Spirit of the Mind.

> *Mt.* 9:1-8: The Healing of the Man with the Palsy.

Twentieth Sunday after Trinity: BWV 54 (also Oculi), 162, 180, 49.

> *Eph.* 5:5-21: Submit yourselves one to another in the fear of God.

> *Mt.* 22:1-14: The King's Wedding Banquet for his Son; Many are called, but few are chosen.

Twenty-first Sunday after Trinity: BWV 109, 38, 98, 188.

> *Eph.* 6:10-17: Put on the whole armor of God.

> *Jn.* 4:47-54: The Healing of the Son of a Nobleman at Capernaum.

Twenty-second Sunday after Trinity: BWV 89, 115, 55.

    Phil. 1:3-11: Paul's Prayer for the Philippians.

    Mt. 18:23-35: The Parable of the Unfaithful Servant.

Twenty-third Sunday after Trinity: BWV 163, 139, 52.

    Phil. 3:17-21: Our citizenship is in heaven.

    Mt. 22:15-22: Deceitful Pharisees; the Parable of the Tribute Penny of Caesar.

Twenty-fourth Sunday after Trinity: BWV 60,.

    Col. 1:9-14: Paul's Prayer for the Colossians.

    Mt. 9:18-26: The Raising of Jairus' Daughter.

Twenty-fifth Sunday after Trinity: BWV 90, 116.

    1 *Th.* 4:13-18: The Coming of Christ and the Raising of the Dead.

    Mt. 24:15-28: The Coming of Christ, the End of the World.

Twenty-sixth Sunday after Trinity: BWV 70.

    2 *Pet.* 3:3-13: The Certainty of Christ's Coming.

    Mt. 25:31-46: Jesus' Description of the Last Judgment.

Twenty-seventh Sunday after Trinity: BWV 140.

    1 *Th.* 5:1-11: Preparation for the Last Judgment.

    Mt. 25:1-13: The Parable of the Ten Virgins.

FEASTS OF THE BLESSED VIRGIN MARY

The Purification (The Presentation of Christ in the Temple, 2 February): BWV 161 (also 16 Sunday after Trinity), 83, 125, 82, 157, 200, 158 (also 3rd Day of Easter).

    Mal. 3:1-4: The Lord shall suddenly come to his temple.

    Lk. 2:22-32: The Presentation of Jesus in the Temple and the Song of Simeon.

The Annunciation (25 March): BWV 182 (also *Palmarum*), *Siehe, eine Jungfrau ist schwanger,* 1.

    Is. 7:10-16: The Prophecy of the Birth of the Messiah.

Lk. 1:26-38: The Angel Gabriel announces the birth
of Jesus to Mary.

The Visitation (2 July): BWV 147, 10, *Meine Seele erhebt den
Herrn.*

> *Is.* 11:1-5: The Prophecy of the Messiah.
>
> *Lk.* 1:39-56: Elizabeth's Salutation to Mary and
> Mary's Song of Praise.

FEASTS OF THE SAINTS AND OTHER SPECIAL OCCASIONS

The Nativity of St. John the Baptist (June 24): BWV 167, 7,
Gelobet sei der Herr, der Israel, 30.

> *Is.* 40:1-5: The Voice of One Crying in the Wilderness.
>
> *Lk.* 1:57-80: The Birth of John and Zacharia's Song
> of Praise.

St. Michael and All Angels (29 September): BWV 130, 19, 149,
50.

> *Rev.* 12:7-12: Michael's Battle with the Dragon.
>
> *Mt.* 18:1-11: The Angels of Children in Heaven.

Reformation (31 October): BWV 76 (also 2nd Sunday after
Trinity, 80, 79.

> 2 *Th.* 2:3-8: Steadfastness against the Lawless One.
>
> *Rev.* 14:6-8: Exhortation to Fear God.

LOCAL OCCASIONS

Wedding: BWV 196, XIV (Anh. 14), 34a, 120a, 195, 197.

Dedication of an Organ: BWV 194.

*Jubilee of the 200th Anniversary of the Augsburg Confession
(25-27 June 1730):* BWV 190a, 120b, XVIb (Anh.
4).

Funeral: BWV 106, 157 (also *The Purification*), 198, 244a,
XXVII (Anh. 16), XX (Anh. 17), 226, ?227, ?228.

Per ogni tempo (For Any Occasion): BWV 21, 51, ?100.

Unspecified Occasion: BWV 131, XIX (223), 150, XIII (Anh.

5), XXI (Anh. 15), 192, 100, 97, 117, 118, 225, ?227,
?228, 229, 230, 232, 233, 234, (242), 235, 236, 237, 238,
239, 240, 241.

A TABLE OF OCCASIONS FOR SECULAR WORKS

The works performed for each type of occasion are listed in relative chronological order.

Inauguration of the New Town Council.
> Mühlhausen: BWV 71, XXIV.
> Leipzig: BWV 119, 137 (also 12th Sunday after Trinity), XVIa, 193, 120, XI, 29, V, 69.

Ceremony for Members of Noble Houses: BWV 208, 66a, 134a, IX (Anh. 6), XII (Anh. 7), XXII, 173a, 184a, 194a, XXIII (Anh. 8), 249a, 36a, X (Anh. 9), 193a, II (Anh. 11), IV (Anh. 12), 213, 214, 205a, 215, 206, 207a, XV (Anh. 13), 208a.

Ceremony for the University and Members of the University: XXVI, BWV 205, 207, 36b.

Ceremony for School and Council: BWV 36c, 216a, III (Anh.18), VIII (Anh. 19).

Homage to Nobility and Townspeople: XXV, BWV 249b, 209, VII (Anh. 10), 30a, 210a, 212.

Marriage Celebration: BWV 202, I, 216, 210.

Unspecified Occasion : BWV 204, 201, 211, 203.

CANTATAS

BWV 1 **Wie schön leuchtet der Morgenstern**

The Annunciation of the Blessed Virgin Mary.

Poet unknown.

1. Philipp Nicolai, verse 1 of the hymn, 1599; 2. based on verse 2; 3. based on verse 3; 4. based on verses 4 and 5; 5. based on verse 6; 6. verse 7, the final verse of the hymn.

25 March 1725, Leipzig.

BG 1; NBA I/28.

1. Chorus [Verse 1] (S, A, T, B)

How beauteous beams the morning star
With truth and blessing from the Lord,
The darling root of Jesse!
Thou, David's son of Jacob's stem,
My bridegroom and my royal king,
Art of my heart the master,
Lovely,
Kindly,
Bright and glorious, great and righteous, rich in blessings,
High and most richly exalted.

2. Recit. (T)

O thou true Son of Mary and of God,
O thou the king of all the chosen,
How sweet to us this word of life,
By which e'en earliest patriarchs
Both years and days did number,
Which Gabriel with gladness there
In Bethlehem did promise!
O sweet delight, O heav'nly bread,
Which neither grave, nor harm, nor death
From these our hearts can sunder.

3. Aria (S)

O fill now, ye flames, both divine and celestial,
The breast which to thee doth in faith ever strive!
The souls here perceive now the strongest of feelings
Of love most impassioned
And savor on earth the celestial joy.

4. Recit. (B)

No earthly gloss, no fleshly light
Could ever stir my soul;
A sign of joy to me from God has risen,
For now a perfect gift,
The Savior's flesh and blood,
Is for refreshment here.
So must, indeed,
This all-excelling blessing,
To us eternally ordained
And which our faith doth now embrace,
To thanks and praise bestir us.

5. Aria (T)

Let our voice and strings resounding
Unto thee
Evermore
Thanks and sacrifice make ready.
Heart and spirit are uplifted,
All life long
And with song,
Mighty king, to bring thee honor.

6. Chorus [Verse 7] (S, A, T, B)

I am, indeed, so truly glad
My treasure is the A and O,
Beginning and the ending;
He will, indeed, the praise be his,
Receive me in his paradise,
For this my hands are clapping
Amen!
Amen!
Come, thou lovely crown of gladness, be not tarry,
I await thee with great longing.

BWV 2 **Ach Gott, vom Himmel sieh darein**

Second Sunday after Trinity.

Poet unknown.

1. Martin Luther, verse 1 of the hymn, based on *Ps.* 12, 1524 (Wackernagel, III, #3); 2-5. based on verses 2-5; 6. verse 6 of the hymn.

18 June 1724, Leipzig.

BG 1; NBA I/16.

---

1. Chorus [Verse 1] (S, A, T, B)

Ah God, from heaven look on us
And grant us yet thy mercy!
How few are found thy saints to be,
Forsaken are we wretches;
Thy word is not upheld as true,
And faith is also now quite dead
Among all mankind's children.

2. Recit. (T)

They teach a vain and false deceit,[1]
Which is to God and all his truth opposed;
And what the willful mind conceiveth,
—O sorrow which the church so sorely vexeth—
That must usurp the Bible's place.
The one now chooseth this, the other that,
And reason's foolishness is their full scope.
They are quite like the tombs of dead men,
Which, though they may be outward fair,
Mere stench and mould contain within them
And all uncleanness show when opened.[2]

3. Aria (A)

God, blot out all teachings
Which thy word pervert now!

          Check, indeed, all heresy
          And all the rabble spirits;

For they speak out free of dread
Gainst him who seeks to rule us!

4. Recit. (B)

The wretched are confused,[3]
Their sighing "Ah," their anxious mourning
Amidst such cross and woe,
Through which the foe to godly souls deals torture,
Doth now the gracious ear of God Almighty reach.
To this saith God: I must their helper be!
I have their weeping heard,
Salvation's rosy morn,
The purest truth's own radiant sunshine bright
Shall them with newfound strength,
The source of life and hope,
Refreshen and make glad.
I will take pity on their suff'ring,
My healing word shall strength be to the wretched.

5. Aria (T)

The fire doth make the silver pure,
The cross the word's great truth revealeth.

Therefore a Christian must unceasing
His cross and woe with patience bear.

6. Chorale [Verse 6] (S, A, T, B)

That[4] wouldst thou, God, untainted keep
Before this wicked people;
And us into thy care commend,
Lest it in us be twisted.
The godless crowd doth us surround,

In whom such wanton people are
Within thy folk exalted.

---

1. This line is verbatim from the hymn.
2. Cf. *Mt.* 23:27.
3. This line is verbatim from the hymn.
4. I.e., the "word."

BWV 3 **Ach Gott, wie manches Herzeleid**

Second Sunday after Epiphany.

Poet unknown.

1. Martin Moller, verse 1 of the hymn, 1587, after Bernard of
Clairvaux, "Jesu dulcis memoria" (Wackernagel, I, #38); 2. verse 2
with interpolated recitative; 3-5. based freely on verses 3-7, 10, 15,
and 16; 6. verse 18 of the hymn.

14 January 1725, Leipzig.

BG 1; NBA I/15.

---

1. Chorus [Verse 1] (S, A, T, B)

Ah God, how oft a heartfelt grief
Confronteth me within these days!
The narrow path is sorrow-filled
Which I to heaven travel must.

2. Chorale [Verse 2] (S, A, T, B) and Recit. (T, A, S, B)

(S, A, T, B)
How hard it is for flesh and blood

(T)
It but for earthly goods and vain things striveth
And neither God nor heaven heedeth,
To be forced to eternal good![1]

(A)
Since thou, O Jesus, now art all to me,
And yet my flesh so stubbornly resists.
Where shall I then my refuge take?

(S)
The flesh is weak, the spirit strong;
So help thou me, thou who my heart dost know.
To thee, O Jesus, I incline.

(B)
Who in thy help and in thy counsel trusts
Indeed hath ne'er on false foundation built;
Since thou to all the world art come to help us
And hast our flesh upon thee taken,
Thy dying shall redeem us
From everlasting ruin.
So savor now a spirit ever faithful
The Savior's graciousness and favor.

3. Aria (B)

Though I feel fear of hell and pain,
Yet must steadfast within my bosom
A truly joyful heaven be.

I need but Jesus' name once utter,
Who can dispel unmeasured sorrows
As though a gentle mist dividing.

4. Recit. (T)

Though both my flesh and soul may languish,
If thou art, Jesus, mine
And I am thine,
I will not heed it.
Thy truthful mouth
And all thy boundless loving,
Which never changed abides forever,
Preserve for me that ancient bond,
Which now my breast with exultation filleth
And even fear of death, the grave's own terror, stilleth.
Though dearth and famine soon from every side oppress,
My Jesus will my wealth and treasure be.

5. Aria (S, A)

When sorrow round me presses,
I will with joyfulness
My song lift unto Jesus.

My cross doth Jesus carry,
So I'll devoutly say now:
It serves me best in every hour.[2]

6. Chorale [Verse 18] (S, A, T, B)

If thou my heart in faith keep pure,
I'll live and die in thee alone.

Jesu, my strength, hear my desire,
O Savior mine, I'd be with thee.

[1.]   An alternate version of this line from a Dresden hymnbook of 1725 is
       cited by Neumann: *sich zwingen zu dem ewgen Gut.*, which avoids the
       heterodyne accentuation of Bach's text.
[2.]   This line is verbatim from the hymn.

BWV 4 **Christ lag in Todes Banden**

First Day of Easter.

Martin Luther, the eight verses of the hymn, 1524 (Wackernagel, III, #15).

Ca. 1707, certainly before 1714.

BG 1; NBA I/9.

---

1. Sinfonia

2. Verse 1 (S, A, T, B)

Christ lay to death in bondage,
For all our sins surrendered;
He is once more arisen
And hath us brought true life now;
For this shall we joyful be,
God giving praise and gratitude
And singing hallelujah.
Hallelujah!

3. Verse 2 (S, A)

That death no one could subdue
Amongst all mankind's children;
This was all caused by our sin,
No innocence was found then.
From this came, then, death so quick
And ruled over us with force,
Held us in his realm as captives.
Hallelujah!

4. Verse 3 (T)

Jesus Christ is God's own Son,
To our abode he cometh
And hath all sin now set aside,
Whereby from death is taken
All his rule and all his might;
Here bideth nought but death's mere form,
His sting hath fully perished.
Hallelujah!

5. Verse 4 (S, A, T, B)

It was an awesome thing that strife,
When death and life[1] did wrestle;
And life did the victory win,
By life hath death been swallowed.
The Scripture foretold it so,[2]
How one death the other ate;
To scorn hath now death been given.
Hallelujah!

6. Verse 5 (B)

Here is the spotless Easter lamb,
Whereof God hath commanded;
It is high on the cross's branch
In ardent love now burning;
The blood signeth now our door,
Our faith doth it to death display,
The strangler can us no more injure.
Hallelujah!

7. Verse 6 (S, T)

So let us keep the great high feast
With heartfelt joy and pleasure,
Which us the Lord makes manifest;
He is himself the sunlight,
And through his own shining grace
Entirely fills our hearts with light,
The sin-filled night now hath vanished.
Hallelujah!

8. Verse 7 (S, A, T, B)

We eat now and live indeed
On this true bread of Easter;
The ancient leaven shall not
Bide with the word of blessing;
Christ would be our sustenance
And nourish the soul alone,
For faith would on none other live.
Hallelujah!

[1.] This and several lines of this hymn have heterodyne meter, i.e., have falsely
accented words. Here *Leben* is accented on the second syllable. Perhaps to

correct this *da* or *das* is added after *Leben* in some parts. Where so, translate: "And life did then the victory win" or "And life, it did the victory win."

2.   All parts but the cantus firmus have *verkündiget* instead of *verkündigt*. With the former translate: "The Scripture foretold of it so."

BWV 5 **Wo soll ich fliehen hin**

Nineteenth Sunday after Trinity.

Poet unknown.

1. Johann Heermann, verse 1 of the hymn, 1630 (Fischer-Tümpel, I, #322); 2-6. based loosely on the inner verses; 7. verse 11 of the hymn.

15 October 1724, Leipzig.

BG 1; NBA I/24.

1. Chorus [Verse 1] (S, A, T, B)

Where shall I refuge find,
For I am burdened low
By sins both great and many?
Where shall I find salvation?
Were all the world here gathered,
My fear it would not vanquish.

2. Recit. (B)

Chaotic sin hath me not merely stained,
It hath, much worse, my soul completely veiled.

God surely would have banished me as sullied;
But since a drop of holy blood
Such mighty wonders doth,
I can still unrejected bide here.
Those wounds are now an open sea,
Wherein I may sink my transgressions,
And when I steer my course into these waters,
Then doth he me of all my stains make free.

3. Aria (T)

Pour forth thine abundance, thou fountain immortal,
Ah, well up with blood-streaming rivers o'er me!

> My heart doth perceive here its moment of comfort,
> Now sink all my burdensome sins to the bottom,
> It purgeth the sin-ridden stains from itself.

4. Recit. (A) with Instrum. Chorale

My faithful Savior comforts me,
Let now within the tomb be buried
All wrongs I have committed;[1]
Though my transgressions be so great,
He makes me free and safe.
When faithful people refuge find beside him,
Shall fear and grief
No longer danger bring
And in a trice shall vanish.
Their spirit's store, their highest wealth
Is Jesus' very priceless blood;
It is their shield gainst devil, death and error;
In it shall they have victory.

5. Aria (B)

Grow silent, host of hell,
Thou mak'st me not afraid!

> If I this blood now show thee,
> Thou must at once be silent,
> For this in God I dare.

6. Recit. (S)

I am, indeed, the world's mere smallest part,
And since that blood's rare liquid hath
Its boundless mighty power
Preserved intact,
So that each drop, however small it be,
Can all the world make clean
Of its transgressions,
Then let thy blood
Upon me bring no ruin,
And me so benefit,
That I, then, heaven may inherit.

7. Chorale [Verse 11] (S, A, T, B)

Lead e'en my heart and will
Through thine own Spirit hence,
That I may shun all perils
Which me from thee could sever,
And I of thine own body
A member bide forever.

[1.]   This line is verbatim from the hymn.

BWV 6 **Bleib bei uns, denn es will Abend werden**

The Second Day of Easter (Easter Monday).

Poet unknown (Christian Weiss?, see Dürr, pp. 42-43).

1. *Lk.* 24:29; 3. the first stanza: Philipp Melanchthon, "Ach bleib bei uns, Herr Jesus Christ," 1579 (the German version of "Vespera iam venit"); the second stanza: Nikolaus Selnecker, "In dieser letzt'n betrübten Zeit," 1572 (Wackernagel, IV, #392); 6. Martin Luther, verse 2 of "Erhalt uns, Herr, bei deinem Wort," 1542 (Wackernagel, III, #1482).

2 April 1725, Leipzig.

BG 1; NBA I/10.

---

1. Chorus [Dictum] (S, A, T, B)

Bide with us, for it will soon be evening, and the day is now declining.

2. Aria (A)

High-exalted Son of God,
Let it thee not be unwelcome
That we now before thy throne
A petition lay before thee:
Bide, oh, bide for us our light,
For the darkness doth steal in.

3. Chorale (S)

Oh, bide with us, Lord Jesus Christ,
For now the evening is at hand,
Thy godly word, that radiant light,
Let in our midst, yea, never fade.
Within this recent time of woe
Grant us, O Lord, steadfastness sure,
That we thy word and sacrament
Keep ever pure until our end.

4. Recit. (B)

Here hath the darkness now
Attained the upper hand in many quarters.
But wherefore is this come upon us?
The cause is simply that the humble and the mighty
Keep not in righteousness
Before thee, God, their pathway
And violate their duty now as Christians.
Thus hast thou e'en the lamp stands overtunéd.[1]

5. Aria (T)

Jesus, keep our sights upon thee,
That we not
Walk upon the sinful pathway.
Let the light
Of thy word o'er us shine brighter,
And forever grant thy favor.

6. Chorale (S, A, T, B)

Reveal thy might, Lord Jesus Christ,
O thou who art the Lord of Lords;

Protect thy wretched Christian folk,
That they praise thee eternally.

---

1.   Cf. *Rev.* 2:5.

BWV 7 **Christ unser Herr zum Jordan kam**

St. John the Baptist.

Poet unknown.

1. Martin Luther, verse 1 of the hymn, 1541 (Wackernagel, I, #218);
2-6. based upon verses 2-6; 7. verse 7 of the hymn.

24 June 1724, Leipzig.

BG 1; NBA I/29.

---

1. Chorus [Verse 1] (S, A, T, B)

Christ did, our Lord, to Jordan come,
His Father's will fulfilling,
And from Saint John baptism took,
His work and charge to accomplish;
Here would he found for us a bath
To wash us clean from error,
To drown as well our bitter death
In his own blood and anguish;
A life restored it gave us.

2. Aria (B)

Mark and hear, O mankind's children,
What God did baptism call.

> True, there must be water here,
> But mere water not alone.
> God's word and Holy Ghost
> Bathes and purifies the sinners.

3. Recit. (T)

This hath God shown
In words and in examples clear to all;
At Jordan's bank the Father plainly let
His voice resound while Christ was being baptized;
He said: This is my own dear Son,[1]
In whom I have now found great pleasure;[2]
He is from heaven's lofty throne
To help the world
In meek and humble form descended
And hath the flesh and blood
Of mankind's children to him taken;
Him take ye now as your Redeemer true
And listen to his precious teaching!

4. Aria (T)

The Father's voice itself resounded,
The Son, who us with blood did buy,
Was as a very man baptized.
The Spirit came, a dove appearing,
So that our faith would never doubt that
It was the Holy Trinity
Which gave baptism unto us.

5. Recit. (B)

When Jesus there endured his passion
And had been raised again,
And from this world would to his Father go,
Spake he to his disciples:
Go forth to all the world and preach to all the gentiles,
He who believes and is baptized on earth now
Shall then be justified and blessed.[3]

6. Aria (A)

Mankind, trust now in this mercy,
That ye not in error die,
Nor in hell's foul pit decay!
Human works and sanctity[4]
Never count before God's throne.
Sins are ours innately given,
We are lost by our own nature;
Faith and baptism[5] make them clean
That they not perdition bring.

7. Chorale (S, A, T, B)

The eye alone the water sees,
As men pour out the water,
But faith alone the power perceives
Christ Jesus' blood hath given;
For faith there is a sea of red
By Christ's own blood now colored,
Which all transgressions healeth well
Which Adam hath bequeathed us
And by ourselves committed.

[1.] This line is almost verbatim from verse 3 of Luther's hymn.

[2.] Cf. *Mt.* 3:17, *Mk.* 1:11, and *Lk.* 3:22.

3. Cf. *Mt.* 28:19 and *Mk.* 16:6.

4. Cf. verse 5 of Luther's hymn: "Nichts hilft sein eigne Heiligkeit."

5. OSt and P also have *Liebe* 'love' instead of *Taufe* 'baptism.' Translate: "Faith and love shall make them clean."

BWV 8 **Liebster Gott, wenn werd ich sterben?**

Sixteenth Sunday after Trinity.

Poet unknown.

1. Caspar Neumann, verse 1 of the hymn, 1697; 2-5. based freely on verses 2-4; 6. verse 6, the final verse, of the hymn.

24 September 1724, Leipzig; transposed from E Major to D Major for a performance in the 1740's.

BG 1; NBA I/23.

1. Chorus [Verse 1] (S, A, T, B)

Dearest God, when will my death be?
Now my days run ever on,
And the heirs of the old Adam,
In whose number I, too, am,
Have this for their legacy,
That they for a little while,
Poor and wretched, earth inhabit
And then are with earth united.

2. Aria (T)

Why wouldst thou then, my soul, be frightened
If that my final hour should strike?

Each day my body draweth earthward,
And there it must its rest discover
Where are so many thousands laid.

3. Recit. (A)

Indeed my weak heart feels
Fear, worry, pain:
Where will my body rest discover?
Who will my soul that day
From its confining yoke of sin
Bring freedom and deliverance?
My goods will be dispersed,
And whither will then all my loved ones
Amid their sad despair
Be torn and banished?

4. Aria (B)

So yield now, ye foolish and purposeless sorrows!
My Jesus doth call me: who would then not go?

>Nought which I desire
>Doth this world possess.
>Appear to me, blessed, exuberant morning,
>Transfigured in glory to Jesus I'll come.

5. Recit. (S)

Then seize, O world, all my possessions!
Thou takest e'en my flesh and this my body,
So take as well my poverty;
Enough, that I from God's abundant store
The highest wealth am yet to have,
Enough, that there I rich and blest shall be.
However, what shall I inherit
Except my God's paternal love?

It is, yea, every morning new[1]
And cannot perish.

6. Chorale [Verse 6] (S, A, T, B)

Ruler over death and living,
Let at last my end be good;
Teach me how to yield my spirit
With a courage firm and sure.
Help me earn an honest grave
Next to godly Christian men,
And at last by earth though covered
May I never ruin suffer!

[1.]   Cf. *Lam.* 3:23.

BWV 9 **Es ist das Heil uns kommen her**

Sixth Sunday after Trinity.

Poet unknown.

1. Paul Speratus, verse 1 of the hymn, 1524 (Wackernagel, III, #55);
2. based freely on verses 2, 3, and the beginning of 4; 4. based freely
on verses 5-7; 5. based freely on verse 8; 6. based freely on verses 9
and 11; 7. verse 12 of the hymn.

1732-1735, Leipzig.

BG 1; NBA I/17.

---

1. Chorus [Verse 1] (S, A, T, B)

Now is to us salvation come
By grace and purest favor.
Our works, they help us not at all,
They offer no protection.
But faith shall Jesus Christ behold,
Who hath enough done for us all;
He is our intercessor.[1]

2. Recit. (B)

God gave to us a law, but we were far too weak
That we could ever hope to keep it.
We followed but the call of sin,
No man could be called godly;
The soul remained to flesh adherent
And ventured not to stand against it.
We were within the law to walk
And there as if within a mirror see
How yet our nature was undisciplined;
And just the same we clung to it.
Of his own strength none had the power
His sinful rudeness to abandon,
E'en though he all his strength might strive to gather.

3. Aria (T)

We were ere then too deeply fallen,
The chasm sucked us fully down,

> The deep then threatened us with death,
> And even still in such distress
> There was no hand to lend us help.

4. Recit. (B)

But somehow was the law to have fulfillment;
And for this came to earth salvation,
The Most High's Son hath it himself fulfilled
And his own Father's wrath made still.
Through his own guiltless dying
He let us win salvation.
Who now in him doth trust
And on his passion build,
He walketh not in peril.
And heaven is for him appointed
Who with true faith himself shall bring
And firmly Jesus' arms embrace.

5. Aria (S, A)

Lord, thou look'st past our good labors
To the heart's believing power,
Nought but faith dost thou accept.

> Nought but faith shall justify,
> Every labor seems too slight
> E'er to bring us any help.

6. Recit. (B)

When we our sin within the law acknowledge,
Our conscience is most sorely stricken;
Yet can we reckon to our comfort
That we within the Gospel's word
Shall soon again
Be glad and joyful:
This gives to our belief new power.
We therefore wait the day
Which God's own graciousness

To us hath firmly pledged,
E'en though, in truth, with purpose wise,
The hour is not told us.
But still we wait with full assurance,
He knoweth when our time is come
And worketh no deceit
On us; we may depend upon him,
And him alone be trusting.

7. Choral [Verse 12] (S, A, T, B)

Though it should seem he were opposed,
Be thou by this not frightened;
For where he is at best with thee,
His wont is not to show it.
His word take thou more certain still,
And though thy heart say only "No,"
Yet let thyself not shudder.

[1.] This translation works only in the cantus firmus. In some parts "our inter-, our intercessor" is required.

BWV 10 **Meine Seel erhebt den Herren**

The Visitation of the Blessed Virgin Mary (The Presentation of Christ in the Temple).

Poet unknown.

1. The German Magnificat (after *Lk.* 1: 46-55), verses 1 and 2; 2. based freely on verse 3; 3. based freely on verses 4 and 5; 4. based freely on verses 6 and 7; 5. verse 8; 6. based freely on verse 9; 7. verses 10 and 11 of the hymn.

2 July 1724, Leipzig.

BG 1; NBA I/28.

---

1. Chorus [Verses 1 and 2] (S, A, T, B)

Now my soul exalts the Master,[1]
And my heart finds in God gladness, in God my Savior;
For he hath on his lowly handmaid looked with favor.
Lo now, from this time forth shall I be called blessed by posterity.[2]

2. Aria (S)

Lord, thou who strong and mighty art,
God, thou whose name most holy is,
How wonderful are all thy labors!
Thou seest me in low estate,
Thou hast for me more blessings wrought
Than I could either know or number.

3. Recit. (T)

The Most High's gracious love
Is every morning new,[3]
Enduring ever more and more
Amongst all those who here
To his salvation look
And him in honest fear do trust.
But he doth also wield great might
With his own arm
Upon all those who neither cold
Nor warm[4]
In faithfulness and love have lived.
Them, naked, bare and blind,
Them, filled with pride and haughtiness,
Shall his own hand like chaff disperse.

4. Aria (B)

God casts the strong down from their seat
Headlong into the sulph'rous pit;
The humble hath God oft exalted,
That they like stars may stand in heaven.
The rich doth God leave void and bare,
The hungry filleth he with blessing,
That they upon his sea of grace
Have riches with abundance ever.

5. Duet [Verse 8] (A, T) with Instrum. Chorale

He's mindful of his mercy's grace
and gives to his servant Israel help.

6. Recit. (T)

What God of old to our forefathers
In promise and in word did give,
He hath fulfilled in all his works and deeds.
What God to Abraham,
When he to him into his tent did come,
Did prophesy and promise,
Is, when the time had been fulfilled, accomplished.[5]
His seed must multiply as much
As ocean sands
And stars of heaven have extended;
For born was then the Savior,
Eternal word was seen in flesh appearing,
That this the human race from death and every evil
And also Satan's slavery
Through purest love might be delivered;
So it remains:
The word of God is full of grace and truth.

7. Chorale [Verses 10 and 11] (S, A, T, B)

Laud and praise be God the Father and the Son
And to the Holy Spirit,
As in the beginning was and ever is
Be from evermore to evermore. Amen.

[1.] *Herren* occurs only in the cantus firmus. The other parts have *Herrn*. Translate there "Lord" instead of "Lord God."

[2.] *Kindeskind* "children's children."

[3.] Cf. *Lam.* 3:22-23.

[4.] Cf. *Rev.* 3:15.

[5.] Cf. *Gen.* 12:2, 15:5, 17:4.

BWV 11 **Lobet Gott in seinen Reichen** (Himmelfahrts-Oratorium) Ascension.

Poet unknown (Picander? See Dürr, p. 289).

2. *Lk.* 24:50-51; 5. based on *Acts* 1:9 and *Mk.* 16:19; 6. Johann Rist, verse 4 of "Du Lebensfürst, Herr Jesu Christ," 1641 (Fischer-Tümpel, II, #188); 7. *Acts* 1:10-11; 9. based on *Lk.* 24:52a, *Acts* 1:12, and *Lk.* 24:52b; 11. Gottfried Wilhelm Sacer, verse 7 of "Gott fähret auf gen Himmel," 1697 (Fischer-Tümpel, IV, #599).

19 May 1735, Leipzig; Parody: 1 ← III, BWV Anhang 18/1; 4, 10 ← I/3, 5; 4: cf. Mass in B Minor, BWV 232/24 (IV,4).

BG 2; NBA II/7.

Ascension Oratorio

---

1. Chorus (S, A, T, B)

Laud to God in all his kingdoms,
Praise to him in all his honors,
In his splendor tell his fame;

> Strive his glory's due to honor
> When ye with assembled choirs
> Make a song to praise his name!

2. Recit. (T) Evangelist

The Lord Jesus then lifted up his hands in blessing on his disciples,
and thereupon, as he was blessing them, he parted from them.

3. Recit. (B)

Ah, Jesus, is thy parting now so near?
Ah, is so soon the moment come
When we shall have to let thee leave us?
Ah, look now, how the burning teardrops
Down these our pallid cheeks are rolling,
How we for thee are yearning,
How nearly all our hope is lost.
Ah, do not yet depart!

4. Aria (A)

Ah, stay with me, my dearest life thou,
Ah, flee thou not so soon from me!

> Thy parting and thine early leaving
> Bring me the most egregious suff'ring,
> Ah yes, then stay yet here awhile;
> Else shall I be with pain surrounded.

5. Recit. (T) Evangelist

And was lifted up manifestly and went up toward heaven, and a cloud did bear him off before their eyes, and he sits at the right hand of God now.

6. Chorale (S, A, T, B)

Now lieth all beneath thy feet,
Thyself the one exception;
The angels must for evermore
To wait upon thee gather.
The princes stand, too, on the way
And are thy willing servants now;
Air, water, earth and fire
Must thee their service offer.

7. Recit. (T, B) Evangelist and Two Men in White Robes

(Evangelist)

And as they looked at him going up to heaven, lo, there standing beside them were two men in shining raiment, and they were saying:

(Both Evangelist and the Two Men)

Ye men of Galilee, why do ye stand and gaze up to heaven? For this Jesus, who hath from you been lifted up unto heaven, shall come again as ye have seen him going up to heaven.

8. Recit. (A)

Ah yes! so come thou soon again:
Efface at last my sad demeanor,

Else will my every moment be
Despised and years in length appearing.

9. Recit. (T) Evangelist

And thereupon they prayed to him, turned around toward
Jerusalem from that mountain which is called Mount of Olives,
that which is not far from Jerusalem and lies only one Sabbath's
day[1] away, and they went up again into Jerusalem filled with great
gladness.

10. Aria (S)

Jesus, thy dear mercy's glances
Can I, yea, forever, see.

> For thy love doth bide among us,
> That I here within these days
> For that future majesty
> Even now my soul may nurture,
> When we'll there before thee stand.

11. Chorale (S, A, T, B)

When shall it ever happen,
When comes the welcome day
In which I shall behold him
In all his majesty?
Thou day, when wilt thou be,
In which we greet the Savior,
In which we kiss the Savior?
Come, make thyself appear!

---

[1]   I.e., "one Sabbath's journey away."

BWV 12 **Weinen, Klagen, Sorgen, Zagen**

Jubilate (Third Sunday after Easter).

Salomo Franck.[1]

3. *Acts* 14:22; 6. Johann Crüger's chorale melody for "Jesu, meine Freude" by Johann Franck, 1650 (cf. BWV 227); 7. Samuel Rodigast, final verse of "Was Gott tut, das ist wohlgetan," 1674 (Fischer-Tümpel, IV, #467).

22 April 1714, Weimar; 30 April 1724, Leipzig; Parody: → Mass in B Minor, BWV 232/16(II,5).

BG 2; NBA I/11.

---

1. Sinfonia

2. Chorus (S, A, T, B)

Weeping, wailing
Grieving, fearing,
Dread and need
Are the Christians' tearful bread,

> Them the sign of Jesus bearing.

3. Recit. [Dictum] (A)

We must pass through great sadness that we come into God's kingdom.

4. Aria (A)

Cross and crown are joined together,
Gem and conflict are made one.

> Christians must at every hour
> Have their torment and their foe,
> But Christ's wounds shall be their comfort.

5. Aria (B)

I'll follow after Christ,
I will not e'er forsake him
In health and in distress,
In living and in dying.
I kiss of Christ his shame,
I'll take his cross unto me.
I'll follow after Christ,
I will not e'er forsake him.

6. Aria (T) with instr. chorale

Be steadfast, every pain
Will have but a trifle been.
After showers
Blessing flowers,
Every tempest will have past.
Be steadfast, be steadfast.[2]

7. Chorale (S, A, T, B)

What God doth, that is rightly done,
To that will I be cleaving,
Though out upon the cruel road
Need, death and suff'ring drive me,
E'en so will God,

All fatherhood,
Within his arms enfold me:
So I yield him all power.

---

1.   So Dürr, p. 263. For further evidence of Franck's authorship see Ambrose, *BJ* (1980), pp. 35-44, and *Bach* (1982), pp. 20-22.

2.   The idea of ameliorative metamorphosis in this movement is so strongly dependent upon the repetition of the sound ai, the sound of lamentation, I have chosen to rhyme the translation. It is particularly interesting that the final verse of Johann Frank's chorale "Jesu, meine Freude" concludes with the same conceit:

> Dennoch bleibst du auch im Leide,
> Jesu, meine Freude.

Eu and *ei* were pronounced virtually alike in Bach's region, allowing the metamorphosis of "sadness" to "gladness" the support of a rhyme. Even without words the wailing of the trumpet, which plays this chorale in this movement, conveys effectively the sound "ai" of the text. This concept is also exploited in the other two cantatas for Jubilate Sunday, BWV 103 and BWV 146.

BWV 13 **Meine Seufzer, meine Tränen**

Second Sunday after Epiphany.

Georg Christian Lehms, *Gottgefälliges Kirchen-Opffer* (Darmstadt, 1711); Facs: Neumann T, p. 258.

3. Johann Heermann, verse 2 of "Zion klagt mit Angst und Schmerzen," 1636 (Fischer-Tümpel, I, #361); 6. Paul Fleming, final verse of "In allen meinen Taten," 1642 (Fischer-Tümpel, I, #489).

20 January 1726, Leipzig.

BG 2; NBA I/5.

---

1. Aria (T)

Of my sighing, of my crying
No one could the sum reveal.

> If each day is filled with sadness
> And our sorrow never passeth,
> Ah, it means that all our pain
> Now the way to death prepareth!

2. Recit. (A)

My dearest Lord hath let
Me long in vain invoke him,
To me in all my weeping
No comfort yet revealing.
The hour even now
Is from afar appearing,
But still I must in vain make my entreaty.

3. Chorale (A)

That God who gave me the promise
Of his helping hand alway
Lets me strive in vain to find him
Now within my sad estate.
Ah! Will he then evermore
Cruel wrath retain for me,
Can and will he to the wretched
Now no longer show his mercy?

4. Recit. (S)

My sorrow ever grows
And robs me of all peace,
My cup of woe is filled
With tears to overflowing,
And my distress will not be dampened
And leaves me full of cold despair.
This night of care and grief
Doth bring my anxious heart oppression,
I sing, thus, only songs of sorrow.
No, spirit, no,
Take only comfort in thy pain:
God can the wormwood's gall
Transform with ease to wine of rapture
And then as well ten thousand joys allow thee.

5. Aria (B)

Moaning and most piteous weeping
Help our sorrow's sickness not;

> But whoe'er to heaven looketh
> And strives there to find his comfort
> Can with ease a light of joy
> In his grieving breast discover.

6. Chorale (S, A, T, B)

Thyself be true, O spirit,
And trust in that one only
Who hath created thee;
Let happen what may happen,
Thy Father there in heaven
Doth counsel in all matters well.

BWV 14 **Wär Gott nicht mit uns diese Zeit**

Fourth Sunday after Epiphany.

Poet unknown.

1. Martin Luther, verse 1 of the hymn, 1524 (Wackernagel, III, #27), an adaptation of *Ps.* 124; 2-4. based freely on verse 2; 5. verse 3 of the hymn.

30 January 1735, Leipzig.

BG 2; NBA I/6.

1. Chorus [Verse 1] (S, A, T, B)

Were God not with us all this time,
Then let Israel say it:
Were God not with us all this time,
We would have surely lost courage,
For such a tiny band we are,
Despised by so much of mankind,
They all oppose us ever.

2. Aria (S)

Our own strength is called too weak,
That our foe we bid defiance.

> Stood by us the Highest not,
> Surely would their tyranny
> Soon our very being threaten.

3. Recit. (T)

Yea, if then God had but allowed it,
We long no more were with the living,
Their vengeance would have ravished us,
Such wrath for us do they intend.
For they had in their rage
Like as a rampant flood
Within its foaming waters spilled upon us,
And no one could have all their might resisted.[1]

4. Aria (B)

God, through thine own strong protection
Are we from our foes set free.

> When they come as raging waters
> In their hate to rise against us,
> With us yet thy hands will be.

5. Chorale [Verse 3] (S, A, T, B)

God praise and thanks, who did not let
Their savage jaws devour us.
As a bird from its snare comes free,
So is our soul delivered:
The snare's in twain, and we are free; The Lord's own name doth stand with us,
The God of earth and of heaven.

[1.]   Cf. *Mt.* 8:24.

BWV 16 **Herr Gott, dich loben wir**

New Year's Day (Feast of the Circumcision).

Georg Christian Lehms, *Gottgefälliges Kirchen-Opffer* (Darmstadt, 1711); Facs: Neumann T, p. 258.

1. Martin Luther, beginning of the German Te Deum, 1529 (Wackernagel, III, #31); 6. Paul Eber, last verse of the New Year's hymn "Helft mir Gotts Güte preisen," ca. 1580 (Wackernagel, IV, #7), added by Bach to Lehm's text.

1 January 1726, Leipzig; re-performed perhaps in 1734 (so Dürr, p. 154), Leipzig.

BG 2; NBA I/4.

1. Chorus (S, A, T, B)

Lord God, we give thee praise,
Lord God, we give thee thanks,
Thee, God Father eternally,
All the world lauds far and wide.

2. Recit. (B)

So we shall raise
Upon this joyful day
Our ardent worship's song
And shall to thee,
O God, for this the fresh new year
Our spirit's first oblation give.
What hast thou not since time began
For our salvation done,

And how much must our breast
Yet of thy love and faith be conscious!
Thy Zion a perfect peace,
Its lot is bliss and happiness;
The temple rings
With sounds of harp and psalt'ry,
And how our soul shall soar
If we but reverent fire to heart and lips shall summon!
Oh, ought there not therefore a new refrain be ringing
And we in fervent love be singing?

3. Aria (S, A, T, B)

(Tutti)
Let us triumph, let's be merry:
God's good will and trust
Shall be every morning new.

(B)
Crown and blessing from his hand,
Ah, be sure that to our clan
Lasting, lasting happiness

4. Recit. (A)

Ah, faithful shield,

Protect as in the past thy precious word,
Protect both church and school now,
Thus shall thy kingdom grow
And Satan's wicked guile fall low;
If thou upholdest order
And our beloved peace,
Our lot, indeed, shall be sufficient,

And we'll have nought but happiness.
Ah! God, thou shalt this land
Bathe still with nurture.
Thou shalt it e'er make better,
Thou shalt it with thy very hand
And very blessing foster.
We're blest, if we
Thee evermore
Shall trust, my Jesus and my Savior.

5. Aria (T)

Beloved Jesus, thou alone
Shalt be the treasure of my soul.
We will before all other riches
Within our faithful heart enthrone thee,
Yea, when the thread of life shall break,
Our spirit shall, in God content,
Again with lips most gladly sing:
Beloved Jesus, thou alone
Shalt be the treasure of my soul.

6. Chorale (S, A, T, B)

We praise all this thy kindness,
Father on heaven's throne,
Which unto us thou showest
Through Christ, who is thy Son,
And beg thee now as well
To make our year be peaceful,
From every woe to guard us,
And nourish us with grace.

BWV 17 **Wer Dank opfert, der preiset mich**

Fourteenth Sunday after Trinity.

Poet unknown (Christoph Helm?);[1] PT (Rudolstadt, 1726).

1. *Ps.* 50:23; 4. *Lk.* 17: 15-16; 7. Johann Gramann, verse 3 of "Nun lob, mein Seel, den Herren," 1530 (Wackernagel, I, #455).

9 September 1726, Leipzig; Parody: 1 ➔ Mass in G Major, BWV 236/6.

BG 2; NBA I/21.

First Part

1. Chorus [Dictum] (S, A, T, B)

Who thanks giveth, he praiseth me, and this is the way that I shall show to him God's healing.

2. Recit. (A)

Thus ought the whole wide world become a silent witness
Of God's exalted majesty,
Air, water, firmament and earth now
While in their order as a line[2] they move;
And nature tells his praise in all the countless blessings
Which he within her lap hath laid;
And all that draweth breath
Shall have a greater portion in him
When it to give him praise both tongue and wing doth stir.

3. Aria (S)

Lord, thy goodwill extends as far as heaven is,
And this thy truth doth reach as far as clouds are coursing.[3]
Knew I no other way how glorious is thy might,
Yet could I with great ease from thine own works observe it.
How could we not with thanks for this forever praise thee?
For thou shalt in return salvation's way then show us.

Second Part

4. Recit. (T)

One, however, in their number, upon seeing that he to health was
restored, turned back again and gave praise to God with a loud
voice then and fell down upon his face before his feet there and gave
thanks to him, and he a Samaritan was.

5. Aria (T)

To me what wealth of favor
Thou dost give!
But what shall thee my spirit
Give in turn?
Lord, I know nought else to offer
Than my thanks and praise to sing thee.

6. Recit. (B)

My purpose now regard, for I know what I am:
Flesh, reason and my life, my health and strength and mind,
Which I through thee enjoy—and tell it gladly,
Are streams of thy dear grace which over me thou pourest.
Love, peace, true righteousness, thy Holy Spirit's joy[4]

Are treasures through which thou to me e'en here dost show
What favor thou dost plan to grant me there in heaven,
In body and in soul to bring me perfect healing.

7. Chorale (S, A, T, B)

As hath a father mercy
For all his children, young and small,
The Lord forgives us also,
When we as children fear him pure.
He knows that we are poor creatures,
God knows we are but dust.
Like as the grass in mowing,
A bud and leaf in fall,
The wind need merely blow it,
And it's no longer there:
E'en so man's life is passing,
His end is ever near.

[1.] W. Blankenburg, BJ (1977) suggests Helm as the possible author.

[2.] Cf. *Ps.* 19:5 which Luther translates "Ihre Schnur gehet aus in alle Lande" ("Their line goeth out into every land"). Luther means here "plumb-line." English versions, following another Hebrew reading, have "voice" or "sound" instead of "line."

[3.] Cf. *Ps.* 57:11 and 36:6.

[4.] Cf. *Rom.* 14:17.

BWV 18 **Gleichwie der Regen und Schnee vom Himmel fällt**

Sexagesima Sunday.

Erdmann Neumeister, *Geistliches Singen und Spielen* (Gotha, 1711); Facs: Neumann T, p. 294.

2. *Is.* 55:10-11; 3. Martin Luther, portions of the Litany, 1528/29, with interpolated recitative; 5. Lazarus Spengler, verse 8 of "Durch Adams Fall ist ganz verderbt," 1524 (Wackernagel, III, #71).

1713 to 24 February 1715 (latest possible date according to Dürr, pp. 209-210), Weimar; revised in A Minor in Leipzig.

BG 2; NBA I/7.

---

1. Sinfonia

2. Recit. [Dictum] (B)

Just as the showers and snow from heaven fall and return again not thither, rather give the earth moisture and make it fertile and fruitful, so it gives seed for the sowing and bread for eating: Just so shall the word that from mine own mouth proceedeth be too; it shall not come again to me empty, but shall do what I have purposed and shall that accomplish for which I send it.

3. Recit. (T, B) and Litany (S, A, T, B)

(T)
My God, here shall my heart abide:
I open it to thee in Jesus' name now[1];
So scatter wide thy seed then
As if on fertile land in me.
My God, here shall my heart abide:
Let it bring forth in hundredfold its harvest.
O Lord, Lord, help! O Lord, O let it prosper![2]

(S, A, T, B)
That thou might to the word thy Spirit add, and power,
O hear us, O good Lord, our God!

(B)
But keep us, faithful Father, keep us,
Both me and any Christian soul,
From Satan's lies attending.
His mind has only one intent,
Of this thy word to rob us
With all our happiness.

(S, A, T, B)
That Satan underneath our feet be trodden,
O hear us, O good Lord, our God!

(T)
Ah! Many, word and faith renouncing,
Do fall away like rotting fruit,
When persecution they must suffer.
Thus they are plunged in everlasting grief
For having passing woe avoided.

(S, A, T, B)
And from all the Turk's and all the Pope's
Most cruel murder and oppression,
Anger and fury, fatherlike protect us.
O hear us, O good Lord, our God!

(B)
One man may but for belly care,
And meanwhile is his soul left quite forgotten;
And Mammon, too,
Hath many hearts' allegiance,
And then the word is left without its power.
How many are the souls
Of pleasure not the captive?
So well seduceth them the world,

The world which must by them instead of heaven be honored,
So that they then from heaven stray and wander.

(S, A, T, B)
All those now who are gone and led astray recover.
O hear us, O good Lord, our God!

4. Aria (S)

My soul's true treasure is God's word;
Otherwise are all those treasures
Mere devices
By the world and Satan woven,
Scornful spirits for beguiling.
Take them all now, take them hence!
My soul's true treasure is God's word.

5. Chorale (S, A, T, B)

I pray, O Lord, with inmost heart,
May thou not take it from me,
Thy holy word not from my mouth;
For thus shall not confound me
My sin and shame, for in thy care
I put all mine assurance:
Who shall steadfast on this rely
Shall surely death not witness.

[1.] Literally, "I open it to thee in the name of my Jesus."

[2.] *Ps.* 118:25.

BWV 19 **Es erhub sich ein Streit**

St. Michael and All Angels.

Poet unknown, a revision of verses 1, 3, 6, and 7 of a Michaelmas poem in Picander's *Sammlung Erbaulicher Gedancken* (Leipzig, 1724/25); Facs: Neumann T, p. 309.

1-2. based upon *Rev.* 12:7-9; 3. verse 3 of Picander with the chorale melody "Herzlich lieb hab ich dich, o Herr," (cf. BWV 174/5); 4. based on verse 4 of Picander; 5. based on the end of verse 6 of Picander and on *Ps.* 34:8, 91:11-13, and 116:8; 6. lines 1-4 of verse 6 and reminiscences of verse 7 of Picander; 7. verse 9 of "Freu dich sehr, o meine Seele," Freiburg, 1620 (Fischer-Tümpel, I, #573).

29 September 1726, Leipzig.

BG 2; NBA I/30.

1. Chorus (S, A, T, B)

There arose a great strife.

> The furious serpent, the dragon infernal,
> Now storms against heaven with passionate vengeance.
> But Saint Michael wins the day,
> And the host which follows him
> Strikes down Satan's cruel might.

2. Recit. (B)

Praise God! The dragon's low.
The uncreated Michael hath
With all his angel host
Him overcome.

He lies there in the darkness' gloom
With fetters bound about him,
And his abode shall be no more
In heaven's realm discovered.
We stand full confident and sure,
And though we by his roar be frightened,
Yet shall our body and our soul
By angels be protected.

3. Aria (S)

God sends us Mahanaim here;[1]
In waiting or departing
We therefore can in safe repose
Before our foes stand firmly.
He is encamped, both near and far,
Round us the angel of our Lord
With fire, horse and wagon.[2]

4. Recit. (T)

What is, then, scornful man, that child of earth?
A worm, a wretched sinner.
Behold how e'en the Lord doth love him so
That he regards him not unworthy
And for him heaven's children,
The host of Seraphim,
To keep him safe and free from harm
For his defense provideth.

5. Aria (T) with instr. chorale[3]

Stay, ye angels, stay by me!

      Lead me so and stay beside me
      That my foot may never stumble!
      But instruct me here as well

How to sing your mighty "Holy"
And the Most High thanks to offer.

6. Recit. (S)

Let us the countenance
Of righteous angels honor
And them with our own sinfulness
Not drive away or even sadden.
And they shall, when the Lord us bids
The world "Farewell" to render,
To our great happiness,
Our chariots be to heaven.

7. Chorale (S, A, T, B)

Let thine angel with me travel
On Elias' chariot red,
This my soul so well protecting
As for Laz'rus when he died.
Let it rest within thy lap,
Make it full of joy and hope
Till from earth shall rise my body
And with it be reunited.

---

1.   Cf. *Gen.* 32:2. Hebrew *Mahanaim* means 'two hosts' or 'two camps.'

2.   Cf. *Ps.* 34:8 and 2 *Cor.* 2:11.

3.   Dürr, p. 774, says that the more knowledgeable members of the congregation, in hearing this melody, would have thought of verse 3 of the hymn: "Ach Herr, laß dein lieb Engelein am letzten End die Seele mein in Abrahams Schoß tragen" ("Ah Lord, allow thine angel dear at the last day to carry this soul of mine to Abraham's bosom").

BWV 20 **O Ewigkeit, du Donnerwort I**

First Sunday after Trinity.

Poet unknown.

1. Johann Rist, verse 1 of the hymn, 1642 (Fischer-Tümpel, II, #204); 2. based closely on verse 2; 3. based on verse 3; 4. based on verses 4 and 5; 5-6. based on verses 5 and 6; 7. verse 8; 8-10. based on verses 9, 10 and 11; 10. also based on *Lk*. 16:19-31; 11. verse 12 of the hymn. These are the verses in the shortened, twelve-verse version of the hymn, not the sixteen-verse original version.

11 June 1724, Leipzig.

BG 2; NBA I/15.

First Part

1. Chorus [Verse 1] (S, A, T, B)

Eternity, thou thundrous word,
O sword that through the soul doth bore,
Beginning with no ending!
Eternity, time lacking time,
I know now faced with deepest grief
Not where to seek my refuge.
So much my frightened heart doth quake
That to my gums my tongue doth cake.

2. Recit. (T)

No sorrow can in all the world be cited
Which lasts eternally.

It must indeed at last in course of time one day end.
Ah! Ah, alas! Eternity hath pain which hath no end;
It carries on and on its torment's game;
Yea, as e'en Jesus saith,
From it there is redemption none.[1]

3. Aria (T)

Endless time, thou mak'st me anxious,[1]
Endless, endless passeth measure![1]
Ah, for sure, this is no sport.[1]
Flames which are forever burning
Are all fires past comparing;
It alarms and shakes my heart
When I once this pain consider
And my thoughts to hell have guided.

4. Recit. (B)

Suppose the torture of the damned should last
As many years as is the sum
Of grass on earth and stars above in heaven;
Suppose that all their pain were just as long to last
As men within the world
Have from the first existed;
There would have been at last
To this an end and limit set:
It would have been at last concluded.
But now, though, when thou hast the dread,[1]
Damned creature, of a thousand million years
With all the demons borne and suffered,
Yet never shall the end be present;
The time which none could ever count[1]
Each moment starts again,
To this thy soul's eternal grief and woe,
Forevermore anew.

5. Aria (B)

The Lord is just in all his dealings:
The brief transgressions of this world[1]
He hath such lasting pain ordained.[1]
Ah, would that now the world would mark it!
Short is the time and death so quick,[1]
Consider this, O child of man!

6. Aria (A)

O man, deliver this thy spirit,
Take flight from Satan's slavery
And make thyself of sin now free,
So that within that pit of sulfphur
The death which doth damned creatures plague
Shall not thy soul forever hound.
O man, deliver this thy spirit!

7. Chorale [Verse 8] (S, A, T, B)

So long a God in heaven dwells
And over all the clouds doth swell,
Such torments shall not be finished:
They will be plagued by heat and cold,
Fear, hunger, terror, lightning's bolt
And still be not diminished.
For only then shall end this pain
When God no more eternal reign.

Second Part

8. Aria (B)

Wake up, wake up, ye straying sheep now,
Arouse yourselves from error's slumber

And better this your life straightway!
Wake up before the trumpet sounds,
Which you with terror from the grave
Before the judge of all the world to judgment calls!

9. Recit. (S)

Forsake, O man, the pleasure of this world,
Pride, splendor, riches, rank and gold;[1]
Consider though
Within thy present time,
While thee the tree of life hath vigor,
What lendeth to thy peace most service!
Perhaps this is the final day,[1]
No man knows when his death may come.
How quick, how soon
Are many dead and cold!
One could this very night
To thine own door the coffin carry.
Hence keep before all matters
Thy soul's salvation in thy thoughts.

10. Aria (A, T)

O child of man,
Now cease forthwith
Both sin and world to cherish,
So that the pain
Where chatt'ring teeth and howling reign
Thee not forever sadden!
See in thyself the wealthy man
Who in his pain
Not even once
A drop of water could receive![2]

11. Chorus [Verse 12] (S, A, T, B)

Eternity, thou thundrous word,
O sword that through the soul doth bore,
Beginning with no ending!
Eternity, time lacking time,
I know now faced with deepest woe
Not where to seek my refuge.
Take me then when thou dost please,
Lord Jesus, to thy joyful tent!

---

[1] From the hymn.
[2] Cf. *Lk.* 16:19-31, the story of Dives and Lazarus. Lazarus, the poor man, is carried to Abraham's bosom. Dives 'the rich man' must endure the torments of Tantalus in Hades.

BWV 21 **Ich hatte viel Bekümmernis**

Third Sunday after Trinity and for any occasion.[1]

Salomo Franck.[2]

2. *Ps.* 94:19; 6. *Ps.* 42:12; 9. *Ps.* 116:7 and Georg Neumark, verses 2 and 5 of "Wer nur den lieben Gott läßt walten," 1657 (Fischer-Tümpel, IV, #365); 11. *Rev.* 5:12-13.

Probably 17 June 1714, Weimar; other performances: ?1720, Hamburg? (See Dürr, p. 344), 13 June 1723, Leipzig (revised).

BG 5, 1; NBA I/16.

First Part

1. Sinfonia

2. Chorus [Dictum] (S, A, T, B)

I had so much distress and woe within my bosom; but still thy
consoling restoreth all my spirit.

3. Aria (S)

Sighing, crying, sorrow, need,
Anxious yearning, fear and death
Gnaw at this my anguished heart,
I am filled with grieving, hurt.

4. Recit. (T)

Why hast thou, O my God,
In my distress,
In my great fear and anguish
Then turned away from me?
Ah! Know'st thou not thy child?
Ah! Hear'st thou not the wailing
Of those who are to thee
In bond and faith allied?
Thou wast once my delight
And to me art now cruel;
I search for thee in every region,
I call and cry to thee,
But still my "Woe and Ah"
Seems now by thee completely unperceived.

5. Aria (T)

Streams of salty tears are welling,
Floods are rushing ever forth.

Storm and waters overwhelm me,
And this sorrow-laden sea
Would my life and spirit weaken,
Mast and anchor are near broken,
Here I sink into the depths,
There peer in the jaws of hell.

6. Chorus [Dictum] (S, A, T, B)

Why art thou distressed, O my spirit, and art so restles within me?
Trust firm in God; for I even yet shall thank him, that he of my
countenance is the help and my God.

Second Part

7. Recit. (S, B) Soul and Jesus

(Soul)
Ah Jesus, my repose,
My light, where bidest thou

(Jesus)
O Soul, behold! I am with thee.

(Soul)
With me?
But here is nought but night.

(Jesus)
I am thy faithful friend,
Who e'en in darkness guards,
Where nought but fiends are found.

(Soul)
Break through then with thy beam and light of comfort here.

(Jesus)
The hour draweth nigh
In which thy battle's crown
Shall thee a sweet refreshment bring.

8. Aria (S, B) Soul, Jesus

(Soul and Jesus)
   Come, my Jesus,
{   } with refreshment
   Yes, I'm coming
   And delight in thine appearing
{   }
   For thee in my grace appearing.
   This my
{   } spirit,
   This thy
         perish
Which shall {   }
       flourish
     flourish
And not {   }
     perish
   And in its misfortune's
{   } cavern
   Here from its afflictions'
   Go to ruin.
{   }
   Shalt thou merit
   I must e'er in sorrow hover,
{   }
   Healing through the grapes' sweet flavor.
   Yes, ah yes, I am forsaken!
{   }
   No, ah no, thou hast been chosen!
   No, ah no, thou hatest me!
{   }

Yes, ah yes, I cherish thee!
Ah, Jesus, now sweeten my spirit and bosom!

{   }

Give way, all ye troubles, and vanish, thou sorrow!

9. Chorus [Dictum] and Chorale (S, A, T, B)

Be now once more contented, O my spirit, for the Lord serves thee
well.
What use to us this heavy sorrow,
What use all this our "Woe and Ah?"
What use that we should every morning
Heap sighs upon our sore distress?
We only make our cross and pain
Grow greater through our discontent.
Think not within the heat of hardship
That thou by God forsaken art,
And that he rests within God's bosom
Who doth on constant fortune feed.
Pursuing time transformeth much
And gives to ev'rything its end.

10. Aria (T)

Be glad, O my spirit, be glad, O my bosom,
Give way now, O trouble, and vanish, thou sorrow.

Transform thyself, weeping, to nothing but wine,
For now shall my sobbing pure triumph become!
Now burneth and flameth most purely the candle
Of love and of hope in my soul and my heart,
For Jesus consoles me with heavenly joy.

11. Chorus [Dictum] (S, A, T, B)

The lamb that is slaughtered now is worthy to have all might and
riches and wisdom and power and honor and praise and fame.

Fame and honor and praise and great might be to our God from
evermore to evermore. Amen, alleluia![3]

---

1.   On the envelope of the autograph score is written *Per ogni Tempo*.

2.   For the text of this cantata see H. Werthemann, BJ (1965). For its parallels
      with the rhetorical features of BWV 12 and Salomo Franck's style in
      general, see Ambrose, BJ (1980).

3.   "Amen, alleluja!" is added, perhaps through the influence of *Rev.* 5:15.

BWV 22 **Jesus nahm zu sich die Zwölfe**

Estomihi (Quinquagesima Sunday).

Poet unknown; PT for re-performance (Leipzig, 1724); Facs:
Neumann T, p. 427.

1. *Lk.* 18:31 and 34; 5. Elisabeth Kreuziger, verse 5 of "Herr Christ,
der einig Gotts Sohn," 1524 (Wackernagel, III, #67f.).

1723, for the audition for the cantorship in Leipzig?; also 2 February
1923, Leipzig.

BG 5, 1; NBA I/8.

---

1. Arioso and Chorus [Dictum]
(T, B, and S, A, T, B)

(T)
Jesus took to him the twelve then and said:

(B)
See now, we shall go up to Jerusalem, and there will all be
accomplished fully which is written now of the Son of man.

(S, A, T, B)
However, they understood nothing and did not grasp what this his saying was.

2. Aria (A)

My Jesus, draw me unto thee,
I am prepared, I will from here
And to Jerusalem to thine own passion go.

> Well me, if I the consequence
> Of this the time of death and pain
> For mine own comfort may completely understand!

3. Recit. (B)

My Jesus, draw me on and I shall hasten,
For flesh and blood completely fail to see,
Like thy disciples then, what this thy saying was.
Our will is with the world and with the greatest rabble;
They would, both of them, when thou transfigured art,
Indeed a mighty tow'r on Tabor's mountain build thee,[1]
But there on Golgotha, which is so full of pain,
In thy distress so low with not an eye behold thee.
Ah, crucify in me, in my corrupted breast,
Before all else this world and its forbidden lust,
And I shall for thy words be filled with understanding
And to Jerusalem with untold gladness journey.

4. Aria (T)

My treasure of treasures, mine infinite store,
Amend thou my spirit, transform thou my heart,
Bring all in subjection
Which to my denial of flesh is resistant!
But when in my spirit I've mortified been,
Then summon me to thee in peace there above!

5. Chorale (S, A, T, B)

Us mortify through kindness,
Awake us through thy grace;
The former man enfeeble,
So that the new may live
E'en in this earthly dwelling,
His will and every purpose
And thought may give to thee.

[1.] Cf. *Mt.* 17:1-9, *Mk.* 9:2-8 and *Lk.* 9:28-36 for the story of the Transfiguration. Though without specific basis in Scripture, Mt. Tabor was the traditional site of the Transfiguration.

BWV 23 **Du wahrer Gott und Davids Sohn**

Estomihi (Quinquagesima Sunday).

Poet unknown.

2. Melody of the German Agnus Dei, Braunschweig, 1524; 4. text of the preceding.

Composed in Cöthen for the audition for the cantorship in Leipzig, 7 February 1723 (whether it was performed is not known, see Dürr, p. 217); also, at the latest, 20 February 1724, Leipzig; again between 1728 and 1731.

BG 5, 1; NBA I/8.

---

1. Aria (S, A)

Thou, very God and David's Son,
Who from eternity and from afar e'en now

My heart's distress and this my body's pain
With caring dost regard, thy mercy give!

And through thine hand, with wonder filled,
Which so much evil hath repelled,
Give me as well both help and comfort.

2. Recit. (T) with instr. chorale

Ah, do not disregard me,
Thou, Savior of all men,
Yea, art appearéd,
The ailing and not to healthy men to give thy succor.[1]
Thus shall I also share in thine almighty power;
I'll see thee now beside the road here,
Where they have
Deigned to leave me lying,
E'en in my sightless state.
I'll rest here firm
And leave thee not
Without thy gracious blessing.

3. Chorus (S, A, T, B)

Every eye now waiteth, Lord,
Thou Almighty God, on thee,[2]
And mine own especially.
Give to them both strength and light,
Leave them not
Evermore to stay in darkness.
Henceforth shall thy nod alone
The belove'd central aim
Of their every labor be,
Till thou shalt at last through death
Once again decide to close them.

4. Chorale (S, A, T, B)

O Christ, Lamb of God, thou,
Who dost bear the world's own sin,
Have mercy on us!
O Christ, Lamb of God, thou,
Who dost bear the world's own sin,
Have mercy on us!
O Christ, Lamb of God, thou,
Who dost bear the world's own sin,
Give us thy peace now. Amen.

[1.] Cf. *Mk.* 2:17.
[2.] Cf. *Ps.* 145:15.

BWV 24 **Ein ungefärbt Gemüte**

Fourth Sunday after Trinity.

Erdmann Neumeister, *Geistliche Poesien* (Eisenach, 1714); Facs: Neumann T, p. 297.

3. *Mt.* 7:12; 6. Johann Heermann, verse 1 of the hymn, 1630 (Fischer-Tümpel, I, #355).

20 June 1723, Leipzig.

BG 5, 1; NBA I/17.

---

1. Aria (A)

An undisguised intention
Of native[1] faith and kindness
Doth us 'fore God and man make fair.

For Christians' work and commerce
Throughout their whole life's compass
Should on this kind of footing stand.

2. Recit.

Sincerity
Is one of God's most gracious blessings.
The fact that in our time
There are but few who have it
Comes from not asking God for it.
For of itself proceeds our heart's contrivance
In nought but evil ways;
If it would set its course on something worthy,
Then must it be by God's own Spirit governed
And in the path of virtue guided.
If God as friend thou seekest,
Thou must thyself no foe be to thy neighbor
Through cunning, ruse and craft!
A Christian[2]
Should strive the way of doves to copy
And live without deceit and malice.
Upon thyself impress the form
Which thou wouldst have thy neighbor own.

3. Chorus [Dictum] (S, A,T, B)

All things now that ye wish to be done by people unto you, that do
ye to them.

4. Recit. (B)

Hypocrisy
Is of the brood which Belial[3] concocteth.
Who self behind its mask concealeth
Doth wear the devil's livery.

What? Do, then, even Christians
Such things as these now covet?
O God, forfend! Sincerity is precious.
And many fiendish monsters
Appear in angel's guise.
We bring the wolf within,
Sheep's clothing don without.
What could be worse than this?
For slander, spite and judgment,
Damnation and destruction
Are ev'rywhere now found.
It is the same, both there and here.
May God above protect me now from this.

5. Aria (T)

Trust and truth should be the base
Of thy every purpose;
As thine outward word and speech,
Be the heart within thee.
Being kind and virtuous
Makes us God and angels like.

6. Chorale (S, A, T, B)

O God, thou righteous God,
Thou fountain of all blessings,
Without whom nought exists,
From whom is all our treasure,
My body grant good health,
And let within my flesh
An uncorrupted soul
And conscience pure e'er dwell.

---

1. Literally, "Of German faith and kindness." *Deutsch* has a sense similar to

that in the idiom *mit jemandem deutsch reden* 'to speak frankly.' Indeed, 'frankly' is a parallel concept in its ethnic connotation.

2. This translation adds one syllable to the line. One may prefer to translate "A man / Of Christ should strive the doves to copy . . ."

3. *Belial* Hebr. 'without use or profit' is identified with Satan in the New Testament.

BWV 25 **Es ist nichts Gesundes an meinem Leibe**

Fourteenth Sunday after Trinity.

Poet unknown.

1. *Ps.* 38:4 with the chorale melody "Herzlich tut mich verlangen nach einem selgen End" (cf. BWV 161/1);[1] 6. Johann Heermann, last verse of "Treuer Gott, ich muß dir klagen," 1630 (Fischer-Tümpel, I, #347).

29 August 1723, Leipzig.

BG 5, 1; NBA I/23, 81.

1. Chorus [Dictum] (S, A, T, B) with instr. chorale

There is nought of soundness within my body, for thou art angry, nor any quiet within these my bones now, for I am sinful.

2. Recit. (T)

Now all the world is but a hospital,
Where mortals in their numbers passing count
And even children in the cradle
In sickness lie with bitter anguish.

The one is tortured in the breast
By raging fever's angry lust;
Another lieth ill
From his own honor's odious foul stench;
The third is torn by lust for gold,
Which hurls him to an early grave.
The first great fall hath ev'ryone polluted
And with its rash of sinfulness infected.
Ah, this great bane doth gnaw as well my members.
Where is a cure for wretched me?
Who will by me within my suff'ring stand?
My healer who, who will restore me?

3. Aria (B)

Ah, where shall this wretch find help?
All my rashes, all my cankers
Can no herb or plaster cure now
But the balm of Gilead.[2]
Healer mine, Lord Jesus, thou
Know'st alone my soul's best cure.

4. Recit. (S)

O Jesus, O dear Master,
To thee I flee:
Ah, strengthen thou my weakened vital spirits!
Have mercy now,
Thou help and doctor of all ailing,
O thrust me not
Hence from thy countenance!
My Healer, make me clean from my great rash of sin,
And I will thee
Give all my heart in turn
In lasting sacrifice
And through my life for all thy help be grateful.

5. Aria (S)

Open to my songs so meager,
Jesus, thy most gracious ear!
When I there in choirs above
Shall be with the angels singing,
Shall my thankful song sound better.

6. Chorale (S, A, T, B)

I will all my days forever
Glorify thy mighty hand,
That thou all my drudge and mourning
Hast so graciously repelled.
Not alone in mortal life
Shall I tell thy glory wide:
I will e'en hereafter tell it
And there evermore extol thee.

[1.] Dürr, p. 431, suggests that the congregation, in hearing this melody, would have thought of its alternative text: "Ach Herr, mich armen Sünder," upon which BWV 135 (for the Third Sunday after Trinity) is based.

[2.] Cf. Jer. 8:22 and 46:11.

BWV 26 Ach wie flüchtig, ach wie nichtig

Twenty-fourth Sunday after Trinity.

Poet unknown.

1. Michael Franck, verse 1 of the hymn, 1652 (Fischer-Tümpel, IV, #254); 2. based on verse 2; 3. based loosely on verses 3-9; 4. based on verse 10; 5. based on verses 11-12; 6. verse 13 of the hymn.

19 November 1724, Leipzig.

BG 5, 1; NBA I/27, 31.

---

1. Chorus [Verse 1] (S, A, T, B)

Ah, how fleeting, ah, how empty
Is the life of mortals!
As a mist which quickly riseth
And again as quickly passeth,
Even thus our life is, witness!

2. Aria (T)

As fast as rushing waters gush,
So hasten on our days of living.
The time doth pass, the hours hasten,
Just as the raindrops quickly break up
When all to the abyss doth rush.

3. Recit. (A)

Our joy will be to sadness turned,
Our beauty falleth like a flower,
The greatest strength will be made weak,
Transformed will be good fortune all in time,
Soon is the end of fame and honor,
What scholarship and what mankind contriveth
Will at the last the grave extinguish.

4. Aria (B)

Upon earthly treasure the heart to be setting
Is but a seduction of our foolish world.
How easily formed are the holocaust's embers,

What thunder and power have waters in floodtime
Till all things collapse into ruin and fall.

5. Recit. (S)

The highest majesty and pomp
Are veiled at last by death's dark night.
Who almost as a god was honored
Escapes the dust and ashes not,
And when the final hour striketh
In which he to the earth is carried
And his own height's foundation falls,
Is he then quite forgotten.

6. Chorale [Verse 13] (S, A, T, B)

Ah, how fleeting, ah, how empty
Are all mortal matters!
All that, all that which we look at,
That must fall at last and vanish.
Who fears God shall stand forever.

BWV 27 Wer weiß, wie nahe mir mein Ende?

Sixteenth Sunday after Trinity.

Poet unknown.

1. Ämilie Juliane von Schwarzburg-Rudolstadt, verse 1 of the hymn, 1686 (Fischer-Tümpel, V, #631) with interpolated recitative; 6. Johann Georg Albinus, verse 1 of the hymn, 1649 (Fischer-Tümpel, IV, #312).

6 October 1726, Leipzig.

BG 5, 1; NBA I/23.

---

1. Chorale (S, A, T, B) and Recit. (S, A, T)

(S, A, T, B)
Who knows how near to me my end is?

(S)
This knows the Lord above alone,
If this my pilgrimage on earth be
Short, or if longer it may be.
Hence fleeth time, here cometh death,

(A)
And at the last the point is reached
When they will surely meet each other.
Ah, with what swiftness and adroitness
Can come to me the trial of death!

(T)
Who knows if e'en today
My mouth its final word might speak.
Thus shall I always pray:
My God, I pray through Christ's own blood,
Allow but that my end be good!

2. Recit. (T)

My lifetime hath no other goal
Than that I may in death be blessed
And this my faith's reward inherit.

Thus shall I always live
For death's grave ready and prepared;
As for the work my hands now do
It is as though I were full certain
That I today were meant to perish:
For all is well that endeth well!

3. Aria (A)

"O welcome!" will I utter
Then when death my bed doth near.

> Gladly will I follow[1]
> To the tomb;
> All of mine afflictions
> Will I bring.

4. Recit. (S)

Ah, would I were in heaven now!
It is my wish to leave now[2]
And with the lamb,
Of all the righteous bridegroom true,
Find in my blessedness a pasture.
Wings come now!
Ah, would I were in heaven now!

5. Aria (B)

O farewell, thou worldly tumult!

> Now I'll take of thee my leave;
> I stand e'en now with one foot
> Nigh our good Lord God in heaven.

6. Chorale (S, A, T, B)

World, farewell! Of thee I weary,
I would unto heaven go,
Where I'll find that perfect quiet
And eternal, glorious rest.
World, with thee are war and strife,
Nought but utter vanity,
But in heaven endlessly
Peace and joy and happiness.

[1.] OP and OSt also have *fröhlich folge ich* for compositional reasons. There translate "gladly following."

[2.] Cf. *Phil.* 1:23.

BWV 28 **Gottlob! nun geht das Jahr zu Ende**

The Sunday after Christmas.

Erdmann Neumeister, *Geistliche Poesien* (Eisenach, 1714); Facs: Neumann T, p. 293.

2. Johann Gramann, verse 1 of the hymn, 1530 (Wackernagel, III, #968ff.); 3. *Jer.* 32:41; 6. Paul Eber, final verse of "Helft mir Gotts Güte preisen," ca. 1590 (Wackernagel, IV, #7).

30 December 1725, Leipzig.

BG 5, 1; NBA I/3.

---

1. Aria (S)

Praise God! For now the year is ending,
The new year draweth quickly nigh.
Consider, O my spirit, this,
How much thee these thy God's own hands have
Within the old year richly blest!
Raise him a happy song of thanks;
And he will further thee remember
And more in this new year reward thee.

2. Chorale (S, A, T, B)

Now praise, my soul, the Master,
All I possess, his name give praise!
His kindness he will increase,
Forget it not, O heart of mine!
He hath thy sin forgiven
And heals thy weakness all,
He saves thy life so wretched,
Takes thee in his embrace;
With comfort rich anoints thee,
Made young with eagle strength.
The King is just and guardeth
Those suff'ring within his realm.[1]

3. Recit. and Arioso (B)

Thus saith the Lord: It shall to me bring pleasure that I unto them
give favor, and them will I within this land in faith establish, with all
my heart now and with all my spirit.

4. Recit. (T)

God is a spring, where nought but kindness wells;
God is a light, where nought but mercy shineth;

God is a store, which nought but blessing gives;
God is a Lord, with loyal, heartfelt purpose.
All him in faith who love, in childlike love adore,
His word sincerely heed
And from all wicked pathways turn,
He gives himself with every blessing.
Who God hath must have every treasure.

5. Aria (A, T)

God hath us in this very year brought such blessing,
That good deed and good health each other encounter.
We praise him sincerely and ask in addition
That he might a happy new year also give us.
Our hope springs from his own unswerving compassion,
We praise him already with most grateful spirit.

6. Chorale (S, A, T, B)

We praise all thy compassion
Father on heaven's throne,
Which thou to us hast proven
Through Christ who is thy Son,
And further ask of thee:
Give us a peaceful year now,
From every woe defend us
And us with kindness feed.

---

1. Although the PT has *Die leid'n in seinem Reich* ("They suffer in his realm"),
   Bach has *Die leiden in seinem Reich*.

BWV 29 **Wir danken dir, Gott, wir danken dir**

Inauguration of the New Town Council.

Poet unknown; PT: Nützliche Nachrichten (Leipzig, 1739); Facs: Neumann T, p. 378; PT: for 1749 performance (Leipzig, 1749); Facs: Neumann T, p. 420.

2. *Ps.* 75:2; 8. Johann Gramann, verse 5 of "Nun lob, mein Seel, den Herren," 1548 (Wackernagel, I, #455).

27 August 1731, 1739, and 1749, Leipzig; Parody: 1 ← BWV 1006 and BWV 120a; 2 ← Mass in B Minor, BWV 232/6 and 25 (I,7 and IV, 5).

BG 5, 1; NBA I/32.

1. Sinfonia

2. Chorus [Dictum] (S, A, T, B)

We give thee thanks, God, we give thee thanks and proclaim to the world thy wonders.

3. Aria (T)

Hallelujah, strength and might
To the name of God Almighty!
Zion is his city still,
Where he doth his dwelling keep,
Where he still with our descendants
Keeps our fathers' covenant.

4. Recit. (B)

Praise God! We are so blest!
God is still our sure confidence,
His shield, his help and light
Protect the town and all its mansions,
His pinions hold the walls unshaken.[1]
He gives us ev'rywhere his blessing,
And faithfulness which kisseth peace
Must evermore
With justice meet together.[2]
Where is a people such as we,
Whom God so near and gracious is?

5. Aria (S)

Remember us with thine affection,
Embrace us in thy mercy's arms!

     Bless all those who us now govern,
     Those who lead us, guard us, guide us,
     Bless those who obey as well!

6. Recit. (A and S, A, T, B)

(A)
Forget not further still with thine own hand
Prosperity to give us;
Thus shall
Now this our town and this our land,
Here with thine honor filled,
With sacrifice and thanks extol thee,
And all the people shall say:

(S, A, T, B)
Amen![3]

7. Aria (A)

Hallelujah, strength and might
To the name of God Almighty!

8. Chorale (S, A, T, B)

Now laud and praise with honor
God Father, Son, and Holy Ghost!
That he in us make flourish
What he to us in mercy pledged,
That we should firmly trust him,
In full on him relying,
Sincerely in him hoping;
That our heart, mind and will
To him with joy be fastened;
To this now let us sing:
Amen, we shall achieve it,
We trust with all our heart.[4]

[1.] Cf. *Ps.* 122:7.
[2.] Cf. *Ps.* 85:11.
[3.] Cf. *Dt.* 27:15-26.
[4.] With *Glauben* translate "We shall trust . . ."

BWV 30 **Freue dich, erlöste Schar**

St. John the Baptist.

Poet unknown, probably Picander.

6. Johann Olearius, verse 3 of "Tröstet, tröstet meine Lieben," 1671
(Fischer-Tümpel, IV, #42).

24 June 1738 or in one of the following years, Leipzig; Parody: 1, 3, 5, 8, 9, 10, 12 ← BWV 30a.

BG 5, 1; NBA I/29.

First Part

1. Aria (S, A, T, B)

Joyful be, O ransomed throng,
Joyful be in Zion's dwellings.

> Thy well-being hath henceforth
> Found a sure and solid means
> Thee with bliss and health to shower.

2. Recit. (B)

We now have rest,
The burden of the law
Has been removed.
Nought shall from this repose distract us,
Which our belove'd fathers oft
Had sought with yearning and with hope.
Come forth,
Be joyful all, whoever can,
And raise to pay their God due honor
A song of praise,
And all the heav'nly choir,
Yea, sing in glad accord!

3. Aria (B)

All praise be to God, all praise for his name's sake,
Who faithfully keepeth his promise and vow!

His faithful servant hath been born now,
Who long had for this been elected,
That he the Lord his way prepare.

4. Recit. (A)

The herald comes and sounds the king's approach,
He calls; so tarry not
And get ye up,
And with a lively pace
Rush to this voice's call!
It shows the way, it shows the light
By which we on those blessed pastures
At last may surely gaze with wonder.

5. Aria (A)

Come, ye sorely tempted sinners,
Haste and run, O Adam's children,
This your Savior calls and cries!
Come ye, all ye errant sheep now,
Rise ye up from sin-filled slumber,
For now is the hour of grace!

6. Chorale (S, A, T, B)

There a voice of one is crying
In the desert far and wide,
Leading mankind to conversion:
For the Lord the way prepare,
Make for God the pathway smooth,
All the world should now arise,
Every valley be exalted,
That the mountains may be humbled.

Second Part

7. Recit. (B)

If thou dost then, my hope, intend
That law which thou didst make
With our own fathers to uphold now
And in thy gracious power to rule o'er us,
Then will I set with utmost care
On this my purpose:
Thee, faithful God, at thy command
In holiness and godly fear to serve now.

8. Aria (B)

I will detest now
And all avoid now
Which thee, my God, doth cause offense.
I will thee not cause sadness,
Instead sincerely love thee,
For thou to me so gracious art.

9. Recit. (S)

And even though the fickle heart
In human weakness is innate,
Yet here and now let this be said:
So oft the rosy morning dawns,
So long one day the next one lets ensue,
So long will I both strong and firm
Through thine own Spirit live,
My God, entirely for thine honor.
And now shall both my heart and voice
According to thy covenant
With well deservéd praise extol thee.

10. Aria (S)

Haste, ye hours, come to me,
Bring me soon into those pastures!
I would with the holy throng
To my God an altar raise,
In the tents of Kedar offered,[1]
Where I'll give eternal thanks.

11. Recit. (T)

Forbear, the loveliest of days
Can no more far and distant be,
When thou from every toil
Of imperfection's earthly burdens,
Which thee, my heart, doth now enthrall,
Wilt come to have thy perfect freedom.
Thy hope will come at last,
When thou with all the ransomed spirits,
In that perfected state,
From death here of the body wilt be freed,
And there thee no more woe will torment.

12. Aria (S, A, T, B)

Joyful be, O hallowed throng,
Joyful be in Zion's pastures!
Of thy joyful majesty,
Of thy full contentment's bliss
Shall all time no end e'er witness.

[1.] Cf. *Ps.* 120:5.

BWV 31 **Der Himmel lacht! die Erde jubilieret**

Easter.

Salomo Franck, Evangelisches *Andachts-Opffer . . . in geistlichen Cantaten* (Weimar, 1715); Facs: Neumann T, p. 278; PT (Leipzig, 1724); Facs: Neumann T, p. 428; PT (Leipzig, 1731); Facs: Neumann T, p. 438.

8. Chorale melody of Nikolaus Herman's "Wenn mein Stündlein vorhanden ist" ("When my hour is at hand"), 1569 (Wackernagel, I, #499); 9. supplementary verse of the preceding, Bonn, 1575.

21 April 1715, Weimar; 9 April 1724?, Leipzig; 25 March 1731, Leipzig.

BG 7; NBA I/9.

---

1. Sonata

2. Chorus (S, A, T, B)

The heavens laugh! The earth doth ring with glory,
And all she bears within her lap;
Our Maker lives! The Highest stands triumphant
And is from bonds of death now free.
He who the grave for rest hath chosen,
The Holy One, sees not corruption.[1]

3. Recit. (B)

O welcome day! O soul, again be glad!
The A and O,[2]
The first and also last one,

Whom our own grievous guilt in death's own prison buried,
Is now torn free of all his woe!
The Lord was dead,
And lo, again he liveth;
As lives our head, so live as well his members.
The Lord hath in his hand
Of death and also hell the keys now![3]
He who his cloak
Blood-red did splash within his bitter passion,[4]
Today will put on finery and honor.

4. Aria (B)

Prince of being, mighty warrior,
High-exalted Son of God!

> Lifteth thee the cross's ladder
> To the highest honor's throne?
> Will what thee once held in bondage
> Now thy finest jewel be?
> Must all these thy wounds of purple
> Of thy radiance be the beams?[5]

5. Recit. (T)

So therefore now, O soul to God devoted,
With Christ in spirit rise!
Set out upon the new life's course!
Rise, leave the works of dying![6]
Make thine own Savior in the world
Be in thy life reflected!
The grape vine which now blooms
Puts forth no lifeless berries!
The tree of life now lets its branches flourish!
A Christian flees

Full speed the tomb and dying!
He leaves the stone,
He leaves the shroud of error
Behind him
And would with Christ alive abide.

6. Aria (T)

Adam must in us now perish,[7]
If the new man shall recover,
Who like God created is.
Thou in spirit must arise now
And from sin's dark cavern exit
If of Christ the limbs thou art.

7. Recit. (S)

For since the head his limbs
By nature takes with him,
So can me nought from Jesus sever.
If I with Christ must suffer,
So shall I also in due time
With Christ again be risen
To glorious majesty
And God in this my flesh then witness.[8]

8. Aria (S) with Instrum. Chorale

Final hour, break now forth,
These mine eyes to close in darkness!
Let me Jesus' radiant joy
And his brilliant light behold then,
Let me angels then be like!
Final hour, break now forth!

9. Chorale (S, A, T, B)

So forth I'll go to Jesus Christ,
My arm to him extending;
To sleep I'll go and rest so fine,
No man could ever wake me,
For Jesus Christ, of God the Son,
He will the heav'nly door unlock,
To life eternal lead me.

---

1. Cf. *Ps.* 16:10.
2. Cf. *Rev.* 1:8.
3. Cf. *Rev.* 1:18.
4. Cf. *Is.* 13:1-2.
5. Two stylistic motifs typical of Franck are combined in this movement: words of adornment and the ameliorative metamorphosis.
6. Bach changes Franck's text from *von den todten Wercken.* Cf. Luther's translation of *Heb.* 9:14: *wieviel mehr wird das Blut Christi, der sich selbst als ein Opfer ohne Fehl durch den ewigen Geist Gott dargebracht hat, unser Gewissen reinigen von den toten Werken, zu dienen dem lebendigen Gott!* RSV: "how much more shall the blood of Christ, who through the eternal Spirit offered himself without blemish to God, purify your conscience from dead works to serve the living God."
7. Cf. *Eph.* 4:24 and 1 *Cor.* 15:42ff.
8. Cf. Job. 19:26.

BWV 32 **Liebster Jesu, mein Verlangen (Dialogus)**

First Sunday after Epiphany.

Georg Christian Lehms, *Gottgefälliges Kirchen-Opffer* (Darmstadt, 1711); Facs: Neumann T, p. 258.

2. After *Lk*. 2:49; 6. added by Bach: Paul Gerhardt, verse 12 of "Weg, mein Herz, mit den Gedanken," 1647 (Fischer-Tümpel, III, #382), to the melody of "Freu dich sehr, o meine Seele" (cf. BWV 70/7).

13 January 1726, Leipzig.

BG 7; NBA I/5.

Dialogue: Soul (S), Jesus (B)

1. Aria (S) Soul

Dearest Jesus, my desiring,
Tell me now where I'll find thee.
Shall I then so quickly lose thee
And no longer feel thee near me?
Ah, my shield, now gladden me,
Let my fondest joy embrace thee.

2. Recit. [Dictum] (B) Jesus

But why wast thou looking for me? Know'st thou not that I must be within my Father's dwelling?[1]

3. Aria (B) Jesus

Here, within my Father's mansion,
Findeth me a downcast soul.

> Here canst thou most surely find me
> And thy heart to me bind firmly,
> For this is my dwelling called.

4. Recit. (S, B) Soul, Jesus

(Soul)
Ah, holy and most mighty God,
Thus I'll for me
Then here with thee
Seek constant help and consolation.

(Jesus)
If thou of earthly trash art scornful
And only to this dwelling go,
Thou canst both here and there fare well.[2]

(Soul)
How lovely is, though, this thy dwelling,
Lord, mighty Sabaoth;[3]
My spirit longs
For that which only in thy court doth shine.
My soul and body are made glad
Within the living God:[4]
Ah! Jesus, this my heart loves thee alone alway.

(Jesus)
Thou canst then happy be,
If heart and soul
With love for me be now with passion filled.

(Soul)
Ah! This reply, which shall henceforth
My heart from Babel's borders tear,
I shall adoring bind within my spirit now.

5. Aria (S, B) Soul, Jesus

(Both)
Now shall vanish every torment
Now shall vanish "Ah and woe."

(Soul)
Now I will not ever leave thee,

(Jesus)
And I'll also e'er embrace thee.

(Soul)
Now contented is my heart

(Jesus)
And can filled with gladness utter:

(Both)
Now shall vanish every torment
Now shall vanish "Ah and woe!"

6. Chorale (S, A, T, B)

My God, open me the portals
Of this grace and kindliness,
In all times and in all places
Let me thy dear sweetness taste!
Love me, too, and lead me on,
That I may as best I can
Once again embrace and love thee
And may now no more be saddened.

[1.] The fact that the Biblical text is from the boyhood of Jesus does
     not affect the conventional assignment of the Vox Christi to a
     bass.

[2.] "Here and there" means "on earth and in heaven."

[3.] *Sabaoth* Hebr. 'armies.' One might substitute "Lord of hosts."

[4.] *Ps.* 84:2-3.

BWV 33 **Allein zu dir, Herr Jesu Christ**

Thirteenth Sunday after Trinity.

Poet unknown.

1. Konrad Hubert, verse 1 of the hymn, 1540 ; 2-3. based loosely on verse 2; 4-5. based loosely on verse 3; 6. verse 4 of the hymn.

3 September 1724, Leipzig.

BG 7; NBA I/21.

1. Chorus [Verse 1] (S, A, T, B)

Alone to thee, Lord Jesus Christ,
My hope on earth regardeth;
I know thou art my comforter,
I have no other comfort.
Since time began, was nought ordained,
On earth there came no man to birth,
Who from my woe could help me flee.
I call to thee,
In whom I have placed all my trust.

2. Recit. (B)

My God and judge thou, by the law if thou wert me to question,
I could no way,
For that my conscience would forbid,
Once in a thousand answer.[1]
In strength of spirit poor am I, of love left bare,

And all my sin is grave and very great,
But since for them my heart repenteth,
Thou wilt, my God and shield,
Through a forgiving word
Again to me bring gladness.

3. Aria (A)

How fearful wavered then my paces,
But Jesus heareth my petition
And doth me to his Father show.

> Though grievous weight of sin depressed me,
> Again hath Jesus' word assured me
> That he for me enough hath done.

4. Recit. (T)

My God, reject me not,
Although against thy law I daily have offended,
From this thy countenance![2]
The smallest law for me to keep is much too hard;
But, if I for no more
Than Jesus' comfort pray now,
There shall no war of conscience rise
Of confidence to rob me;
Give me but of thy mercy's store
A faith both true and Christian![3]
And it shall come with rich rewards to me
And then through love its work achieve.[4]

5. Aria (T, B)

God, thou who art love now called,
Ah, enkindle this my soul,
Let for thee before all matters

This my love be strongly yearning!
Grant that I with pure devotion
As myself my neighbor cherish;
Should the foe disturb my rest,
Then to me assistance send!

6. Chorale [Verse 4] (S, A, T, B)

Now praise God on the highest throne,
The Father of all goodness,
And Jesus Christ, his dearest Son,
Who us alway protecteth,
And God the Holy Spirit, too,
Who us his help alway doth give,[5]
That we may ever him obey,
Here within this time
And then in all eternity.

[1.] Cf. *Job* 9:3.
[2.] Cf. *Ps.* 51:13.
[3.] This and the preceding line are almost verbatim from the hymn.
[4.] Cf. *Gal.* 5:6.
[5.] The meter of this and the preceding line is heterodyne.

BWV 34 **O ewiges Feuer, o Ursprung der Liebe**

Pentecost (Whitsunday)

Poet unknown.

After 1740; Parody: 1,3,5 ← BWV 34a/1, 5, 4.

BG 7; NBA I/13

1. Chorus (S, A, T, B)

O fire everlasting, O fountain of loving,
Enkindle our hearts now and consecrate them.

> Let heavenly flames now envelop and flood them,
> We wish now, O Highest, thy temple to be,
> Ah, let thee our spirits in faith ever please thee.

2. Recit. (T)

Lord, these our hearts hold out to thee
Thy word[1] of truth to see:
Thou wouldst midst mankind gladly be,
Thus let my heart be thine;
Lord enter graciously.
For such a chosen holy shrine
Hath e'en the greatest fame.

3. Aria (A)

Rejoice, all ye, the chosen spirits,
Whom God his dwelling did elect.
Who can a greater bliss be wanting?
Who can his blessings; number reckon?
And this is by the Lord fulfilled.[2]

4. Recit. (B)

If God doth choose the holy shelters
Where he with health doth dwell,
Then must he, too, his blessing pour upon them,

> And thus the holy temples seat reward.
> The Lord proclaims above his hallowed house
> His word of blessing now:

5. Chorus (S, A, T, B)

Peace be over Israel.
Thank the lofty hands of wonder,
Thank, God hath you in his heart.
Yea, his blessing works with might,
Peace be over Israel,
Peace upon you all he sendeth.

---

1   I.e., the words of the Gospel, *Jn*. 14:23.
2.   Cf. *Ps*. 118:23.
3.   Cf. *Ps*. 128:6

BWV 34a **O ewiges Feuer, o Ursprung der Liebe**

Wedding

Poet unknown; music only partly extant.

3. *Ps*. 128:4-6 with interpolations; 4. first line: *Ps*. 128:6; 7. *Num*. 24-26 with interpolations.

1726?, Leipzig; Parody: 1, 4, 5 → BWV 34/1, 5, 3.

BG 41; NBA I/33.

Part One

1. Aria (S, A, T, B)

O fire everlasting, O fountain of loving,
Enkindle our hearts at the sacred altar.

Let heavenly fires envelop and flood them,
Ah, let upon this our dear couple made one
The rays of the noblest emotions now shower.

2. Recit. (B)

What, doth then love's exalted force
In every human spirit
A paradise on earth create?
What moveth thee, O highest creature,
Affection's influence to elect thee?
A darling for thy house to choose thee?

3. Aria (T) and Recit. (A)

Lo now, e'enso shall be blessed the man who the Lord God feareth.[1]
    Why doth the soul with faithful eyes now press?
    Why seeketh he good fortune's fountain,
    Of faithful souls the wedded state
    As though a prosperous, and promised land's
    Full worth it sought to capture?
The Lord shall so bless thee from Zion,
    But what thy God proposed for thee?
    Thee, whose good works in God's own house await?
    What will thy turn in holy temples
    On thee for blessings shower?
That thou seest Jerusalem prosperous thy whole life long,[2]
    Since Zion's weal did first thy heart concern,
    Then shall e'en earthly goods and pleasures
    To meet thy heart's desires attend thee.
    For God doth here a chosen child to thee now bring,
    That thou in year unnumbered yet
    Renewed prosperity discover.
And thou shat see thy children's children.[3]
    Thus do we cry to bless this moment
    Sincerely with united voices:

4. Aria (S, A, T, B)

Peace be over Israel[4]
Haste unto that holy stairway,
Haste, the Highest bends his ear.

> And our longing welleth up,
> "Peace be over Israel,"
> "Peace be over you" invoking.

Part Two

5. Aria (A)

Well you, ye chosen of the shepherd,
Whom a devoted Jacob loves.

> His wage will there be greatest ever,
> Which him on earth the Lord hath given
> Through this his Rachel's charm and grace.[5]

6. Recit. (S)

This is for thee, O honor-worthy man,
The loftiest of wages
That can thee pleasure give.
God, who since time began hath love itself been called
And did a good and virtuous child thy heart allow to touch,
Make full now with his blessing this thy swelling
As that of Oben Edom was,[6]
And fulfill his benediction, too.

7. Aria (S, A, T, B)

Give, Most high God, once more thy word the strength
Which so much good amongst thy people brings:
The Lord bless thee now and watch over thee[7]

His blessing must upon that one be falling
Who songs like this in holy places singeth:
/A song of thanks unto thy throne be lifted
And at his feet a joyful offering render:/
The Lord shall brighten his countenance upon thee and be thee
gracious,[8]
The deeds of him who in the temple serves
Call forth the Lord's attention and his grace.
/He signeth thee with his paternal hand,
Which thee with many blessing hath endowed.
The Lord lift up his countenance upon thee and give the peace.[9]
The Lord by whom all passion pure is kindled
Preserve them both and speak his mighty Amen.
/Thy health doth stem from God's own name and bosom.
So be now blessed through his most holy Amen.

[1.] *Ps.* 128:4
[2.] *Ps.* 128:5
[3.] *Ps.* 128:6
[4.] *Ps* 128:6
[5.] Cf. *Gen.* 29:15 ff.
[6.] Cf. 2 *Sam.* 6:10-12.
[7.] *Num.* 6:24
[8.] *Num.* 6:25
[9.] *Num.* 6:26

BWV 35 **Geist und Seele wird verwirret**

Twelfth Sunday after Trinity.

Georg Christian Lehms, *Gottgefälliges Kirchen-Opffer* (Darmstadt, 1711);
Facs: Neumann T, p. 261.

8 September 1726, Leipzig; 1 ← a concerto from the Cöthen period,

of which a fragment survives in a version for harpsichord, BWV
1059.

BG 7; NBA I/20.

First Part

1. Concerto

2. Aria (A)

Soul with spirit is bewildered
When it thee, my God, beholds.[1]

> For the wonders, which it knoweth,
> Which the folk with triumph telleth,
> Have it deaf and dumb now made.

3. Recit. (A)

I am amazed;
For ev'rything we see
Must give us cause to marvel.
Regarding thee,
Thou precious Son of God,
From me
My reason and my sense do flee.
Thou art the reason
That even miracles next thee so wretched seem.
Thou art
In name and deed and office truly wonderful,
There is no thing of wonder on the earth like thee.
For hearing givest thou the deaf,
The dumb thou dost return their speaking,
Yea, more than this,

Dost open the lids of eyes unseeing.
These, these are works of wonder,
And to their power
Doth e'en the angel choir lack strength to give expression.

4. Aria (A)

God hath all so well achieved.
His devotion, his good faith
We see every day renewed.
When both fear and toil oppress us,
He hath ample comfort sent us,
For he tendeth us each day.
God hath all so well achieved.

Second Part

5. Sinfonia

6. Recit. (A)

Ah, mighty God, let me
Then this alway remember,
And then I can
Content within my soul implant thee.
For me let thy sweet Hephata[2]
My heart so obstinate now soften;
Ah, lay thou but upon mine ear thy gracious finger,
Or else I soon must perish.
Touch, too, my tongue's restraint
With thine own mighty hand,
That I may all these signs of wonder
In sacred worship praise now,
Myself thine heir and child revealing.

7. Aria (A)

I seek alone with God to live now,
Ah, would that now the time were come,
To raise a glad hallelujah
With all the angels in rejoicing.
My dearest Jesus, do release
This sorrow-laden yoke of pain
And let me soon within thy bosom
My life so full of torment finish.

---

1. Frequently in the cantata texts there is a singular verb with a compound subject, especially when, as here, the two subjects *Geist* and *Seele* have virtually the same meaning (a rhetorical figure called *congeries verborum*). While this might have been allowable in the English of Bach's period, it is probably preferable to avoid the inconcinnity. I have placed one of the subjects in a prepositional phrase and kept a singular verb.

2. *Hephata* Hebr. 'be opened!'

BWV 36 **Schwingt freudig euch empor**

First Sunday in Advent.

Perhaps Picander.

2. Martin Luther, verse 1 of "Nun komm, der Heiden Heiland" (the translation of "Veni redemptor gentium"), 1524 (Wackernagel, III, #16); 4. Philipp Nicolai, verse 6 of "Wie schön leuchtet der Morgenstern," 1599; 6. verse 6 of "Nun komm, der Heiden Heiland"; 8. final verse of the preceding.

2 December 1731, Leipzig; Parody: 1, 3, 5, 7 ← BWV 36c/1, 3, 5, 7.

BG 7; NBA I/1.

First Part

1. Chorus (S, A, T, B)

Soar joyfully aloft amidst the starry grandeur,
Ye voices, ye who now in Zion gladly dwell!
No, wait awhile! Your sound shall not have far to travel,
To you draws nigh himself the Lord of majesty.

2. Chorale (S, A)

Come now, the nations' Savior,
As the Virgin's child made known,
At this marvels all the world,
That God this birth gave to him.

3. Aria (T)

Now love doth draw with gentle paces
Its true beloved more and more

　　　Like as it brings the bride enchantment
　　　When she the bridegroom near beholdeth,
　　　E'en so the heart for Jesus yearns.

4. Chorus (S, A, T, B)

Raise the viols in Cythera
And let now charming Musica
With joy and gladness echo,
That I may with my Jesus-child,

With this exquisite groom of mine,
In constant love e'er journey.
Sing now,
Dance now,
Jubilation cry triumphant, thank the Lord now!
Great is the king of all honor.

Second Part

5. Aria (B)q

O welcome, dearest love!
My love and faith prepare a place
For thee within my heart that's pure,
Come dwell in me!

6. Chorale (S, A, T, B)

Thou who art the Father like,
Lead the conquest o'er the flesh,
That thy God's eternal power
May by our sick flesh be held.

7. Aria (S)

E'en with our muted, feeble voices
Is God's great majesty adored.

> For sound nought but our soul alone,
> This is to him a mighty shout,
> Which he in heaven itself doth hear.

8. Chorale (S, A, T, B)

Praise to God, the Father, be,
Praise to God, his only Son,

Praise to God, the Holy Ghost,
Ever and eternally!

BWV 36a **Steigt freudig in die Luft**

Birthday of Charlotte Friederike Amalie, second wife of Prince Leopold of Anhalt-Cöthen.

Christian Friedrich Henrici (Picander), *Ernst-Schertzhaffte und Satyrische Gedichte*, Teil I (Leipzig, 1727; 2nd ed., 1732; 3rd ed., 1736); Facs: Neumann T, p. 312; Music lost.

?30 November 1726, Leipzig; Parody: 1, 3, 5, 7, 9 ← BWV 36c/1, 3, 5, 7, 9.

BG 34; NBA I/1, Krit. Bericht and NBA I/35.

Bey der Ersten Geburths-Feyer

Der Durchlauchtigsten Fürstin zu
Anhalt-Cöthen. 1726

[1.] Aria

Steigt freudig in die Lufft zu den erhabenen Höhen,
Ihr Wünsche, die ihr ietzt in unsern Hertzen wallt;
Doch bleibet hier; Ihr dürfft so weit nicht von uns gehen,
Die Theure Hertzogin ist euer Auffenthalt.

[2. Recit.]

Durchlauchtigste,
Die tieffgebückte Schuldigkeit
Erscheint zu Deinen Füssen,

Die Hulde, so Dein Eigenthum,
Dein Glantz, Dein Welt bekannter Ruhm
Macht uns von aller Schüchternheit
Und allen Fürchten frey,
Daß wir der Lippen Melodei
Mehr halten, als befördern müssen.

[3.] Aria

Die Sonne zieht mit sanfften Triebe
Die Sonnen-Wende zu sich hin.
So, Grosse Fürstin, Deinen Blicken,
Die unser gantzes Wohl beglücken,
Folgt unser stets getreuer Sinn.

Da Capo.

[4. Recit.]

Die Danckbarkeit,
So Tag und Nacht
In unsern Hertzen nachgedacht,
Ein Merckmahl ihrer Pflicht zu zeigen,
Macht dieser Tag erfreut,
Das Dich du Kleinod unsrer Zeit,
Das Licht der Erden hat erblicket.
Und da Dein Theurer Leopold,
Und jedes, was Dir treu und hold,
Sich über dieses Fest erquicket.
So können wir auch nicht
Die Demuths-volle Pflicht
Vor Deinen Ohren ietzt verschweigen.

[5.] Aria

Sey willkommen, schönster Tag!
Wer Zung und Odem noch vermag,

Der stimm in diese Harmonie:
Charlotte blüh!

[6. Recit.]

Wiewohl das ist noch nicht genung,
Die Demuth, Treu und Unterthänigkeit,
Die wir vor Dich in unsern Hertzen hegen,
Dir völlig also darzulegen.
Denn daß das Hertz Dir süsse Wünsche streut,
Der Mund Dir lauter Heyl verspricht,
Das ist, Durchlauchtste, unsrer Pflicht
Nur ein Erinnerung;
Und trügen wir uns selbst Dir eigen an,
So wird der Pflicht noch nicht genung gethan,
Doch wir Dir unser schwaches lallen
In Gnaden wohl gefallen.

[7.] Aria

Auch mit gedämpfften schwachen Stimmen
Wird, Fürstin, dieses Fest verehrt.
Denn schallet nur der Geist darbey,
So heisset solches ein Geschrey,
Das man im Himmel selber hört.

Da Capo.

[8. Recit.]

Doch ehe wir
Noch Deinen Thron verlassen,
Soll unser Geist,
Der, Grosse Fürstin, Dir
Auf ewig eigen heist,
Den Wunsch in solche Worte fassen:

[9.] Aria

Grüne, blühe, lebe lange,
Grosse Fürstin, sey beglückt!
Wiewohl wer so, wie Du,
Den Himmel liebt,
Hat lauter Heyl und Ruh,
Dieweil darauf der Himmel Achtung giebt.
Was Dein Hertze kan begehren,
Müsse Dir das Glück beschehren!
Doch will es Deine hohen Gaben
Zum Maasse seines Wohltuns haben;
Sonst ist es selbst zu arm darzu.
Dieses Licht, das Du erblickt,
Wisse nichts vom Untergange!
Diß treue Seuffzen wird erlanget,
Dieweil daran
Die Helffte Deiner Brust,
Des Milden Leopoldens Lust,
Der Wunsch und Wohl von jedem Unterthan
Und Deiner Diener Wohlfarth hanget.
Grüne, blühe, lebe lange,
Grosse Fürstin, sey beglückt!

1. Aria

Soar gladly through the air to the lofty grandeur,
Ye wishes, ye which now within our hearts well up;
But wait ye here; ye may so far not from us journey,
The worthy Duchess offers cause for your delay.

2. Recit.

Serenest one,
Our deeply humble gratitude
Appears before thy presence;

Thy favor and thy character,
Thy grace, thy world-acknowledged fame
Make us from ev'ry bashfulness
And ev'ry worry free,
That we should our lips' melody
Restrain more than advance before thee.

3. Aria

The sun doth draw with soft insistence
The solar eclipse to itself.
Thus, lofty Princess, to thy glances,
Which make our whole well-being prosper,
Attend our ever faithful hearts.

Da Capo.

4. Recit.

The gratitude
Which day and night
Within our hearts hath pondered how
A token of its debt to show thee,
Is by this day made glad,
Since thee, thou jewel of our time,
The light of earth now hath regarded;
And since thy precious Leopold
And all, who thee are true and dear,
Are by this festival enlivened,
So we as well cannot
Our humble duty's task
Before thine ears now leave unspoken.

5. Aria

Receive our welcome, finest day!
Who tongue and breath still yet possess

Join in now this our harmony:
Charlotte, bloom!

6. Recit.

In truth this is not yet enough,
The humble faith and loyal servitude
Which we for thee within our bosoms nurture
Sufficiently to lay before thee.
For that our hearts to thee sweet wishes cast,
Our mouths thee nought but health extend,
This is, Serenest, of our debt
But faint suggestion,
For if we gave our very selves to thee,
We would our debt not yet in full have met;
Yet will in thee our feeble stammer
Most graciously find favor.

7. Aria

E'en with our muted, feeble voices
Is, Princess, this great feast revered.
For sound nought but our soul alone,
It cometh as a very shout
Which doth in heav'n itself resound.

Da Capo.

8. Recit.

But ere we yet
Hence from thy throne have parted,
Our spirit must,
Which, lofty Princess, thine
Forever shall be called,
Its wish in words like these now offer.

9. Aria and Recit.

Flourish, blosom, live thou long yet,
Lofty Princess, be thou blest!
Although, who so, as thou,
Doth heaven love,
Hath nought but health and peace,
So long as this doth heaven's care receive.
What thy heart could ever long for,
Must to thee good fortune offer!
But it would thine own noble blessings
As measure of its kindness reckon,
Or else it is for this too poor.
May this light which thou dost see
Nought e'er know of any setting!
Our faithful sighing will be granted
As long thereto
The half of thine own heart,
The gentle Leopold's delight,
The hope and wish of ev'ry loyal liege
And this thy servant's welfare tendeth.
Flourish, blosom, live thou long yet,
Lofty Princess, be thou blest!

BWV 36b **Die Freude reget sich**

Congratulatory Cantata for the Leipzig scholar Johann Florens Rivinus (probably for his inauguration as Rector of the University).

Perhaps Picander.

?October 1735, Leipzig; Parody: 1, 3, 5, 7, 8 ← BWV 36c/1, 3, 5, 7, 9.

BG 34; NBA I/38.

1. Chorus (S, A, T, B)

Now gladness doth arise, doth raise the lively music,
For this most lovely day hath no one left unstirred.
Pursue our wish, be quick, ye loyal sons of muses,
And pay in full the toll of your good wishes now!

2. Recit. (T)

Ye see how the good fortune
Of our revered Rivin through its familiar glances
At this occasion's happy hour
Is for his house's weal renewed.
For blessing crowneth all the labors
Which our fond jurist hath so much advantage brought.
And all this blessing doth through its own mighty pow'r
Make woe and all distress flee from his very presence.

3. Aria (T)

From God's own gentle hands paternal
Flows this his children's happiness.

> He can both truth and goodness give us,
> He gives us more than we imagine
> And better than we understand.

4. Recit. (A)

Thy friends are most content
This feast and day of praise to witness;
They can, indeed, their hopes on certain grounds establish,
Upon his grace, who wisely all directs,
Whose many tests have shown already
That this most godly man a thousand times hath praised him.
What? May we also be in his good fortune glad?
Disdain us not, thou good and kind Rivin,

If we as well take pains
And cause here now, to pay thee honor,
E'en our own songs to echo.

5. Aria (A)

That favor which thy God doth grant
And which on thee today doth fall
Makes thy most welcome happiness
For us shine too.

6. Recit. (A)

If now the world doth to thy glory tend,
Which through thy learne'd labor e'er to grow is wont,
If thine own righteousness a worthy model giveth
How one his neighbor serves and God thereby yet loveth,
If thine own noble house upon thy forethought stands,
Through which as well the poor it helps,
We witness this but with admiring awe,
For our own poverty can nothing higher dare.

7. Aria (A)

With tender and contented feelings
We honor thy dear graciousness.

> If echo, though, could once a song,
> Which thee from mortal state could free,
> We are for this as well prepared.

8. Aria (S, A, T, B) and Recit. (T, A, S)

(S, A, T, B)
What good fortune we have wished thee,
We would wish thee ten times more.

(T)
Oh yes! This thou hast earned:
Who thee from thy repute doth know
Transgression's scourge doth name,
But of the righteous the defense and shield,
Who doth all need and woe defy.
Thee shall no misfortune torment,
Nought for thine own welfare lacking.

(A)
May all thy house
Now like a temple seem,
Where one more praise than anxious sighing hears,
In which no harm its sweet repose disturbs.
All this joy delights too much,
More than we have pow'r to utter.

(S)
Thus wilt thou, honored Sir, forgive us
If meanwhile we, who trust our teacher's faith,
Ourselves with him at this thy feast take pleasure;
And too, that we be bound
No more good wishes here to speak.
What good fortune we have wished thee,
We would wish thee ten times more.

BWV 36c **Schwingt freudig euch empor**

Birthday Cantata for a teacher

Poet perhaps Picander; original format for BWV 36a (so Dürr, p. 46);

April or May? 1725, Leipzig; 1, 3, 5, 7, 9 Parody → BWV 36b and 1, 3, 5, 7 Parody → BWV 36.

BG 7, Anhang, and 34; NBA I/39.

---

1. Chorus (S, A, T, B)

With gladness rise aloft, unto the stars press onward,
Good wishes, till you God before his throne beholds!
Yet, pause awhile! a heart need not span such great distance
That gratitude and duty to its teacher sends.

2. Recit. (T)

A heart that's filled with soft affections,
That in him endless joy awakes,
Is almost overwhelmed in its own pleasure,
For to it hope doth ever more reveal.
It riseth like a brilliant light,
Devotions ardor to God's holy shrine;
How true, the worthy teacher's fame
Is his own pole, to which, a magnet like,
His hopes and his deep longing tend.

3. Aria (T)

Love's force doth guide with gentle paces
A heart that its dear teacher loves.

Where others to excess are yielding,
This heart more cautiously is stirring
For to it reverence measure bids.

4. Recit. (B)

Thou art, indeed, O much deserving Sir,
The man who in unbroken teaching
With highest honors
The senior badge of silver can display.
Thanks, veneration, fame,
They all come here together;
And since thou these our hearts
As light and leader must direct,
Thou wilt this joyful commendation not disfavor.

5. Aria (B)

The day that thee long hence did bear
Appears to us so blessed now
As that day when our Maker saith:
Let there be light!

6. Recit. (S)

Just this one thing doth worry us:
Our offering may be too imperfect;
Yet, if it but by thee,
O honored teacher, kindly be accepted,
Its worth, however poor, will rise
As high as our devoted hearts desire.

7. Aria (S)

E'en with our muted, feeble voices
Proclaim we this our teacher's praise.

> It echoes forceful in our breast
> Although the joy which we here feel
> But partly know itself to tell.

8. Recit (T)

In such delightful joyful moments
Is our well-wishing's aim fulfilled,
Which all in all
But for thy life doth hope.

9. Chorus (S, A, T, B) and Recit. (T, B, S)

As the years find their renewal
So renewed be now thy fame!

> But yet, why do we wish,
> For this will of itself come true,
> And since indeed thy fame,
> Which our own Helicon[1] knoweth best,
> Is seen as well in other climes?

Thy deserts' full proclamation
Summons more than we are able.

> So we shall hush
> And show thereby to thee
> Our gratitude though not within our mouths
> Is all the more within our hearts expressed.

This thy life's most holy shrine
Can completely give us pleasure.

> When gratitude our mouths doth open,
> Then every limb doth in the pleasure share;
> The eye extends beyond its wonted limits
> And sees thy coming happy fate.

As the years find their renewal,
So renewed by now thy fame!

---

1. The tenor refers to the chorus as Muses or children of Muses, the express
roll of the chorus in BWV 36b/1.

BWV 37 **Wer da gläubet und getauft wird**

Ascension.

Poet unknown.

1. *Mk.* 16:16; 3. Philipp Nicolai, verse 5 of "Wie schön leuchtet der
Morgenstern," 1599; 6. Johann Kolrose, verse 4 of "Ich dank dir,
lieber Herre," ca. 1535 (Wackernagel, III, #114).

18 April 1724, Leipzig.

BG 7; NBA I/12.

---

1. Chorus [Dictum] (S, A, T, B)

He who trusteth[1] and is baptized, he shall have salvation.

2. Aria (T)

Belief doth guarantee the love now
Which Jesus for his people keeps.

> Thus hath he from pure love's emotion,
> When he into life's book enrolled me,
> On me this precious gem bestowed.

3. Chorale (S, A)

Lord God, Father, my champion strong!
Thou hast me e'er before the world
In thine own Son belove'd.
Thy Son hath me himself betrothed,
He is my store, I am his bride,
Most high in him rejoicing.
Eia!
Eia!
Life in heaven shall he give to me supernal;
Ever shall my heart extol him.

4. Recit. (B)

Ye mortal folk, do ye now long
With me
God's countenance to see before you?
Then ye should not be on good works dependent;
For though a Christian ought
Indeed in good works ever labor,
Because this is the solemn will of God,
Yet doth our faith alone assure
That we 'fore God be justified and saved.

5. Aria (B)

Belief provides the soul with pinions,
On which it shall to heaven soar,
Baptism is the seal of mercy
Which us God's saving blessing brings;
And thus is called the Christian blest
Who doth believe and is baptized.

6. Chorale (S, A, T, B)

Belief bestow upon me
In thy Son Jesus Christ,
My sins as well forgive me
While I am in this life.
Thou wilt not e'er deny me
What thou hast promised me,
That he my sin shall carry
And loose me of its weight.

---

1. The central theme of this cantata is *der Glaube* 'belief.' Where the music allows, I have translated it with "belief," but have substituted "trust" or "faith" where necessary.

BWV 38 **Aus tiefer Not schrei ich zu dir**

Twenty-first Sunday after Trinity.

Poet unknown.

1. Martin Luther, verse 1 of the hymn, 1524 (Wackernagel, I, #188), after *Ps.* 130; 2-3. based freely on verses 2-3; 4. based loosely on verse 3 and 4 and *Jn.* 4:47-54, with the chorale melody; 5. based freely on verse 4; 6. verse 5 of the hymn.

29 October 1724, Leipzig.

BG 7; NBA I/25.

---

1. Chorus [Verse 1] (S, A, T, B)

In deep distress I cry to thee,
Lord God, hear thou my calling;
Thy gracious ear bend low to me
And open to my crying!
For if thou wilt observance make
Of sin and deed unjustly done,
Who can, Lord, stand before thee?

2. Recit. (A)

In Jesus' mercy will alone
Our comfort be and our forgiveness rest,
Because through Satan's craft and guile
Is mankind's whole existence
'Fore God a sinful outrage found.
What could then now
Bring peace and joy of mind to us in our petitions
If Jesus' Spirit's word did not new wonders do?

3. Aria (T)

I hear amidst my very suff'ring
This comfort which my Jesus speaks.

> Thus, O most anguished heart and spirit,
> Put trust in this thy God's dear kindness,
> His word shall stand and never fail,
> His comfort never thee abandon!

4. Recit. (S) with instr. chorale

Ah!
That my faith is still so frail,
And that all my reliance

On soggy ground I must establish!
How often must I have new portents
My heart to soften!
What? Dost thou know thy helper not,
Who speaks but one consoling word,
And then appears,
Before thy weakness doth perceive,
Salvation's hour.
Just trust in his almighty hand and in his mouth so truthful.

5. Aria (S, A, B)

When my despair as though with fetters
One sorrow to the next doth bind,
Yet shall no less my Savior free me,
And all shall sudden from me fall.
How soon appears the hopeful morning
Upon the night of woe and sorrow!

6. Chorale [Verse 5] (S, A, T, B)

Though with us many sins abound,
With God is much more mercy;
His hand's assistance hath no end,
However great our wrong be.
He is alone our shepherd true,
Who Israel shall yet set free
Of all his sinful doings.

BWV 39 Brich dem Hungrigen dein Brot

First Sunday after Trinity.

Poet unknown, Christoph Helm?;[1] PT (Rudolstadt, 1726).

1. *Is.* 58:7-8; 4. *Heb.* 13:16; 7. David Denicke, verse 6 of "Kommt, laßt euch den Herren lehren," 1648 (Fischer-Tümpel, II, #404).

23 June 1726, Leipzig.

BG 7; NBA I/15.

First Part

1. Chorus [Dictum] (S, A, T, B)

Break with hungry men thy bread and those who in want are found take in thy house! If thou dost a man see naked, then cover him and withdraw thyself not from thy flesh. And then shall thy light through all break forth like the rosy morning, and thy recovery shall wax quickly, and thine own righteousness shall go forth before thee, and the majesty of the Lord God shall receive thee.

2. Recit. (B)

The bounteous God casts his abundant store
On us, those who without him were not even breathing.
His is all that we are; he gives us but the use,
But not that us alone
Should these his treasures comfort.
They as a touchstone serve
By which he hath revealed
That he to poor men also need hath freely given,
And hath with open hand,
Whate'er the poor require, to us so richly proffered[2].
We are required for all the wealth he lends
No interest into his barns to carry;
But mercy which is to one's neighbor shown
Can more than any gift be to his heart compelling.

3. Aria (A)

One's creator while on earth yet
Even dimly to resemble
Is a foretaste of true bliss.
His compassion's way to follow
Scatters here the seeds of blessing
Which in heaven we shall reap.

Second Part

4. Aria [Dictum] (B)

To do good and share your blessings forget ye not; for these are
off'erings well-pleasing to God.

5. Aria (S)

Highest, my possessions
Are but what thou givest.
If before thy countenance
I with what I have now
Grateful seek to venture,
Thou wouldst not an offering have.

6. Recit. (A)

How shall I then, O Lord, sufficiently repay thee
All that for flesh and soul thou hast bestowed on me?
Yea, what I yet receive, and that by no means seldom,
Since I at every hour still can thy praises tell?[3]
I own nought but my soul which I to thee may offer,
To neighbor nought but hope that I shall serve him well,
To poor men, all thou me hast giv'n within my lifetime,
And, if it be thy will, my feeble flesh to earth.

I'll offer what I can, Lord, let it find thy favor,
That I all thou hast pledged from them e'en yet may gather.

7. Chorale (S, A, T, B)

Blessed those who through compassion
Bear the weight of others' woe,
Who with pity for the wretched
Pray steadfast for them to God.
They who helpful are in word,
And if possible in deed,
Shall in turn receive thy succor
And themselves obtain compassion.

[1.] Helm is suggested by W. Blankenburg, BJ (1977).

[2.] I.e., God has created the poor to test our generosity and compassion: He gives us what we should pass on to the poor.

[3.] This is punctuated as a rhetorical question expecting an affirmative response.

BWV 40 **Dazu ist erschienen der Sohn Gottes**

Second Day of Christmas (St. Stephen).

Poet unknown.

1. 1 *Jn*. 3:8; 3. Kaspar Füger, verse 3 of "Wir Christenleut," 1592; 6. Paul Gerhardt, verse 2 of "Schwing dich auf zu deinem Gott," 1653 (Fischer-Tümpel, III, #445); 10. Christian Keymann, "Freuet euch, ihr Christen alle," 1646 (Fischer-Tümpel, IV, #8).

26 December 1723, Leipzig; Parody: 1 → Mass in F Major, BWV 233/6.

BG 7; NBA I/3.

---

1. Chorus [Dictum] (S, A, T, B)

For this is appearéd the Son of God, that he destroy all the works of
the devil.

2. Recit. (T)

The word was flesh and dwelleth in the world,[1]
The world's true light doth shine throughout the earth now,
The mighty Son of God
Hath left the throne of heaven,
And in his majesty would be
A little child of human nature.
Give thought to this exchange, all ye who thought possess:
The king a subject is become,
The Lord as servant doth appear
And for this mortal race of man
—O sweetest word to all who hear it—
Is born to heal and comfort.

3. Chorale (S, A, T, B)

Though sin brings pain,
Our Christ brings joy,
For as our comfort he this world hath entered.
With us is God
Now in our need:
Who could us now as Christians bring damnation?

4. Aria (B)

Hell's very serpent,
Art thou not anxious?
He who thy head as a victor shall dash
Is to us born now,
And all the fallen
Shall in eternal repose be made glad.

5. Recit. (A)

The serpent that in paradise
Upon all Adam's children
The bane of souls did cause to fall
Brings us no danger more;
The woman's seed is manifest,[2]
The Savior is in flesh appearéd
And hath from it[3] removed all venom.
Take comfort then, O troubled sinner!

6. Chorale (S, A, T, B)

Shake thy head now and declare:
Flee, thou ancient serpent!
Why renewest thou thy sting
For my fear and anguish?
Now indeed thy head is dashed,
And I've through the passion
Of my Savior fled from thee
To the hall of gladness.

7. Aria (T)

Christian children, now rejoice!
Raging now is hell's domain,

> You would Satan's fury frighten:
> Jesus, who can rescue bring,
> Would embrace his little chicks
> And beneath his wings protect them.[4]

8. Chorale (S, A, T, B)

Jesus, take now these thy members
Henceforth with thy loving grace;

Pour out all that we could ask
To the comfort of thy brethren;
Give to all the Christian throng
Concord and a blessed year!
Gladness, gladness after gladness!
Christ shall ward off every sadness.
Rapture, rapture after rapture!
For he is the sun of favor.

[1.] Cf. *Jn.* 1:14.
[2.] Cf. *Gen.* 3:15.
[3.] I.e., the serpent.
[4.] Cf. *Mt.* 23:37.

BWV 41 **Jesu, nun sei gepreiset**

New Year's Day (Feast of the Circumcision)

Poet unknown.

1. Johannes Herman, verse 1 of the hymn, 1593; 2-5. based freely on verse 2; 6. 6th and final verse of the hymn.

1 January 1725; again after 1732 (Neumann Hb).

BG 10; NBA I/4.

---

1. Chorus [Verse 1] (S, A, T, B)

Be praised now, O Lord Jesus,
At this the newborn year
For thy help which thou showest
In all our dread and stress,[1]

That we ourselves have witnessed
The new and joyful age
Which full of blessing bideth,
And lasting happiness;
That we in goodly stillness
The old year have completed.
Ourselves we'd[2] thee surrender
For now and evermore,
Protect[3] life, soul and body
Henceforth through all the year![4]

2. Aria (S)

Let us, O highest God, the year accomplish
That it be ended even as it was begun.

Beside us let thy hand abide,
That later, when the year hath closed,
We be midst blessing's rich excess,
As now, a hallelujah singing.

3. Recit. (A)

Ah, thine own hand, thy blessing must alone
The A and O, beginning and the ending be!
Our whole life holdest thou within thy hand,
The number of our days with thee stands written;
Thine eye doth watch o'er town and land;
Thou tellest all our weal and knowest all our sorrow,
Ah, give from both now,
Whate'er thy wisdom will, wherever thy great mercy thee hath prompted.

4. Aria (T)

For just as thou hast noble concord
To this our flesh and state allotted,
So grant my soul as well thy gracious, healing word.

If us this health befalleth,
We shall be here most blessed
And thine elected there![5]

5. Recit. (B) and Chorus (S, A, T, B)

(B)
But since the foe both day and night
To do us harm doth watch
And our tranquillity would ruin,
May it please thee, O Lord our God, to hear us
When we in sacred congregation beg thee:

(S, A, T, B)
That Satan underneath our feet be trampled.[6]

(B)
And we'll forever to thy praise
As thine elect belong to thee
And also after cross and passion
From here depart into great glory.

6. Chorale (S, A, T, B)

Thine is alone the honor,
Thine is alone the praise;
To bear the cross now teach us,
And rule our every deed,
Till we depart with rapture
To heaven's eternal realm,
Into true peace and gladness,
The saints of God made like.
With us deal in the meanwhile
According to thy pleasure:
Thus sing today in earnest

The Christ-believing throngs
And wish with voice and spirit
A new and blessed year.

[1.] Where necessary, in the lower parts read "In all our dread and distress."

[2.] Where necessary, in the lower parts read "Ourselves we would thee surrender."

[3.] Where necessary, in the lower parts read "Protect our life, soul and body."

[4.] From the Litany of Martin Luther, 1528/29.

[5.] I.e., both here on earth and there in heaven.

[6.] From the Litany of Martin Luther, 1528/29.

BWV 42 **Am Abend aber desselbigen Sabbats**

Quasimodogeniti (First Sunday after Easter). Poet unknown; PT (Leipzig, 1731); Facs: Neumann T, p. 442.

2. *Jn.* 20:19; 4. Jakob Fabricius, verse 1 of "Verzage nicht, o Häuflein klein," (ascribed to M. Altenburg in Fischer-Tümpel, II, #56); 7. Martin Luther, verse 1 of "Verleih uns Frieden gnädiglich" ("Da pacem Domine"), 1529 (Wackernagel, III, #35ff.) with the traditional supplement based on 1 *Tim.* 2:2, "Gib unsern Fürsten und aller Obrigkeit" by Johann Walter, 1566.

8 April 1725, Leipzig; re-performance 1731 and after 1735 (Neumann Hb).

BG 10; NBA I/11.

---

1. Sinfonia

2. Recit. [Dictum] (T)

The evening, though, of the very same Sabbath, the disciples
assembled, and the doors had been fastened tightly for fear of the
Jews when Jesus came and walked among them.

3. Aria (A)

Where two and three assembled are[1]
For Jesus' precious name's sake,
There cometh Jesus in their midst
And speaks o'er them his Amen.
For that which love and need have caused
Doth not the Highest's order break.

4. Aria (S, T)

Do not despair, O little flock,
E'en though the foe may well intend
Thee fully to destroy
And seek a way to bring thee down,
Wherefore thou shalt know fear and dread:
It shall not long be lasting.

5. Recit. (B)

One can from this a fine example summon,
From that which in Jerusalem did happen;
When the disciples had assembled that day
In gloomy shadows
Because they feared the Jews then,[2]
There came my Savior in their midst
To witness that he for his church its shield would be.
Thus, leave the foe his fury!

6. Aria (B)

Jesus shall now shield his people
When them persecution strikes.
For their sake the sun must shine forth
With the golden superscript:
Jesus shall now shield his people,
When them persecution strikes.

7. Chorale (S, A, T, B)

Now grant us concord graciously,
Lord God, in our own season;
For there indeed no other is
Who for us could do battle
Than thou, our God, thou only.
Give to our princes and all magistrates
Peace and good governance,
So that we beneath them
A most peaceful and quiet life may lead forever
In godliest devotion and honesty.
Amen.

[1.]   Cf. *Mt.* 18:20.
[2.]   Cf. *Jn.* 20:19.

BWV 43 **Gott fähret auf mit Jauchzen**

Ascension.

Poet unknown (Christoph Helm?);[1] PT (Rudolstadt, 1726).

1. *Ps.* 47:6-7; 4. *Mk.* 16:19; 5-10. based upon the six verses of the
poem "Mein Jesus hat nunmehr"; 11. Johann Rist, verses 1 and

13 of "Du Lebensfürst, Herr Jesu Christ," 1641 (Fischer-Tümpel, II, #188).

30 May 1726, Leipzig.

BG 10; NBA I/12.

First Part

1. Chorus [Dictum] (S, A, T, B)

God goeth up with shouting and the Lord with ringing of trumpets. Sing praises, sing praise to God, sing praises, sing praises to our Lord and King.

2. Recit. (T)

Now would the Highest his own victory-song make ready,
For he captivity himself hath captive led.[2]
Who haileth him? Who is it who the trumpets sound?
Who goeth at his side now?
Is it not God's own host,
Which for his name's great praise,
Strength, fame, rule, power and might with open voices singeth
And him now evermore a hallelujah bringeth.

3. Aria (T)

Yea, thousands on thousands in convoys of wagons,[3]
The great King of Kings shall sing praises, proclaiming
That both earth and heaven beneath him now bend,
And all he hath conquered now fully submits.

4. Recit. (S)

And the Lord, once that he amongst them had finished speaking, was there lifted up into heaven and sitteth at the right hand of God.

5. Aria (S)

My Jesus hath henceforth
Salvation's work completed
And makes now his return
To that one who had sent him.
He ends his earthly course,
Ye heavens, open wide
And take him once again!

Second Part

6. Recit. (B)

The hero's hero comes,
Who Satan's prince and terror,
Who even death did fell,
Erased the stain of error,
Dispersed the hostile horde;
Ye powers, come with haste
And lift the victor up.

7. Aria (B)

'Tis he who all alone
The wine press hath betrodden[4]
Of torment, pain and woe,
The lost to bring salvation
Through purchase at great price.
Ye thrones all, stir yourselves
And on him laurels set!

8. Recit. (A)

The Father hath him, yea,
A lasting kingdom given:
Now is the hour at hand

When he the crown receiveth
For countless hardship borne.
I stand here by the path
And to him gladly gaze.

9. Aria (A)

I see within my soul
How he at God's own right hand
Doth all his foes strike down
To set free all his servants
From mourning, woe and shame.
I stand here by the path
And on him yearn to gaze.

10. Recit. (A)

He would beside himself
A dwelling for me ready,
In which for evermore
I shall stand close beside him,
Made free of "woe and ah!"
I stand here by the path
And to him grateful call.

11. Chorale (S, A, T, B)

Thou Prince of life, Lord Jesus Christ,
Thou who art taken up now
To heaven, where thy Father is
And all the faithful people,
How shall I thy great victory,
Which thou through a most grievous strife
Hast merited, praise rightly
And thy full honor pay thee?
Draw us to thee and we shall run,
Give us of faith the pinions!

Help us our flight from here to make
To Israel's true mountains!
My God! When shall I then depart
To where I'll ever happy dwell?
When shall I stand before thee,
Thy countenance to witness?

[1.]   Helm is suggested by W. Blankenburg, BJ (1977).
[2.]   Cf. *Ps.* 68:18 and *Eph.* 4:8.
[3.]   Cf. *Dan.* 7:10 and *Ps.* 68:17.
[4.]   Cf. *Is.* 63.3.

BWV 44 **Sie werden euch in den Bann tun I**

Exaudi (The Sunday after Ascension).

Poet unknown.

1-2. *Jn.* 16:2; 4. Martin Moller, verse 1 of "Ach Gott, wie manches
Herzeleid," 1587; 7. Paul Fleming, final verse of "In allen meinen
Taten," 1642 (Fischer-Tümpel, I, #489).

21 May 1724, Leipzig.

BG 10; NBA I/12.

---

1. Aria [Dictum] (T, B)

In banishment they will cast you.[1]

2. Chorus [Dictum] (S, A, T, B)

There cometh, yea, the time when he who slays you will think that he
doeth God a good deed in this.

3. Aria (A)

Christians must, while on earth dwelling,
Christ's own true disciples be.

>On them waiteth every hour
>Till they blissfully have conquered
>Torment, ban and grievous pain.

4. Chorale (T)

Ah God, how oft a heartfelt grief
Confronteth me within these days.
The narrow path is sorrow-filled
Which I to heaven travel must.

5. Recit. (B)

Now doth the Antichrist,
That huge and mighty monster,
With sword and fire
Hound Christ's own members with oppression,
Since what they teach to him is odious.
He is, indeed, meanwhile convinced
That all his actions God's approval have.
But yet, the Christians are so like the palm tree branches,
Which through their weight just all the higher tower.[2]

6. Aria (S)

It is and bides the Christians' hope
That God o'er this his church doth watch.

>For when so quick the tempests tower,
>Yet after all the storms of sorrow
>The sun of gladness soon doth laugh.[3]

7. Chorale (S, A, T, B)

Thyself be true, O spirit,
And trust in him alone now
Who hath created thee.
Let happen what may happen,
Thy Father there in heaven
Doth counsel in all matters well.

[1.] I.e., excommunicate you.

[2.] Detlef Gojowy, "Zur Sprache in Bachs Kantaten," *Das Kantatenwerk*, Vol. 10, pp. 3-4, with English translation, pp. 8-9, explains that these lines refer to a common view that weights applied to palm branches make them grow higher. This theory is represented in an emblem printed by Andrea Alciate and may be seen in Albrecht Schöne, *Emblemata. Handbuch zur Sinnbildkunst des XVI and XVII Jahrhunderts* (Stuttgart: Metzler, 1967), p. 68.

[3.] The transformation of tempest to sunshine is a common motif of the cantatas for Jubilate Sunday. This motif is also represented in the emblematic tradition (see note 2, above), and specifically in a collection by Johann Mannich, *Sacra Emblemata*, Nürnberg, 1624, p. 15 (shown in *Das Kantatenwerk*, Vol. 10, p. 6). Cf. BWV 12/6 for Jubilate.

BWV 45 **Es ist dir gesagt, Mensch, was gut ist**

Eighth Sunday after Trinity.

Poet unknown (Christoph Helm?);[1] PT (Rudolstadt, 1726).

1. *Mic.* 6:8; 4. *Mt.* 7:22-23; 7. Johann Heermann, verse 2 of "O Gott, du frommer Gott," 1630 (Fischer-Tümpel, I, #355).

11 August 1726, Leipzig.

BG 10; NBA I/18.

First Part

1. Chorus [Dictum] (S, A, T, B)

It hath thee been told, Man, what is good and what the Lord of thee asketh, namely: God's word to hold fast and love to practise, to be humble before this thy God.

2. Recit. (T)

The Highest lets me know his will and purpose
And what him pleaseth well;
His word he gave to be a guide for life,
By which my foot shall be most careful
At all times to proceed
With fear, with rev'rence and with love now
As tests of the obedience which I practise,
That I his servant true in days to come be proved.

3. Aria (T)

I know God's true justice,
What it is which me can help
When from me as his own servant
He demands strict reckoning.
Spirit, ponder thy salvation,
To obedience comes reward;
Pain and scorn
Threaten thee in thy transgression!

Second Part

4. Arioso [Dictum] (B)[2]

There will be many who will say unto me on that day: Lord, Lord, have we then not in thine own name been prophesying, have we then not in thine own name been exorcising devils, have we then not in thine own name performed many labors?

Then unto them all shall I say this: I recognize not one of you, get ye all hence from me, ye evildoers.

5. Aria (A)

Who God doth own
With honest heart's intent
Will he in turn acknowledge.[3]

> For he shall burn forever
> Who merely with the mouth
> Doth call him Lord.

6. Recit. (A)

Thus will the heart and mouth themselves my judges be,
And God will the reward which I have sought allot me:
Should now my conduct his commandments not fulfill,
Who would thereafter heal my soul's misfortune?
Why do I make mine own impediment?
The Lord's desire must be fulfilled,
But his support is also sure,
That he his work through me might see in full accomplished.

7. Chorale (S, A, T, B)

Grant that I do with care
What I to do am given,
To that which thy command
Me in my station leadeth!
Grant that I do it quick,
Just at the time I ought;

And when I do, then grant
That it may prosper well!

---

1. Helm is suggested by W. Blankenburg, BJ (1977).

2. Representing the vox Christi.

3. Cf. *Mt.* 10:32.

BWV 46 **Schauet doch und sehet, ob irgendein**

Tenth Sunday after Trinity.

Poet unknown.

1. *Lam.* 1:12; 6. Johann Matthäus Meyfart, a supplemental verse 9 added in 1633 to Balthasar Schnurr's "O großer Gott von Macht" (Fischer-Tümpel, III, #321).

1 August 1723, Leipzig; Parody: 1 → Mass in B Minor, BWV 232/8.

BG 10; NBA I/19.

---

1. Chorus [Dictum] (S, A, T, B)

Look indeed and see then if there be a grief like to my grief which hath stricken me. For the Lord hath me with sorrow made full on that day of his furious wrath.

2. Recit. (T)

Then cry aloud, thou fallen town of God,
Thou wretched heap of stone and ashes!
Let brimming streams of tears be flowing,

For thee hath stricken now
An irreplaceable loss
Of that most precious grace
Which thou must do without
Through thine own fault.
Thou wast just like Gomorra sternly dealt with,
Albeit not destroyed.
Oh, better hadst thou been leveled low
Than that the foe of Christ should blaspheme now in thee.
Though thou wouldst Jesus' tears not heed,
Yet heed thou still the tidal wave of passion
Which thou upon thyself dost summon,
For God, who long forbears,
The rod of judgment wields.

3. Aria (B)

Thy tempest gathered from great distance,
But now its fires at last break loose

And must thee surely overwhelm,
For surfeit of transgression
Shall lightning's wrath enkindle
And send its certain doom upon thee.

4. Recit. (A)

And yet thou must, O sinner, not suppose
That now Jerusalem alone
Is more than others filled with error!
To you already one may read this judgment:
Since ye shun amendment
And daily your sins are increasing,
Ye shall every one meet that dreadful destruction.[1]

5. Aria (A)

Yet Jesus shall e'en midst the judgment
The righteous' shield and helper be,
He gathers them as his own sheep now,
As his own chicks, so dear, to him.[2]
When tempests of vengeance are sinners rewarding,
He helps the righteous dwell securely.

6. Chorale (S, A, T, B)

O faithful God, so great,
Before thee none hath weight
But thy Son Jesus Christ,
Who thy great wrath hath stilled;
So gaze upon those wounds of his,
His torment, fear and grievous pain;
And for his sake protect us,
Nor for our sins repay us

[1.]   Cf. *Lk.* 13:5.

[2.]   Cf. *Mt.* 23:37.

BWV 47 **Wer sich selbst erhöhet, der soll erniedriget werden**

Seventeenth Sunday after Trinity.

Johann Friedrich Helbig, *Auffmunterung Zur Andacht* (Eisenach, 1720); Facs: Neumann T, p. 304.

1. *Lk.* 14:11 and 18:14; 5. verse 11 of "Warum betrübst du dich, mein Herz?," ca. 1560 (Wackernagel, IV, #90).

13 October 1726, Leipzig.

BG 10; NBA I/23.

---

1. Chorus [Dictum] (S, A, T, B)

Who himself exalteth, he shall be made to be humble, and who doth make himself humble, he shall be made exalted.

2. Aria (S)

He who would be called true Christian
Must to meekness give much practice;
Meekness comes from Jesus' realm.

> Haughty pride is devil's fare,
> God treats all those with his hatred
> Who their pride do not abandon.

3. Recit. (B)

Mankind is dirt, stench,[1] earth and ashes;
How could it be by arrogance,
Born of the devil's brood,
Still yet so fascinated?
Ah, Jesus, God's own Son,
Creator of all nature,
Became for our sake humble and most lowly,
Enduring spite and scorn;
And thou, thou wretched worm, wouldst thou be boastful?
Beseemeth such as this a Christian?
Go, shame thyself, thou prideful creature man,
Repent and follow Christ's own path;
Prostrate thyself to God with faithful spirit!
In his own time he shall again exalt thee.

4. Aria (B)

Jesus, humble yet my spirit
Under thy most mighty hand,
That I not salvation forfeit
As a foretaste of hell's fire.
Let me thine own meekness follow
And on pride set condemnation;
Give to me a humble heart,
That I may thy favor find!

5. Chorale (S, A, T, B)

All temporal praise would I glad forsake
If thou me but eternity give,
Which thou hast won for us
Through thine own painful, bitter death.
This do I ask, my Lord and God.

[1.]   OSt emends *Stank* 'stench' to *Staub 'dust.'*

BWV 48 **Ich elender Mensch, wer wird mich erlösen**

Nineteenth Sunday after Trinity.

Poet unknown.

1. Romans 7:24, with the chorale melody of "Herr Jesu Christ,"
Freiburg, 1620; 3. Martin Rutilius, verse 4 of "Ach Gott und Herr,"
1604 (Fischer-Tümpel, I, #52); 7. verse 12 of "Herr Jesu Christ,"
Freiburg, 1620 (Fischer-Tümpel, I, #574).

3 October 1723, Leipzig.

BG 10; NBA I/24.

---

1. Chorus [Dictum] with instr. chorale

A poor man am I; who will set me free from the body of this dying?

2. Recit. (A)

Such pain, such sorrow strike at me
While poison born of sin
Within my breast and veins is raging:
My world a house of death and sickness is,
My flesh must all its torments
Into the very grave bear with it.
But yet the soul perceiveth the poison most
With which it is infected;
Thus, when by pain the flesh of death is struck
And soul tastes cross's bitter chalice,
That cup doth force from it a fervent sigh.

3. Chorale (S, A, T, B)

If it need be
That judgment's pain
Our sins must ever follow,
Continue on,
Refine me there
And let me here do penance.[1]

4. Aria (A)

Ah, put off that Sodom from my sinful members,
Whenever thy purpose it bringeth to ruin!

Refine, though, my soul now and render it pure,
Before thee a hallowéd Zion to be.

5. Recit. (T)

But here doth work the Savior's hand
Amidst the very dead its wonders.[2]
If thy soul nigh to death appeareth,
Thy body weak and fully broken,
Yet we shall Jesus' power know:
He can the weak in spirit,
The body sound, the soul robust yet render.

6. Aria (T)

Forgive me Jesus my transgressions,
So shall my flesh and soul be well.
He can the dead to life awaken
And shows his power in our weakness;[3]
He keeps the long contracted bond,
That we in faith shall find salvation.

7. Chorale (S, A, T, B)

Lord Jesus Christ, my only help,
In thee will I take refuge;
My heart's distress is thee well known,
Thou canst and wilt dispel it.
Upon thy will let all depend,
Deal, O my God, as thou dost please:
Thine am I now and ever.

[1.] I.e., there in heaven and here on earth.

[2.] Cf. *Ps.* 88:11.

[3.] Cf. 2 *Cor.* 12:9.

BWV 49 **Ich geh und suche mit Verlangen (Dialogus)**

Twentieth Sunday after Trinity.

Poet unknown.

6. Philipp Nicolai, verse 7 of "Wie schön leuchtet der Morgenstern," 1599, with interpolated aria.

3 November 1726, Leipzig.

BG 10; NBA I/25.

Dialogue

1. Sinfonia

2. Aria (B) Jesus

I go and search for thee with longing,
Thee, O my doveling,[1] fairest bride.
Tell me, where art thou left and gone now
That thee my eye no more can find?

3. Recit. and Arioso (B, S) Jesus, Soul

(Jesus)
My feast is now prepared,
And this my marriage table ready,
But still my bride is not yet in attendance.

(Soul)
My Jesus speaks of me;
O voice that maketh me so glad!

(Jesus)
I go and seek for thee with longing,
Thee, O my doveling, fairest bride.

(Soul)
My bridegroom dear, I fall before thy feet now.

(Jesus, Soul)
Come, fairest, come and let me kiss thee,
  Thou shalt my
{   } sumptuous meal² enjoy now.
  Let me thy
  Come, O my bride, and
{   } hasten now,
 My bridegroom dear, I
The wedding raiment to put on.

4. Aria (S) Soul

I am glorious, I am fair,³
And my Savior I've impassioned.
His salvations's righteousness
Is my cloak of honor bright;
And in it will I be dressed
When I unto heaven go.

5. Recit. (S, B) Soul, Jesus

(Soul)
My faith now holds me with such deep emotion.

(Jesus)
As to thee bides my heart's devotion,
So will I plight to thee
For evermore my troth and pledge of marriage.⁴

(Soul)
How well for me!
For heaven is to me provided:
Its majesty doth call and sends its very servants[5]
So that the fallen generations
To heaven's hall
At our salvation's meal
As guests may come to dine,
I'm here now, Jesus, let me in!

(Jesus)
So keep till death thy faith,
And I'll to thee the crown of life bequeath.[6]

6. Aria (B) and Choral (S) Jesus, Soul

(Jesus)
Thee have I loved with love eternal,[7]
(Soul)
How am I now so truly glad
My treasure is the A and O,
Beginning and the ending.
And therefore draw thee unto me.
He'll me, indeed, to his great praise
Receive into his paradise;
For this I'll clap my hands now.
I'm coming soon,
Amen! Amen!
I stand before the door,[8]
Come, thou lovely crown of gladness, do not tarry.
Unlock it, mine abode!
I await thee with great longing.
Thee have I loved with love eternal,
And therefore draw thee unto me.

---

1.   Cf. *S. of S.* 5:2; 6:9.
2.   Cf. *Is.* 25:6.

3.   Cf. *Mt.* 22:11-14.
4.   *Hos.* 2:21.
5.   Cf. *Mt.* 22:2.
6.   Cf. *Rev.* 2:10.
7.   Cf. *Jer.* 31:3.
8.   Cf. *Rev.* 3:20.

BWV 50 **Nun ist das Heil und die Kraft**

St. Michael and All Angels.

Poet unknown.

1. *Rev.* 12:10 (altered).

Date uncertain.

BG 10; NBA I/30.

Chorus [Dictum] (S, A, T, B)

Now is the health and the strength and the kingdom and might of our God and of his Christ come to us, for he is cast down now who was accusing them day and night to God.

BWV 51 **Jauchzet Gott in allen Landen!**

Fifteenth Sunday after Trinity and For any occasion (et in ogni tempo).

4. Substitute verse to Johann Gramann's "Nun lob, mein Seel, mein Seel, den Herren," Königsberg, 1548 (Wackernagel, III, #968ff.)

Probably 17 September 1730, Leipzig.

BG 12, 2; NBA I/22.

---

1. Aria (S)

Praise ye God in every nation!
All that heaven and the world
Of created order hold
Must be now his fame exalting,
And we would to this our God
/ With the angels let's today /[1]
Likewise now present an off'ring
/ To our God a song of praise sing/[2]
For that he midst cross and woe
/ For that he midst spite and pain /[3]
Always hath stood close beside us.

2. Recit. (S)

In prayer we now thy temple face,[4]
Where God's own honor dwelleth,[5]
Where his good faith,
Each day renewed,
The purest bliss dispenseth.
We praise him for what he for us hath done.
Although our feeble voice before his wonders stammers,
Perhaps e'en modest praise to him will yet bring pleasure.

3. Aria (S)

Highest, make thy gracious goodness
Henceforth every morning new.
/ E'en in our dominion new. /[6]

Thus before thy father's love
Should as well the grateful spirit
Through a righteous life show plainly
That we are thy children truly.

4. Chorale (S)

Now laud and praise with honor
God Father, Son, and Holy Ghost!
May he in us make increase
What he us with grace hath pledged,
So that we firmly trust him,
Entirely turn to him,
Make him our true foundation,
That our heart, mind and will
Steadfast to him be cleaving;
To this we sing here now:
Amen, we shall achieve it,
This is our heart's firm faith!

5. Aria (S)

Alleluia![7]

[1.] This line is found in the OSt as an alternate text to the immediately preceding line.

[2.] This line is found in the OSt as an alternate text to the immediately preceding line.

[3.] This line is found in the OSt as an alternate text to the immediately preceding line.

[4.] Cf. *Ps.* 138:2.

[5.] Cf. *Ps.* 26:8.

[6.] This line is found in the OSt as an alternate text to the immediately preceding line.

[7.] Bach adds the *Alleluia*, probably as an etymology of the opening words of the cantata: in Hebrew *hallelu-yah* means 'praise ye Jehovah," i.e., *Jauchzet Gott*.

BWV 52 **Falsche Welt, dir trau ich nicht!**

Twenty-third Sunday after Trinity.

Poet unknown.

6. Adam Reusner, verse 1 of the hymn, 1533 (Wackernagel, III, #170).

24 November 1726, Leipzig; Parody: 1 ← First Brandenburg Concerto, BWV 1046/1.

BG 12, 2; NBA I/26.

1. Sinfonia

2. Recit. (S)

Treacherous world, I trust thee not!
Here must I in the midst of scorpions
And midst deceitful serpents sojourn.
Thy countenance,
Which, ah, so friendly is,
Now plots in secret a destruction:
At Jacob's kiss
Must come a righteous Abner's ruin.[1]
Sincerity is from the world now banned,
Duplicity hath driv'n it from us,
And now hypocrisy
Here in its stead abideth.
The best of friends is found untrue,
O what a wretched state!

3. Aria (S)

Just the same, just the same,
Though I be expelled with blame,

> Though the false world me offend,
> Oh, yet bideth God my friend,
> Who doth true for me intend.[2]

4. Recit. (S)

God is e'er true!
He shall, he can me not abandon;
E'en though the world and all its raging seek
Within its coils to seize me,
Yet near to me his help shall stand.
Upon his friendship I will build now
And give my spirit, soul and mind
And ev'rything I am
To him for keeping.

5. Aria (S)

I'll side with my dear God above,
The world may now alone continue.
God with me, and I with God,
And I'll myself find scorn
For the treacherous tongues about me.

6. Chorale (S, A, T, B)

In thee I've placed my hope, O Lord,
Help me not be to ruin brought,
Nor evermore derided!
This I pray thee,

Uphold thou me
In thy true love, Almighty!

[1.]   Cf. 2 *Sam.* 3:27.

[2.]   Here the translation is made to rhyme in order to draw attention to the
       interesting rhyme of the original: Feind, Freund, meint.

BWV 53 Schlage doch, gewünschte Stunde

Funeral?

Poet unknown.

Not by Bach, probably by Georg Melchior Hoffmann (see BJ 1956,
p. 155 and Dürr, p. 1003.) ca. 1730, Leipzig (so Schmieder, p. 71).

BGA 122., 53.

Aria (A)

Schlage doch, gewünschte Stunde,
Brich doch an, du schöner Tag!

> Kommt, ihr Engel, auf mich zu.
> Öffnet mir die Himmelsauen,
> Meinen Jesum bald zu schauen
> In vergnügter Seelenruh.
> Ich begehr von Herzens Grunde
> Nur den letzten Seigerschlag.

Aria (A)

Strike then thou, O blessed hour,
Break forth thou, O glorious day!

Come, ye angels, unto me.
Open to me heavens' pastures;
I my Jesus soon would gaze at
In contented soul's repose.
I desire with heart and spirit
But the final tolling stroke!

BWV 54 **Widerstehe doch der Sünde**

Oculi (Third Sunday in Lent), First and Twentieth Sundays after Trinity, and probably for the Seventh Sunday after Trinity.

Georg Christian Lehms, *Gottgefälliges Kirchen-Opffer* (Darmstadt, 1711); Facs: Neumann T, p. 259.

?15 July 1714, Weimar; Parody: 1 → St. Mark Passion, BWV 247/53.

BG 12, 2; NBA I/18.

---

1. Aria (A)

Stand steadfast against transgression,
Or its poison thee will seize.

> Be thou not by Satan blinded,
> For God's glory to dishonor
> Brings a curse of fatal doom.

2. Recit. (A)

The shape of vile transgression
In sooth is outward wondrous fair;

But yet one must
Receive with sorrow and dismay
Much toil and woe thereafter.
The outside is pure gold,
But, should one look within,
Appears nought but an empty shadow
And whited sepulcher.[1]
It is the Sodom's apple like,[2]
And those who are with it united
Shall never reach God's heav'nly realm.
It is just like a sharpened sword
Which doth our soul and body pierce.

3. Aria (A)

Who sin commits is of the devil,[3]
For he it was who brought it forth.
But if one gainst its haughty fetters
With true devotion stand steadfastly,
Shall it at once from here take flight.

[1.] Cf. *Mt.* 23:27.

[2.] Josephus, *Bellum Judaicum*, IV. 8. 4, writes that apples of Sodom looked
      like edible fruit, but turned to smoke and ashes when picked.

[3.] Cf. Dürr, p. 369, and BWV 179/3.

[3.] Cf. 1 *Jn.* 3:8.

BWV 55 Ich armer Mensch, ich Sündenknecht

Twenty-second Sunday after Trinity.

Poet unknown.

5. Johann Rist, verse 6 of "Werde munter, mein Gemüte," 1642
(Fischer-Tümpel, II, #199).

17 November 1726, Leipzig.

BG 12, 2; NBA I/26.

---

1. Aria (T)

I, wretched man, I, slave to sin,
I go before God's very presence
With fear and trembling unto judgment.
E'er just is he, unjust am I,
I, wretched man, I, slave to sin.

2. Recit. (T)

I have against my God offended
And have upon the path
Which he did once prescribe for me
Not steadfast traveled.
Where now? Should I the rosy morning's pinions
For this my flight elect now,
To take me to the ocean's limits,
Yet would e'en still the hand of God Almighty find me
And with the rods of sin chastise me.[1]
Ah yes!
If even hell a bed could[2]
For me and all my sins make ready,
Yet would indeed the wrath of God be there.
The earth protects me not,
It threatens wicked me to swallow;
And I would lift myself to heaven,
Where God doth dwell, who shall my judgment tell.

3. Aria (T)

Have mercy, Lord!
Let my tears now make thee soften,

Let them reach into thy bosom;
Let for Jesus Christ's own glory
All thy zealous wrath grow calm now!
Have mercy, Lord!

4. Recit. (T)

Have mercy, Lord!
However,
I now hope
That I'll not stand before his judgment,
But rather to the throne of grace
Of this my righteous Father venture.
I'll offer him his Son,
His passion, his redemption then,
And how he for my sin
Hath all repaid sufficiently,
And beg him to forbear,
Henceforth will I my sin forswear.
Thus take me God into thy grace again.

5. Chorale (S, A, T, B)

Though I now from thee have fallen,
I will come again to thee;
For now hath thy Son redeemed us
Through his fear and pain of death.
I do not deny my guilt,
But thy mercy and thy grace
Are much greater than my sins are,
Which I ever find within me.

---

1.   Cf. *Ps.* 139:7-10.
2.   Cf. *Ps.* 139:7-10.

BWV 56 **Ich will den Kreuzstab gerne tragen**

Nineteenth Sunday after Trinity.

Poet unknown.[1]

5. Johann Franck, verse 6 of "Du, o schönes Weltgebäude," 1653 (Fischer-Tümpel, IV, #99).

27 October 1726, Leipzig.

BG 12, 2; NBA I/24.

---

1. Aria (B)

I will the cross-staff gladly carry,
It comes from God's belove'd hand,
It leadeth me so weak and weary
To God, into the promised land.
When I in the grave all my trouble once lay,
Himself shall my Savior my tears wipe away.[2]

2. Recit. (B)

My sojourn in the world
Is like a voyage at sea:
The sadness, cross and woe
Are billows which have overwhelmed me
And unto death
Each day appall me;
My anchor, though, which me doth hold,
Is that compassion's heart
With which my God oft makes me glad.
He calleth thus to me:

I am with thee,
I will not e'er abandon or forsake thee![3]
And when the raging ocean's shaking
Comes to an end,
Into my city from the ship I'll go
It is the heav'nly realm
Which I with all the righteous
From deepest sadness will have entered.[4]

3. Aria (B)

One day, one day shall my yoke
Once again be lifted from me.

> Then shall I in the Lord find power,
> And with the eagle's features rare,
> There rise above this earthly bound'ry[5]
> And soar without becoming weary.
> This I would today invoke!

4. Recit. and Arioso (B)

I stand here ready and prepared,
My legacy of lasting bliss
With yearning and with rapture
From Jesus' hands at last to capture.
How well for me that day
When I the port of rest shall come to see.
When I in the grave all my trouble once lay,
Himself shall my Savior my tears wipe away.

5. Chorale (S, A, T, B)

Come, O death, of sleep the brother,
Come and lead me hence now forth;

Loosen now my small bark's rudder,
Bring thou me secure to port!
Others may desire to shun thee,
Thou canst all the more delight me;
For through thee I'll come inside
To the fairest Jesus-child.

---

1. Neumann T, p. 141, notes a remote similarity to E. Neumeister's cantata for the Twenty-first Sunday after Trinity, "Ich will den Kreuzweg gerne gehen," *Geistliche Cantaten* (Weißenfels, 1700), and Dürr, p. 477, suggests that the librettist is the same one who imitated Neumeister in BWV 27.
2. Cf. *Rev.* 7:17.
3. Cf. *Heb.* 13:5.
4. Cf. *Rev.* 7:14.
5. Cf. *Is.* 40:31.

BWV 57 **Selig ist der Mann (Dialogus)**

Second Day of Christmas (St. Stephen).

Georg Christian Lehms, *Gottgefälliges Kirchen-Opffer* (Darmstadt, 1711); Facs: Neumann T, p. 257.

1. *Jas.* 1:12; 8. Ahasverus Fritsch, verse 6 of "Hast du denn, Jesus, dein Angesicht," 1668 (Fischer-Tümpel, V, #569).

26 December 1725, Leipzig.

BG 12, 2: NBA I/3.

Dialogue

Soul (S), Jesus (B)

1. Aria [Dictum] (B) Jesus

Blessed is the man who bears temptation with patience; for when he hath withstood the test, he shall the crown of true life then be given.

2. Recit. (S) Soul

Ah! this sweet comfort doth
Restore my heart as well,
Which nought but "Ah and woe"
In endless sorrow findeth
And is just like a worm in its own blood now writhing.
I must just like the sheep
Midst countless savage wolves be living;
I am a true forsaken lamb
And must now to their rage
And cruelty surrender.
What Abel once befell,[1]
Evokes from me as well a flood of tears.
Ah! Jesus, had I here
No strength from thee,
My courage and my heart would fail me
And say with deepest sorrow:

3. Aria (S) Soul

I would now yearn for death, for death,
If thou, my Jesus, didst not love me.

> Yea, if thou me wouldst still leave saddened,
> I'd suffer more than pain of hell.

4. Recit. (B, S) Jesus, Soul

(Jesus)
I stretch to thee my hand,
My heart as well comes with it.

(Soul)
Ah! Sweetest bond of love,
Thou canst my foes bring ruin
And their great rage diminish.

5. Aria (B) Jesus

Yes, yes, I can thy foes destroy now
Who have before me e'er accused thee,
So have no fear, O anxious soul.

O anxious soul, cease now thy weeping,
The sun will soon be brightly shining,
Which thee now clouds of trouble sends.

6. Recit. (B, S) Jesus, Soul

(Jesus)
Within my lap life's peace abideth,
This I will once give thee forever.

(Soul)
Ah, Jesus, were I now with thee!
Ah, if the wind
Did now graze o'er my tomb and grave,
I could then every sorrow conquer.
How blest are they within the coffin
Who to the sound of angels hearken!
Ah, Jesus, open for me too,
As Stephen once, the gates of heaven![2]

My heart is now prepared
To soar aloft to meet thee.
Come, come, O blessed hour!
Thou canst the tomb and grave
And mine own Jesus show me.

7. Aria (S) Soul

I'd quit now so quickly[3] mine earthly existence,
With gladness to part now I long at this moment.
My Savior, I'd die now with greatest of joy,
Here hast thou my spirit, what dost thou give me?

8. Chorale (S, A, T, B)

Bring, my belovéd, my hopes to fulfillment, confiding
That I'll thy bosom friend always and ever be biding,
Who thee hath pleased
And into heaven hath brought
Out of this thy tortured body.[4]

[1.]   Cf. *Mt.* 23:35.

[2.]   Cf. Act. 7:55.

[3.]   "Quit now so quickly" is meant to reflect the jingle in *ende . . . behende.*

[4.]   The text of the final chorale represents the response of Jesus to the
       Soul's question in 7: "What dost thou give me?"

BWV 58 **Ach Gott, wie manches Herzeleid II (Dialogus)**

New Year's Day (Feast of the Circumcision).

Poet unknown.

1. Martin Moller, verse 1 of the hymn, 1587, after "Jesus dulcis memoria" of Bernard of Clairvaux (Wackernagel, I, #38); 5. Martin Behm, verse 2 of "O Jesu Christ, meins Lebens Licht," 1610.

5 January 1727, Leipzig; again in 1733 or 1734.

BG 12, 2; NBA I/4.

Dialogue

1. Chorale (B) and Aria (S)

(B)
Ah God, how oft a heartfelt grief
(S)
Just forbear, forbear, my spirit,
Confronteth me within these times!
This is such an evil age!
The narrow path is sorrow-filled
Yet the road to blessedness
Which I to heaven travel must.
Leads to pleasure after sorrow.
Just forbear, forbear, my spirit,
This is such an evil age!

2. Recit. (B)

Pursue thee though the wicked world,
Yet thou hast even God as ally,
Who shall, thy foes opposing,
E'er cover thy retreat.
And when enraged the furious Herod
The judgment of a death most scornful
Upon our Savior once pronounced,
There came an angel in the night

Who sent a dream to Joseph,
That he the strangler should be fleeing
And Egypt's refuge seeking.
God hath a word which thee with trust doth fill.
He saith: Though hill and mountain fall in ruin,
E'en though the bloodshed's waters seek to drown thee,
Yet will I still not e'er forsake thee or neglect thee.[1]

3. Aria (S)

I am content in this my sorrow,
For God is my true confidence.

> I have a certain seal and charter,
> And this abides a mighty barrier,
> Unrest in truth by hell itself.

4. Recit. (S)

E'en though the world refrain not
To pursue me and to hate me,
God's hand doth show to me
Another land.
Ah, could today it only happen
That I my Eden might behold yet!

5. Chorale (S) and Aria (B)

(S)
I stand before a toilsome road

(B)
Just take heart, take heart, ye spirits,
To thee in heaven's paradise;
Here is fear, there glory reigns!
There is my proper fatherland,

And the pleasure of that day
For which thou thine own blood hast shed.
Overcometh every sorrow.
Just take heart, take heart, ye spirits,
Here is fear, there glory reigns!

---

1. Cf. *Is.* 54:10 and *Heb.* 13:5.

BWV 59 **Wer mich liebet, der wird mein Wort halten I**

First Day of Pentecost (Whitsunday).

Erdmann Neumeister, *Geistliche Poesien*(Eisenach, 1714) and *Fünffache Kirchenandachten* (Leipzig, 1717); Facs: Neumann T, p. 296.

1. *Jn.* 14:23; 3. Martin Luther, verse 1 of the hymn (Wackernagel, III, #19).

16 May 1723 or 28 May 1724, Leipzig; Parody: 4 → BWV 74/2.

BG 12, 2; NBA I/13.

---

1. Aria [Dictum] (S, A, T, B)

He who loves me will keep my commandments, and my Father, too, will love him, and we shall unto him come then and make our dwelling with him.

2. Recit. (S)

Oh, what are then these honors
To which us Jesus leads?

He finds in us such worth,
That he hath pledged
With Father and the Holy Ghost
Within our hearts to make his dwelling.
Oh, what are then these honors:
For man is dust,
Of vanity the prey,
Of toil and work a tragedy,
Of every woe the end and goal.
What then? The Lord Almighty saith:
He will within our spirits
Elect to make his dwelling.
Ah, what doth God's dear love not do?
Ah, would that, as he wanted,
Now each and every man should love him.

3. Chorale (S, A, T, B)

Come Holy Spirit, God the Lord,
And fill with thy most precious grace
Thy believers in heart, will and mind.
Thine ardent love ignite in them.
O Lord, through thine own brilliant light
To faith thou hast assembled now
The folk of every tongue and clime;
May this, O Lord, be sung to praise thee.
Alleluia, alleluia.

4. Aria (B)

The world with all its realms and kingdoms,
The world with all its majesty
Is to this majesty no equal
Through which our God doth make us glad:
That he's enthroned within our spirits
And there as in a heaven dwelleth.

Ah God, though blessed we may be,
How blessed shall we still become
When we, our earthly time completed,
With thee in heaven shall be dwelling.[1]

[1.] The bass part has *Chorale segue.* The chorale was probably the one in
Neumeister's text, verse 3 of "Erhalt uns, Herr, bei deinem Wort" by
Martin Luther (Wackernagel, III, #44ff. or #1482):

Gott Heil'ger Geist, du Tröster werth,
gieb dein'm Volck ein'rley Sinn auf Erd.
Steh bey uns in der letzten Noth,
gleit uns ins Leben aus dem Tod.

God Holy Ghost, thou helper dear,
Make thy folk of one mind on earth.
Stand by us in our final need,
Lead us to life and free from death.

In Neumeister's text Movement 6 is *Rom.* 15:13 and Movement 7 the aria
"Ich bin der Seligkeit gewiss" ("I am of blessedness assured").

BWV 60 **O Ewigkeit, du Donnerwort II (Dialogus)**

Twenty-fourth Sunday after Trinity.

Poet unknown.

1. Johann Rist, verse 1 of the hymn, 1642 (Fischer-Tümpel, II, #204)
and *Gen.* 49:18 = *Ps.* 119:166; 4. *Rev.* 14:13 with interpolated recitative;
5. Franz Joachim Burmeister, verse 5 of "Es ist genug, so nimm,
Herr, meinen Geist," 1662 (Fischer-Tümpel, IV, #533).

7 November 1723, Leipzig.

BG 12, 2; NBA I/27, 3.

Dialogue

Fear (A), Hope (T), Christ (B)

1. Chorale and Aria [Dictum]
(A, T) Fear and Hope

(Fear)
Eternity, thou thundrous word,
O sword that through the soul doth bore,
Beginning with no ending!
Eternity, time lacking time,
I know now faced with deepest grief
Not where to seek my refuge.
So much my frightened heart doth quake
That to my gums my tongue doth cake.

(Hope)
Lord, I wait now for thy help.

2. Recit. (A, T) Fear and Hope

(Fear)
O toilsome road to final strife and battle!

(Hope)
My sponsor is at hand,
My Savior stands nearby
With help beside me.

(Fear)
The fear of death, the final pain
Rush on and overwhelm my heart
And torture all my members.

(Hope)
I lay before the Lord in sacrifice my body.
And though the fire of grief be hot,
Enough! It cleanseth me to God's own praise.

(Fear)
But now will stand my sins' own grievous guilt before my face
accusing.

(Hope)
God will on their account not sentence thee to death, though.
He sets a limit to temptation's torments
So that we can endure them.

3. Aria (A, T) Fear and Hope

(Fear)
My final bed would bring me terror,

(Hope)
But yet the Savior's hand will guard me,

(Fear)
My faith's own weakness faileth near,

(Hope)
My Jesus bears with me the weight.

(Fear)
The open grave so cruel appears,

(Hope)
It will be yet my house of peace.

4. Recit. and Arioso [Dictum] (A, B) Fear and Christ

(Fear)
But death abides to human nature most perverse
And hurleth nigh
All hope to its destruction.

(Christ)
Blessed are the dead men.

(Fear)
Ah, ah, alas! What jeopardy
The soul will have to face
In making death's last journey!
Perhaps the jaws of hell will threaten
Its death to fill with terror
When they attempt to swallow it;
Perhaps it is already cursed
To everlasting ruin.

(Christ)
Blessed are the dead, those who in the Lord have diéd.

(Fear)
If in the Lord I die now,
Can then salvation be my lot and portion?
My flesh, indeed, the worms will nurture!
Yea, change will all my members,
To dust and earth returning,
For I a child of death am reckoned
And seem, in truth, within the grave to perish.

(Christ)
Blessed are the dead, those who in the Lord have diéd, from now on.

(Fear)
Lead on!
If from now on I shall be blest,
Present thyself, O Hope, again to me!
My body may unfearing rest in sleep,
My spirit can a glance into that bliss now cast.

5. Chorale (S, A, T, B)

It is enough;
Lord, if it be thy will,
Then let me rest in peace!
My Jesus comes;
To thee, O world, good night!
I fare to heaven's house,
I fare in peace henceforth securely,
My great distress shall bide behind me.
It is enough.

BWV 61 **Nun komm, der Heiden Heiland I**

First Sunday in Advent.

Erdmann Neumeister, *Geistliche Poesien* (Eisenach, 1714) and *Fünffache Kirchenandachten* (Leipzig, 1717); Facs: Neumann T, p. 293.

1. Martin Luther, verse 1 of the German adaptation of Veni redemptor gentium, 1524 (Wackernagel, III, #16); 4. *Rev.* 3:20; 6.

Philipp Nicolai, conclusion (Abgesang) of the last verse of Wie schön
leuchtet der Morgenstern, 1599.

2 December 1714, Weimar.

BG 16; NBA I/1.

---

1. Ouverture [Chorale] (S, A, T, B)

Now come, the gentiles' Savior,
As the Virgin's child revealed,
At whom marvels all the world
That God him this birth ordained.

2. Recit. (T)

To us is come the Savior,
Who hath our feeble flesh and blood
Himself now taken
And taketh us as kinsmen of his blood.
O treasure unexcelled,
What hast thou not for us then done?
What dost thou not
Yet daily for thy people?
Thy coming makes thy light
Appear with richest blessing.

3. Aria (T)

Come, Jesus, come to this thy church now
And fill with blessing the new year!

Advance thy name in rank and honor,
Uphold thou every wholesome doctrine,
The pulpit and the altar bless!

4. Recit. [Dictum] (B)[1]

See now, I stand before the door and on it knock. If anyone my voice will render heed and make wide the door, I will come into his dwelling and take with him the evening supper, and he with me.

5. Aria (S)

Open wide, my heart and spirit,
Jesus comes and draws within.

> Though I soon be earth and ashes,
> Me he will yet not disdain,
> That his joy he find in me
> And that I become his dwelling.
> Oh, how blessed shall I be!

6. Chorale (S, A, T, B)

Amen, amen!
Come, thou lovely crown of gladness, do not tarry[2].
Here I wait for thee with longing.

---

[1]   Representing the vox Christi.

[2]   In the alto and tenor parts where necessary: "come, and do not tarry."

BWV 62 **Nun komm, der Heiden Heiland II**

First Sunday in Advent.

Poet unknown.

1. Martin Luther, verse 1 of the German adaptation of "Veni redemptor gentium," 1524 (Wackernagel, III, #16); 2. based loosely

on verses 2-3; 3. based on verses 4-5; 4. based on verse 6; 5. based on verse 7. 6. final verse of the hymn.

3 December 1724, Leipzig; again after 1732.

BG 16; NBA I/1.

---

1. Chorus [Verse 1] (S, A, T, B)

Now come, the gentiles' Savior,
As the Virgin's child revealed,
At whom marvels all the world,
That God him this birth ordained.

2. Aria (T)

Admire, all ye people, this mystery's grandeur:
The highest of rulers appears to the world.

> Here are all the treasures of heaven discovered,
> Here for us a manna divine is ordained,
> O wonder! Virginity bideth unblemished.

3. Recit. (B)

Now comes from God's great majesty and throne
His one begotten Son.
The man from Judah now appears
To run his course with gladness[1]
And us the fallen bring redemption.
O splendid light,
O sign of grace most wonderful!

4. Aria (B)

Fight victorious, hero strong!
Show for us in flesh thy power!

> Ever striving
> Our own power, now so feeble,
> Strong to temper.

5. Recit. (S, A)

We honor this great majesty
And venture nigh now to thy cradle
And praise thee now with lips of gladness
For what thou us hast brought;
For darkness did not trouble us
When we beheld thy lasting light.

6. Chorale [Verse 8] (S, A, T, B)

Praise to God, the Father, be,
Praise to God, his only Son,
Praise to God, the Holy Ghost,
Always and eternally!

---

1.   Cf. *Ps.* 19:5; "The man from Judah," should properly be "The hero from
      Judah, if the music allowed."

BWV 63 **Christen, ätzet diesen Tag**

Christmas Day.

Possibly Johann Michael Heineccius (see Dürr, p. 108); PT (Halle,
1717); Facs: Neumann T, p. 303.

Between 1713 and 1716, Halle; again 25 December 1723, Leipzig.
BG 16; NBA I/2.

---

1. Chorus (S, A, T, B)

Christians, etch ye now this day
Both in bronze and stones of marble!

> Come, quick, join me at the manger
> And display with lips of gladness
> All your thanks and all you owe;
> For the light which here breaks forth
> Shows to you a sign of blessing.

2. Recit. (A)

O blessed day! O day exceeding rare, this,
On which the world's true help,
The Shiloh,[1] whom God in the Paradise[2]
To mankind's race already pledged,
From this time forth was perfectly revealed
And seeketh Israel now from the prison and the chains of slav'ry
Of Satan to deliver.
Thou dearest God, what are we wretches then?
A people fallen low which thee forsaketh;
And even still thou wouldst not hate us;
For ere we should according to our merits lie in ruin,
Ere that, must deity be willing,
The nature of mankind himself assuming,
Upon earth dwelling,
In shepherd's stall to be a child incarnate.
O inconceivable, yet blessed dispensation!

3. Aria (S, B)

God, thou hast all well accomplished
Which to us now comes to pass.

> Let us then forever trust him
> And rely upon his favor,
> For he hath on us bestowed
> What shall ever be our pleasure.

4. Recit. (T)

Transformed be now today
The anxious pain
Which Israel hath troubled long and sorely burdened
To perfect health and blessing.
Of David's stem the lion now appeareth,
His bow already bent, his sword already honed,
With which he us to former freedom brings.

5. Aria (A, T)

Call and cry to heaven now,
Come, ye Christians, come in order,
Ye should be in this rejoicing
Which God hath today achieved!

> For us now his grace provideth
> And with such salvation sealeth,
> More than we could thank him for.

6. Recit. (B)

Redouble then your strength, ye ardent flames of worship,
And come in humble fervor all together!
Rise gladly heavenward
And thank your God for all this he hath done!

7. Chorus (S, A, T, B)

Highest, look with mercy now
At the warmth of rev'rent spirits!

> Let the thanks we bring before thee
> To thine ears resound with pleasure.
> Let us e'er in blessing walk,
> But yet / Let it / never come to pass
> That we Satan's torments suffer.

[1.] Cf. *Gen.* 49:10. Luther translates *Shiloh* with *Held* 'hero.' English versions
include "champion" and "strong man." Cf. BWV 62/3.

[2.] The "Paradise" (Persian for 'garden') is the Garden of Eden.

BWV 64 **Sehet, welch eine Liebe hat uns der Vater erzeiget**

Third Day of Christmas (St. John, Apostle and Evangelist).

Johann Oswald Knauer, *Gott-geheiligtes Singen und Spielen des Friedensteinischen Zions* (Gotha, 1720); Facs: BJ (1981), p. 19; Bach uses, with substantial alterations, six of Knauer's twelve movements.[1]

1. 1 *Jn.* 3:1; 2. Martin Luther, final verse of "Gelobet seist du, Jesu Christ," 1524 (Wackernagel, III, #19); 4. Balthasar Kindermann, verse 1 of "Was frag ich nach der Welt," 1667 (Fischer-Tümpel, IV, #218); 6. Johann Franck, verse 5 of "Jesu, meine Freude," 1650 (Fischer-Tümpel, IV, #104). 27 December 1723, Leipzig.

BG 16; NBA I/3.

---

1. Chorus [Dictum] (S, A, T, B)

Mark ye how great a love this is that the Father hath shown us, that
we should be called God's children.

2. Chorale (S, A, T, B)

This hath he all for us now done
His great love to show alone.
Rejoice then all Christianity,
Give thanks for this eternally.
Kyrieleis!

3. Recit. (A)

Hence, world! Retain then thy possessions.
I seek and want to gain nought from thee,
Now heaven is my possession,
In which my soul shall find its true refreshment.
Thy gold, it is mere passing wealth,
Thy riches are but borrowed.
Their owner hath exceeding scant provisions.
I say thus with new strength of heart:

4. Chorale (S, A, T, B)

What need I of this world
And all its idle treasures,
If I may but in thee,
My Jesus, find my pleasure!
Thee have I, only thee,
Envisioned as my joy:
Thou, thou art my delight;
What need I of this world!

5. Aria (S)

What the world
Doth contain
Must as though mere smoke soon vanish.[2]

> But what I from Jesus have
> And that which my soul doth love,
> Bides secures and lasts forever.

6. Recit. (B)

That heaven waits for me is sure,
Which I possess in faith already.
Nor death, nor world, nor error,
In truth, nor all the host of hell
Can rob me, one of God's own children,
Of heaven, now or anytime,
And from my spirit take it.
But this, but this one thing doth cause me yet remorse,
That I still longer here within this world should linger;
For Jesus would a share of heaven grant me,
And it was for this that he chose me,
For this was he as man begotten.

7. Aria (A)

From the world I long for nought,
If I but inherit heaven.

> All, yea, all I offer up,
> For I enough assurance have
> That I'll never know destruction.

8. Chorale (S, A, T, B)

Now good night, existence
Which the world hath chosen!
Thou dost please me not.
Now good night, transgression,
Get thee far behind me,
Come no more to light!
Now good night, thou pomp and pride!
Once for all, thou life of trouble,
Thee 'good night' be given!

---

1.   See H. K. Krausse, BJ (1981), pp. 7-22, esp. p. 14.
2.   Cf. *Ps.* 37:20 and passim.

BWV 65 **Sie werden aus Saba alle kommen**

Epiphany.

Poet unknown.

1. *Is.* 60:6; 2. Johann Spangenberg, verse 4 of "Ein Kind geborn zu Bethlehem" (the German version of "Puer natus in Bethlehem"), 1545 (Wackernagel, III, #1110); 7. Paul Gerhardt, verse 10 of "Ich hab in Gottes Herz und Sinn," 1647 (Fischer-Tümpel, III, #393).

6 January 1724, Leipzig.

BG 16; NBA I/5.

---

1. Chorus [Dictum] (S, A, T, B)

They shall from out Sheba all be coming, gold and incense bringing,
and the Lord's great praise then tell abroad.

2. Chorale (S, A, T, B)

The kings from out Sheba came then forth,
Gold, incense, myrrh did they then bring forth.
Alleluia!

3. Recit. (B)

What there Isaiah did once foretell,
That is in Bethlehem fulfilled.
Here gather round the wise men
At Jesus' manger now,
And seek him as their very king to honor.
Gold, incense, and myrrh are
The rare and costly presents
With which they this the Jesus-child
In Bethlehem's poor stall do honor.
My Jesus, if I now my duty well consider,
Must I myself before thy manger venture
And likewise show my thanks:
For this one day I deem a day of gladness,
When thou, O Prince of life,
The light of nations
And their Redeemer art.
But what could I bring thee, thou King of heaven?
If thou my heart deem not too little,
Accept it with thy grace,
No nobler gift could I bring thee.

4. Aria (B)

Gold from Ophir[1] is too slight,
Off, be off with empty off'rings,
Which ye from the earth have torn!
Jesus seeks the heart to own now,
Offer this, O Christian throng,
Jesus thank for the new year!

5. Recit. (T)

Disdain then not,
Thou light unto my soul,
My heart, which I now humbly to thee offer;
It doth indeed such objects
Within it now contain
Which of thy Spirit are the fruits.
The gold of faith, the frankincense of pray'r,
The myrrh of patience, these now are my off'rings,
Which thou shalt, Jesus, evermore,
Have as thy property and as my presents.
But give thyself as well to me,
And thou shalt make me earth's most wealthy mortal.
For, having thee, I must
The most abundant store of wealth
One day above in heaven inherit.

6. Aria (T)

Take me for thine own now hence,
Take my heart as my true present,
All, yes, all that now I am,
All I utter, do and ponder,
Shall, my Savior, be alone
To thy service offered now.

7. Chorale (S, A, T, B)

Ah now, my God, I fall here thus
Consoled into thy bosom.
Take me and deal thou thus with me
Until my final moment,
As thou well canst, that for my soul
Thereby its good be fostered
And thy true honor more and more
Be in my soul exalted.

[1.] Cf. *Is.* 13:12. *Ophir* is a region thought of in the Old Testament as a source of gold, cf. *Kg.* 10.11.

BWV 66 **Erfreut euch, ihr Herzen (Dialogus)**

Second Day of Easter.

Poet unknown; PT (Leipzig, 1724); Facs: Neumann T, p. 429; PT (Leipzig, 1731); Facs: Neumann T, p. 440.

6. Verse 3 of "Christus ist erstanden," Passau, c. 1090 (Wackernagel, II, #948).

10 April 1724 and 26 March 1731, Leipzig; Parody: 1-5 ← BWV 66a/1-4, 8.

BG 16; NBA I/10.

Dialogue

Fear (A) and Hope (T)

1. Chorus (S, A, T, B)

Rejoice, all ye spirits,
Depart, all ye sorrows,
Alive is our Savior and ruling in you.
Ye can now dispel all

> That grieving, that fearing, that faint-hearted anguish,
> Our Savior restoreth his rule o'er the soul.

2. Recit. (B)

The grave is broken and therewith our woe,
My mouth doth publish God's own labors;
Our Savior lives, and thus in woe and death
For faithful folk is all made perfect.

3. Aria (B)

Raise to the Highest a song of thanksgiving
For his dear mercy and lasting good faith.

> Jesus appeareth with peace to endow us,
> Jesus now summons us in life to join him,
> Daily is his gracious mercy made new.

4. Recit. and Arioso (T, A) Hope and Fear

(Hope)
In Jesus' life to live with joy
Is to our breast a brilliant ray of sun.
With comfort filled to look upon their Savior,

And in themselves to build a heav'nly kingdom
Of all true Christians is the wealth.
But since I here possess a heav'nly rapture,
My soul doth seek here its true joy and rest;
My Savior clearly calls to me: "My grave and dying bring you
    living,
My rising is your true hope."
My mouth indeed would bring an off'ring,
My Savior, though so small,
Though meager, though so very little,
It will to thee, O mighty victor, come,
When I bring thee a song of thanks and triumph.

(Hope and Fear)
{Mine/No} eye hath seen the Savior raised from sleep,
Him holdeth {not/still} that death in bondage.

(Hope)
What? Can yet fear in any breast arise?

(Fear)
Can then the grave give up the dead?

(Hope)
If God within a grave be lying,
The grave and death constrain him not.

(Fear)
Ah God! Thou who o'er death art victor,
For thee the tombstone yields, the seal doth break,
I trust thee, but support my weakness,
Thou canst my faith make stronger;
Subdue me and my weak and doubting heart;
The God of wondrous works
Hath this my soul with comfort's might so strengthened,
That it the resurrected Jesus knoweth.

5. Aria (A, T) Fear and Hope

(Fear and Hope)
I {feared in truth/feared no whit} the grave and all its darkness
And {made complaint/kept my hope} my rescue was {now/not}
stolen.

> Now is my heart made full of hope,
> And though a foe should show his wrath,
> I'll find in God victorious triumph.

6. Chorale (S, A, T, B)

Alleluia! Alleluia! Alleluia!
For this we all shall be glad:
Christ shall be our true comfort.
Kyrie eleis.

BWV 66a **Der Himmel dacht auf Anhalts Ruhm und Glück (Serenata)**

Birthday of Prince Leopold of Anhalt-Cöthen.

Christian Friedrich Hunold (Menantes), *Auserlesene und theils noch nie gedruckte Gedichte* (Halle, 1719); Facs: Neumann T, p. 264; Music lost, except in parodied movements.

10 December 1718, Cöthen; Parody: 8, 1-4 → BWV 66/1-5.

NBA I/35.

Serenata

Die Glückseeligkeit Anhalts, Fama

[1. Recit.] Glückseeligkeit

Der Himmel dacht' auf Anhalts Ruhm und Glück,
So ward Fürst Leopold gebohren.
Das Land gedenckt an diese Zeit zurück,
Und hat sie sich zum Jubel-Fest erkohren.

[2.] Aria [Glückseeligkeit]

Traget ihr Lüffte den Jubel von hinnen,
Bringet dem Himmel unsterbliches Lob.
Leopold lebet, in welchem wir leben[,]
Leopold herrschet, dem Himmel ergeben,
Welcher den göttlichen Printzen erhob.
Traget ihr Lüffte den Jubel von hinnen,
Bringet dem Himmel unsterbliches Lob.

[3. Recit. Glückseligkeit, Fama]

(Fama)
Die Klugheit auf dem Thron zu sehn,
Und Tugenden, wie sie im Purpur gehn,
Ja Gnad, und Huld, die Land und Leut erquicken,
Bey der Gewalt des Scepters zu erblicken[,]
Hab' ich der Grossen Burg beschaut.
Ich bin umsonst zu manchem Thron geflogen[,]
Der nur auf Weh' und Ach gebaut.
Kaum, daß ich hier den Edlen Hof bezogen,
So lebt mein Wunsch; Diß Kleinod treff ich an;
Man hat von jener Sternen-Bahn
Der Klugheit, Tugend, Gnad' und Güte,
Die Macht und Hoheit anvertraut.

"O Fürst, von Fürstlichem Gemüthe!
Wie herrlich, wohl und fest
Hast Du den Fürsten-Stuhl gesetzet!
Der Grund ist Gott, der ihn nie wancken läst,
Der dich o Fürst nach seinem Sinn ergetzet.

(Fama, Glückseeligkeit)
{Ich/Du} aber {will/kanst} auf {meinem/deinem} Ehren[-
]Wagen
{Dein/Sein} Lob zu allen Völckern tragen.

(Fama)
Wie? Find ich dich Glückseeligkeit allhier?

(Glückseeligkeit)
Ist dieses ein so seltsam Ding?

(Fama)
Kaum, sah' ich dich noch auf dem Landen,
Als ich durch Anhalt Cöthen gieng.

(Glückseeligkeit)
Mir gab bey seinem Fürsten-Stande
Zwar Leopold am Hofe das Quartier;
Doch auf des Landes sehnlichs Flehen,
Mich auch bey sich zu sehen,
Hat mir der Fürst, der seinen Unterthan
Nicht höher lieben kan,
Viel Wohnungen im Fürstenthum erbauet,
Du findest mich, wohin dein Auge schauet.

[4.] Aria [Fama, Glückseeligkeit]

(Fama, Glückseeligkeit)
Ich weiche {nun; ich will/nicht; du solst} der Erden sagen:
Nur Tugend kan {Glückseeligkeit/des Landes wohl} erjagen[.]

{Dir/Mir} Anhalt {sey/bleibt} der Himmel hold,
{Ich will/Und wird} den Theuren Leopold
Mit Ruhm auf {meinen/Adlers} Flügeln tragen.
Ich weiche {nun, ich will/nicht, du solst} der Erden sagen,
Nur Tugend kan {Glückseeligkeit/des Landes wohl} erjagen.

[5. Recit. Glückeeligkeit, Fama]

(Glückseeligkeit)
Wie weit bist du mit Anhälts Götter-Ruhm,
Die noch die Welt in ihren Thaten ehrt,
Die schon im grauen Alterthum
Die Kunst zu herrschen wohl gelehrt,
Wie weit bist du mit ihrem Ruhm geflogen?

(Fama)
Biß an der Sternen-Bogen.

(Glückseeligkeit)
Nun dieser Fürsten Tugend-Gold
Gläntzt in dem Theuren Leopold.
So bringe dann bis an der Sternen Achsen
Den edlen Zweig der Hochgepriesnen Sachsen.
Wie offt hat Gott das Land zuvor ergetzt?

(Fama)
So offt ein Fürst sein Heil auf Gott gesetzt.

(Glückseeligkeit)
Sprich: Leopold hat himmlische Gedancken;
Gott wird von ihm und er von Gott nie wancken.
Was hat vor dem das Land so hoch geziert,
Und ihm des Fürsten Huld verschrieben?

(Fama)
Gehorsam, treu zu seyn und lieben.

(Glückseeligkeit)
Sprich: Daß noch nie ein Herr regiert,
Der im Triumph die Hertzen mehr geführt.
Nenn ihn der Unterthanen Lust;
Sprich, daß sie ihm den Namen Vater geben.
Geh! Aller Welt sey unser heil bewust.

(Fama)
So sprich mit mir:

(Fama, Glückseeligkeit)
Fürst Leopold soll leben.

[6.] Aria [Fama?]

Beglücktes Land von süsser Ruh und Stille!
In deiner Brust wallt nur ein Freuden-Meer.
Du siehst von fern die Krieges-Fluthen schlagen,
Und Sturm und Noth so manches Ufer plagen[,]
Hier weht allein ein Gnaden-West daher.
Beglücktes Land von süsser Ruh und Stille,
In deiner Brust wallt nur ein Freuden-Meer.

[7. Recit. Glückseeligkeit, Fama]

(Glückseeligkeit)
Nun theurer Fürst! der seinen Purpur schmücket,
Gott mache dich je mehr und mehr beglücket.

(Fama)
Ein Palmen-Baum blüht schön bey seines gleichen:
Jedoch vielleicht denckt dieser Herr allein
Unsterblichkeit durch Tugend zu erreichen.

(Glückseeligkeit)
Die hat er schon.

(Fama)
Ja, die ist ungemein.
Wird aber Anhalts Götter-Zahl
Nicht durch sein theures Fürsten-Blut
Annoch unsterblich seyn?

(Glückseeligkeit)
Du wünschest ein unschätzbahr Gut.

(Fama)
Man preist der holden Sonnen Strahl.
Die ihren Glantz auch Mond und Sternen giebt.

(Glückseeligkeit)
Ich weiß, daß mich der Himmel liebt;
Ich weiß, daß der die Zeit ersehn,
In welcher noch ein himmlisch Licht
Wird neben unsrer Sonne stehn.
Diß ist ein Wunsch, der durch die Wolcken bricht:

(Glückseeligkeit, Fama)
Es blühe denn durch ihn diß Götter-Haus,
Es blüh und sterbe nimmer aus.

[8.] Aria [Glückseeligkeit, Fama, Tutti]

(Glückseeligkeit)
Es strahle die Sonne,

(Fama)
Es lache die Wonne,

(Tutti)
Es lebe Fürst Leopold ewig beglückt.

(Glückseeligkeit, Fama)
Ach Himmel wir flehen;
{Diß holde Licht/Die frohe Zeit} sechzigmahl wieder zu sehen.

(Tutti)
Gib Höchster was unsern Regenten erquickt.

(Glückseeligkeit)
Es strahle die Sonne,

(Fama)
Es lache die Wonne,

(Tutti)
Es lebe Fürst Leopold ewig beglückt.

Serenade

The Happiness of Anhalt, Fama[1]

[1. Recit.] Happiness

Since heaven cared for Anhalt's fame and bliss,
Prince Leopold was born amongst us,
This land doth call now that same hour to mind,
And hath it for a joyful feast selected.

[2.] Aria [Happiness]

Waft hence, ye breezes, your glad jubilation,
Lift up to heaven undying great praise.
Leopold liveth, who gives our life meaning, Leopold ruleth, to heaven
    devoted,
Which him to princes immortal did raise.

[3. Recit. Happiness, Fama]

Great wisdom on the throne to see,
And virtues rare, as they in purple walk,
Yea, grace and charm, which land and folk enliven,
Joined with the force of scepter, to discover,
Have I the mighty's tow'rs beheld.
I have in vain to many thrones yet flown now
Which but on 'Woe and Ah' are built.
But when I here the noble court first entered,
My hope revived; this jewel did I meet;
Here were from yonder starry course
To wisdom, virtue, grace and kindness
Both might and high rank put in trust.
"O Prince, of princely heart and spirit,
How glorious, well and firm
Hast thou the princely throne been sitting!
On God it rests, who holds it e'er unmoved,
Who thee, O Prince, as he intends, give favor.

(Fama, Happiness)
{I will/Thou canst} therefore in this {my/thy} honor-chariot
{Thy/His} praise to all the nations carry.

(Fama)
What? Is it thee, O Happiness, I see?

(Happiness)
Is this indeed so rare a thing?

(Fama)
No, I saw thee even in the country
As I through Anhalt-Cöthen went.

(Happiness)
Though me among his fellow princes
Did Leopold at court make resident,

Upon the land's sincere petition
That it as well receive me,
For me the Prince, who could his subjects here
Not hold in higher love,
Hath many dwellings built in his dominion,
Thou findest me where'er thine eye observeth.

[4.] Aria [Fama, Happiness]

(Fama, Happiness)
I'll leave then {now; I would/not; thou shouldst} all earth be
     telling
Just virtue can {true happiness/the land's true health} accomplish.
{Thy/My} Anhalt {be/bides} to heaven dear,
{I will/Which shall} the worthy Leopold
With fame on {these my/eagle's} pinions carry.

[5. Recit. Happiness, Fama]

(Happiness)
How far hast thou with Anhalt's fame divine,
Which all the world in action doth revere,
Which e'en in dim antiquity
The art of ruling well did learn,
How far hast thou with her great fame been flying?

(Fama)
E'en to the starry heavens.

(Happiness)
Now doth a princely virtue's gold
Shine forth in precious Leopold.
So carry then into the starry axis
The noble branch of the exalted Saxons.
How oft hath God this land before this blessed?

(Fama)
As oft a Prince his hope in God doth rest.

(Happiness)
Say: Leopold hath heavenly intentions;
God shall from him and he from God ne'er waver.
What hath ere this the land so highly graced,
And it this Prince's charm alloted?

(Fama)
Obedience, faithfulness and honor.

(Happiness)
Say: Ere this time no lord hath ruled
Who hath the hearts of all more led in triumph. Name him his subjects'
     pride and joy;
Say that they now the name of father give him.
Go! All the world of our good health should know.

(Fama)
So say with me:

(Fama, Happiness)
Prince Leopold shall prosper!

[6.] Aria [Fama?]

O happy land of sweet repose and quiet!
Within thy breast wells but a sea of joy.
Thou see'st far off the floods of warfare crashing,
And storms and need so many shores oppressing,
But here alone a gracious west wind blows.

     Da Capo.

[7. Recit. Happiness, Fama]

(Happiness)
Now worthy Prince! God who adorns his purple,
God give to thee e'er more and more good fortune.

(Fame)
A palm of praise doth bloom beside such nature:
Perhaps, indeed, doth this one lord intend
His immortality to win through virtue.

(Happiness)
He hath it now!

(Fama)
Yes, exceedingly!
But will not Anhalt's godlike host
Through his most precious princely blood
As well immortal be?

(Happiness)
Thy wish is for a pricelss gift.

(Fama)
We praise the gracious sunlight's rays
Which give their light to moon and stars as well.[2]

(Happiness)
I know that I'm by heaven loved;
I know that it the time foresees
In which another heav'nly light
Will take its place beside our sun.
This is our wish which through the clouds breaks forth:

(Both)
Let flourish then through him this godlike house,
Let bloom, and perish nevermore.

[8.] Aria [Happiness, Fama, Tutti]

(Happiness)
Let sun shine forever,

(Fama)
Let pleasure bring laughter,

(Tutti)
Let prosper Prince Leopold ever in bliss.

(Happiness, Fama)
Ah heaven, we pray now:
{This gracious light/This happy day} sixty times over to witness.

(Tutti)
Grant, Highest, to all these our rulers good health.

[1.] The Latin for 'fame' or 'rumor.' In this Dialogue Fama will carry the fame of Prince Leopold throughout the universe.

[2.] Just as the sun shares it light with the moon, so will the immortality of Leopold be shared by his subjects.

BWV 67 Halt im Gedächtnis Jesum Christ

Quasimodogeniti (The Sunday after Easter).

Poet unknown; PT (Leipzig, 1724); Facs: Neumann T, p. 431.

1. 2 *Tim.* 2:8; 3b (4). Nikolaus Herman, "Erschienen ist der herrlich Tag," 1560 (Wackernagel, III, #1374); 4 (6). *Jn.* 20:19 with interpolated aria; 5 (7). Jakob Ebert, verse 1 of "Du Friedefürst, Herr Jesu Christ," 1601.

16 April 1724, Leipzig; Parody: 4 → BWV 234/2.

BG 16; NBA I/11.

---

1. Chorus [Dictum] (S, A, T, B)

Hold in remembrance Jesus Christ, who is arisen from death's bondage.[1]

2. Aria (T)

My Jesus is arisen,
But still, why fear I yet?
My faith the Savior's triumph sees,
But still my heart feels strife and war,
Appear, my Savior, now!

3a (4).[2] Recit. (A)

My Jesus, thou art called the bane to death,
And unto hell a plague and torment;[3]
Ah, am I still by dread and terror struck?
Thou set upon our very tongues then
The song of praise we have been singing:[4]

3b (5). Chorale (S, A, T, B)

Appeared is now the glorious day
When no one hath his fill of joy:
Christ, he our Lord, today triumphs,
Who all his foes hath captive led.
Alleluia!

3c (6). Recit. (A)

It seems as though
The remnant of my foe,

Whom I too strong and frightful still consider,
Will leave me not in peace.
But if for me the victory thou hast won,
Contend thyself with me, with thine own child now:
Yes, yes, we feel in faith already
That thou, O Prince of peace,
Thy word and work in us shalt yet fulfill.

4 (6). Aria (S, A, T, B)

(B)
Peace be unto you!

> (S, A, T)
> O joy! Jesus helps us battle
> And the foes' great rage to dampen,
> Hell and Satan, yield!

(B)
Peace be unto you!

> (S, A, T)
> Jesus summons us to peace now
> And restores in us so weary
> Soul and flesh alike.

(B)
Peace be unto you![5]

(S, A, T)
> O Lord, help as we endeavor
> E'en through death to press our journey
> To thy glorious realm!

(B)
Peace be unto you!

5 (7). Chorale (S, A, T, B)

Thou Prince of peace, Lord Jesus Christ,
True man and very God,
A helper strong in need thou art
In life as well as death:
So we alone
For thy name's sake
Are to thy Father crying.

[1.] Literally but unsuitable as underlay: "from the dead." "Bondage" is added in the translation by way of allusion to the context of the passage (2 *Tim.* 2:8-10): "Remember Jesus Christ, risen from the dead, descended from David, as preached in my gospel, the gospel for which I am suffering and wearing fetters like a criminal. But the word of God is not fettered."

[2.] 3a, 3b, and 3c have usually been listed as 3, 4, and 5, but they form a single section in which the faithful, yet frightened soul speaks to Jesus. 3. *Hos.* 13:14. Jesus is the death of death.

[3.] 3. Cf. *Hos.*13:14. Jesus is the death of death.

[4.] Following the PT, this is punctuated as a rhetorical question. The believer asks how he could feel such anguish when Jesus himself inspired the ensuing Easter hymn, which would have been sung first one week ago. The verb tenses are critical here.

[5.] The bass part represents the vox Christi in the repetition of *Jn* 20:19.

BWV 68 **Also hat Gott die Welt geliebt**

Second Day of Pentecost.

Christiane Mariane von Ziegler, *Versuch in Gebundener Schreibart, Teil I* (Leipzig, 1728); Facs: Neumann T, p. 363.

1. Salomo Liscow, verse 1 of the hymn, 1675 (Fischer-Tümpel, IV, #160), after *Jn.* 3:16; 5. *Jn.* 3:18.

21 May 1725, Leipzig; Parody: 2, 4 ← BWV 208/14, 7.

BG 16; NBA I/14.

1. Chorus [Chorale] (S, A, T, B)

In truth hath God the world so loved
That he to us his Son hath given.
Who gives in faith himself to him
With him shall always live in heaven.
Who trusts that Jesus is born for him
Shall be forever unforsaken,
And there's no grief to make him sad,
Whom God, his very Jesus, loves.

2. Aria (S)

My heart ever faithful,
Exulting, sing gladly,
Thy Jesus is here!

    Hence sorrow! Hence grieving!
    I will simply tell you:
    My Jesus is near!

3. Recit. (B)

I am like Peter not mistaken,[1]
I am consoled and filled with joy,
That I'm by Jesus not forgotten.
He came not in the world to judge it,
No, no, he wanted sin and guilt,
As arbiter 'twixt God and man, here now to straighten.

4. Aria (B)

Thou art born man to my advantage,
This is my faith, I am contented,
Since thou for me hath done enough.

> The ball of earth may soon be shattered,
> And Satan arm himself against,
> But I'll to thee, my Savior, pray.

5. Chorus [Dictum] (S, A, T, B)

Who in him trusteth will not judged guilty; but who doth not trust
him is already judged guilty; for he trusteth not in the name of the
one-born Son of God the Father.

[1.] Cf. *Acts* 10:26 and 47.

BWV 69 **Lobe den Herrn, meine Seele I**

Inauguration of the New Town Council (Twelfth Sunday after Trinity).

Poet unknown; based on a cantata by Johann Oswald Knauer, *Gott-geheiligtes Singen und Spielen des Friedensteinischen Zions* (Gotha, 1720), which was adapted to form BWV 69a.

1. *Ps.* 103:2; 6. Martin Luther, after *Ps.* 67, verse 3 of "Es woll uns Gott genädig sein," 1524 (Wackernagel, I, #189).

Later years at Leipzig; Parody: 1, 3, 5 ← BWV 69a/1, 3, 5.
BG 16; NBA I/32.

---

1. Chorus [Dictum] (S, A, T, B)

Praise thou the Lord, O my spirit, and forget not the goodness that
he hath shown thee.

2. Recit. (S)

How great is God's dear kindness though!
He brought us to the light,
And he sustains us yet.
Where can one find a single creature now
Which doth for sustenance yet lack?
Consider though, my soul,
Almighty God's unhidden trace
Which e'en in small things proves to be so great.
Ah, would that I, Most High God, had the power
A worthy song of thanks to bring thee!
But, should in me for this the strength be lacking,
I will e'en still, Lord, thy great fame be telling.

3. Aria (A)

O my spirit,
Rise and tell it,
All that God hath shown to thee!

Glorify his wondrous work,
To the Most High bring now pleasure,
Make thy song of thanks ring gladly.

4. Recit. (T)

The Lord hath mighty things for us achieved.
For he provideth and sustains,
Protecteth and ruleth all the world.
He doth more than could e'er be told.
But still, just one thing now consider:

What better thing could God have giv'n us
Than that he to our governors
The soul of wisdom granteth,
Who then forevermore
Both ill rebuke and goodness cherish?
Yea, who both day and night
For our well-being watch?
Let us in turn the Most High praise now:
Rise! Call to him,
That he may also ever yet such favor wish to show us.
From all that would our land do harm,
Wouldst thou, O Most High God, defend us,
And thy most welcome help now send us.
Indeed, though thou with cross and suff'ring
May punish us, thou wilt not slay us.

5. Aria (B)

My Redeemer and Sustainer,
Keep me in thy care and watch!
Stand by me in cross and suff'ring,
And my mouth shall sing with gladness:
God hath all things set aright!

6. Chorale (S, A, T, B)

Let thank, O God, and honor thee
The people through good service.
The land bears fruit, amends itself,
Thy word is well commended.
Us bless the Father and the Son,
And bless us God, the Holy Ghost,
Whom all the world doth[1] glorify
And hold in rev'rence unexcelled,
And say sincerely: Amen!

---

[1]   With the subjunctive form *thu*, found in the older hymnbooks, translate "let."

BWV 69a **Lobe den Herrn, meine Seele**

Twelfth Sunday after Trinity.

Johann Oswald Knauer, *Gott-geheiligtes Singen und Spielen des Friedensteinischen Zions* (Gotha, 1720); Facs: BJ (1981), p. 20; Bach adapts with substantial alterations six of Knauer's ten movements.[1]

15 August 1723, Leipzig; 1, 3, 5—> BWV 69/1, 3, 5.

BG 16, Anhang; NBA I/20.

1. Chorus [Dictum] (S, A, T, B)

Praise thou the Lord, O my spirit, and forget not the goodness that he hath shown thee.

2. Recit. (S)

Ah, would I had a thousand tongues now!
Ah, would as well my mouth
Of empty words were free!
Ah, could I nothing utter
But what to God's renown intended were!
Then would I make the Most High's kindness known;
For he hath all my life so much for me achieved,
That through eternity I could not thank him full.

3. Aria (T)

O my spirit,
Rise and tell it,
All that God hath shown to thee!

Glorify his wondrous work,
To the Most High bring now pleasure,
Make thy song of thanks ring gladly.

4. Recit. (A)

If I but now think back
To what, my God, from tender childhood on
Until this moment thou
For me hast done,
I could then all thy wonders, Lord
So little as the stars e'er number.
For all thy care, which thou dost on my spirit
At ev'ry hour bestow,
From which thou only[2] out of love dost rest,
I could not ever fully give thee thanks.
My mouth is weak, my tongue is mute
To tell thy praise and fame.
Ah! Be near me
And speak thy mighty "Hephata,"[3] / gracious "yes," /
Then shall my mouth with thanks be filled.

5. Aria (B)

My Redeemer and Sustainer,
Keep me in thy care and watch!
Stand by me in cross and suff'ring,
And my mouth shall sing with gladness:
God hath all things set aright!

6. Chorale (S, A, T, B)

What God doth, that is rightly done,
To that will I be cleaving.

Though out upon the cruel road
Need, death and suff'ring drive me,
E'en so will God,
All fatherhood,
Within his arms enfold me;
So I yield him all power.

---

1. For a full account of Bach's use of this and two other cantatas of Knauer, see H. K. Krausse, BJ (1981), pp. 7-22, esp. p. 13.
2. BG has *nie*: to be translated with "never."
3. Hebr. 'be opened!'

BWV 70 **Wachet! betet! betet! wachet!**

Twenty-sixth Sunday after Trinity.

Recitatives by unknown poet, arias by Salomo Franck, *Evangelische Sonn- und Fest-Tages-Andachten* (Weimar and Jena, 1717); Facs: Neumann T, p. 290.

7. Final verse of "Freu dich sehr, o meine Seele," Freiberg, 1620 (Fischer-Tümpel, I, #573); 9. chorale melody of "Es ist gewißlich an der Zeit"; 11. Christian Keymann, verse 5 of "Meinen Jesum laß ich nicht," 1658 (Fischer-Tümpel, IV, #13).

21 November 1723, Leipzig; Parody: 1, 3, 5, 8, 10, 11 ← BWV 70a/1-6.

BG 16; NBA I/27.

First Part

1. Chorus (S, A, T, B)

Watch ye, pray ye, pray ye, watch ye!

> Keep prepared
> For the day
> When the Lord of majesty
> To this world its ending bringeth!

2. Recit. (B)

Be frightened, O ye stubborn sinners!
A day shall dawn
From which no one can hope to hide:
It speeds thee to a stringent judgment,
O sinful generation,
To lasting lamentation.
But you, God's own elected children,
It brings the onset of true gladness.
The Savior summons you, when all else shall collapse,
Before his own exalted face:
So fear ye not!

3. Aria (A)

When comes the day of our deliv'rance
From this the Egypt of our world?
Ah, let us soon from Sodom flee now,
Ere us the fire hath overwhelmed!
Wake up, ye souls, from your repose,
And trust, this is the final hour!

4. Recit. (T)

In spite of all our heav'nly longing
Our body holds the spirit captive;
The world doth set through all its cunning
For good men traps and meshes.
The soul is willing, but the flesh is weak;[1]
This forces out our sorrowful "Alas!"

5. Aria (S)

Leave to mocking tongues their scorning,
For it will and has to happen
That we Jesus shall behold yet
In the clouds, in the heavens.
World and universe may perish,
Christ's word must still stand unshaken.
Leave to mocking tongues their scorning,
For it will and has to happen!

6. Recit. (T)

And yet amidst this savage generation
God careth for his servants,
That this most wicked breed
Might cease henceforth to harm them,
For he doth hold them in his hand secure
And to a heav'nly Eden bring them.

7. Chorale (S, A, T, B)

Now be glad, O thou my spirit,
And forget all need and fears,
For thee now doth Christ, thy Master,
Summon from this vale of tears!

His great joy and majesty
Shalt thou see eternally,
Join the angels' jubilation
In eternal exultation.

Second Part

8. Aria (T)

Lift high your heads aloft[2]
And be consoled, ye righteous,
That now your souls may bloom!

> Ye shall in Eden flourish
> In God's eternal service.

9. Recit. (B) with instr. chorale[3]

Ah, ought not this most awful day,
The world's collapse,
The sounding trumpet's peal,
The strange, unequaled final stroke,
The sentence which the judge proclaimeth,
The open jaws of hell's own portals
Within my heart
Much doubting, fear and terror
In me, the child of sin I am,
Awaken?
And yet, there passeth through my spirit
A glint of joy, of light of hope doth rise.
The Savior can his heart no more keep hidden,
It doth with pity break,
His mercy's arm forsakes me not.
Lead on, thus shall I end with gladness now my course.

10. Aria (B)

O most blest refreshment day,
Lead me now into thy mansions!
Sound and crack, O final stroke,
World and heavens, fall in ruins!
Jesus leadeth me to stillness,
To that place where joy hath fullness.

11. Chorale (S, A, T, B)

Not for world, for heaven not,
Doth my spirit yearn with longing;
Jesus seek I and his light,
Who to God hath reconciled me,
Who from judgment sets me free;
My Lord Jesus I'll not leave.

[1.] *Mt.* 26:41.

[2.] *Lk.* 21:28.

[3.] The text of this chorale is by Bartholomäus Ringwaldt, 1582, and is found in Bach's four-part chorale BWV 307:

> Es ist gewisslich an der Zeit,
> Daß Gottes Sohn wird kommen
> In seiner grossen Herrlichkeit,
> Zu richten Bös' und Frommen.
> Dann wird das Lachen werden theu'r,
> Wann Alles soll vergehn im Feu'r,
> Wie Petrus davon zeuget.

> Now is in truth the time at hand
> For God's own Son's appearing
> Within his glorious majesty
> To judge the good and wicked.
> Then shall all laughter be most dear,

When all must perish in the fire,
As Peter testifieth.

5.   Cf. *Ps.* 16:11.

BWV 70a **Wachet! betet! betet! wachet!**

Second Sunday in Advent.

Salomo Franck, *Evangelische Sonn-und Fest-Tages-Andachten* (Weimar and Jena, 1717); Facs: Neumann T, p. 290.

6. Christian Keymann, verse 5 of "Meinen Jesum laß ich nicht," 1658 (Fischer-Tümpel, IV, #13).

6 December 1716, Weimar; 1-6—> BWV 70/1, 3, 5, 8, 10, 11.

NBA I/1, Krit. Bericht.

---

1. Chorus (= BWV 70/1)

2. Aria (= BWV 70/3)

3. Aria (= BWV 70/5)

4. Aria (= BWV 70/8)

5. Aria (= BWV 70/10)

6. Chorale (= BWV 70/11)

---

1.   Unlike Weimar, Leipzig permitted no cantatas on the second, third, and fourth Sundays in Advent. Hence, this cantata in its enlarged version was designed for the Twenty-sixth Sunday after Trinity.

BWV 71 **Gott ist mein König**

Inauguration of the New Town Council.

Poet unknown; PT (Mühlhausen, 1708); Facs: Neumann T, p. 384.

1. *Ps.* 74:12; 2. Johann Heermann, verse 6 of "O Gott, du frommer Gott," 1630 (Fischer-Tümpel, I, #355), with interpolated aria based on 2. *Sam.* 19:35 and 37; 3. *Dt.* 33:25 and *Gen.* 21:22; 4. *Ps.* 74:16-17; 6. *Ps.* 74:19.

4 February 1708, Mühlhausen.

BG 18; NBA I/32.

---

1. Chorus [Dictum]

God is my Sovereign since ancient days, who all salvation brings which on earth may be found.

2. Aria [Dictum] (T) and Chorale (S)

(T)
I have lived eighty years, wherefore shall thy thrall still more complain, then?

(S)
If I should in this world
My life extend yet longer,
Through countless bitter steps
Into old age advancing,
I would return now, that I die within my own town,
Help me forbear, from sin
And scandal me defend,
So that I may wear well beside my father's and mine own mother's grave.
With honor my gray hair.

3. Chorus [Dictum] (S, A, T, B)

Thine old age be like to thy childhood, and God is with thee in every deed thou dost.

4. Arioso [Dictum] (B)

Day and night are thine. Thou makest them both, the sun and the stars, their own appointed course follow.

5. Aria (A)

With powerful might
Dost thou preserve our borders,
Here shall then peace be radiant,
Though death and raging war
May all around appear.
Though crown and scepter shake,
Hast thou salvation brought
With powerful might!

6. Chorus [Dictum] (S, A, T, B)

May'st thou to the foe not deliver thy turtledoves' own very spirits.

7. Chorus (S, A, T, B)

This our new government
In every endeavor
Here crown with thy blessing!
Concord, peace and prosp'rous fortune
Must alway be in attendance
On our new government
Joy, health, great victory
Must each day continue
O Joseph,[1] to please thee,
That in every clime and country

Ever steadfast may attend thee
Joy, health, great victory!

---

1. Emperor (Kaiser) Joseph I (1705-1711).

BWV 72 **Alles nur nach Gottes Willen**

Third Sunday after Epiphany.

Salomo Franck, *Evangelisches Andachts-Opffer* (Weimar, 1715); Facs: Neumann T, p. 277.

6. Margrave Albrecht von Brandenburg, verse 1 of the hymn, 1547 (Wackernagel, III, #1240).

27 January 1726, Leipzig; Parody: 1 → Mass in G Minor, BWV 235/2.

BG 18; NBA I/6.

---

1. Chorus (S, A, T, B)

All things but as God is willing,
Both in joy and deepest grief,
Both in good and evil times.
God's own will shall be my solace
Under cloud and shining sun.
All things but as God is willing,
This shall hence my motto be.[1]

2. Recit. (A)

O Christian blest who always doth his own will
In God's own will submerge, no matter what may happen,

In health and sickness!
Lord, if thou wilt,[2] must all things be obedient!
Lord, if thou wilt, thou canst bring me contentment!
Lord, if thou wilt, shall vanish all my pain!
Lord, if thou wilt, will I be well and clean!
Lord, if thou wilt, all sadness will be gladness!
Lord, if thou wilt, I'll find midst thorns a pasture!
Lord, if thou wilt, will I be blest at last!
Lord, if thou wilt, (let me express in faith this sentence
To make my soul be quiet!)
Lord, if thou wilt, I'll perish not,
Though life and limb have me forsaken,
If to my heart thy Spirit speaks this word![3]

3. Aria (A)

With ev'rything I have and am
I'll trust myself to Jesus;

> E'en though my feeble soul and mind
> The will of God not fathom,
> Still may he lead me ever forth
> On roads of thorns and roses!

4. Recit. (B)

So now believe!
Thy Savior saith: "This will I!"[4]
He shall his gracious hand
Most willingly extend thee
When cross and suff'ring thee have frightened;
He knoweth thy distress and lifts the cross's bond,
He helps the weak
And would, the humble roof
Of poor in spirit not despising,
Therein deign graciously to enter.

5. Aria (S)

My Jesus will[5] do it, he will thy cross now sweeten.
E'en though thy heart may lie amidst much toil and trouble,
Shall it yet soft and still within his arms find rest
If him thy faith doth grasp! My Jesus will do it.

6. Chorale (S, A, T, B)

What my God will, be done alway,
His will, it is the best will;
To help all those he is prepared
Whose faith in him is steadfast.
He frees from want, this righteous God,
And punisheth with measure:
Who trusts in God, on him relies,
Him will he not abandon.

[1.]   This motto is similar to one which influenced so much of Salomo Franck's
       poetry: *mihi omnia Jesus* (Augustine).
[2.]   This ninefold anaphora, "Lord, if thou wilt," is based on the words of the leper
       at *Mt.* 8:2 from the Gospel for this day: "Domine, si vis potes me mundare."
       The translation of *Wohl und Wehe* with "health and sickness" is meant to draw
       attention to Jesus' miraculous healing. One may prefer "In joy and sorrow."
[3.]   BG has a colon here to introduce the ensuing aria.
[4.]   Cf. *Mt.* 8:3, Jesus' response to the leper.
[5.]   Cf. *Mt.* 8:3, Jesus' response to the leper.

BWV 73 **Herr, wie du willt, so schick's mit mir**

Third Sunday after Epiphany.

Poet unknown; PT (Leipzig, 1724); Facs: Neumann T, p. 424.

1. Kaspar Bienemann, verse 1 of the hymn, 1582 (Wackernagel, IV,

#1046), to the chorale melody "Wo Gott, der Herr, nicht bei uns hält" (cf. BWV 178), with interpolated recitative; 5. Ludwig Helmbold, final verse of "Von Gott will ich nicht lassen," 1563.

23 January 1724, Leipzig.

BG 18; NBA I/6.

---

1. Chorale (S, A, T, B) and Recit. (T, B, S)

(S, A, T, B)
Lord, as thou wilt, so deal with me
In living and in dying!

(T)
Ah! Ah, alas! How much
Thy will doth let me suffer!
My life hath been misfortune's prey,
For sorrow and dismay
Must plague me all my days,
Nor will yet my distress in dying even leave me.
Alone for thee is my desire,
Lord, leave me not to perish!

(B)
Thou art my helper, strength and shield,
Who every mourner's tears dost number,
And dost their confidence,
That fragile reed, no way corrupt;
And since thou me hast chosen,
So speak to me of hope and joy!
Maintain me only in thy grace,
But as thou wilt, let me forbear,
For thy will is the best will.

(S)
Thy will, in truth, is like a book that's sealed,
Which human wisdom cannot read;
Thy grace oft seems to us a curse,
Chastisement, oft a cruel judgment,
The rest which thou hast in our dying slumber
One day ordained,
To hell an introduction.
Thy Spirit, though, our error doth dispel
And show that thy true will doth make us well.
Lord, as thou wilt!

2. Aria (T)

Ah, pour thou yet thy joyful Spirit
Into my heart!

> For often through my spirit's sickness
> Both joyfulness and hope would falter
> And yield to fear.

3. Recit. (B)

Ah, our own will remains perverse,
Now haughty, now afraid,[1]
With death e'er loathe to reckon.
But men of Christ, through God's own Spirit taught,
Submit themselves to God's true purpose
And say:

4. Aria (B)

Lord, if thou wilt,
Suppress, ye pains of dying,
All sighing in my bosom,

If this my pray'r thou dost approve.
Lord, if thou wilt,
Then lay to rest my body
In dust and ashes lowly,
This most corrupted shape of sin.
Lord, if thou wilt,
Then strike, ye bells of mourning,
I follow quite unfrightened,
My sorrow is forever stilled.

5. Chorale (S, A, T, B)

This is the Father's purpose,
Who us created hath;
His Son hath plenteous goodness
Gained for us, and much grace;
And God the Holy Ghost
In faith o'er us yet ruleth,
To heaven's kingdom leadeth.
To him laud, honor, praise!

[1.]   Cf. *Jer.* 17:9.

BWV 74 **Wer mich liebet,**
der wird mein Wort halten II

Pentecost (Whitsunday).

Based on Christiane Mariane von Ziegler, *Versuch in Gebundener Schreibart, Teil I* (Leipzig, 1728); Facs: Neumann T, p. 362.

1. *Jn.* 14:23; 4. *Jn.* 14:28; 6. *Rom.* 8:1; 8. Paul Gerhardt, verse 2 of "Gott Vater, sende deinen Geist," 1653 (Fischer—Tümpel, III, #414).

20 May 1725, Leipzig; Parody: 1, 2 ← BWV 59/1, 4.

BG 18; NBA I/13.

---

1. Chorus [Dictum] (S, A, T, B)

He who loves me will keep my commandments, and my Father, too, will love him, and we shall unto him then come and make our dwelling with him.

2. Aria (S)

Come, come, my heart to thee is open,
Ah, let it now thy dwelling be!
I do love thee and must be hopeful:
Thy word is now in me fulfilled;
For who thee seeks, fears, loves and honors,
With him the Father is content.
I do not doubt that I am favored
And shall in thee my comfort find.

3. Recit. (A)

Thy dwelling is prepared.
Thou hast my heart, to thee alone devoted,
So let me never suffer
That thou shouldst mean from me to part,
For I will never let, ah, never let it happen.

4. Aria [Dictum] (B)

I go from here and come again unto you. If I had your love, ye would be now rejoicing.

5. Aria (T)

Come, hasten, tune your strings and anthems
In lively and rejoicing song.
Though he now leaves, again he cometh,
The high-exalted Son of God.

> But Satan will be now attempting
> Thy people to bring condemnation.
> He is my obstacle,
> My faith is, Lord, in thee.

6. Recit. [Dictum] (B)

There is nought destructible in any who in Christ, Lord Jesus, live.

7. Aria (A)

Nought could me deliver
From hell's very shackles
But, Jesus, thy blood.

> Thy passion, thy dying
> Are mine to inherit:
> I'll laugh at hell's wrath.

8. Chorale (S, A, T, B)

No child of man here on the earth
Is worthy of this noble gift,
In us there is no merit;
Here nought doth count but love and grace
Which Christ for us hath merited
With sacrifice and healing.

BWV 75 **Die Elenden sollen essen**

First Sunday after Trinity.

Poet unknown, possibly Christian Weiss.

1. *Ps.* 22:27; 7. Samuel Rodigast, verse 5 of "Was Gott tut, das ist wohlgetan," 1674 (Fischer-Tümpel, IV, #467); 14. Samuel Rodigast, last verse of "Was Gott tut, das ist wohlgetan."

30 May 1723, Leipzig.

BG 18; NBA I/15.

Part One

1. Chorus [Dictum] (S, A, T, B)

The hungering shall be nourished till they be sated, and they who desire the Lord shall tell his praises. And your heart shall evermore flourish.

2. Recit. (B)

What use is purple's majesty
When it is gone?
What use the greatest store of wealth
Since all things in our vision
Must disappear?
What use the stirring of vain yearnings,
Since this our flesh itself must perish?
Alas, how swiftly doth it happen
That riches, pleasure, pomp,
The soul to hell condemn![1]

3. Aria (T)

My Jesus shall be all I own![2]

> My purple is his precious blood,
> Himself my most exalted wealth,
> And this his Spirit's fire of love
> My most delicious wine of joy.

4. Recit. (T)

God humbleth and exalteth
Both now and for all time.
Who in the world would heaven seek
Shall here be cursed.[3]
However, who here hell's power overcometh
Shall there[4] find joy.

5. Aria (S)

I take up my sadness with gladness to me.

> Who Lazarus' torments
> With patience endureth
> Be taken by angels above.

6. Recit. (S)

A conscience clear hath God provided
So that a Christian can
In simple things find great delight and pleasure.
Yea, though he lead through long distress
To death,
Yet is it in the end done right and well.

7. Chorale (S, A, T, B)

What God doth, that is rightly done;
Must I the cup soon savor,
So bitter after my mad plight,
I shall yet feel no terror,
For at the last
I will find joy,
My bosom's sweetest comfort,
And yield will ev'ry sorrow.

Part Two

8. Sinfonia

9. Recit. (A)

Just one thing grieves
A Christian in the spirit:
When he upon his soul's own want doth think.
Though he trust God's great kindness,
Which all things new doth make,
Yet doth he lack the strength,
For life above in heaven,
His increase and his fruits to offer.

10. Aria (A)

Jesus makes my spirit rich.
If I can receive his Spirit,
I will nothing further long for;
For my life doth grow thereby.
Jesus makes my spirit rich.

11. Recit. (B)

Who bides in Christ alone
And self-denial keeps,
That he in God's affection
His faith may practise,
Hath, when all earthly things have vanished,
Himself and God discovered.

12. Aria (B)

My heart believes and loves.[5]

> For Jesus' flames of sweetness,
> From which mine own have risen,
> Engulf me altogether,
> Because he loveth me.

13. Recit. (T)

O poorness which no wealth can match!
When from my bosom
Shall all the world withdraw
And Jesus all alone shall rule,
Thus is a Christian led to God!
Grant, God, that we this hope not squander!

14. Chorale (S, A, T, B)

What God doth, that is rightly done,
To that will I be cleaving.
Though out upon the cruel road
Need, death and suff'ring drive me;
E'en so shall God,
All fatherhood,

In his dear arms enfold me;
So I yield him all power.

---

1. It is curious that there are several stylistic and thematic features of this
cantata which are characteristic of Salomo Franck. Among them is this
noun series with asyndeton. The central theme, which Dürr calls the
"Gegensatz Armut—Reichtum," is also Franckian.

2. This translation of Augustine's *mihi omnia Jesus* was a life-motto of Salomo
Franck. Cf. also BWV 132/5:

> Christus gab zum neuen Kleide
> Roten Purpur, weiße Seide,
> Diese sind der Christen Staat.

3. Cf. *non est mortale quod opto,* the other life-motto of Salomo Franck, and
Ambrose in *BACH* (1982), pp. 20-22.

4. I.e., in heaven.

5. For the ameliorative metamorphosis with paronomasia, a favorite
technique of Franck, see BWV 21/10 and BWV 146/footnote 2.

BWV 76 **Die Himmel erzählen die Ehre Gottes**

Second Sunday after Trinity (later, Reformation).

Poet unknown, possibly Christian Weiss.

1. *Ps.* 19:1 and 3; 7. Martin Luther, verse 1 of an imitation of *Ps.* 67
(Wackernagel, III, #7); 14. Martin Luther, verse 3 of "Es soll uns
Gott genädig sein," 1524 (Wackernagel, III, #7).

6 June 1723, Leipzig; Part One, again 31 October 1724 or 1725, Leipzig.

BG 18; NBA I/16.

Part One

1. Chorus [Dictum] (S, A, T, B)

The heavens are telling the glory of God, and the firmament publisheth all his handiwork.

There is neither language nor speaking, for one cannot perceive their voices.

2. Recit. (T)

Himself doth God leave not unproven!
Both grace and nature to all mankind proclaim:
This, all this, did, yea, God achieve
So that the heavens waken
And soul and body have their motion.
God hath himself to you inclined
And calls through heralds passing count:
Rise, come ye to my feast of love!

3. Aria (S)

Hear, ye nations, God's voice calling,
Haste ye to his mercy's throne!

      Of all things the root and limit
      Is his one begotten Son:
      That all nature to him gather.

4. Recit. (B)

Who, though, doth hear,
When now the greatest numbers
To other gods give heed?
The ancient idols' wayward lust

Controls the human breast.
The wise are brooding foolishness,
And Belial[1] sits firm in God's own house,
For even Christians, too, from Christ are running.

5. Aria (B)

Get hence, idolatrous band!

> Though all the world be perverted,
> Will I still Christ render honor,
> He is the light of the mind.

6. Recit. (A)

Thou didst us, Lord, from every pathway
To thee call forth
When we in darkness sat amongst the heathen.
And, just as light the air
Makes radiant with new life,
Thou hast illumined and renewed us,
Yea, with thyself both nourished and refreshed us,
And thine own Spirit given,
Who dwells within our spirits ever.
Therefore, let this our pray'r most humbly come to thee:

7. Chorale (S, A, T, B)

May to us God his mercy show
And his salvation give us;
His face on us with radiant beams
Pour light for life eternal,
That we discern his handiwork;
And what on earth he loveth
And Jesus Christ's own healing strength

Be known to all the nations
And they to God converted!

Part Two

8. Sinfonia

9. Recit. (B)

God bless then all the faithful throng,
That they his fame and honor
Through faith and love and holiness
Make manifest and greater.
They are like heaven on earth dwelling
And must, through constant strife
With hate and with great dread,
Within this world be purifiéd.

10. Aria (T)

Hate me then, hate me full well,
O hostile race!

> Christ by faith to be embracing
> Would I all delights relinquish.

11. Recit. (B)

I feel now in my soul
How Christ to me
His love's true sweetness doth reveal
And me with manna feed,
So that amongst us here may be
The bond of loyal brothers
E'er strengthened and renewéd.

12. Aria (A)

Love, ye Christians, in your works!

> Jesus dieth for his brothers,
> Now they're dying for each other,
> For he doth them bind to this.

13. Recit. (T)

Thus ought Christianity
The love of God sing praises
And in themselves reveal it:
Until the end of time,
When heaven's righteous spirits
God and his praise are telling.

14. Chorale (S, A, T, B)

Let thank, O God, and give thee praise
The people in good labors;
The land bears fruit, its ways it mends,
Thy word doth thrive and prosper.
Bless us the Father and the Son,
And bless us God, the Holy Ghost,
Whom all the world should glorify,
To him pay rev'rence unexcelled
And say sincerely: Amen.

[1.]   Hebrew, 'a thing without profit, wickedness.' In the *New Testament* Belial
         = Satan.

BWV 77 **Du sollt Gott, deinen Herren, lieben**

Thirteenth Sunday after Trinity.

Johann Oswald Knauer, *Gott-geheiligtes Singen und Spielen des Friedensteinischen Zions* (Gotha, 1720); Facs: *BJ* (1981), p. 22; Bach uses only the second half of the cantata and makes several substantial changes.

1. *Lk.* 10:27 and the chorale melody "Dies sind die heilgen zehn Gebot"[1]; 6. Chorale without text, for which Neumann T suggests verse 8 of David Denicke, "O Gottes Sohn, Herr Jesus Christ," 1657 (Fischer-Tümpel, II, #438); BG follows Zelter's suggestion: verse 8 of David Denicke, "Wenn einer alle Ding verstünd," 1657 (Fischer-Tümpel, II, #436); the chorale melody is "Ach Gott, vom Himmel sieh darein" (cf. BWV 2/1).

22 August 1723.

BG 18; NBA I/21, 3.

1. Chorus [Dictum] (S, A, T, B) with instr. chorale

Thou shalt thy God and master cherish with all thy bosom, with all thy spirit, with all thy power and with all thine affection, as well thy neighbor as thyself.[2]

2. Recit. (B)

So must it be!
God would our hearts himself possess completely.
We must the Lord with all our spirit
Elect as he requireth,
And never be content

But when he doth our spirits
Through his own Spirit fire,
For we, of all his grace and kindness,
Are only then completely sure.

3. Aria (S)

My God, with all my heart I love thee,
And all my life depends on thee.
But help me thy great law to fathom
And with love to be so kindled
That I thee evermore may love.

4. Recit. (T)

Make me as well, my God, Samaritan in heart
That I may both my neighbor cherish
And be amidst his pain
For his sake also troubled,
That I may never merely pass him by
And him to his distress abandon.
Make me to self-concern contrary,
For then thou shalt one day the life of gladness
That I desire in thy dear mercy grant me.

5. Aria (A)

Ah, there bideth in my loving
Nought but imperfection still!
Though I often may be willing
God's commandments to accomplish,
'Tis beyond my power yet.

6. Chorale (S, A, T, B)

Lord, through my faith come dwell in me,
Make it grow ever stronger,

That it be fruitful more and more
And rich in righteous labors;
That it be active in my love,
In gladness and forbearance skilled,
My neighbor ever serving.[3]
Lord Jesus, thou dost make thyself
A model of true loving:
Now grant that I may follow this
And love of neighbor practise,
That I, in every way I can,
Love, trust, and help to ev'ryone,
As I should wish, may offer.[4]

[1.]   Knauer's cantata used the final verse of this chorale by Martin Luther
       (Wackernagel, III, #22) as the final chorale. For a full account of Bach's
       treatment of Knauer's cantatas see H. K. Krausse, BJ (1981), pp. 7-22.
[2.]   The graceful simplicity of the traditional wording from *Lk*. 10:27 is not
       allowed by the syllabic requirements of the original:

       "Thou shalt love the Lord thy God with all thy heart, and with all thy soul,
       and with all thy strength, and with all thy mind, and thy neighbor as thyself."

[3.]   The Denicke text suggested by Neumann T.
[4.]   The Denicke text suggested by BG.

BWV 78 **Jesu, der du meine Seele**

Fourteenth Sunday after Trinity.

Poet unknown.

1. Johann Rist, verse 1 of the hymn, 1641 (Fischer-Tümpel, II, #189);
2. based freely on verse 2; 3. based on verses 3, 4, and 5; 4. based
freely on verses 6 and 7; 5. based on verses 8-10; 6. based freely on
verse 11; 7. verse 12, the final verse of the hymn.

10 September 1724, Leipzig.

BG 18; NBA I/21.

---

1. Chorus [Verse 1] (S, A, T, B)

Jesus, thou who this my spirit
Hast through thy most bitter death
From the devil's murky cavern
And that grief which plagues the soul
Forcefully brought forth to freedom
And of this hast well assured me
Through thy most endearing word,
Be e'en now, O God, my shield!

2. Aria (S, A)

We hasten with failing but diligent paces,
O Jesus, O master, to thee for thy help.

> Thou seekest the ailing and erring most faithful,
> Ah, hearken, as we
> Our voices are raising to beg thee for succor!
> Let on us thy countenance smile ever gracious!

3. Recit. (T)

Ah! I am a child of error,
Ah! I wander far and wide.[1]
The rash[2] of error which o'er me is coursing,
Leaves me no peace in these my mortal days.
My will attends alone to evil.
My soul, though, saith: ah, who will yet redeem me?
But both flesh and blood to conquer,

And bring goodness to fulfillment,[3]
Surpasseth all my power and strength.[4]
Though I my error would not bury,
Yet I cannot my many failures number.
Therefore, I take my sinful grief and pain
And all my sorrow's burden,
Which would be past my power to carry:
I yield them to thee, Jesus, with a sigh.
Reckon not the sinful deed,
Which, O Lord, hath angered thee![5]

4. Aria (T)

That blood which through my guilt doth stream,
Doth make my heart feel light again
And sets me free.
Should hell's own host call me to battle,
Yet Jesus will stand firm beside me,
That I take heart and victory gain.

5. Recit. (B)

The wounding, nailing, crown and grave,
The beating, which were there the Savior giv'n
For him are now the signs of triumph
And can endow me with new strength and power.
Whene'er an awful judgment seat
A curse upon the damned doth speak,
Thou changest it to blessing.
There is no grief nor any pain to stir me,
For them my Savior knows;
And as thy heart for me with love doth burn,
So I in turn would offer
Whate'er I own before thee.
This my heart, with grief acquainted,

Which thy precious blood hath quickened,
Shed upon the cross by thee,
I give thee, Lord Jesus Christ.[6]

6. Aria (B)

Now thou wilt this my conscience quiet
Which gainst my will for vengeance cries;
Yea, thine own faithfulness will fill it,
Because thy word bids me have hope.
When Christian folk shall trust thee,
No foe in all eternity
From thine embrace shall steal them.

7. Chorale [Verse 12] (S, A, T, B)

Lord, I trust thee, help my weakness,
Let me, yea, not know despair;
Thou, thou canst my strength make firmer
When by sin and death I'm vexed.
Thy great goodness I'll be trusting
'Til that day I see with gladness
Thee, Lord Jesus, battle done,
In that sweet eternity.

[1.] This and the preceding line are verbatim from verse 3.

[2.] *Aussatz* 'rash' is any kind of skin disease, such as leprosy, eczema, or boils.

[3.] This and the preceding line are verbatim from verse 4.

[4.] Cf. *Rom.* 7:18 and 24.

[5.] This and the preceding line are verbatim from verse 5. Cf. Martin Luther, verse 1 of "Mitten wir im Leben" (Wackernagel, III, #12).

[6.] The last four lines of this movement are verbatim from verse 10.

BWV 79 **Gott der Herr ist Sonn und Schild**

Reformation Sunday.

Poet unknown.

1. *Ps.* 84:12; 3. Martin Rinckart, verse 1 of the hymn, 1636 (Fischer-Tümpel, I, #526). 6. Ludwig Helmbold, last verse of "Nun lasst uns Gott, dem Herren," 1575 (Wackernagel, IV, #932).

31 October 1725, Leipzig; revised after 1728.

BG 18; NBA I/31.

1. Chorus [Dictum] (S, A, T, B)

God the Lord is sun and shield. The Lord gives blessing and honor, he will no worthy thing withhold from the righteous.

2. Aria (A)

God is our true sun and shield!

> We thus tell abroad his goodness
> With our spirits ever thankful,
> For he loves us as his own.
> And he shall still further guard us
> Though our foes their arrows sharpen,
> And the hound of hell should howl.

3. Chorale (S, A, T, B)

Now thank ye all our God
With heart and tongue and labor,

Who mighty things doth work
For us in all endeavor,
Who since our mother's womb
And our first toddling steps
Us countless benefit
Until this day hath brought.

4. Recit. (B)

Thank God we know it,
The proper path to blessedness,
For Jesus, thou hast shown it to us through thy Gospel,
Wherefore thy name in every age is honored.
But since so many still
Until this day
An alien yoke
For blindness' sake must carry,
Ah, such compassion give
E'en these, Lord, graciously,
That they the proper path acknowledge
And call thee their one intercessor.

5. Aria (S, B)

God, O God, forsake thy people
Nevermore!
Let thy word o'er us shine brightly;
Even though
Sorely rage our foes against us,
Yet shall these our mouths extol thee.

6. Chorale (S, A, T, B)

Preserve us in the true path,
Grant everlasting freedom
To raise thy name in glory
Through our Christ Jesus. Amen.

BWV 80 **Ein feste Burg ist unser Gott**

Reformation Sunday.

In part, Salomo Franck, *Evangelisches Andachts-Opffer . . . in geistlichen Cantaten* (Weimar, 1715) = BWV 80a; Facs: Neumann T, p. 278.

1. Martin Luther, verse 1 of the hymn (Wackernagel, I, #210); 2. verse 2 with interpolated aria; 5. verse 3 of the hymn; 8. verse 4 of the hymn.

31 October 1724?, Leipzig; Parody: 2, 3, 4, 6, 7 ← BWV 80a/2, 3, 4, 6, 7.

BG 18; NBA I/31.

1. Chorus [Verse 1] (S, A, T, B)

A mighty fortress is our God,[1]
A sure defense and armor;
He helps us free from every need
Which us till now hath stricken.
The ancient wicked foe,
Grim is his intent,
Vast might and deceit
His cruel weapons are,
On earth is not his equal.

2. Aria (B) and Chorale [Verse 2] (S)

(B)
All that which of God is fathered[2]
Is for victory intended.

(S)
With our own might is nothing done,
We face so soon destruction.

He strives for us, the righteous man,
Whom God himself hath chosen.

(B)
Who hath Christ's own bloodstained flag
In baptism sworn allegiance
Wins in spirit ever more.

(S)
Ask thou who he is?
His name: Jesus Christ,
The Lord of Sabaoth,
There is no other god,
The field is his forever.

(B)
All that which of God is fathered
Is for victory intended.

3. Recit. (B)

Consider well, O child of God, this love so mighty,
Which Jesus hath
In his own blood for thee now written;
By which he thee
For war opposing Satan's host, opposing world and error,
Enlisted thee!
Yield not within thy spirit
To Satan and his viciousness!
Let not thy heart,
Which is on earth God's heav'nly kingdom,
Become a wasteland!
Confess thy guilt with grief and pain,
That Christ's own soul to thine be firm united!

4. Aria (S)

Come in my heart's abode,
Lord Jesus, my desiring!

> Drive world and Satan out,
> And let thine image find in me new glory!
> Hence, prideful cloud of sin!

5. Chorale [Verse 3] (S, A, T, B)

And were the world with devils filled,
Intending to devour us,
Our fear e'en yet would be not great,
For we shall win the victory.
The prince of this world,
How grim may he be,
Worketh us no ill,
That is, he is destroyed.
One little word can fell him.

6. Recit. (T)

So stand then under Christ's own bloodstained flag and banner,
O spirit, firm,
And trust that this thy head betrays thee not,
His victory
E'en thee the way to gain thy crown prepareth!
March gladly on to war!
If thou but God's own word
Obey as well as hearken,
Then shall the foe be forced to leave the battle;
Thy Savior is thy shield.

7. Aria (A, T)

How blessed though are those who God hold in their voices,
More blessed still the heart which him in faith doth hold!
Unconquered it abides, can deal the foe destruction,
And shall at last be crowned when it shall death defeat.

8. Chorale [Verse 4] (S, A, T, B)

That word they must allow to stand,
No thanks to all their efforts.
He is with us by his own plan,
With his own gifts and Spirit.
Our body let them take,
Wealth, rank, child and wife,
Let them all be lost,
And still they cannot win;
His realm is ours forever.

---

[1] The first line of this verse follows the translation of Henry Hedge, 1852.

[2] Cf. 1 *Jn.* 5:4.

BWV 81 **Jesus schläft, was soll ich hoffen?**

Fourth Sunday after Epiphany.

Poet unknown; PT (Leipzig, 1724); Facs: Neumann T, p. 425.

4. *Mt.* 8:26; 7. Johann Franck, verse 2 of "Jesu, meine Freude," 1650 (Fischer-Tümpel, IV, #103).

30 January 1724, Leipzig.

BG 20, 1; NBA I/6.

---

1. Aria (A)

Jesus sleeps, what should my hope be?

> See I not
> With an ashen countenance
> Death's abyss e'en now stand open?

2. Recit. (T)

Lord, why dost thou remain so distant?
Why dost thou hide thyself in time of need?[1]
When all doth me a dreadful end portend?
Ah, will thine eye then not by my distress be troubled,
Whose wont is ne'er to rest in slumber?
Thou showed indeed with one star's brightness
Ere now the newly convert wise men
The proper path to travel.
Ah, lead then me with thine own eyes' bright light,
Because this course doth nought but woe forebode.

3. Aria (T)

The foam-crested billows of Belial's[2] waters
Redoubled their rage.
A Christian, true, like waves must rise
When winds of sadness him surround,
And strive doth the waters' storm
The strength of faith to diminish.

4. Arioso [Dictum] (B)

Ye of little faith, wherefore are ye so fearful?

5. Aria (B)

Still, O thou tow'ring sea!
Be silent, storm and wind!

> On thee is set thy limit,
> So that this mine own chosen child
> No mishap e'er may injure.

6. Recit. (A)

I'm blest, my Jesus speaks a word,
My helper is awake;
Now must the waters' storm, misfortune's night
And every woe depart.

7. Chorale (S, A, T, B)

Under thy protection
Am I midst the tempests
Of all foes set free.
Leave then Satan raging,
Let the foe grow bitter,
By me Jesus stands.
Though at once the lightning crack
Though both sin and hell strike terror,
Jesus will protect me.

[1.] Cf. *Ps.* 10:1.

[2.] Belial = Satan.

BWV 82 **Ich habe genung**

The Purification of the Blessed Virgin Mary (The Presentation of Christ in the Temple).

Poet unknown.

2 February 1727, Leipzig; again 2 February 1731, perhaps also in 1730, transposed to E minor for flute and soprano.

BG 20, 1; NBA I/28.

1. Aria (B)

I have now enough,
I have now my Savior, the hope of the faithful
Within my desiring embrace now enfolded;
I have now enough!

> On him have I gazed,
> My faith now hath Jesus impressed on my heart;
> I would now, today yet, with gladness
> Make hence my departure.

2. Recit. (B)

I have now enough.
My hope is this alone,
That Jesus might belong to me and I to him.
In faith I hold to him,
For I, too, see with Simeon
The gladness of that life beyond.
Let us in this man's burden join!

Ah! Would that from the bondage of my body
The Lord might free me.
Ah! My departure, were it here,
With joy I'd say to thee, O world:
I have now enough.

3. Aria (B)

Slumber now, ye eyes so weary,
Fall in soft and calm repose!

> World, I dwell no longer here,
> Since I have no share in thee
> Which my soul could offer comfort.
> Here I must with sorrow reckon,
> But yet, there, there I shall witness
> Sweet repose and quiet rest.

4. Recit. (B)

My God! When comes that blessed "Now!"
When I in peace shall walk forever
Both in the sand of earth's own coolness
And there within thy bosom rest?
My parting is achieved,
O world, good night!

5. Aria (B)

Rejoicing do I greet my death,
Ah, would that it had come already.

> I'll escape then all the woe
> Which doth here in the world confine me.

BWV 83 **Erfreute Zeit im neuen Bunde**

The Purification of the Blessed Virgin Mary (The Presentation of Christ in the Temple).

Poet unknown; PT (Leipzig, 1724); Facs: Neumann T, p. 425.

2. *Lk.* 2:29-31 with interpolated recitative; 5. Martin Luther, verse 4 of "Mit Fried und Freud ich fahr dahin" ("Simeon's Song of Praise" = "Nunc dimittis," *Lk.* 2:29-31), 1524 (Wackernagel, I, #205).

2 February 1724, Leipzig; again 2 February 1727.

BG 20, 1; NBA I/28.

---

1. Aria (A)

O joyous day of the new order,
When our belief doth Jesus hold.

> How gladly is at that last moment
> That resting place, the grave, prepared![1]

2. Aria [Dictum] and Recit. (B)

Lord, now lettest thou this thy servant in peace depart now, according to thy word.
What to us mortals seems so dire
Gives us an entrance unto living.
In truth is death
A limit to this time and woe,

A pledge to us the Lord hath given,
A token that he meaneth well
And then, when once the fight is over,
To peace would lead us.
And since the Savior now
The eyes' true hope, the heart's refreshment is,
What wonder that a heart the fear of death forgets?
It can with joy this utt'rance make:
For mine own eyes now have indeed thy Savior regarded, him whom
thou hast here brought forth before all nations.

3. Aria (T)

Hasten, heart, with joyfulness[2]

> 'Fore the throne of grace to venture![3]
> Thou must now receive salvation
> And compassion's grace discover,
> Yea, when trouble fills thy days,
> Strong in spirit, pray with vigor.

4. Recit. (A)

Yea, if thy faith doth see much darkness yet,
Thy Savior can the doubting shadows scatter;
Yea, when the tomb's dark night
The final hour fills with dread,
Then shalt thou, still secure,
His radiant light in death itself encounter.

5. Chorale (S, A, T, B)

He is salvation's blessed light
To the gentiles,
To illumine those who know thee not,

And give nurture.
He's thy people's Israel,
The praise, fame, joy, and glory.

---

1. This aria alludes to the prophecy made to Simeon that he would not die
before he had seen the Messiah. *Im neuen Bund* is properly "In the New
Covenant," but this translation is not allowed by the meter.
2. Where the text has *voller Freudigkeit* read "with all joyfulness."
3. Cf. *Heb.* 4:16.

BWV 84 **Ich bin vergnügt mit meinem Glücke**

Septuagesima Sunday.

Christian Friedrich Henrici (Picander), *Ernst-Schertzhaffte und Satyrische
Gedichte, Teil III* (Leipzig, 1732); Facs: Neumann T, p. 338; the author
of this adaptation unknown.

5. Ämilie Juliane von Schwarzburg-Rudolstadt, verse 12 of "Wer
weiß, wie nahe mir mein Ende," 1686 (Fischer-Tümpel, V, #631).

Probably 9 February 1727, Leipzig.

BG 20,1; NBA I/7.

---

1. Aria (S)

I am content with my good fortune,
On me by God himself bestowed.

> Should I possess no sumptuous treasures,
> I'll thank him just for simple favors
> Yet merit not the worth of these.

2. Recit. (S)

Indeed God owes me nothing,
And with his every gift
He shows to me his love for me;
I can acquire nought in his service,
For what I do I owe to him.
Indeed, however good my deeds' appearance,
I have, no less, nought worthy brought to pass.
However, man is so impatient,
That he is often sad
If on him God above excessive wealth not shed.
Hath he not us through all these years
Both freely nourished and beclothed?
And will he us one day to bliss
Before his majesty not raise?
It is enough for me
That I not hungry must to bed retire.

3. Aria (S)

I eat now with gladness my humblest of bread
And grant to my neighbor sincerely what he hath.

A conscience e'er quiet, a spirit e'er gay,
A heart ever thankful, exalting with praise,
Increaseth one's blessings and sweetens one's need.

4. Recit. (S)

With sweat upon my countenance
I will meanwhile my bread enjoy,
And when my life's full course,
My life's last evening, once is finished,
Then God will deal me all my pence,

As sure as heaven stands!
Oh, if I may this favor
As my reward of mercy savor
I shall nought further need.

5. Chorale (S, A, T, B)

I live meanwhile in thee contented
And die, all troubles laid aside;
Sufficient is what my God gives me,
Of this I am in faith convinced:
Through thy dear grace and Christ's own blood
Mak'st thou mine own life's finish good.

BWV 85 **Ich bin ein guter Hirt**

Misericordias Domini (Second Sunday after Easter).

Poet unknown.

1. *Jn.* 10:12; 3. Cornelius Becker, verse 1 of an adaptation of *Ps.* 23, 1598; 6. Ernst Christoph Homburg, verse 4 of "Ist Gott mein Schild und Helfersmann," 1658 (Fischer-Tümpel, IV, #342).

15 April 1725, Leipzig.

BG 20,1; NBA I/11.

1. Aria [Dictum] (B)

I am a shepherd true, a shepherd true will give up his life for his sheep.

2. Aria (A)

Jesus is a shepherd true,
For he hath his life already
For his sheep now freely given,
Which shall no man steal from him.
Jesus is a shepherd true.

3. Chorale (S)

The Lord my faithful shepherd is,
Him do I trust entirely,
He leads to pasture me, his lamb,
To green and lovely meadow,
To waters fresh he leads me,
My soul to nourish with his strength
And gracious word of blessing.

4. Recit. (T)

If e'er the hirelings slumber,
There watcheth o'er the flock this faithful shepherd,
So that each member in most welcome rest
Enjoyment have of mead and pasture,
In which life's streams are ever flowing.
For should the wolf of hell strive there to enter,
The sheep for to devour,
Is he by this good shepherd from his wrath restrained.

5. Aria (T)

See what his love hath wrought!

>   My Jesus holds with kindly care
>   His flock securely in his keeping
>   And on the cross's branch hath poured out
>   For them his precious blood.

6. Chorale (S, A, T, B)

With God my refuge, shepherd true,
No danger will me e'er befall:
Yield, all ye who despise me,
All ye who cause me dread and pain,
It will to your own harm yet lead,
For God is my companion.

BWV 86 **Wahrlich, wahrlich ich sage euch**

Rogate (Fifth Sunday after Easter or Rogation Sunday).

Poet unknown.

1. *Jn.* 16:23; 3. Georg Grünwald, verse 16 of "Kommt her zu mir, spricht Gottes Sohn," 1530 (Wackernagel, III, #1461); 6. Paul Speratus, verse 11 of "Es ist das Heil uns kommen her," 1524 (Wackernagel, III, #55).

14 May 1724, Leipzig.

BG 20,1; NBA I/12.

1. Arioso [Dictum] (B)

Truly, truly, I say to you, if any ask for something from the Father, and ask in my name, he will give it to you.

2. Aria (A)

I in truth would roses gather,
Even though the /now/ thorns should prick me.

For of this I'm confident:
My petition and my prayer
God most sure to heart is taking,
For this me his word hath pledged.

3. Chorale (S)

And what the ever gracious God[1]
In his own word hath promised us,
And sworn on his name's honor,
This keeps and gives he verily.
His help lift us to angel-choirs
Through Jesus Christ, Lord. Amen!

4. Recit. (T)

God doth not act as doth the world,
Which much doth pledge and little keep;
For what he pledgeth must be granted,
That we thereby may his true will and pleasure witness.

5. Aria (T)

God's help is sure;
Although that help may sometimes tarry,
It will e'en still not be abolished.
For God's own word declareth this:
God's help is sure!

6. Chorale (S, A, T, B)

Our hope awaits the proper time
For what God's word doth promise;
When that should happen to our joy
Gods sets no certain moment.
He knows well when it best shall be

And treats us not with cruel guile;
For this we ought to trust him.

[1.]   Cf. *Jn.* 14:27.

BWV 87 **Bisher habt ihr nichts gebeten in meinem Namen**

Rogate (Fifth Sunday after Easter or Rogation Sunday).

Christiane Mariane von Ziegler, *Versuch in Gebundener Schreibart, Teil I* (Leipzig, 1728); Facs: Neumann T, p. 360).

1. *Jn.* 16:24; 2. differs substantially from Ziegler's text; 4. not in Ziegler's text; 5. *Jn.* 16:33; 6. some departures from Ziegler's text; 7. Heinrich Müller, verse 9 of "Selig ist die Seele," 1659 (Fischer-Tümpel, V, #539), to the chorale melody of "Jesu, meine Freude."

6 May 1725, Leipzig.

BG 20, 1; NBA I/12.

---

1. Aria [Dictum] (B)

Till now have ye nought been asking in my name's honor.

2. Recit. (A)

O word that heart and soul alarms!
Ye mortals, mark his bidding, what behind it lies!
Ye have both Law and Gospel message with purpose sore offended
And therefore ought ye not delay
To pray with grief and worship.[1]

3. Aria (A)

Forgive, O Father, all our sin
And even still with us forbear,
As we in worship pray now

> And ask thee: Lord to thy command,
> (Ah, speak no more in figures now),
> Help us much more be faithful![2]

4. Recit. (T)

When all our guilt e'en unto to heaven climbs,
Thou seest and knowest, too, my heart, which nought from thee conceals;
Thus, seek to bring me comfort!

5. Arioso [Dictum] (B)

In the world ye have fear; but ye should be glad, I have now the
world overpowered.

6. Aria (T)

I will suffer, I'll keep silent,
Jesus shall his comfort show me.
For he helps me in my pain.
Yield, ye sorrows, sadness, grieving,[3]
For wherefore should I lose courage?
Calm thyself, o trouble heart!

7. Chorale (S, A, T, B)

Must I be so troubled?
For if Jesus loves me,
Is my every grief

Sweeter e'en than honey,
Countless dulcet kisses
Plants he on my heart.
And whenever pain appears,
His dear love doth turn to gladness
Even bitter sadness.[4]

---

1. The recitative responds to the words of Jesus as though to a reproval. In context Jesus continues: "Ask, and ye will receive, that your joy may be full."

2. Cf. *Jn.* 16:25.

3. Ziegler's text: *Weicht, ihr Sorgen! flieht ihr Klagen! Seele, du darffst nicht verzagen....* The change in BWV 87 uses asyndeton somewhat in the style of BWV 12.

4. The ameliorative metamorphosis from *Leiden* to *Freuden* is expressed with the paronomasia of the two nouns. Cf. BWV 146/footnote 2.

BWV 88 Siehe, ich will viel Fischer aussenden

Fifth Sunday after Trinity.

Poet unknown (Christoph Helm?)[1]; PT (Rudolstadt, 1726).

1. *Jer.* 16:16; 3. *Lk.* 5:10; 7. Georg Neumark, "Wer nur den lieben Gott läßt walten," 1657 (Fischer-Tümpel, IV, #365).

21 July 1726, Leipzig.

BG 20, 1; NBA I/17.

First Part

1. Aria [Dictum]

See now, I will send out many fishers, saith the Lord, whose work is to catch them.[2] And then I will many hunters send also, whose work is to catch them on all the mountains and on all the highlands and in all of the hollows.

2. Recit.

How easily, though, could the Highest do without us
And turn away his mercy from us,
When our perverted hearts in evil from him part
And in their stubbornness
To their destruction run.
But what response
From his paternal spirit?
Withhold his loving kindness
From us, and, just as we from him, withdraw,
And then betray us to the foe's deceit and spite?

3. Aria (T)

No, God is all the time intending
On the proper path to keep us,
Sheltered by his glory's grace.
Yea, when we have gone astray
And the proper way abandon,
He will even have us sought for.

Second Part

4. Recit. and Aria [Dictum] (T, B)

(T)
Jesus spake to Simon:

(B)
Fear have thou none; for from now on men wilt thou be catching.

5. Aria (S, A)

If God commands, then must his blessing
In all that we may do
Abundantly endure,
E'en though both fear and care oppose us.
The talent he hath given us
Would he with int'rest have returned him;
If only we ourselves not hide it,
He gladly helps, that it may bear its fruit.[3]

6. Recit. (S)

What can then thee in all thy dealings frighten,
If thee, my heart, God doth his hands extend?
Before his merest nod doth all misfortune yield,
And he, most huge in might, can shelter and protect thee.
When trouble, hardship's toil, grudge, plague and falsehood come,
Intending all thou dost to harass and to hinder,
Let passing discontent thy purpose not diminish;
The work which he assigns will be for none too hard.
With steadfast joy go forth, thou shalt see at the finish
That what before caused pain occurred to bring thee blessing.

7. Chorale (S, A, T, B)

Sing, pray, and walk in God's own pathways,
Perform thine own work ever true,
And trust in heaven's ample blessing,
Then shall he stand by thee anew;
For him who doth his confidence
Rest in God, he forsaketh not.

---

1. Helm is suggested by W. Blankenburg, BJ (1977).
2. I.e., "bring back the people of Israel."
3. Of Bach's librettists Salomo Franck and Picander are the most frequent users of banking metaphors.

BWV 89 **Was soll ich aus dir machen, Ephraim?**

Twenty-second Sunday after Trinity.

Poet unknown.

1. *Hos.* 11:8; 6. Johann Heermann, verse 7 of "Wo soll ich fliehen hin," 1630 (Fischer-Tümpel, I, #322).

24 October 1723, Leipzig.

BG 20, 1; NBA I/26.

---

1. Aria [Dictum] (B)

What shall I make of thee now, Ephraim[1]? Shall I protect thee, Israel?
Shall I not simply an Admah[2] make out of thee now, and like a

Zeboim[3] transform thee? But this my heart is other-minded, and my compassion's love is too ardent.

2. Recit. (A)

Yea, surely oweth God
To speak his word of judgment
And for his name's disdain
Against his foes take vengeance.
Past counting is the sum of thy transgressions,
And even though God should forbear,
Rejecteth yet the ill-will of thy spirit
The offer of his kindness
And to thy neighbor shifts the guilt;
For this his vengeance must be kindled.

3. Aria (A)

An unforgiving word of judgment
Will over thee most surely come.

> For vengeance will with those begin
> Who have not mercy exercised,[4]
> Reducing them like Sodom to mere nothing.

4. Recit. (S)

Well, then, my heart will lay wrath, rage, and strife aside;
It is prepared my neighbor to forgive now.
But yet, what terror doth my sinful life afford me,
That I 'fore God in debt must stand!
But Jesus' blood
Doth my account make good,
If I to him, who is the law's foundation,[5]
In faith take refuge.

5. Aria (S)

O righteous God, ah, judgest thou?
I shall then for my soul's salvation
The drops of Jesus' blood be counting.
Ah! Put the sum to my account!
Yea, since no one can ever tell them,
They cover now my debt and failings.

6. Chorale (S, A, T, B)

My failings are so great,
But all that I would have
Is fully in my favor
By thine own blood accomplished,
So that I shall now conquer
Death, devil, hell, and error.

---

1. *Ephraim* was the most powerful tribe of Israel.
2. For *Admah* 'red lands' cf. *Gen.* 10:19; 14:2 and 8; *Dt.* 29:33. It was overthrown in the destruction of Sodom and Gomorrah.
3. *Zeboim* 'hyena' was one of the five Cities of the Plain. Cf. *Gen.* 10:19 and *Dt.* 29:23.
4. Cf. *Jas.* 2:13.
5. Cf. *Rom.* 10:4.

BWV 90 **Es reißet euch ein schrecklich Ende**

Twenty-fifth Sunday after Trinity.

Poet unknown.

5. Martin Moller, verse 7 of "Nimm von uns, Herr, du treuer Gott," 1584.

14 November 1723, Leipzig.

BG 20, 1; NBA I/27.

---

1. Aria (T)

To ruin you an end of terror,
Ye blasphemous disdainers, brings.

> Your store of sin is full in measure,
> But your completely stubborn minds
> Have him, your judge, now quite forgotten.

2. Recit. (A)

The Highest's kindness is from day to day renewed,[1]
But ingrates always sin against such mercy.
Oh, what a desp'rate act of mischief
Which thee to thy destruction leads.
Ah! Is thy heart not to be touched?
That God's dear kindness may
To true repentance guide thee?[2]
His faithful heart reveals itself
In countless works of grace appearing:
Now doth he build the lofty temples,[3]
Now is the verdant pasture readied[4]
On which the word's true manna falls
To give thee strength.
And yet, O wicked life of mortals,
Good deeds are spent on thee for nothing.

3. Aria (B)

Extinguish with haste will the judge in his vengeance
The lamp of his word as his sentence in full.[5]

Ye must then, O sinners for your own transgressions
The outrage on your sacred places now suffer,
Ye make of the temples a house full of death.[6]

4. Recit. (T)

Yet God's observant eye regards us as his chosen:[7]
And though no man the hostile host may number,
The hero shields us yet in Israel,
His arm restrains the foe's attack
And helps us stand;
In peril is his word's great strength
Just that much more perceived and manifest.

5. Chorale (S, A, T, B)

Lead us with thine own righteous hand
And bless our city and our land,
Give us alway thy holy word,
Protect from Satan's craft and death;
And send a blessed hour of peace,
That we forever be with thee!

---

[1]   Cf. *Lam.* 3:22-23.

[2]   Cf. *Rom.* 2:4.

[3]   Cf. *Zech.* 6:12-15.

[4]   Cf. *Ps.* 23:2.

[5]   Cf. *Rev.* 2:5.

[6]   Cf. *Lk.* 19:46, *Mt.* 21:13 and passim.

[7]   Cf. *Mt.* 24:22.

BWV 91 **Gelobet seist du, Jesu Christ**

Christmas Day.

Poet unknown.

1. Martin Luther, verse 1 of the hymn, 1524 (Wackernagel, III, #9); 2. verse 2 of the hymn with interpolated recitative; 6. verse 7 of the hymn.

25 December 1724, Leipzig.

BG 22; NBA I/2.

---

1. Chorus [Verse 1] (S, A, T, B)

All glory to thee, Jesus Christ,
For thou man today wast born,
Born of a virgin, that is sure,
Thus joyful is the angel host.
Kyrie eleis!

2. Recit. and Chorale [Verse 2] (S)

The light of highest majesty,
The image of God's very being,
Hath, when the time was full,
Himself a dwelling found and chosen.
        Th'eternal Father's only child
Th'eternal light of light begotten,
        Who now in the crib is found.
Ye mortals, now behold
What here the power of love hath done!
        Within our wretched flesh and blood,

And was this flesh then not accursed, condemned, and fallen?
　　　Doth veil itself eternal good.
Yet is it, yea, for grace and blessing chosen.

3. Aria (T)

God, for whom earth's orb is too small,
Whom neither world nor heaven limits,
Would in the narrow crib now lie.

　　　Revealed to us this lasting light,
　　　Thus henceforth will us God not hate,
　　　For of this light we are the children.

4. Recit. (B)

O Christian world,
Now rise and get thyself prepared
To thee thy maker now to welcome.
The mighty Son of God
Comes as a guest to thee descended.
Ah, let thy heart by this his love be smitten;
He comes to thee, that he before his throne
Through this deep vale of tears may lead thee.

5. Aria (S, A)

The weakness which God hath assumed
On us eternal health bestowed,
The richest store of heaven's treasures.

　　　His mortal nature maketh you
　　　The angels' glory now to share,
　　　You to the angels' choir appointeth.

6. Chorale [Verse 7] (S, A, T, B)

All this he hath for us achieved,
His great love to manifest;
Rejoice then all Christianity
And thank him for this evermore.
Kyrie eleis!

BWV 92 Ich hab in Gottes Herz und Sinn

Septuagesima Sunday.

Poet unknown.

1. Paul Gerhardt, verse 1 of the hymn, 1647 (Fischer-Tümpel, III, #393); 2. verse 2 of the hymn with interpolated recitative; 3. loosely related to verse 4; 4. verse 5;

5. loosely related to verses 6 and 8; 6. loosely related to verse 9; 7. verse 10 with interpolated recitative; 8. loosely related to verse 11; 9. verse 12 of the hymn.

28 January 1725, Leipzig.

BG 22; NBA I/7.

1. Chorus [Verse 1] (S, A, T, B)

I have to God's own heart and mind
My heart and mind surrendered;
What seemeth ill is for my gain,
E'en death itself, my living.
I am a son of him who laid

The throne of heaven open;
Though he strike me and cross impose,
His heart keeps yet its favor.

2. Chorale [Verse 2] and Recit. (B)

It cannot fail me anytime!
Needs be ere that,
As e'en our truthful witness saith,
With cracking and with awesome thunder
The mountains and the hills have fallen:[1]
My Savior, though, betrayeth not,
My Father surely loves me.
Through Jesus' crimson blood am I into his hand committed;
He guards me well!
Though he should cast me in the sea,
The Lord doth live on mighty waters, too,
He did to me himself my life allot,
The waters therefore shall not drown me.
Although the waves already hold me
And in their wrath rush with me to the depths,
Yet would he only test me,
If I of Jonah shall be mindful,
Or if I shall like Peter to him turn my spirit.
He would me strong in faith establish,
He would for my soul's sake be watchful
And this my heart,
Which ever faints and yields, in his dear care,
Which in steadfastness nought can match,
Accustom to stand firmly.
My foot shall firm
Until the end of all the days
Be here upon this rock established.
If I stand sure,
And gird myself in faith as firm as craggy mountains, his hand will
know,

Which he to me from heaven extends,
The proper time
For me to be exalted.

3. Aria (T)

Mark, mark! it snaps, it breaks, it falls,
What God's own mighty arm holds not.
Mark, though, the firm and unremitting glory
Of all our hero with his might surroundeth.
Leave Satan furious, raving, raging,
Our mighty God will us unconquered ever render.

4. Chorale [Verse 5] (A)

And too are wisdom and judgment
With him beyond all measure;
Time, place, and hour him are known
For action and inaction.
He knows when joy, he knows when grief,
Would us his children profit,
And what he doth is always good,
However sad it seemeth.

5. Recit. (T)

We therefore would no longer falter
And us with flesh and blood,
While we're in God's own care,
So sorely as till now be bothered.
I think on this,
How Jesus had no fear of all his myriad sorrows;
He looked to them
As but a source of endless pleasure.
My Christian, thee
Shall thine own fear and grief, thy bitter cross and pain

For Jesus' sake thy health and sweetness be.
So trust the grace of God
And mark henceforth what thou must do:
Forbear! Forbear!

6. Aria (B)

The raging /storming/ of the winds so cruel
Lets us the richest harvest gather.[2]

> The cross's turbulence doth yield the Christians fruit,
> So let us, ev'ryone, our living
> To our wise ruler fully offer.
> Kiss ye his own Son's hand, revere his faithful care.[3]

7. Chorale [Verse 10] (S, A, T, B) and Recit. (B, T, A, S)

(S, A, T, B)
Ah now, my God, thus do I fall
Assured into thy bosom.

(B)
Thus speaks the soul which trusts in God
When he the Savior's brotherhood
And God's good faith in faith doth praise.
Take me and work thy will with me
Until my life is finished.

(T)
I know for sure
That I unfailing blest shall be
If my distress, and this my grief and woe,
By thee will thus an end be granted:
For thou dost know that to my soul
Thereby its help ariseth,

(A)
That in my earthly lifetime,
To Satan's discontent,
Thy heav'nly realm in me be manifest
And thine own honor more and more
Be of itself exalted.

(S)
Thus may my heart as thou commandest
Find, O my Jesus, blessed stillness,
And I may to these muted lyres
The Prince of peace a new refrain now offer.[4]

8. Aria (S)

To my shepherd I'll be true.
Though he fill my cross's chalice,
I'll rest fully in his pleasure,
He stands in my sorrow near.
One day, surely, done my weeping,
Jesus' sun again will brighten.
To my shepherd I'll be true.
Live in Jesus, who will rule me;
Heart, be glad, though thou must perish,
Jesus hath enough achieved.
Amen: Father, take me now!

9. Chorale [Verse 12] (S, A, T, B)

If I then, too, the way of death
And its dark journey travel,
Lead on! I'll walk the road and path
Which thine own eyes have shown me.
Thou art my shepherd, who all things

Will bring to such conclusion,
That I one day within thy courts
Thee ever more may honor.

---

1. Cf. *Is.* 54:10.

2. For the ameliorative metamorphosis of showers to flowers, cf. BWV 12/6.

3. *Treue Zucht* has a double sense here: 'stock bred true to kind' (sustaining the plant-imagery of the aria) and 'honest discipline' (sustaining the theme of fruitful hardship).

4. Neumann T notes the pizzicato accompaniment of the strings appropriate to this text.

BWV 93 **Wer nur den lieben Gott läßt walten**

Fifth Sunday after Trinity.

Poet unknown.

1. Georg Neumark, verse 1 of the hymn, 1657 (Fischer-Tümpel, IV, #365); 2. verse 2 with interpolated recitative; 3. based freely on verse 3; 4. verse 4; 5. verse 5 with interpolated recitative; 6. based freely on verse 6; 7. verse 7 of the hymn.

9 July 1724, Leipzig.

BG 22; NBA I/17.

---

1. Chorus [Verse 1] (S, A, T, B)

The man who leaves to God all power
And hopeth in him all his days,
He will most wondrously protect him
Through every cross and sad distress.

Who doth in God Almighty trust
Builds not upon the sand his house.

2. Chorale [Verse 2] and Recit. (B)

What help to us are grievous worries?
They just oppress the heart
With heavy woe, with untold fear and pain.
What help to us our "woe and ah!"?
It just brings bitter, sad distress.
What help to us that every morning
With sighing from our sleep to rise
And with our tearstained countenance at night to go to bed?
We make ourselves our cross and grief
Through anxious sadness only greater.
So fares a Christian better;
He bears his cross with Christ-like confidence and calm.

3. Aria (T)

If we be but a little quiet,[1]
Whene'er the cross's hour draws nigh,
For this our God's dear sense of mercy[2]
Forsakes us ne'er in word or deed.
God, who his own elected knows,
God, who himself our "Father" names,
Shall one day every trouble banish
And to his children send salvation.

4. Aria [Verse 4] (S, A) with instr. chorale

He knows the proper time for gladness,
He knows well when it profit brings;
If he hath only faithful found us
And marketh no hypocrisy,
Then God comes, e'en before we know,
And leaves to us much good result.

5. Chorale [Verse 5] and Recit. (T)

Think not within thy trial by fire,
When fire and thunder crack
And thee a sultry tempest anxious makes,
That thou by God forsaken art.
God bides e'en in the greatest stress,
Yea, even unto death
With his dear mercy midst his people.
Thou may'st not think then
That this man is in God's lap sitting
Who daily, like the wealthy man,
In joy and rapture life can lead.
Whoe'er on constant fortune feeds,
Midst nought but days of pleasure,
Must oft at last,
When once he hath of idle lust his fill,
"The pot is poisoned!"[3] utter.
Pursuing time transformeth much!
Did Peter once the whole night long
With empty labors pass the time
And take in nothing?
At Jesus' word he can e'en yet a catch discover.[4]
Midst poverty then trust, midst cross and pain,
Trust in thy Jesus' kindness
With faithful heart and spirit.
When rains have gone, he sunshine brings,[5]
Appointing every man his end.

6. Aria (S)

I will to the Lord now look
And e'er in my God put trust.
He worketh truly wonders rare.[6]
He can wealthy, poor and bare,
And the poor, both rich and great,
According to his pleasure make.

7. Chorale [Verse 7] (S, A, T, B)

Sing, pray, and walk in God's own pathways,
Perform thine own work ever true
And trust in heaven's ample blessing,
Then shall he stand by thee anew;
For who doth all his confidence
Rest in God, he forsaketh not.

[1.]   This line is verbatim from verse 3.
[2.]   This line is verbatim from verse 3.
[3.]   Cf. 2 *Kg*. 4:40.
[4.]   Cf. *Lk*. 5:5-7.
[5.]   Cf. BWV 12/6 and BWV 92/6 and 8.
[6.]   This line is verbatim from verse 6.

BWV 94 **Was frag ich nach der Welt**

Ninth Sunday after Trinity.

Poet unknown.

1. Georg Michael Pfefferkorn, verse 1 of the hymn, 1664 (Fischer-Tümpel, IV, #218); 2. based loosely on verse 2; 3. verse 3 with interpolated recitative; 4. based loosely on verse 4; 5. verse 5 with interpolated recitative; 6 and 7. based loosely on verse 6; 8. verses 7 and 8 of the hymn.

6 August 1724, Leipzig; again around 1732 and 1735.

BG 22; NBA I/19.

---

1. Chorus [Verse 1] (S, A, T, B)

What need I of this world
And all its idle treasures,
If I may but in thee,
My Jesus, find my pleasure?
Thee have I, only thee,
Envisioned as my joy;
Thou, thou art my delight;
What need I of this world?

2. Aria (B)

The world is like a haze and shadow,
Which soon doth vanish and subside,
For it but briefly doth endure.
When, though, the world shall fall and break,
Shall Jesus bide my confidence,
To whom my very soul shall cleave.
Therefore: what care I for the world?

3. Chorale [Verse 3] and Recit. (T)

The world seeks praise and fame
Midst high and lofty people.
The proud man buildeth palaces most splendid,
He seeks the highest offices,
He dresses in the finest,
In purple, gold, in silver, velvet, silk.
His name before all people
In every region must be echoed.
His tower of pride
Must through the air unto the clouds be pressing,
His aim is on but lofty matters
And thinks not once on this:
How soon indeed these vanish.

Oft bloweth sear and vapid air
The prideful flesh asudden to the grave,
And therewith vanisheth all pomp
Of which this wretched earthly worm
Here in the world so much display hath made.
Ah! All such idle trash
Is far from me, from this my breast, now banned.
However, what my heart
Before all else exalts,
Which Christians true respect and proper honor giveth,
And which my soul,
As it from vanity breaks free,
Instead of pride and splendor loveth,
Is Jesus, him alone,
And this one shall it ever be.
Although I by the world
For this a fool be deemed,
What need I of this world?

4. Aria (A)

Deluded world, deluded world!
E'en thy riches, wealth, and gold
Are a snare and false pretense.
Thou may'st thine idle mammon treasure,
I will instead my Jesus favor;
Jesus, Jesus shall alone
Of my soul the treasure be.
Deluded world, deluded world!

5. Chorale [Verse 5] and Recit. (B)

The world is sore distressed.
What must, indeed, its trouble be?
O folly! This doth cause it pain:
Lest it should be dishonored.

World, shame on thee!
For God indeed so much did love thee,
That he his one begotten child
For all thy sin
To worst disgrace for thy fame's sake subjecteth,
And yet thou wouldst for Jesus' sake not suffer?
The sadness of the world is never greater,
Than when one doth with guile
For all its honors try it.
Indeed, much better
I suffer Christ's disgrace
As long it doth him please.
It is, indeed, but sorrow for a time,
I know full well that once eternity,
For this, with praise and fame will crown me;
Though me the world
Despiseth and derideth,
Though it as well put me to scorn,
If me my Jesus praise,
What need I of this world?

6. Aria (T)

The world can its delight and joy,
The tricks of scornful vanity,
Not high enough pay honor.

> It gnaws, mere yellow rot to gather,
> Just like a mole within its burrow
> And leaves for its sake heaven untended.

7. Aria (S)

Let him tend to the world so blind
Who nought for his own soul doth care,
With earth I am disgusted.

I will alone my Jesus love now
And works of faith and penance practise,
That I may be both rich and blessed.

8. Chorale [Verses 7 and 8] (S, A, T, B)

What need I of this world?
Asudden must it vanish,
Its pose cannot at all
Put pallid death in bondage.
Possessions must give way,
And every pleasure fade;
If Jesus bide with me,
What need I of this world?

What need I of this world?
My Jesus is my being,
My store, my property,
To whom I am devoted,
My realm of heav'nly bliss,
And all else I hold dear.
Thus do I say once more:
What need I of this world!

BWV 95 **Christus, der ist mein Leben**

Sixteenth Sunday after Trinity.

Poet unknown.

1a. Anonymous, verse 1 of the hymn, ca. 1609; 1c. Martin Luther, verse 1 of "Mit Fried und Freud ich fahr dahin," an adaptation of "Simeon's Song of Praise" = "Nunc dimittis," 1524 (Wackernagel, I, #205 and III,

#25); 3. Valerius Herberger, verse 1 of "Valet will ich dir geben," 1613 (Fischer-Tümpel, I, #125); 7. Nikolaus Herman, verse 4 of "Wenn mein Stündlein vorhanden ist," 1560 (Wackernagel, I, #499).

12 September 1723, Leipzig.

BG 22; NBA I/23.

1a. Chorale (S, A, T, B)

Lord Christ, he is my being,
My death is my reward;
To it I will surrender,
With joy will I depart.

1b. Recit. (T)

With gladness,
Yea, with joyful heart,
I'll take hence my departure.
E'en if today were said: "Thou must!",
Yet am I willing and prepared
My wretched flesh, my fully wasted members,
The dress of mortal rank,
To earth returning,
Into her lap to offer.
My dying song e'en now is made;
Ah, I today would sing it!

1c. Chorale (S, A, T, B)

With peace and joy do I depart,
As God doth will it;
Consoled am I in heart and mind,
Calm and quiet,

As God me his promise gave:
My death is to sleep altered.

2. Recit. (S)

Now, treacherous world!
Now I'll have nothing more with thee to do;
My house is now prepared,
I'll much more softly rest
There than I could with thee,
Beside thy Babel's waters,
Where passion's salt I'm forced to swallow,
And when within thy paradise
Mere Sodom's apples I could gather.[1]
No, no! I can now with collected courage say it:

3. Chorale (S)

"Valet"[2] would I now give thee,
Thou wicked, treacherous world;
Thy sinful, evil, living
Doth fully me displease.
In heaven is my fair dwelling,
Whereto my hopes arise.
There will God ever favor
Those who have served him here.

4. Recit. (T)

Ah, if it could for me now quickly come to pass
That I my death,
The end of all my woe,
Within my body could behold,
I would, indeed, for my own body's dwelling[3] choose it
And every moment by it number.

5. Aria (T)

Ah, strike thou, then, soon, happy hour,
That last and final tolling stroke![4]

> Come, come, to thee I reach my hands out,
> Come, set to all my woe an ending,
> Thou long desire'd day of death.

6. Recit. (B)

For I know this
And hold it ever true,
That from my very grave I
Have a most certain entrance to my heav'nly Father.
My death is but a sleep
Through which my flesh, which here by sorrow was diminished,
To rest might journey.
If here the shepherd seeks his errant sheep,
How could then Jesus once again not find me,
For he's my head, and I his form possess!
So I can now with happy spirit
My blessed resurrection ground upon my Savior.

7. Chorale (S, A, T, B)

Since thou from death arisen art,
I'll in the grave not tarry;
Thy final word my rising is,
Death's fear canst thou now banish.
For where thou art, there will I come,
That I e'er with thee live and be;
So I depart with pleasure.

[1.] Josephus, *Bellum Judaicum,* IV. 8. 4, writes that the apples of Sodom, though appearing to be edible, turned to smoke and ashes when picked. Cf. Dürr, p. 363, and BWV 179/3.

2.   *Valet,* 'he fares well' in Latin, in German is used as a noun meaning 'a farewell.'

3.   *Leibgedinge* = *Leiberente* 'rent for a lifetime.'

4.   Bach expresses the knell of death as the ticking of a clock rather than a tolling bell, here and elsewhere. Cf. BWV 74/4.

BWV 96 **Herr Christ, der einge Gottessohn**

Eighteenth Sunday after Trinity.

Poet unknown.

1. Elisabeth Kreuziger, verse 1 of the hymn, 1524 (Wackernagel, I, #236); 2. based freely on verse 2; 3. based freely on verse 3; 4 and 5. based freely on verse 4; 6. verse 5 of the hymn.

8 October 1724, Leipzig; again 1744/1748 (Dürr), 1734 and 1745 (Neumann Hb).

BG 22; NBA I/24.

---

1. Chorus [Verse 1] (S, A, T, B)

Lord Christ, the only Son of God,
Father's, eternally,
From his own heart /bosom/ descended,
Just as the scripture saith;
He is the star of morning,
Whose light he spreads so broadly,
Beyond all stars, more bright.

2. Recit. (A)

O love of wondrous power,
When God for his own creatures careth,
When now his majesty
Until the end of time[1]
To earth is bending;
O inconceivable, mysterious might!
A chosen body now doth bear
The mighty Son of God,
Whom David's heart
Already as his Lord did honor,
While this, a woman favored well,
In chastity unsullied bideth.
O gen'rous saving power! which is on us o'erflowing,
For he hath opened heaven, and hell he hath shut tightly.

3. Aria (T)

Ah, draw close my spirit with bonds of affection,

> O Jesus, show thyself strongly in it!
> Illumine it that it in faith thee acknowledge,
> Grant that it with holiest passion grow ardent,
> Ah, make it in faith ever thirst to find thee!

4. Recit. (S)

Ah, lead thou me, O God, to righteous pathways,
Me, for I am in darkness now
And, seeking what my flesh desires,
So oft in error wander;
But yet, if thou but walk beside me,
If thou wouldst only with thine eyes now guide me,
Then surely will my course
Secure to heaven lead.

5. Aria (B)

To the right side, to the left side,
Wend their way my wayward steps.
Walk with me, my Savior, still,
Let me not in peril falter,
Make me, yea, of thy wise guidance
Until heaven's portals conscious!

6. Chorale [Verse 5] (S, A, T, B)

O'erwhelm us with thy kindness,
Arouse us with thy grace;
The ancient man now weaken,
So that the new may live
And, here on earth now dwelling,
His mind and every yearning
And thought may raise to thee.

[1.] Verbatim from verse 2 of the hymn.

BWV 97 **In allen meinen Taten**

Unspecified occasion.

Based on the nine verses of the hymn by Paul Fleming, 1642 (Fischer-Tümpel, I, #439).

1734, Leipzig.

BG 22; NBA I/34.

---

1. Chorus [Verse 1] (S, A, T, B)

In all my undertakings
I let the Master counsel,
Who all things can and owns;
He must in every matter,
If it's to be accomplished,
Himself advise and act.

2. Aria [Verse 2] (B)

Nought is too late or early
Despite my toil and labor,
My worry is in vain.
He may with all my dealings
Dispose as he is willing,
I give it to his care.

3. Recit. [Verse 3] (T)

For I can nought accomplish
But what he hath provided,
And what shall make me blest:
I take it as he gives it;
What he of me desireth
Is also what I choose.

4. Aria [Verse 4] (T)

I trust in his dear mercy,
Which me from every danger,
From every evil guards.
If I love by his commandments,
There will be nought to harm me,
Nought lacking that I need.

5. Recit. [Verse 5] (A)

May he seek from my error
In mercy to release me,
Extinguish all my wrongs!
He will for my transgressions
Not strict be in his judgment
And yet with me forbear.

6. Aria [Verse 6] (A)

Though I be late retiring,
Arise in early morning,
Rest or continue on,
In weakness and in bondage,
With every blow about me,
Yet comforts me his word.

7. Aria [Verse 7] (S, B)

For if he hath decided,
Then will I uncomplaining
Unto my fate press on!
No mishap midst the many
Will seem to me too cruel,
I will them overcome.

8. Aria [Verse 8] (S)

To him I am committed
For dying and for living
Whene'er he me doth bid.
If this day or tomorrow
I leave to his attention;
He knows the proper time.

9. Chorale [Verse 9] (S, A, T, B)

To thee be true, O spirit,
And trust in him alone now
Who hath created thee;
Let happen what may happen,
Thy Father who's in heaven
In all things counsels well.

BWV 98 **Was Gott tut, das ist wohlgetan I**

Twenty-first Sunday after Trinity.

Poet unknown.

1. Samuel Rodigast, verse 1 of the hymn, 1674 (Fischer-Tümpel, IV, #467).

10 November 1726, Leipzig.

BG 22; NBA I/25.

1. Chorale (S, A, T, B)

What God doth, that is rightly done,
His will is just forever;
Whatever course he sets my life,
I will trust him with calmness.
He is my God,
Who in distress
Knows well how to support me;
So I yield him all power.

2. Recit. (T)

Ah, God! When shalt thou me at last
From my torment and pain,
And from my fear deliver?
How long then must I day and night
For help be crying?
And there's no savior here!
The Lord is to them all so near
Who in his might
And in his grace are trusting.
So I will all my confidence
On God alone establish,
For he betrays his people not.

3. Aria (S)

Cease, ye eyes now, all your weeping!
For I bear
And endure my heavy yoke.
God, the Father, liveth still,
Of his people
None betraying.
Cease, ye eyes now, all your weeping!

4. Recit. (A)

God hath a heart which with forgiveness overflows;
And when our voices in his hearing moan
And him the cross's pain
In faith and confidence recall,
So doth his heart then break,
That he must for our sake then pity take.
He keeps his word;
He saith: Knock ye here,
And opened will it be![1]

So let us from this day,
When in supreme distress we hover,
Our hearts to God alone be lifting!

5. Aria (B)

I my Jesus shall not leave
Till me first his countenance
Shall give favor or its blessing.

>He alone
>Shall my shield in all things be
>Which with danger may confront me.

[1.] Cf. *Mt.* 7:7.

BWV 99 **Was Gott tut, das ist wohlgetan II**

Fifteenth Sunday after Trinity.

Poet unknown.

1. Samuel Rodigast, verse 1 of the hymn, 1674 (Fischer-Tümpel, IV, #467); 2-5. based freely on verses 2-5; 6. verse 6 of the hymn.

17 September 1724, Leipzig.

BG 22; NBA I/22.

---

1. Chorus [Verse 1] (S, A, T, B)

What God doth, that is rightly done,
His will is just forever;

Whatever course he sets my life,
I will trust him with calmness.
He is my God,
Who in distress
Knows well how to support me.
So I yield him all power.

2. Recit. (B)

His word of truth doth stand secure
And will not e'er betray me,[1]
For it the faithful lets not fall or to their ruin go.
Yea, since it on the path to life doth lead me,
My heart doth calm itself and findeth satisfaction
In God's paternal faith and care
And shall forbear
When I'm by mishap stricken.
God can with his own hands almighty
Change my misfortune.

3. Aria (T)

Disturb thyself do not, discouraged spirit,
If thee the cross's cup so bitter tastes!
God is thy wise physician, his wonders great,
Who can no fatal poison pour for thee,
E'en though its sweetness may quite hidden lie.[2]

4. Recit. (A)

Now, the eternally contracted bond
Bides e'er my faith's firm base.
It saith with confidence
In death and living:
God is my light,
To him I am committed.[3]

And though each day should offer
Its own peculiar torment,[4]
Yet for the pain which is endured,
When we have done with weeping,
At last shall come salvation's day,
When God's true loyal will appeareth.

5. Aria (S, A)

When the cross's bitter sorrows
With the flesh's weakness struggle,
It is ne'erless rightly done.
Who the cross through folly base
For himself too heavy reckons
Will e'en later have no pleasure.

6. Chorale [Verse 6] (S, A, T, B)

What God doth, that is rightly done,
To that will I be cleaving.
Though out upon the cruel road
Need, death and suff'ring drive me,
E'en so will God,
All fatherhood,
Within his arms enfold me;
So I yield him all power.

[1.] Except for *und*, verbatim from verse 2 of the hymn.

[2.] The doctor who disguises the healing, but bitter medicine with honey is for Lucretius (ca. 99-44 B.C.) analogous to the poet who sweetens the difficult doctrine of Epicurus with the charm of the muses (*De Rerum Natura* 1. 933-950).

[3.] Verbatim from verse 4 of the hymn.

[4.] Cf. *Mt.* 6:34.

BWV 100 **Was Gott tut, das ist wohlgetan III**

Unspecified occasion (or For any occasion, Per ogni tempo?, cf. Dürr, p. 639).

The six verses of the hymn by Samuel Rodigast, 1674 (Fischer-Tümpel, IV, #467).

After 1732, Leipzig; again after 1735 (Neumann Hb).

BG 22; NBA I/34.

---

1. Chorus [Verse 1] (S, A, T, B)

What God doth, that is rightly done,
His will is just forever;
Whatever course he sets my life,
I will trust him with calmness.
He is my God,
Who in distress
Knows well how to support me;
So I yield him all power.

2. Aria [Verse 2] (A, T)

What God doth, that is rightly done,
He will not e'er betray me;
He leads me on the proper path,
So I will find contentment
Within his care
And then forbear,
He shall turn my misfortune,
In his hands rests the outcome.

3. Aria [Verse 3] (S)

What God doth, that is rightly done,
He will me well consider;
He doth, my healer, wonders work
And will no poison give me
As healing balm.
God keepeth faith,
I'll make him my foundation
And to his mercy trust me.

4. Aria [Verse 4] (B)

What God doth, that is rightly done,
He is my light, my being,
Who me no evil can allow;
I'll be to him committed
In joy and woe!
The time is nigh
When manifest appeareth
How faithful is his favor.

5. Aria [Verse 5] (A)

What God doth, that is rightly done;
Though I the cup must savor
Soon, bitter to my maddened sense,
I will yet be not frightened,
For at the last
I will find joy
And sweet hope in my bosom;
And yield shall all my sorrow.

6. Chorale [Verse 6] (S, A, T, B)

What God doth, that is rightly done,
To that will I be cleaving.

Though out upon the cruel road
Need, death, and suff'ring drive me,
E'en so God will,
All fatherhood,
Within his arms enfold me;
So I yield him all power.

BWV 101 **Nimm von uns, Herr, du treuer Gott**

Tenth Sunday after Trinity.

Poet unknown.

1. Martin Moller, verse 1 of the hymn (after the Latin "Aufer immensam"), Wittenberg, 1541; 2. based on verse 2; 3. verse 3 with interpolated recitative; 4. based on verse 4; 5. verse 5 with interpolated recitative; 6. based on verse 6; 7. verse 7 of the hymn.

13 August 1724, Leipzig.

BG 23; NBA I/19.

1. Chorus [Verse 1] (S, A, T, B)

Take from us, Lord, thou faithful God,
The punishment and great distress
Which we for sins beyond all count
Have merited through all our days.
Protect from war and times of dearth,
Contagion,[1] fire and grievous pain.

2. Aria (T)

Do not deal by thine own justice
With us wicked thralls of error,
Let the hostile sword now rest!
Master, hearken to our crying,
That we not through sinful deeds,
Like Jerusalem, be ruined.

3. Chorale [Verse 3] and Recit. (S)

Ah, Lord God, through thy faithfulness
Will this our land in peace and quiet bide.
When us misfortune's storms approach,
When so we call,
O gracious God, to thee
In such distress:
Appear with saving strength to us!
Thou canst the foe and his destruction
Through thy great might and help keep from us.
Reveal in us thy great store of grace,
Us punish not amidst our deeds,
If e'er our feet would stagger,
And in our weakness we should stumble.
Attend us with thy favor dear,
And grant that we
Strive only after goodness,
And in the life hereafter
Thy wrath and rage far from us stay.

4. Aria (B) with instr. chorale

Wherefore wouldst thou so wrathful be?[2]
The flames of thy great zeal and ardor
Already o'er our heads are falling.

Ah, moderate thy sentence now
And from a father's loving grace
With this our feeble flesh forbear!

5. Chorale [Verse 5] and Recit. (T)

Our sin hath us corrupted much.
E'en must the godliest admit it
And with their tearful eyes bewail it:
The devil plagues us still much more.
Yea, this most evil soul,
Who was e'en from the start a murderer,[3]
Seeks to deprive us of salvation
And like a lion to devour us.[4]
The world, our very flesh and blood,
Doth all the time lead us astray.
Here we encounter on this narrow path
So many obstacles against the good.
Such sorrow know'st thou, Lord, alone:
Help, helper, help us weak ones,
For thou canst make us stronger!
Ah, let us thee commended be!

6. Aria (S, A)

Consider Jesus' bitter death!
Take, Father, these thy Son's great sorrows
And this his wounds' great pain to heart now,
They are in truth for all the world
The payment and the ransom price;[5]
And show me, too, through all my days,
Forgiving God, forgiving ways!
I sigh alway in my distress:
Consider Jesus' bitter death!

7. Chorale [Verse 7] (S, A, T, B)

Lead us with thine own righteous hand
And bless our city and our land,
Give us alway thy holy word,
Protect from Satan's craft and death;
And send a blessed hour of peace,
That we forever be with thee.

[1.] This hymn was written during a period of plague.

[2.] This line is verbatim from verse 4.

[3.] Cf. *Jn.* 8:44.

[4.] Cf. 1 *Pet.* 5:8.

[5.] This and the preceding line are verbatim from verse 6 of the hymn.

BWV 102 **Herr, deine Augen sehen nach dem Glauben!**

Tenth Sunday after Trinity.

Poet unknown (Christoph Helm?)[1]; PT (Rudolstadt, 1726).

1. *Jer.* 5:3; 4. *Rom.* 2:4-5; 7. Johann Heermann, verses 6 and 7 of "So wahr ich lebe, spricht dein Gott," 1630 (Fischer-Tümpel, I, #318).

25 August 1726, Leipzig; Parody:1 → Mass in G Minor, BWV 235/1; 3 and 5 → Mass in F Major, BWV 233/4 and 5.

BG 23; NBA I/19.

Part One

1. Chorus [Dictum] (S, A, T, B)

Lord, thine eyes look after true believing! Thou smitest them, but
they feel not the blow; thou vexest them, but they reform themselves
not. Their countenance is more obstinant than a rock and they would
not be converted.

2. Recit. (B)

Where is the image true which God hath stamped within us,
If our perverted will hath set itself against it?
Where is the power of his word,
If all amelioration doth the heart desert?
The Highest doth in truth with mildness seek to tame us,
So that the errant soul wish yet to be obedient;
But if it doth maintain its stubborn will,
He yieldeth it unto the heart's conceit.

3. Aria (A)

Woe that spirit which its mischief
No more knows,
And, inviting its own judgment,
Pell-mell runs,
Yea, from its God's very mercy stands apart.

4. Arioso [Dictum] (B)

Despisest thou the richness of his mercy, his patience and forbearance?
Knowest thou not that God's kindness thee to repentance calleth?
But thou dost, because of thy stubbornness and impenitent spirit,
store for thyself great wrath on the day of wrath and the revelation
of the righteous judgment of God.

Part Two

5. Aria (T)

Be frightened yet,
Thou all too trusting spirit!
Think what it shall once cost thee,
This sinful yoke.
For God's forbearance walketh with a foot of lead,
So that his wrath at last o'er thee much graver fall.

6. Recit. (A)

In waiting danger lurks;
Wouldst thou this chance then forfeit?
The God who e'er was merciful
With ease can lead thee to his seat of judgment.
Where is thy penitence? A twinkle of an eye
Eternity and time, the flesh and soul divideth;
O blinded sense, ah, turn thyself around,
Lest thee this very hour discover unprepared.

7. Chorale (S, A, T, B)

Alive today, today repent,
Ere morning comes, the times can change;
Today who's fresh and safe and sound
Tomorrow's sick or even dead.
If thou now diest uncontrite,
Thy soul and body there[2] must burn.
Help, O Lord Jesus, help thou me,
That I e'en this day come to thee,
Contrition in that moment make
Before me sudden death should take,

That I today and evermore
For my home-coming be prepared.

---

1.   W. Blankenburg, BJ (1977), reports the discovery of the PT for BWV 17, 39, 43, 45, 88, 102, and 187 and suggests Christoph Helm as the possible author, pp. 22-25.

2.   I.e., in hell.

BWV 103 **Ihr werdet weinen und heulen**

Jubilate(Third Sunday after Easter).

Christiane Mariane von Ziegler, *Versuch in Gebundender Schreibart, Teil I* (Leipzig, 1728); Facs: Neumann T, p. 359.

1. *Jn.* 16:20; 6. Paul Gerhardt, verse 9 of "Barmherz'ger Vater, höchster Gott," 1653 (Fischer-Tümpel, III, #449).

22 April 1725, Leipzig; again 15 April 1731.

BG 23; NBA I/11.

---

1. Chorus and Arioso [Dictum] (S, A, T, B, and B)

(S, A, T, B)
Ye will be weeping and wailing, although the world will be joyful.

(B)
But ye will be most sorrowful. Yet all your sadness shall into gladness find transformation.

2. Recit. (T)

Who ought then not in lamentation sink,
If our belove'd is torn from us?
Our souls' true health, the refuge of sick spirits,
Pays no heed to our sorrow.

3. Aria (A)

There is besides thee no physician,
Though I should search all Gilead;[1]
Who'll heal the wounds of my transgressions,
While here there is no balm for me?
If thou dost hide, then I must perish.
Have mercy now, ah, hear my prayer!
Thou seekest, yea, not my destruction,
So come, in hope my heart's yet firm.

4. Recit. (A)

When once my fear is past, thou shalt again restore me;[2]
Thus will I me for thine approach get ready,
I trust in what thy word assures,
That all my sadness now
To gladness shall find transformation.[3]

5. Aria (T)

Recover now, O troubled feelings,
Ye cause yourselves excess of woe.
Leave off your sorrowful beginning,
Ere I in tears collapse and fall,
My Jesus is again appearing,
O gladness which nought else can match!

What good to me thereby is given,
Take, take my heart, my gift to thee!

6. Chorale (S, A, T, B)

I have thee but a little while,
O dearest child, forsaken;
But lo, now, lo, with fortune fair
And comfort past all measure,
Will I for sure the crown of joy
Put on thee for thine honor.
And thy brief pain shall be to joy
And lasting health converted.

---

1.   Cf. *Jer.* 8:22: "Is there no balm in Gilead? Is there no physician there? Why then has the health of the daughter of my people not been restored?"

2.   Cf. *Ps.* 138:7.

3.   Ziegler's printed edition is as follows:

Du wirst, mein Heyland, mich schon nach der Angst erquicken.
Wohlan! ich will mich auch zu deiner Ankunfft schicken.
Ich traue dem Verheissung-Wort,
Daß meine Traurigkeit,
Und diß vielleicht in kurtzer Zeit,
Nach bäng-und ängstlichen Gebehrden,
In Freude soll verkehret werden.

Thou shalt, my Savior, when once my fear is past, restore me.
So come! I will me also for thy coming ready.
I trust in what thy word assures,
That all my sadness shall,
And this perhaps in briefest time,
With timid, anxious gestures over,
To gladness find its transformation.

Bach's abbreviation focuses on the Gospel text in the first movement.

BWV 104 **Du Hirte Israel, höre**

Misericordias Domini (Second Sunday after Easter).

Poet unknown; PT (Leipzig, 1724); Facs: Neumann T, p. 431.

1. *Ps.* 80:2; 6. Cornelius Becker, verse 1 of an adaptation of *Ps.* 23, 1598.

23 April 1724, Leipzig.

BG 23; NBA I/11.

1. Chorus [Dictum] (S, A, T, B)

Thou guide[1] of Israel, hear me, thou who like the sheep dost shelter
Joseph, appear thou who dost sit above the Cherubim.

2. Recit. (T)

The highest shepherd cares for me,
What use is all my sorrow?
Appear will every morning
The shepherd's kindness new.
My heart, compose thyself,
For God is true.

3. Aria (T)

Whene'er my shepherd too long hideth,
The desert makes me all too anxious,
My feeble steps run ever on.
My tongue cries to thee,
And thou, my shepherd, stir'st in me
A faithful "Abba" through thy word[2]

4. Recit. (B)

Yea, this same word is to my soul its nurture,
A balm unto my breast,
The pasture which I call my joy,
A taste of heaven, yea, my very being.
Ah! Gather then, O kindly shepherd,
Thy wretched, straying people;
Ah, bring our path straightway unto its end
And lead thou us into thy sheepfold soon!

5. Aria (B)

Ye herds, so blessed, sheep of Jesus,
The world is now your kingdom come.
Here taste ye Jesus' goodness now.
And hope ye, too, for faith's reward,
When once ye rest in death's soft slumber.

6. Chorale (S, A, T, B)

The Lord my faithful shepherd is,
Him do I trust entirely,
He leads to pasture me, his lamb,
To green and lovely meadow,
To waters fresh he leadeth me,
My soul to nourish with his strength
And gracious word of blessing.

---

1. Though the Scottish *herd* 'shepherd' could be substituted for "guide," it
   might cause confusion. "Shepherd" violates the meter.
2. Cf. *Rom.* 8:15 and *Gal.* 4:6.

BWV 105 Herr, gehe nicht ins Gericht mit deinem Knecht

Ninth Sunday after Trinity.

Poet unknown.

1. *Ps.* 143:2; 6. Johann Rist, verse 11 of "Jesu, der du meine Seele," 1641 (Fischer-Tümpel, II, #189).

25 July 1723, Leipzig.

BG 23; NBA I/19.

1. Chorus [Dictum] (S, A, T, B)

Lord, go thou not into court with this thy thrall, since with thee there is no living person just.

2. Recit. (A)

My God, reject me not,
While I myself now humbly bow before thee,
From thine own countenance.[1]
I know, though great thy wrath and mine own wickedness,
That thou art both a ready witness
And a most righteous judge as well.
I give to thee my free confession now
And cast myself not in great risk,
That I my soul's own failings
Disclaim now, or keep hidden.

3. Aria (S)

How tremble and waver
The sinners' intentions,
In that they do often accuse one another
And then turn around and would dare make excuses.[2]
Just so is the scrupulous conscience
Because of its own torments shattered.

4. Recit. (B)

Blest though is he who doth his bonder know,
Who every debt redeemeth;
Then is the mortgage canceled out,
When Jesus with his blood doth drench it.[3]
He doth it on the cross himself affix,
He will of thy possessions, life and body,
When once thy dying hour doth strike,
Himself transmit the record to his Father.
E'en though thy body will, when borne unto the grave,
With sand and dust be covered,
Thy Savior opens thee eternal shelter.

5. Aria (T)

If I but Jesus as my friend may number,
Then counteth Mammon nought with me.
For I can find no pleasure here
Amidst this empty world and earthly treasures.

6. Chorale (S, A, T, B)

Now, I know, thou shalt make quiet
This my conscience, plaguing me.
Thy good faith will bring fulfillment
To what thou thyself hast said:

That in all these earthly reaches
No one shall be lost forever,
But instead have life eternal,
If he but with faith be full.

---

1.   Cf. *Ps.* 51:13.

2.   Cf. *Rom.* 2:15.

3.   Cf. *Col.* 2:14.

BWV 106 **Gottes Zeit ist die allerbeste Zeit**

Actus Tragicus

A Funeral (possibly of Bach's uncle, Tobias Lämmerhirt, d. 10 August 1707).

Poet unknown.

2a. Adaptation of *Acts* 17:28; 2b. *Ps.* 90:12; 2c. *Is.* 38:1; 2d. *Ecclus.* 14:17 and *Rev.* 22:20 with instrumental chorale: "Ich hab mein Sach Gott heimgestellt" ("I have put my life in God's hands"), Johann Leon, 1582/1589; 3a. *Ps.* 31:6; 3b. *Lk.* 23:43 and Martin Luther, verse 1 of "Mit Fried und Freud ich fahr dahin" (an adaptation of "Simeon's Song of Praise" = "Nunc Dimittis"), 1524 (Wackernagel, I, #205, and III, #25); 4. Adam Reusner, verse 4 of "In dich hab ich gehoffet, Herr," 1533 (Wackernagel, III, #170).

Probably 1707, Mühlhausen.

BG 23; NBA I/34.

A Tragic Performance

1. Sonatina

2a. Chorus [Dictum] (S, A, T, B)

God's own time is the very best of times.
In him living, moving, we exist, as long as he wills. In him shall we die at the right time, when he wills.

2b. Arioso [Dictum] (T)

Ah, Lord, teach us to remember that our death is certain, that we might gain wisdom.

2c. Aria [Dictum] (B)

Set ready thine house; for thou shalt perish and not continue living!

2d. Chorus and Arioso [Dictum] (S, A, T, B and S) with instr. chorale (S, A, T, B)

This is the ancient law: man, thou must perish!

(S)
Yes, come, Lord Jesus!

3a. Aria [Dictum] (A)

Into thine hands now do I commit my soul; for thou hast redeemed me, Lord, thou my faithful God.

3b. Arioso [Dictum][1] (B) and Chorale (A)

(B)
This day shalt thou with me in paradise be.

(A)
In peace and joy do I depart,
As God doth will it;
Consoled am I in heart and mind,
Calm and quiet.
As God me his promise gave:
My death is changed to slumber.

4. Chorale (S, A, T, B)

Glory, laud, praise and majesty
To thee, God, Father, and Son, be giv'n,
The Holy Ghost, with these names!
May godly strength
Make us triumph
Through Jesus Christ, Lord, Amen.

[1.]   Representing the *vox Christi*.

BWV 107 **Was willst du dich betrüben**

Seventh Sunday after Trinity.

The seven verses of the hymn by Johann Heerman, 1630 (Fischer-Tümpel, I, #342).

1. The chorale melody "Von Gott will ich nicht lassen" ("From God will I depart not"), 1690.

23 July 1724, Leipzig.

BG 23; NBA I/18.

---

1. Chorus [Verse 1] (S, A, T, B)

Why wouldst thou then be saddened,
O thou my very soul?
Devote thyself to love him
Who's called Immanuel!
Put trust in him alone,
He will set all in order
And further what concerns thee
As thee will blessed make

2. Recit. [Verse 2] (B)

For God forsaketh no one
Who doth in him put trust;
He bides true to his people
Who in him firmly trust.
Though life deal strange with thee,
Yet thou ought not be frightened!
With gladness wilt thou marvel
How God will rescue thee.

3. Aria [Verse 3] (B)

With him thou canst act boldly,
E'er undismayed at heart,
Thou wilt with him discover
What thee doth serve and help.
What God resolves to do,
That can no one hinder
Of /Midst/ all of mankind's children;
All goes as he commands.

4. Aria [Verse 4] (T)

Although soon from hell's cavern
The devil should himself desire to rise against thee

And rage before thy face,
Yet must he, put to scorn,
Desist from his deceptions,
With which he hopes to catch thee;
For thy cause God assists.

5. Aria [Verse 5] (S)

He sets all for his honor
And for thy blessedness;
God's will no man can hinder,
Him though it bring much pain.
But what God will not have,
This can no one continue,
It must remain unfinished,
For what God wills is done.

6. Arias [Verse 6] (T)

Thus I'm to him devoted,
On him will I rely;
For nought would I yet struggle
But what he doth approve.
Awaiting this, I rest,
For his will is the best way,
I hold this sure and firmly,
God act howe'er he would!

7. Chorale [Verse 7] (S, A, T, B)

Lord, grant that I thine honor,
Yea, all my living days,
With heart unfeigned may augment,
And give thee praise and thanks!

O Father, Spirit, Son,
Thou, who with purest mercy
Avertest need and danger,
For evermore be praised!

BWV 108 Es ist euch gut, daß ich hingehe

Cantate (Fourth Sunday after Easter).

Christiane Mariane von Ziegler, *Versuch in Gebundener Schreibart, Teil I* (Leipzig, 1728); Facs: Neumann T, p. 360.

1. *Jn.* 16:7; 4. *Jn.* 16:13; 6. Paul Gerhardt, verse 10 of "Gott, Vater, sende deinen Geist," 1653 (Fischer-Tümpel, III, #414).

29 April 1725, Leipzig.

BG 23; NBA I/12.

1. Aria [Dictum] (B)

It is for you that I depart now, for were I not departing, would your Comforter not come. But since I am leaving, I will send him unto you.

2. Aria (T)

There shall no doubt deter me,
To thy word, Lord, I'll hearken.
I trust that if thou go'st,
I can in this find comfort,
That I'll amongst the rescued
Come, at the welcome port.

3. Recit. (T)

Thy Spirit will in such wise rule me
That I the proper road shall walk;
Through thy departure he shall come to me.
I ask, though, anxiously: Ah, is he not now here?

4. Chorus [Dictum] (S, A, T, B)

When he, however, truth's very Spirit, will have come, will he into
every truth then lead you. For he will not of himself be speaking,
rather all that he hath heard will he be speaking; and what the future
holds will he proclaim abroad.

5. Aria (A)

What my heart of thee doth seek,
Ah, shall on me be bestowed.
Pour upon me thy rich blessing,
Lead me now upon thy pathways,
That I in eternity
Look upon thy majesty!

6. Chorale (S, A, T, B)

Thy Spirit God from heaven sends,
He leadeth all that him do love
Upon a well-laid pathway.
He sets and ruleth all our steps,
That they not elsewhere ever tread
But where we find salvation.

BWV 109 Ich glaube, lieber Herr, hilf meinem Unglauben!

Twenty-first Sunday after Trinity.

Poet unknown.

1. *Mk.* 9:24; 6. Lazarus Spengler, verse 7 of "Durch Adams Fall ist ganz verderbt," 1524 (Wackernagel, III, #71).

17 October 1723, Leipzig.

BG 23; NBA I/25.

1. Chorus [Dictum] (S, A, T, B)

I have faith, O dear Lord, help my unbelieving.

2. Recit. (T)

The Lord's own hand, indeed, has not grown short,[1]
I can receive his help yet.
Ah no, I sink to earth already
With sorrow, to the ground am I cast down.[2]
The Highest yearns, his father's heart doth break.[3]
Ah no! He hears the sinners not.
He will, he must come to thy rescue quickly
And to thy need bring healing.
Ah no, I still remain for help most anxious;[4]
Ah Lord, how long then?[5]

3. Aria (T)

How filled with doubting is my hoping,
How wavering my anxious heart!

> Of faith the wick but dimly glows,
> Now snaps the almost broken reed,[6]
> And fear doth ever cause new grief.

4. Recit. (A)

Compose thyself, thou doubt-beridden heart,
For Jesus still doth wonders work!
The eyes of faith e'en yet shall witness
God's healing power;
Though the fulfillment distant seem,
Thou canst, indeed, rely upon his promise.

5. Aria (A)

The Savior knows, indeed, his people,[7]
Whene'er their hope doth helpless lie.

> When flesh and will within them quarrel,
> He shall himself yet stand beside them,
> That at the last their faith triumph.

6. Chorale (S, A, T, B)

Who hopes in God and in him trusts
Shall never be confounded;
For who upon this rock doth build,
E'en though there may surround him
Great danger here,

I've[8] yet known ne'er
That man to fall in ruin,
Who doth rely upon God's help;
He helps his faithful always.

---

1. Cf. *Num.* 11;23 and *Is.* 59:1. This recitative sets up a dialogue within the
    soul between faith and doubt which lends a dramatic character to the
    whole cantata.
2. Cf. *Mk.* 9:18.
3. Cf. *Jer* 31:20: "Is Ephraim my dear son? Is he my darling child? For
    as often as I speak against him, I do remember him still. Therefore
    my heart yearns for him; I will surely have mercy on him, says the
    Lord."
4. Cf. *Is.* 38:17.
5. Cf. *Ps.* 6:3.
6. Cf. *Is.* 42:3 and *Mt.* 12:20.
7. Cf. *Jn.* 10:14 and 27.
8. The "I" interjects a declaration of personal faith appropriate to the
    central theme of the cantata. Erdmann Neumeister includes this verse
    in "Gelobet sey der Herr" in *Geistliches Singen und Spielen* (Gotha
    1711), for which Bach probably wrote music. This translation follows
    the colometry of that edition (9 lines instead of the 8 in Neumann T,
    p. 144).

BWV 110 **Unser Mund sei voll Lachens**

Christmas Day.

Georg Christian Lehms, *Gottgefälliges Kirchen-Opffer* (Darmstadt, 1711);
Facs: Neumann T, p. 257.

1. After *Ps.* 126:2-3; 3. *Jer.* 10:6; 5. *Lk.* 2:14; 7. Kaspar Füger, verse 5
of "Wir Christenleut," 1592.

25 December 1725, Leipzig; Parody: 1 ← Overture in D Major, BWV 1069; 5 ← Magnificat in E flat Major, BWV 243a/D.

BG 23; NBA I/2.

---

1. Chorus [Dictum]1 (S, A, T, B)

Make our mouth full with laughter and make our tongue full with praises. For the Lord hath great things for us achieved.[1]

2. Aria (T)

All ye thoughts and all ye senses,
Lift yourselves aloft this moment,
Soaring swiftly heavenward,
And bethink what God hath done!
He is man[2] for this alone,
That we heaven's children be.

3. Recit. [Dictum] (B)

Thee, Lord, is no one like. Thou art great and thy name, too, is great and thou with thy works canst prove it.

4. Aria (A)

Ah Lord, what is a child of man[3]
That thou wouldst through such pain redeem him?
A worm thy curse tormenteth
While hell and Satan round him stand;
But yet, thy Son, whom heart and soul
In love call their inheritance.

5. Aria [Dictum] (S, T)

Glory to God in the highest and peace be on earth, now, and to mankind a sign of favor!

6. Aria (B)

Wake up, ye nerves and all ye members,
And sing those very hymns of gladness
Which to our God with favor come.
And ye, ye strings[4] of deep devotion,
To him a song of praise now offer
In which the heart and soul rejoice.

Da Capo.

7. Chorale (S, A, T, B)

Alleluia! All praise to God
We all sing forth now from our heart's foundation.[5]
For God today hath wrought that joy
Which we shall not forget at any moment.

---

1. This is only a paraphrase of *Ps.* 126:2-3.
2. More literally: "He becomes man . . ."
3. Cf. *Ps.* 8:4.
4. That the oboes cease to double the violins here calls attention to *Saiten* "strings."
5. In another musical context one might translate *Herzens Grunde* more metaphorically, e.g. "sincerely," but the descending line of the continuo is inspired too clearly by *Grunde* to let pass unnoticed the sense of "bottom" or "foundation" of the heart.

BWV 111 **Was mein Gott will, das g'scheh allzeit**

Third Sunday after Epiphany.

Poet unknown.

1. Margrave Albrecht von Brandenburg, verse 1 of the hymn, 1547 (Wackernagel, III, #1240f.); 2-5. based freely on verses 2 and 3; 6. verse 4 of the hymn.

21 January 1725, Leipzig

BG 24; NBA I/6.

---

1. Chorus [Verse 1] (S, A, T, B)

What my God will, be done alway,
His will, it is the best will;
To help all those he is prepared
Whose faith in him is steadfast.
He frees from want, this righteous God,
And punisheth with measure:
Who trusts in God, on him relies,
Him will he not abandon.

2. Aria (B)

Be frightened, O my bosom, not,
God is thy strength and confidence[1]
And to thy soul life bringeth.
Yea, what his wisdom doth decide,
Can by the world and human might
In no way be resisted.

3. Recit. (A)

O foolish one, who doth from God withdraw
And, like a Jonas once,
Before the face of God doth flee![2]
Our very thoughts to him are manifest,
And of our head's own hairs
He hath the number.
Blest he who this protection chooseth
In faithfulness and trusting:
To look to his command
With patience and with expectation.

4. Aria (A, T)

I'll walk, then, with emboldened paces,
E'en when me God to grave shall lead.
As God my days hath set in writing,
So shall, when me his hand hath touched,
The bitterness of death be banished.[3]

5. Recit. (S)

So when by death at last my soul
Is with great force hence from its body torn,
Receive it, God, in faithful hands paternal!
When devil, death and sin on me make war,
And my own deathbed's pillow
Must be a field of battle,
Bring help, so that in thee my faith triumph!

6. Chorale [Verse 4] (S, A, T, B)

Just this, Lord, will I ask of thee,
Thou wilt me not deny it:
When me the evil spirit tries,

Let me still not be anxious.
Help, guide, defend, ah God, my Lord,
To thy name's fame and honor.
Who this doth seek, him is it giv'n;
And I say gladly: Amen.

[1.]   This line is verbatim from the hymn.

[2.]   Cf. *Jon.* 1:3.

[3.]   Cf. 1 *Sam.* 15:32.

BWV 112 Der Herr ist mein getreuer Hirt

Misericordias Domini (Second Sunday after Easter).

?Wolfgang Meuslin, an imitation of *Ps.* 23, 1530; PT (Leipzig, 1731);
Facs: Neumann T, p. 443.

1-5. Verses 1-5 of the hymn.

8 April 1731, Leipzig.

BG 24; NBA I/11.

---

1. Chorus [Verse 1] (S, A, T, B)

The Lord is now my shepherd true,
He holds me in his shelter,
Wherein for nothing shall I want,
Possessing any value;
He gives me pasture endlessly,
Whereon grows the sweet-tasting grass
Of his word's healing Gospel.

2. Aria [Verse 2] (A)

To water pure he leadeth me,
Which me refreshment bringeth.
It is his sacred Holy Ghost,
Which makes me strong in courage.
He guides me on the proper road
Of his commandments evermore
For sake of his own name and honor.

3. Recit. [Verse 3] (B)

And though I wander in darkness' vale,
I'll fear[1] no evil fortune,
Persecution, suff'ring, sadness,
Nor this world's callous whimsy;
For thou art with me constantly,
Thy staff and rod, they comfort me,
To thy word I commend me.

4. Aria [Verse 4] (S, T)

Thou preparest a table for me
Midst the foes[2] which stand about me,
Dost my heart make unafraid and fresh,
My head hast thou anointed
With thine own spirit's joyful oil,
And thou dost pour full this my soul
With thy spiritual gladness.

5. Chorale [Verse 5] (S, A, T, B)

His goodness and his mercy shall
Attend me through my lifetime,
And I will evermore abide
Within the Lord's own dwelling,

On earth in Christian company,
And after death there will I be
With Christ, my Lord and Master.

---

1. With *Fürcht ich doch* read "I'll fear yet."
2. With *Für meinen Feind* read "Amidst the foes."

BWV 113 **Herr Jesu Christ, du höchstes Gut**

Eleventh Sunday after Trinity.

Poet unknown.

1. Bartholomäus Ringwaldt, verse 1 of the hymn, 1599 (Wackernagel, IV, #1523); 2. verse 2; 3. based on verse 3; 4. verse 4, slightly modified, with interpolated recitative; 5-7. based on verses 5, 6 and 7; 8. verse 8 of the hymn.

20 August 1724, Leipzig.

BG 24; NBA I/20.

---

1. Chorus [Verse 1] (S, A, T, B)

Lord Jesus Christ, thou highest good,
Thou wellspring of all mercy,
O see how I within my heart
With sorrows am sore laden
And bear the pangs of many darts,
Which in my conscience endlessly
Oppress this wretched sinner.

2. Chorale [Verse 2] (A)

Have mercy on me in such grief,
This weight lift from my bosom,
Since thou for it hast paid in full
Upon death's tree of sorrow,
That I may not with grievous woe
Amidst my sins to ruin go,
Nor evermore lose courage.

3. Aria (B)

In truth, when I before me see[1]
The wrongs I unto God committed,
How daily I've him sore offended,
I'm vexed by trembling, fear and pain.
I know my heart would now be broken,
If me thy word no hope did promised.

4. Chorale [Verse 4] and Recit. (B)

But now thy healing word assures,
Within me sweetly singing,
That this my breast,
Which once did nought but anguish know,
Shall find again new strength and courage.
My sorrow-laden heart
Perceiveth now, the many tears of pain now past,
The radiant beams of Jesus' eyes of mercy;
His word to me hath so much comfort brought,
That once again my heart doth laugh
As though it would be dancing.
How blest is now my spirit!
My conscience, faint and fearful, can me no longer torture,

Since now God all his grace hath pledged,
Who soon the faithful and the righteous
Shall heaven's manna feed,
If we but with remorseful souls
Draw nigh to Jesus' presence.

5. Aria (T)

Jesus sinners doth accept:
Soothing word of life and comfort!

He gives to all their soul's true peace
And calls with comfort to each one:
Thy sin is thee forgiven.

6. Recit. (T)

The Savior sinners doth accept:
How lovely to mine ears this sentence ringeth!
He calls: "Come unto me,
All ye who labor and are burdened,[2]
Come to the wellspring of all mercy,
For I have chosen you as my companions!"
Upon this word I would to thee
Come forth just like the contrite taxman
And with a humble heart "God grant me mercy!" beg thee.[3]
Ah, comfort this my foolish mind
And make me through the blood which thou hast poured
From all my sins now clean,
And I will follow David[4] and Manasseh,[5]
When I like them
Have e'er in love and trust
Within mine arms of faith embraced thee
And shall a child of heaven be.

7. Aria (S, A)

Ah Lord, my God, forgive me still,[6]
For all I've done to stir thine anger,
And break the heavy yoke of sin
Which Satan now hath laid upon me,
So that my heart may rest contented
And to thy praise and fame henceforth
Be to thy word
With childlike faith and trust obedient.

8. Chorale [Verse 8] (S, A, T, B)

Firm me with thine own Spirit's joy,
Heal me with thine own wounding,
Wash me with thine own sweat of death
At my last hour's coming;
And take me then, when thou dost please,
Sincere in faith hence from the world
Unto thy chosen people!

[1.] This line is taken verbatim from verse 3.
[2.] Cf. *Mt.* 11:29.
[3.] Cf. *Lk.* 18:13.
[4.] Cf. 2 *Sam.* 12:13.
[5.] Cf. 2 *Chr.* 33:12-13.
[6.] This line is taken verbatim from verse 7.

BWV 114 **Ach, lieben Christen, seid getrost**

Seventeenth Sunday after Trinity.

Poet unknown.

1. Johannes Gigas, verse 1 of the hymn, 1561 (Wackernagel, I, #511

and IV, #257), to the chorale melody "Wo Gott, der Herr, nicht bei uns hält" (cf. BWV 178); 2-3. based freely on verse 2; 4. verse 3; 5-6. based freely on verses 4 and 5; 7. verse 6 of the hymn.

1 October 1724, Leipzig.

BG 24; NBA I/23.

---

1. Chorus [Verse 1] (S, A, T, B)

Ah, fellow Christians, be consoled,
Why are ye so despondent!
Since now the Lord doth punish us,
Let us sincerely say it:
Chastisement have we well deserved,
This must we one and all confess,
Let no one be excepted.

2. Aria (T)

Where will within this vale of sorrow
My spirit find its refuge now?

> Alone in Jesus' hands paternal
> Will I in weakness seek my refuge;
> I know no other place to go.[1]

3. Recit. (B)

O sinner, bear with patient heart
What thou through thine own fault
Upon thyself hast summoned!
Injustice dost thou drink
Like water to thyself,
And this, thy thirsting after sin,
Is for corruption made

And will lead thee to death.
For pride did long ago eat of forbidden fruit,
To be God's equal;
How oft thou risest up with proud and pompous bearing,
And must be humbled in thy turn!
Go forth, make ready now thy heart
That it may death and grave not fear,
Then shalt thou come through death most blessed
Forth from thy sin's corrupt condition
To innocence and majesty.

4. Chorale [Verse 3] (S)

No fruit the grain of wheat will bear
Unless to earth it falleth;[2]
So must as well our earthly flesh
Be changed to dust and ashes,
Before it gain that majesty
Which thou, Lord Christ, for us hast made
Through thy path to the Father.

5. Aria (S)

Thou shalt, O death, make me no longer anxious.
If I through thee my freedom would accomplish,
Then I, indeed, one day must death endure.

    With Simeon will I in peace then journey,
    My Savior shall within the grave protect me
    And summon me at last transformed and pure.

6. Recit. (T)

Till then be mindful of thy spirit
And give it to thy Savior's care;
Return thy body and thy limbs to
God, who himself did give them to thee.

He cares and tends.
And thus will his own love's great might
In death and life be manifest.

7. Chorale [Verse 6] (S, A, T, B)

In waking or in slumbering
We are, indeed, God's children;
In Christ baptism we receive,
And he can ward off Satan.
Through Adam to us cometh death,
But Christ frees us from all our need.
For this we praise the Master.

[1.]   Literally: "I know neither where to come out or in."
[2.]   Cf. *Jn.* 12:24.

BWV 115 **Mache dich, mein Geist, bereit**

Twenty-second Sunday after Trinity.

Poet unknown.

1. Johann Burchard Freystein, verse 1 of the hymn, 1697, to the chorale melody "Straf mich nicht in deinem Zorn" ("Punish me not in thy wrath"), 1681; 2. based on verse 2; 3. based on verses 3-6; 4. the first two lines verbatim, the rest based on verse 7; 5. based on verses 8 and 9; 6. verse 10 of the hymn.

5 November 1724, Leipzig.

BG 24; NBA I/26.

---

1. Chorus [Verse 1] (S, A, T, B)

Get thyself, my soul, prepared,
Watching, begging, praying,
Lest thou let the evil day
Unforeseen o'ertake thee.
For in truth
Satan's guile
Often to the righteous
With temptation cometh.

2. Aria (A)

Ah slumbering spirit, what? Still at thy rest?
Arouse thyself now!

> For well may damnation thee sudden awaken
> And, if thou not watchest,
> In slumber of lasting perdition obscure thee.

3. Recit. (B)

God, who for this thy soul doth watch,
Hath loathing for the night of sin;
He sendeth thee his gracious light
And wants for all these blessings,
Which he so richly thee assures,
Alone the open eyes of spirit.
In Satan's craft there is no end
Of charm to snare the sinner;
If thou dost break the bond of grace,
Thou shalt salvation ne'er discover.
The whole wide world and all its members
Are nought but untrue brothers;

Yet doth thy flesh and blood from them
Seek nought but flattery.

4. Aria (S)

Pray though even now as well,
Even in thy waking!¹

> Beg now in thy grievous guilt
> That thy Judge with thee forbear,
> That he thee from sin set free
> And unspotted render.

5. Recit. (T)

He yearneth after all our crying
He bends his gracious ear to us;
When foes respond to all our woe with gladness,
We shall triumph within his might:
For this his Son, in whom we ask it,
Us strength and courage sends
And will advance to be our Helper.

6. Chorale [Verse 10] (S, A, T, B)

Therefore let us ever be
Watching, begging, praying,
Since our fear, need, and great dread
Press on ever nearer;
For the day
Is not far
When our God will judge us
And the world demolish.

---

1. These two lines are taken verbatim from verse 7 of the hymn.

BWV 116 **Du Friedefürst, Herr Jesu Christ**

Twenty-fifth Sunday after Trinity.

Poet unknown.

1. Jakob Ebert, verse 1 of the hymn, 1601; 2-4. based loosely on verses 2-4 respectively; 5. based loosely on verse 5 and 6; 6. verse 7 of the hymn.

26 November 1724, Leipzig.

BG 24; NBA I/24.

1. Chorus [Verse 1] (S, A, T, B)

Thou Prince of peace, Lord Jesus Christ,
True man and very God,
A helper strong in need thou art
In life as well as death.
So we alone
In thy dear name
Are to thy Father crying.

2. Aria (A)

Ah, past all telling is our woe
And this our angry judge's menace!

  Scarce may we, while in our great fear,
  As thou, O Jesus, dost command,
  To God in thy dear name be crying.

3. Recit. (T)

Remember though,
O Jesus, thou art still
A prince of peace considered!
For love thou didst desire thy word to send us.
Would then thy heart so suddenly turn from us,
Thou who such mighty help before didst show us?

4. Aria (S, T, B)

Ah, we acknowledge all our guilt
And pray for nought but to forbear
And for thy love surpassing measure.
For broke, yea, thy forgiving heart,
As then the fallen's pain
To us into the world did drive thee.

5. Recit. (A)

Ah, let us through the stinging lashes
Not all too fiercely bleed now!
O God, thou who a God of order art,[1]
Thou know'st within our foe's vast rage
What cruelty and wrong abide.
Come then, and stretch out thine own hand
O'er this alarmed and harried land.
It can the foe's great might now conquer
And us a lasting peace then offer!

6. Chorale [Verse 7] (S, A, T, B)

Illumine, too, our minds and hearts
With grace thy Spirit sends,
That we not be a cause for scorn
Unto our souls' regret.
O Jesus Christ,

Alone thou art
Who can such good accomplish.

[1.]   Cf. 1 *Cor.* 14:33.

BWV 117 **Sei Lob und Ehr dem höchsten Gut**

Unspecified occasion.

Johann Jakob Schütz, 1675.

1-9. The nine verses of the hymn.

Ca. 1728/1731, Leipzig.

BG 24; NBA I/34.

---

1. Chorus [Verse 1] (S, A, T, B)

Give laud and praise the highest good,
The Father of all kindness,
The God who every wonder works,
The God who doth my spirit
With his rich consolation fill,
The God who makes all sorrow still.
Give to our God all honor!

2. Recit. (B) [Verse 2]

To thee give thanks the heav'nly host,
O ruler o'er all thrones,[1] thou,
And those on earth and air and sea,
Within thy shadow dwelling,
These honor thy creative power,

Which all things hath so well designed.
Give to our God all honor!

3. Aria [Verse 3] (T)

Whate'er our God created hath,
This, too, would he keep safely;
O'er all this shall he morn and night
With his dear grace be master.
Within his kingdom far and wide
Are all things just and all things fair.
Give to our God all honor!

4. Chorale [Verse 4] (S, A, T, B)

I called to God in my distress:
Ah Lord, pay heed my crying!
Then saved my Savior me from death
And let my comfort flourish.
My thanks, O God, my thanks to thee;
Ah thank ye, thank ye God with me!
Give to our God all honor!

5. Recit. [Verse 5] (A)

The Lord is not and never was
From his own people severed;
He bideth e'er their confidence,
Their blessing, peace, and rescue;
With mother's hands he leadeth sure
His people ever here and there.
Give to our God all honor!

6. Aria [Verse 6] (B)

When strength and help must fail at times,
As all the world doth witness,

He comes, he helps abundantly,
The maker comes, inclining
His father's eyes below to them
Who else would nowhere find repose.
Give to our God all honor!

7. Aria [Verse 7] (A)

I will thee all my life's extent,
O God, from henceforth honor;
One shall, O God, the song of praise
In every region hearken.
My heart be fully stirred with life,
My soul and body let rejoice.
Give to our God all honor!

8. Recit. [Verse 8] (T)

Ye, who on Christ's own name do call,
Give to our God all honor!
Ye, who do God's great might confess,
Give to our God all honor!
All those false idols put to scorn,
The Lord is God, the Lord is God:
Give to our God all honor!

9. Chorale [Verse 9] (S, A, T, B)

So come before his countenance
With glad, triumphant dancing;
Discharge ye now your solemn oath
And let us sing with gladness;
God hath all things so well designed
And all things, all things rightly done,
Give to our God all honor!

[1.] Dionysius, the Pseudo-Areopagite (ca. 500), in the *Celestial Hierarchy* gives the following orders within the heavenly host: Seraphim, Cherubim, Thrones, Dominions, Virtues, Powers, Principalities, Archangels, Angels.

BWV 118 O Jesu Christ, meins Lebens Licht

Occasion unknown.

Martin Behm, verse 1 of the hymn, 1610.

1736/1737, Leipzig.

BG 24; NBG XVII,1; NBA III/1.

1. Chorus [Verse 1] (S, A, T, B)

O Jesus Christ, my life's true light,
My prize, my strength, hope to my sight,
On earth here am I but a guest
And by sin's burden sore oppressed.

BWV 119 Preise, Jerusalem, den Herrn

Inauguration of the New Town Council.

Poet unknown.

1. *Ps* 147:12-14; 9. Martin Luther, part of verse 4 of the German Te Deum, 1529 (Wackernagel, I, #212).

30 August 1723, Leipzig.

BG 24; NBA I/32.

---

1. Chorus [Dictum] (S, A, T, B)

Praise, O Jerusalem, the Lord, laud, O Zion, him thy God! For he maketh fast the bars across thy doorway and blesseth all thy children therein, he bringeth peace within thy borders.

2. Recit. (T)

O happy land, O city blest,
Where e'en the Lord his hearth and fire doth keep!
Can God show greater favor
Than where he honor gives within a land a dwelling?
Can he a city give
With richer force his blessing
Than where he troth and kindness cause to meet each other,
And where, that righteousness and peace ought
To kiss, he never tireth,[1]
Untiring, never done,
That they be ever cherished, and hath his promise here fulfilled?
Therefore we must conclude: O happy land, O city blest!

3. Aria (T)

Well thee, thou linden people,[2]
Well thee, thou art well off!

How much of God's true blessing
And of his gracious favor,
Which overfloweth here,
Thou canst in thee discover.

4. Recit. (B)

Thou dost in glory stand, dear town!
Thou folk which God did choose for his inheritance![3]
How good! How very good! Where one to heart would take it
And rightly recognize
Through whom the Lord his blessing's increase sponsored.
True!
Need there more be said?
The witness is at hand,
The heart and conscience will convince us quickly
That all the good we near us see,
First God, then wise authority
By means of prudent government inspired.
So now, beloved folk, thy steadfast thanks prepare,
Else would of all these things not e'en thy walls keep silent![4]

5. Aria (A)

Authority is God's endowment,
Indeed, of God an image true.

> Who would its might not duly measure
> Must also be of God unmindful:
> How would else be his word fulfilled?[5]

6. Recit. (S)

Now! We acknowledge this and bring to thee,
O God on high, an off'ring of our thanks for this.
And so, whereas this very day,
The day which us the Lord hath made,[6]
You, cherished elders, partly from your toil delivered,
And partly, too,
Brought sleepless hours of worry

Which with a new election come,
Thus sighs a loyal throng with heart and tongue alike:

7. Chorus [S, A, T, B)

The Lord hath good for us achieved,
For this we're all rejoicing.

> May he our cherished elders tend
> And keep them for uncounted
> And long-enduring years on end
> Within their house of government,
> And we will gladly praise him.

8. Recit. (A)

And last!
Since thou didst, Lord, us to thy people join,
Then let from these thy faithful
Still one more humble pray'r
Before thine ears to come now.
And hear us! Oh yes, hear us!
The mouth, the heart and soul are sighing deeply.

9. Chorale (S, A, T, B)

Thy people help, Lord Jesus Christ,
And bless them, thine inheritance.
Guard and tend them at every hour
And raise them high forever more!
Amen.

---

1. Cf. *Ps.* 85:10.
2. This expression alludes to the etymology of Leipzig from the Slavic *lipa* 'linden tree.' This rhetorical figure (*locus notationis* 'play on names') on

Leipzig occurs in several of Bach's cantatas. Cf. BWV 215/8a and BWV 207a/1.

3. Cf. *Ps.* 33:12.

4. Cf. *Lk.* 19:40.

5. Cf. *Rom.* 13:1-7. The unity of the God-given authority is emphasized in the unison flauto [dolce] I and II.

6. Cf. *Ps.* 118:24.

BWV 120 **Gott, man lobet dich in der Stille**

Inauguration of the New Town Council.

Poet unknown, probably Picander.

1. *Ps.* 65:1; 6. Martin Luther, part of verse 4 of the German Te Deum, 1529 (Wackernagel, I, #212).

1728 or 1729, Leipzig.

BG 24; NBA I/32.

1. Aria [Dictum] (A)

God, we praise thee now in the stillness of Zion, and thee we pay our solemn pledges.

2. Chorus (S, A, T, B)

Triumph, all ye joyous voices,
Soaring into heaven, rise!

> Praise God in his holy shrine
> And exalt ye his great fame;
> All his kindness,

His forgiving heart of mercy,
Shall at no time ever cease!

3. Recit. (B)

Wake, thou beloved linden town,[1]
Come, fall before thy master humbly,
Acknowledge how he thee,
In all thy splendor's state,
So fatherly
Supports, protects, and guards,
And doth his hand of love
Still over thee steadfastly hold.
Rise up,
And pay thy solemn pledges, which thou the Highest now hast vowed,
And sing thy songs of thanks most humble!
Come, pray now that he town and land
Unending wish e'en more to foster
And this its honored government,
Today with seats and vote renewed,
Through many splendors wish to favor.

4. Aria (S)

Health and blessing
Shall and must at every hour
Bide with our high government,
In their proper fullness dwelling,

> So that faith and justice shall be
> Led as friends to kiss each other.[2]

5. Recit. (T)

O Lord, so consecrate this government with thine own blessing now,
That every malice may flee from us,
And that true righteousness within our dwellings flourish,

That thine own Father's seed unspotted
And thy most blessed name's due honor
With us in glory ever reign!

6. Chorale (S, A, T, B)

Now help us, Lord, these servants thine,
Whom with thy blood thou hast redeemed!
Let us in heaven have a share
With the saints forever saved!
Thy people help, Lord Jesus Christ,
And bless them, thine inheritance;
Guard and tend them at every hour
And raise them high forever more!

[1.] The expression "linden town" is a rhetorical play on the etymology of
Leipzig: < Slavic *lipa* 'linden.' Cf. BWV 119, note 2, BWV 215/8a and
BWV 207a/1.

[2.] Cf. *Ps.* 85:10.

BWV 120a **Herr Gott, Beherrscher aller Dinge**

A Wedding.

Poet unknown.

2. *Ecclus.* 50:24 with recitative; 5. Martin Luther, response from the
Litany, 1528/1529 (after the recitative); 9. Joachim Neander, verses 4
and 5 of "Lobe den Herren, den mächtigen König der Ehren," 1689.

Ca. 1729; Parody: 1, 3, 6 ← BWV 120/2, 4, 1.

BG 41; NBA I/33.

First Part

1. Chorus (S, A, T, B)

Lord God, thou ruler of all nature,
Who all doth own, control and bear,
Through whom what breath doth draw is moved,

> We all deserve now much too little
> The kindness and forgiving heart,
> Through which thou us since toddling children
> Until this instant hast made glad.

2. Recit. (B, T) and Chorus [Dictum] (S, A, T, B)

(B)
How marvelous, O God, is thy creation,
How great indeed thy might,
How past all telling is thy faith!
Thou didst display thy boundless power
Before thou brought us in the world.
That time
When we were nothing still
And of ourselves knew nothing,
Was thy dear kindness, thy forgiving love,
To our prosperity
Most zealously devoted.
Our very name and length of life
By thee are set in writing,
While we are still in darkness waiting;
Yea, thy dear kindness is prepared,
When it us in the world once brings,
Forthwith with loving arms to hold us tightly.
And that we may ne'er be of thee unmindful,
For our sake is thy gracious might
With every morning new.

Therefore when we perceive this,
We must with hearts unfeignéd sing thy praises:

(S, A, T, B)
Now thank ye all our God, who mighty wonders works in every region.

(T)
Now, Lord, grant, too, that this love and troth
For this day's bridal pair be new;
And since here this betrothéd couple
Before thy holy countenance are coming
And, filled with worship, praying,
Give ear to them before thy throne now,
And let, to our own pleasure
And their reward, them prosper and be happy.

3. Aria (S)

Lead, O God, through thy love's kindness
This the new betrothéd pair.

> Make in them exceeding true
> What thy word to us promised,
> That thou to all who adore thee
> Wouldst give favor evermore.[1]

Second Part (Post Copulationem)

4. Sinfonia

5. Recit. (T) and Chorus (S, A, T, B)

(T)
Lord Sabaoth,
Lord, our forefathers' God,

Give heed to this our cry;
Bestow thy blessing and success
Upon this new-made marriage,
That all their deeds be in and from and with thee.
Let ev'rything through thee arising
In thee its blessing find;
Both banish all distress
And guide as well the wedded couple
Thus, as thou will'st,
E'er nearer thee.
Thus will this couple more and more
With truly joyful spirits,
And with thy ample blessing,
That blessing all things in the world depend on,
Be filled and satisfied.

(S, A, T, B)
O hear us, O good Lord and God.

6. Aria (A, T)

Lord, now begin and speak thy blessing
Upon this thine own servant's house.

> Let them unto thy fear be cleaving,
> And they shall live in endless blessing;
> Upon them set thy gaze and vision,
> And all shall sure in blessing end.

7. Recit. (B)

The Lord, the Lord our God, so be with you
As he with your forefathers' throng
Was always and now also is;[2]

And you like Ephraim and like Manasseh plant;[3]
And leave you not,
Nor take from you his caring hand;
May he incline your heart and mind
Alway to him,
That ye may journey in his pathways,
And in your dealings may act wisely;
His Spirit ever favor you;
If all this now is done,
Then will your every deed and action
Fill its intention.
And your devoted parents' blessing
Will rest in twofold store upon you.
But meanwhile we would God bring praise and singing,
A sacrifice of glad thanksgiving.

8. Chorale (S, A, T, B)

Praise the Almighty, who thine estate clearly hath favored,
Who doth from heaven with streams of his love blessing shower.
Think now on this,
What the Almighty can do,
Who doth with love ever greet thee.
Praise the Almighty, all that I own, praise his name's honor.
All things that breath possess, praise him with Abraham's children!
He is thy light,
Spirit, yea, this forget not;
Praising him, close thou with "Amen."

---

1.   Cf. *Ex.* 20:6.

2.   Cf. 1 *Kg.* 8:57.

3.   Cf. *Gen.* 48:20.

BWV 120b **Gott, man lobet dich in der Stille**

Bicentennial of the Augsburg Confession.

Christian Friedrich Henrici (Picander), *Ernst-Schertzhaffte und Satyrische Gedichte*, *Teil III* (Leipzig, 1732); Reprint: Sicul,*Annales Lipsienses, Sectio XXXVIII*, 1731, and *Das Jubilierende Leipzig*, 1731; Facs: Neumann T, p. 333.

1. *Ps.* 65:2; 6. Martin Luther, verse 3 of "Komm, Heiliger Geist, Heere Gott," 1524 (Wackernagel, I, #199).

26 June 1730, Leipzig; Parody: 1, 2, 4 ← BWV 120/1, 2, 4.

On the Second Day of the Festival

1. (Arioso) [Dictum]

God, we praise thee now in the stillness of Zion, and thee we pay our solemn pledges.

2. Aria

Pay, O Zion, all thy pledges,
Pay the vows to God on high.[1]
Now thy hope doth serve thee well,
Source and fountains are still pure;
His steadfastness
Builds and lays a new foundation
For his name's great fame and house.

Da Capo.

3. Recit.

Ah! Thou the city loved of God,
May God by thee yet further stand,
Thy hearth and altar and thy fire
Are in great danger and oppressed;
So for thine own sake watch with care.
Be firm in faith and waver not
As though a mere broken reed, as though a fading light.
Maintain the hope of thy confession:
God is steadfast
Who sealed it with his pledge.

4. Aria

True and faithful,
Never falt'ring in distress,
True in living, true in death,
Must be real Christians always,
That they after welcome dying
Of true life the crown inherit.
Da Capo.

5. Recit.

Rise up, thou sacred congregation,[2]
Now act true to thy word
And hasten more and more
To kindness, to the works of goodness,
That all who now oppose thee
Thy covenant
And its true word's foundation firm
In service of the town may witness.

6. Chorale

O thou holy flame, comfort sweet,
Now help us, joyful and content,
To bide forever in thy service,
That sadness may not disperse us;
O Lord, through thy might us prepare;
Make strong the weakness of our flesh,
That we here gallantly struggle
Through death and life to reach thy presence.
Alleluia, alleluia.

[1.]   This text is closer than that of BWV 120/2 to the sense of the first
movement.

[2.]   *Gemeinde* = 'community' or 'congregation.' In Bach's Leipzig the two
were virtually one. The last line of this recitative contains the word
Gemeinschaft 'community.' For metrical reasons it is here translated with
"town."

BWV 121 **Christum wir sollen loben schon**

Second Day of Christmas (St. Stephen).

Poet unknown.

1. Martin Luther, verse 1 of the translation of "A solis ortus cardine"
(Coelius Sedulius, 5th c.), 1524 (Wackernagel, III, #17ff.); 2-5. based
freely on verses 2-7; 6. 8th and final verse of the hymn.

26 December 1724, Leipzig.

BG 26; NBA I/3.

---

1. Chorus [Verse 1] (S, A, T, B)

To Christ we should sing praises now,
The spotless maid Maria's Son,
As far as our dear sun gives light
And out to all the world doth reach.

2. Aria (T)

O thou whom God created and extolled,
With reason not, no, no, with wonder see:

> God would through flesh the flesh's health accomplish.
> Though great is he, the maker of all nature,
> And though thou art despiséd and unworthy,
> That thou by this be rescued from corruption.

3. Recit. (T)

The nature of unbounded favor
Hath chosen heaven not
To be its only dwelling,
For it no limits can contain.
Why wonder that in this all sense and reason fail
So great a mystery to fathom,
When grace into a virgin heart is poured?
God chooseth him this body pure to make a temple for his honor,
That to mankind he might in awe-inspiring form be present.

4. Aria (B)

Then John's own glad and joyful leaping
Acknowledged thee, my Jesus, first.[1]

> Now while an arm of faith holds thee,
> So would my heart escape this world
> And to thy cradle press with fervor.

5. Recit. (S)

But how doth it regard thee in thy cradle?
My heart doth sigh: with trembling and almost unopened lips now
It brings its grateful sacrifice.
God, who all limits did transcend,
Bore servile form and poverty.
And since he did this for our benefit,
Thus raise now[2] with the choirs of angels
Triumphant sounds of thankful singing!

6. Chorus [Verse 8] (S, A, T, B)

Laud, praise, and thanks to thee be giv'n,
Christ, now born of the spotless maid,
With Father and the Holy Ghost
From now until eternity.

[1.]   Cf. *Lk* 1:44.

[2.]   OP and BG have *laß ich*. Translate "I'll raise."

BWV 122 **Das neugeborne Kindelein**

The Sunday after Christmas (not present in every year).

Poet unknown.

1. Cyriakus Schneegaß, verse 1 of the hymn, 1597; 2. based freely on verse 2; 3. beginning lines based on verse 2; 4. verse 3 with interpolations; 5. based loosely on verse 4; 6. verse 4 of the hymn.

31 December 1724, Leipzig.

BG 26; NBA I/3.

---

1. Chorus [Verse 1] (S, A, T, B)

The newly born, the tiny child,
The darling, little Jesus-child,
Doth once again the year renew
For this the chosen Christian throng.

2. Aria (B)

O mortals, ye each day transgressing,
Ye ought the angels' gladness share.

> Your jubilation's joyful shout
> That God to you is reconciled
> Hath you the sweetest comfort published.

3. Recit. (S) with instr. chorale

The angels all who did before
Shun you, as though the cursed avoiding,
Make swell the air now in that higher choir,
That they at your salvation tell their gladness.
God, who did you from paradise
And angels' sweet communion thrust,
Lets you again, on earth now dwelling,
Through his own presence perfect blessedness recover:
So thank him now with hearty voices
For this awaited day in his new order.[1]

4. Chorale [Verse 3] (A) and Aria (S, T)

(A)
If God, appeased, is now our friend,

(S, T)
How blest are we in him believing,

(A)
How can us harm the cruel foe?

(S, T)
His rage our comfort cannot ravish;

(A)
'Spite devil and the gate of hell,

(S, T)
Their fury will them little profit,

(A)
The Jesus-child is now our shield.

(S, T)
God is with us and shall protect us.

5. Recit. (T)

This is a day himself the Lord hath made,[2]
Which hath his Son into this world now brought.
O blessed day, here now fulfilled!
O faithful waiting, which henceforth is past!
O faith here, which its goal doth see!
O love here, which doth draw God nigh!
O joyfulness, which doth through sadness press
And God our lips' glad off'ring bring.

6. Chorus [Verse 4] (S, A, T, B)

It brings the year of Jubilee,
Why do we mourn then anymore?

Quick, rise! Now is the time for song,
The Jesus-child fends off all woe.

---

1.   "His new order" = the new covenant.
2.   Cf. *Ps.* 118:24.

BWV 123 **Liebster Immanuel, Herzog der Frommen**

Epiphany.

Poet unknown.

1. Ahasverus Fritsch, verse 1 of the hymn, 1679 (Fischer-Tümpel, V, #593); 2-5. based loosely on verse 2-5, respectively; 6. verse 6 of the hymn.

6 January 1725, Leipzig.

BG 26; NBA I/5.

---

1. Chorus [Verse 1] (S, A, T, B)

Dearest Emanuel, Lord[1] of the faithful,
Thou Savior of my soul, come, come now soon!
Thou hast, my highest store, my heart won over;
So much its love doth burn and for thee seethe.
On earth can nothing
Be dearer to me
Than that I my Jesus e'er may hold.

2. Recit. (A)

Now heaven's sweet delight, the chosen people's joy,
Doth fill e'en here on earth my heart and breast,
When I the name of Jesus utter
And recognize his secret manna:
Like as the dew an arid land revives,
Just so my heart
In peril and in pain
To joyfulness doth Jesus power transport.

3. Aria (T)

E'en the cruel cross's journey
And my fare of bitter weeping
Daunt me not.

> When the raging tempests bluster,
> Jesus sends to me from heaven
> Saving light.

4. Recit. (B)

No fiend of hell can e'er devour me,
The crying conscience now is still.
How shall indeed the hostile host surround me?
E'en death itself hath lost its might,
And to my side the victory now inclines,
For Jesus is to me, my Savior, shown.

5. Aria (B)

Leave me, world, for thou dost scorn me,
In my grievous loneliness!

Jesus, now in flesh appearing
And my sacrifice accepting,
Shall be with me all my days.

6. Chorale [Verse 6] (S, A, T, B)

Be gone, then, evermore, ye idle fancies!
Thou, Jesus, thou art mine, and I am thine;
I would depart this world and come before thee;
Thou shalt within my heart and mouth be found.
My whole existence
Shall thee be offered,
Until at last they lay me in the grave.

[1.] *Herzog* 'duke' seems inappropriate in its literal sense. Its etymological meaning, 'leader of the army' (cf. *Herr* and *ziehen*), is similar to that of its Latin cognate *dux*. One might prefer to translate with "leader" or "guide," but "Lord" seems to have the proper connotations of rank and function.

BWV 124 **Meinen Jesum laß ich nicht**

First Sunday after Epiphany.

Poet unknown.

1. Christian Keymann, verse 1 of the hymn, 1658 (Fischer-Tümpel, IV, #13); 2-5. based loosely on verses 2-5, respectively; 6. verse 6 of the hymn.

7 January 1725, Leipzig.

BG 26; NBA I/5.

1. Chorus [Verse 1] (S, A, T, B)

This my Jesus I'll not leave,
Since his life for me he offered;
Thus by duty I am bound
Limpet-like to him forever.
He is light unto my life,
This my Jesus I'll not leave.

2. Recit. (T)

As long as yet a drop of blood
In heart and veins is stirring,
Shall Jesus, he alone,
My life and my existence be.
My Jesus, who for me such wond'rous things hath done.
I can, indeed, nought but my life and body
To him as presents offer.

3. Aria (T)

And when the cruel stroke of death
My thoughts corrupt, my members weaken,
And comes the flesh's hated day,
Which only fear and terror follow,
My comfort is my firm resolve:
I will my Jesus never leave.

4. Recit. (B)

Alas!
What grievous toil and woe
Perceiveth here e'en now my spirit?
Will not my sore-offended breast
Become a wilderness and den of yearning
For Jesus, its most painful loss?

But still, my soul with faith looks up,
E'en to that place where faith and hope shine radiant,
And where I, once my course is run,
Shall, Jesus, evermore embrace thee.

5. Aria (S, A)

Withdraw thyself quickly, my heart, from the world,
Thou shalt find in heaven thy true satisfaction.

> When one day thine eye shall the Savior behold,
> At last shall thy passionate heart be restored,
> Where it will in Jesus contentment receive.

6. Chorus [Verse 6] (S, A, T, B)

Jesus I'll not let leave me,
I will ever walk beside him;
Christ doth let me more and more
To the spring of life be guided.
Blessed he who saith with me:
This my Jesus I'll not leave.

BWV 125 Mit Fried und Freud ich fahr dahin

Purification of St. Mary the Virgin (The Presentation of Christ in the Temple).

Poet unknown.

1. Martin Luther, verse 1 of the hymn (an adaptation of "Nunc dimittis"), 1524 (Wackernagel, III, 25); 3. verse 2 with interpolated recitative; 4-5. based on elements of verse 3; 6. verse 4 of the hymn.

2 February 1725, Leipzig.

BG 26; NBA I/28.

---

1. Chorus [Verse 1] (S, A, T, B)

In peace and joy do I depart,
As God doth will it;
Consoled am I in mind and heart,
Calm and quiet;
As God me his promise gave,
My death is to sleep altered.

2. Aria (A)

I would e'en with my broken vision
To thee, my faithful Savior, look.

When once my body's form shall break,
Yet shall my heart and hope not fall.
My Jesus cares for me in dying
And shall let me no grief attend.

3. Recit. and Chorale [Verse 2] (B)

O wonder, that one's heart
Before the flesh's hated tomb and even death's distress
Should not be frightened!
This Christ hath done, God's own true son,
The faithful Savior,
Who o'er my dying bed now stands
With heaven's sweet repose my soul to comfort,
Whom thou, O Lord, hast let me see,
When at the final hour an arm of faith shall grasp the Lord's salvation;
Thou hast revealed

Of the Almighty God, creator of all nature,
That he salvation is and life,
Of men the hope and share,
Their Savior from corruption
In death as well in dying.

4. Aria (T, B)

A great mysterious light hath filled the orb of all the earth now.

> There echoes strongly on and on
> A word of promise most desired:
> In faith shall all be blessed.

5. Recit. (A)

O unexhausted store of kindness,
Which to us mortals is revealed: one day the world,
Which wrath's curse on itself hath summoned,
A throne of mercy[1]
And sign of triumph shall receive,
And every faithful heart and spirit
Shall to his realm of grace be summoned.

6. Chorale [Verse 4] (S, A, T, B)

He is that grace and blessed light,
Which the nations
Shall illumine, all who know thee not,
And shall nurture;
To Israel, thy people,
The praise, laud, joy and gladness.

---

[1]   Cf. *Rom.* 3:25.

BWV 126 Erhalt uns, Herr, bei deinem Wort

Sexagesima Sunday.

Poet unknown.

1. Martin Luther, verse 1 of the hymn, 1542 (Wackernagel, III, #44ff.);
2. based on verse 2; 3. verse 3 with interpolated recitative; 4-5. based
on two supplemental verses to Luther's hymn by Justus Jonas (1493-
1555), "Ihr Anschläg, Herr" and "So werden sie"; 6. Martin Luther,
German version of "Da pacem Domine," 1529 (Wackernagel, III,
#35ff.), with its traditional supplementary verse by Johann Walter,
1566 (after 1 *Tim.* 2:2).

4 February 1725, Leipzig.

BG 26; NBA I/7, 157.

1. Chorus [Verse 1] (S, A, T, B)

Maintain us, Lord, within thy word,
And fend off murd'rous Pope and Turk,
Who Jesus Christ, thy very Son,
Strive to bring down from his throne.

2. Aria (T)

Send down thy great strength from heaven,
Prince of princes, mighty God,

>This thy church to fill with gladness
>And the foe's most bitter scorn
>In an instant far to scatter!

3. Recit. and Chorale [Verse 3] (A, T)

(A)
All human will and might will little help us,
If thou wouldst not protect thy wretched people,

(Both)
God, Holy Ghost, dear comforter;

(T)
Thou see'st that this tormented city of God
The worst of foes but in itself doth have
Through the great danger posed by untrue brothers.

(Both)
Thy people make of one mind on earth,

(A)
That we, the members of Christ's body,
In faith agree, in life united be.

(Both)
Stand by us in extremity!

(T)
Although e'en now the final foe break in
And seek thy comfort from our hearts to sever,
Yet in that moment show thyself our helper.

(Both)
Lead us to life and free from death!

4. Aria (B)

Crash down in ruin, arrogant bombast!
Hurl to destruction what it conceives!

> Let the abyss now quickly devour them,
> Fend off the raging of the foe's might,
> Let their desires ne'er find satisfaction.

5. Recit. (T)

Thus will thy word and truth be manifest
And set themselves in highest glory forth,
Since thou dost for thy church keep watch,
Since thou thy holy Gospel's teachings
To prosp'rous fruit dost bring;
And if thou dost as helper seek our presence,
To us will then in peacetime
Abundant blessing be apportioned.

6. Chorale (S, A, T, B)

Grant to us peace most graciously,
Lord God, in our own season;
For there is surely no one else
Who for us could do battle
Than thou who our God art only.
Give to our lords and all authority
Peace and good governance,
So that we beneath them
A most calm and quiet life may lead forever
In godliest devotion and honesty.
Amen.

BWV 127 **Herr Jesu Christ, wahr' Mensch und Gott**

Estomihi (Quinquagesima Sunday).

Poet unknown.

1. Paul Eber, verse 1 of the hymn, 1562 (Wackernagel, IV, #2); 2. based freely on verses 2 and 3; 3. based freely on verse 4; 4. first part based freely on verse 5, second part on verse 6 and 7; 5. verse 8 of the hymn.

11 February 1725, Leipzig.

BG 26; NBA I/8.

---

1. Chorus [Verse 1] (S, A, T, B)

Lord Jesus Christ, true man and God,
Thou, who bore torture, fear and scorn,
For me on cross at last didst die
And me thy Father's grace didst win,
I beg by thy most bitter pain:
For all my sins be merciful.

2. Recit. (T)

When ev'rything at that last hour strikes terror,
And when a chilling sweat of death
My limbs, all stiff with torpor, moistens,
When this my tongue can nought but feeble sighing speak,
And this my heart doth break:
Enough is it that faith doth know
That Jesus by me stands,

Who with great patience to his passion goes
And through this toilsome way doth lead me also
And my repose is now preparing.

3. Aria (S)

My soul shall rest in Jesus' bosom,[1]
When earth doth this my body hide.

> Ah, call me soon, O deathly tolling,
> I am at dying undismayed,
> For me my Jesus shall awake.

4. Recit. and Aria (B)

When once at last the trumps have sounded,
And when the world's own frame
With heaven's firm foundation
Is smashed and sunk in ruin,
Then think on me, my God, with favor;
When once thy thrall before thy court doth stand,
Where e'en my thoughts seek to accuse me,[2]
Then may'st thou wish alone,
O Jesus, my defense to be
And to my spirit speak with comfort:

In truth, in truth, I say to you:[3]
When heaven and earth shall in fire have perished,
Yet shall all believers eternally prosper.[4]

> They will not come into the court[5]
> And death eternal shall not taste.[6]
> But ever cleave,
> My child, to me:
> I'll break with my mighty and rescuing hand
> The violent bonds of encompassing death.

5. Chorale [Verse 8] (S, A, T, B)

Ah, Lord, forgive us all our sins,
Help us with patience to abide
Until our hour of death shall come,
And help our faith e'er steadfast be,
Thy word to trust tenaciously,
Until we rest in blessed sleep.

---

1.   OP usually has *Wunden* instead of *Hünden*. Translate "wounds then" or
     "sorrows."

2.   Cf. *Rom.* 2:15.

3.   Verbatim from the hymn.

4.   Cf. *Mt.* 24:35.

5.   Cf. *Jn.* 5:24; verbatim from the hymn.

6.   Cf. *Jn.* 8:52; verbatim from the hymn.

BWV 128 **Auf Christi Himmelfahrt allein**

Ascension.

Christiane Mariane von Ziegler, *Versuch in Gebundener Schreibart, Teil I*
(Leipzig, 1728); Facs: Neumann T, p. 361. 1. Ernst Sonnemann,
verse 1 of the hymn (after Josua Wegelin), 1661 (Fischer-Tümpel,
III, #304); 2-4. several departures from Ziegler's PT; 5. Matthäus
Avenarius, verse 4 of "O Jesu, meine Lust," 1673 (Fischer-Tümpel,
IV, #452).

10 May 1725, Leipzig.

BG 26; NBA I/12.

1. Chorus [Chorale] (S, A, T, B)

On Christ's ascent to heaven alone
I base my journey to him,
And all my doubting, fear and pain
Thereby I'll ever conquer;
For as the head in heaven dwells,
So shall its members Jesus Christ
In all due time recover.

2. Recit. (T)

I am prepared, come, summon me!
Here in the world
Is trouble, fear and pain;
But there instead, in Salem's tent,
Will I transfigured dwell.
There I'll see God from countenance to countenance,
As me his holy word assures.[1]

3. Aria and Recit. (B)

Up, up, with lively sound
Announced to all the world:
My Jesus sits beside him!
Who seeks now to oppose me?
Though he is taken from me,
I shall one day come thither
Where my redeemer lives.
With mine own eyes will I in perfect clearness see him.
If I could but before that time a shelter build me!
But why? O useless wish!
He dwelleth not on hill, in vale,
His power is o'er all revealed;
So hush, presumptuous mouth,
And do not strive this very might to fathom!

4. Aria (A, T)

His boundless might to fathom
No mortal will be able,
My mouth falls dumb and still.

> I see, though, through the heavens
> That he e'en at this distance
> At God's right hand appears.[2]

5. Chorale (S, A, T, B)

Therefore then shalt thou me
Upon thy right hand station[3]
And me as to thy child
A gracious judgment render,
Bring me into that joy
Where on thy majesty
I will hold fast my gaze
For all eternity.

---

[1] Cf. 1 *Cor.* 13:12.
[2] Cf. *Acts* 7:55.
[3] Cf. *Mt.* 25:33.

BWV 129 **Gelobet sei der Herr, mein Gott**

Trinity.

Johann Olearius, the five verses of the hymn, 1665 (Fischer-Tümpel, IV, #398).

16 June 1726 or 8 June 1727, Leipzig.

BG 26; NBA I/15.

1. Chorus [Verse 1] (S, A, T, B)

Give honor to the Lord,
My God, my light, my being,
My maker, who hath me
My soul and body given,
My Father, who hath kept
Me since my mother's womb,
Who every moment hath
Much good for me fulfilled.

2. Aria [Verse 2] (B)

Give honor to the Lord,
My God, my health, my being,
The Father's dearest Son,
Himself for me hath given,
Himself hath me redeemed
With his own precious blood,
Who me through faith doth give
Himself, the highest good.

3. Aria [Verse 3] (S)

Give honor to the Lord,
My God, my hope, my being,
The Father's Holy Ghost,
Whom me the Son hath given,
Who doth my heart restore,
Who me doth give new strength,
Who me in all distress
Word, hope and help provides.

4. Aria [Verse 4] (A)

Give honor to the Lord,
My God, who always liveth,

Whom all things honor which
In every sphere now hover;
Give honor to the Lord,
Whose name is holy called,
God Father, God the Son
And God the Holy Ghost.

5. Choral [Verse 5] (S, A, T, B)

Whom we that "Holy" now
With gladness make to echo
And with the angels' host
Are "Holy, Holy" singing,
Whom deeply laud and praise
Doth all Christianity:
Give honor to my God
For all eternity!

BWV 130 **Herr Gott, dich loben alle wir**

St. Michael and All Angels.

Poet unknown.

1. Paul Eber, verse 1 of the hymn, ca. 1561 (Wackernagel, IV, #1), an adaptation of Philipp Melanchthon's "Dicimus grates tibi," 1539; 2. based freely on verses 2 and 3; 3. based freely on verses 4-6; 4. based freely on verse 7-10; 5. Neumann T: based on other Michaelmas hymns (cf. BWV 19/7); Dürr: based freely on verse 10 of the hymn.

29 September 1724, Leipzig.

BG 26; NBA I/30.

1. Chorus [Verse 1] (S, A, T, B)

Lord God, we praise thee every one
And shall give willing thanks to thee
For this thy work, the angels, now,
Which round thee flock about thy throne

2. Recit. (A)

Their radiance and lofty wisdom show
How God doth to us mortals bend,
Who such defenders, such great armor
For us hath fashioned.
In praising him they take no rest;
Their whole endeavor hath but one intent,
That they, Lord Christ, round thee be
And round thy wretched company:[1]
How needed is indeed this care
Midst Satan's rage and might?

3. Aria (B)

The ancient serpent burns with spite,
Contriving e'er to bring new pain,
To bring our little band division.

He seeks to crush what God doth own,
And ply deceit,
For he no rest or slumber knoweth.

4. Recit. (S, T)

Well though for us that day and night
The host of angels watch,
That Satan's onslaught might be broken!

A Daniel who amidst the lions sits[2]
Doth learn how him the hand of angels guards.
As once the coals
In Babel's furnace did no injury,[3]
So let the faithful raise their thankful voices,
That still in danger's midst
E'en now the angels' help comes forth.

5. Aria (T)

Let, O Prince of holy Cherubs,
This heroic lofty throng
Evermore
O'er thy faithful flock be tending.

    That they on Elijah's chariot
    Them to thee in heaven carry.

6. Chorale (S, A, T, B)

For this we give thee willing praise
And give thee thanks, God, evermore,
Just as thine own dear angel host
Thee laud today and ever shall.
And ask that thou shouldst ever wish
To order them to be prepared
To shelter this thy tiny flock,
Which keeps thy sacred word intact.

[1.] This and the preceding line are verbatim from the hymn.
[2.] Cf. *Dan.* 6:16.
[3.] Cf. *Dan.* 3.

BWV 131 **Aus der Tiefen rufe ich, Herr, zu dir**

Unspecified Occasion.

Perhaps by Georg Christian Eilmar.

1. *Ps.* 130:1-2; 2. *Ps.* 130:3-4 and Bartholomäus Ringwaldt, verse 2 of "Herr Jesus Christ, du höchstes Gut," 1582 (Wackernagel, IV, #1523); 3. *Ps.* 13:5; 4. *Ps.* 130:6 and Ringwaldt, verse 5 of the hymn; 5. *Ps.* 130:7-8.

1707-1708, Mühlhausen.

BG 28; NBA I/34.

---

1. Chorus [Dictum] (S, A, T, B)

From the depths now do[1] call, Lord, to thee. Lord, hear my voice's crying, and let thine ears consider well the voice of my complaining.

2. Arioso [Dictum] (B) and Chorale (S)

(B)
If thou willt, Lord, mark what is sinful, Lord, who will abide it?

(S)
Have mercy on me in such grief,
Remove it from my bosom,
Because thou hast now paid for it
On wood with pains of dying,

(B)
For with thee there is forgiveness, that we might fear thee.

(S)
So that I might with grievous woe
Within my sinful state not die,
Nor give up hope forever.

3. Chorus [Dictum] (S, A, T, B)

I wait for the Lord, this my spirit waiteth, and I put trust in his word.

4. Aria (T) and Choral (A)

(T)
This my spirit waiteth for the Lord before one morning watch until the next watch.

(A)
Especially that in my heart,
As I have long lamented,
I, too, an anxious sinner am,
Who is by conscience rankled,
And would so glad within thy blood
From sinfulness be washed and pure
Like David and Manasseh.[2]

5. Chorus [Dictum] (S, A, T, B)

Israel, trust now in the Lord; for with the Lord there is mercy, and much redemption with him.
And he shall Israel deliver from all of his transgressions.

[1.] With *ruf' ich* omit "do."
[2.] Cf. 2 *Sam.* 12:13 and 2 *Chr.* 33:13.

BWV 132 **Bereitet die Wege, bereitet die Bahn!**

Fourth Sunday in Advent.

Salomo Franck, *Evangelisches Andachts-Opffer . . . in geistlichen Cantaten* (Leipzig, 1715); Facs: Neumann T, p. 275.

6. Elisabeth Kreuziger, verse 5 of "Herr Christ, der einig Gotts Sohn," 1524 (Wackernagel, III, #67).

22 December 1715, Weimar.

BG 28; NBA I/11.

1. Aria (S)

Make ready the pathways, make ready the road![1]

> Make ready the pathways
> And make every byway
> In faith and in living
> Now smooth for the Highest,
> Messiah shall come!

2. Recit. (T)

If thou wouldst call thyself God's child and Christ's own brother,
Then freely thy heart and mouth the Savior must acknowledge.
Yes, man, thy life entirely
Must by its faith give constant witness!
If Christ's own word and teaching
E'en through thy blood is to be sealed,
Thyself then willing give!
Because this is the Christian's crown and glory.

Meanwhile, my heart, make ready,
Today yet,
To God the way of faith
And clear away the high hills and the mountains
Which in the path oppose him!
Roll back the heavy stones of error,
Receive thy Savior now,
That he with thee in faith may be united!

3. Aria (B)

Who art thou? Question thine own conscience,
Thou shalt without hypocrisy,
If thou, O man, art false or true,
Thy proper judgment have to hear now.
Who art thou? Question the commandment
Which will then tell thee who thou art,
A child of wrath in Satan's clutches,
A Christian false and hypocrite.

4. Recitative (A)

I will, my God, to thee make free confession, I have not thee till now
in truth confessed.
Although my mouth and lips have named thee Lord and Father,
My heart no less hath from thee turned away.
I have thee disavowed within my living!
How canst thou then for me good witness offer?
When, Jesus, me thy Spirit's waters bathed
And made me clean of all my sinful deeds,
I did in truth swear constant faith unto thee;
Ah! Ah, alas! Baptism's bond is broken.
I rue my faithlessness!
Ah God, be merciful,
Ah, help that I with loyalty unswerving
The bond of grace through faith renew forever!

5. Aria (A)

Christ's own members, ah, consider
What the Savior you hath granted
Through baptism's cleansing bath![2]
By this spring of blood and water
Are your garments all made radiant
Which were stained by sinful deeds.
Christ then gave as your new raiment
Crimson purple, silken whiteness,[3]
These now are the Christians' dress.

[6. Chorale (S, A, T, B)][4]

Us mortify through thy kindness,
Arouse us through thy dear grace;
The ancient man make weaker,
So that the new may live
E'en here while on earth dwelling,
His mind and every yearning,
His thoughts inclined to thee.

[1.]   *Is.* 40:3.
[2.]   Cf. BWV 162 for the baptismal theme.
[3.]   Cf. *Rev.* 7:13-14 and BWV 162/4.
[4.]   This is the chorale Franck intended. Bach's score lacks the final chorale.

BWV 133 **Ich freue mich in dir**

Third Day of Christmas (St. John, Apostle and Evangelist).

Poet unknown.

1. Kaspar Ziegler, verse 1 of the hymn, 1697 (Fischer-Tümpel, I,

#567); 2-3. based freely on verse 2; 4-5. based freely on verse 3; 6. 4th and final verse of the hymn.

27 December 1724, Leipzig; Neumann Hb: again after 1735.

BG 28; NBA I/3.

---

1. Chorus [Verse 1] (S, A, T, B)

I find my joy in thee
And bid thee hearty welcome,
My dearest Jesus-child!
Thou hast here undertaken
My brother dear to be.
Ah, what a pleasing sound!
How friendly he appears,
This mighty Son of God!

2. Aria (A)

Take hope! A holy body holds
Almighty God's mysterious being.

> I have now God—how well for me this moment!—
> From countenance to countenance regarded.
> Ah, this my soul must now recover.

3. Recit. (T)

An Adam may when filled with terror
From God's own countenance
In paradise seek hiding![1]
But here Almighty God himself doth come to us:
And thus no fear oppresseth now my heart:

It knoweth his forgiving disposition.
Of his unbounded kindness
He's born a tiny babe
Who's called my Jesus-child.[2]

4. Aria (S)

How lovely to my ears it ringeth,
This word: for me is born my Jesus!
How this doth reach into my heart!

> Who Jesus' name can't comprehend,
> He whom it strikes not to the heart,
> He must of hardest rock be made.

5. Recit. (B)

Well then, to fear and pain of death
No thought will give my strengthened heart.
If he from heaven would
The road to earth now journey,
Then will he, too, of me
Within my tomb be mindful.
Who Jesus truly knows
Will die not when he dies,
If he calls Jesus' name.[3]

6. Chorale (S, A, T, B)

Lead on, 'tis my desire
To cleave to thee, O Jesus,
E'en though the world should break
Into a thousand pieces.
O Jesus, thou, just thou,
Thou art my life alone;

428   CANTATAS

In thee, alone in thee,
My Jesus, will I sleep.

[1.] Cf. *Gen.* 3:8.
[2.] This and the preceding line are verbatim from verse 2 of the hymn.
[3.] This and the two preceding lines are verbatim from verse 3 of the hymn.

BWV 134 **Ein Herz, das seinen Jesum leben weiß**

Third Day of Easter (Easter Tuesday).

Poet unknown; PT (Leipzig, 1724); Facs: Neumann T, p. 430; PT (Leipzig, 1731); Facs: Neumann T, p. 441.

11 April 1724, Leipzig; again after 1731, Leipzig; Parody: ← BWV 134a/1-4, 7, 8.

BG 28; NBA I/10.

---

1. Recit. (T, A)

(T)
A heart which doth its Jesus clearly know
Perceiveth Jesus' new compassion
And fashions nought but for his Savior praise.

(A)
How happy is a faithful heart and spirit!

2. Aria (T)

Rise, ye of faith, sing ye the songs of rejoicing,
Upon you now glorious a new light doth shine.

The living Redeemer bestows times of blessing;
Rise, spirits, ye must now a sacrifice offer
And pay to the Highest your duty with thanks.

3. Recit. (T, A)

(T)
Well thee, God hath remembered thee,
O thou, God's hallowed property;
The Savior lives and wins with might,
To bring thee health, to his own praise
Here now must Satan fear and tremble
And even hell itself be shaken.
The Savior dieth for thy sake
And for thy sake to hell doth journey;
He even poureth out his precious blood,
That thou within his blood prevail,
For this is what the foe shall vanquish,
And whene'er strife about thy soul doth press,
That thou e'en then not be o'ercome and fall.

(A)
The power of love, this shall my standard be
For bravery, for strength amidst the battle:
To gain for me the crown of triumph
Didst thou the crown of thorns accept,
My Lord, my God, my Savior now aris'n,
And now no foe on me may work his harm.

(T)
The foes, indeed, are past all counting.

(A)
God guards the souls to him e'er faithful.

(T)
The final foe is tomb, and death.[1]

(A)
God maketh it the end of all our woe.

4. Aria (A, T)

We thank thee and praise thee for thy warm affection
And bring now an off'ring from our lips to thee.

> The victor awakens the songs of rejoicing,
> The Savior appeareth and comforts us further[2]
> And strengthens the church, now divided, himself.

5. Recit. (T, A)

(T)
But rouse, thyself, the thanks within our voices,
When they too much to earth are bound;
Yea, bring to pass that every moment
Thee and thy work no mortal heart forget;
Yea, let in thee refreshment of our breasts
And joy and comfort of all hearts
Which trust in thy protecting mercy
Both perfect and unending be.
And may thy hand now us embrace,
That we the end may clearly witness
Which us thy death and triumph win,
And that we after thine own resurrection
Not die, although we die in time,
And we thereby to thy great majesty now enter.

(A)
All in our power exalts thee, mighty God,
And lauds thee for thy grace and faith;

Thy resurrection hath these now renewed,
Thy mighty triumph us from foe doth free
And into life doth bring us;
To thee, thus, praise and thanks be given.

6. Chorus (S, A, T, B)

O echo, ye heavens, O earth, be thou gladdened,
Sing praise to the Highest, thou throng of great faith!
Now seeth and tasteth each spirit among us
The infinite kindness of our living Savior;
With comfort he comes as a victor to us.

[1.]   Cf. 1 *Cor.* 15:26.

[2.]   Cf. *Lk.* 24:36.

BWV 134a **Die Zeit, die Tag und Jahre macht**

New Year's Congratulations for the Princely House of Anhalt-Cöthen.

Adapted from Christian Friedrich Hunold (Menantes), *Auserlesene und theils noch nie gedruckte Gedichte . . ., 11.-20. Stück* (Halle, 1719); Facs: Neumann T, p. 267.

1 January 1719, Cöthen; Parody: 1-4, 7, 8 → BWV 134.

BG 29 (incomplete); NBA I/35.

[Serenata]¹

Divine Providence (A), Time (T)

1. Recit. (T, A) Time, Divine Providence

(Time)
Now time, which day and year doth make,
Hath Anhalt many hours of blessing
And even now hath new salvation brought.
(Divine Providence)
O noble time, with God's own grace united!

2. Aria (T) Time

Up, mortal ones, let now your triumph be sounding;
Upon you now doth a new light divine shine!
With mercy is heaven now crowning the ages,
Up, spirits, ye must now a sacrifice offer
And pay to the Highest your duty with thanks!

3. Recit. (T, A) Time, Divine Providence

(Time)
As soon thou didst the stars' grace hold,
O much admiréd princely house,
Did I bring forth dear Leopold.²
To thy good health, to his great fame
Have I him many years now favored
And him to those a new year added.
I still adorn this godly house,
Bedecking Anhalts princely heaven
With fresh new light and radiant beams of grace;
Still doth all dearth these borders widely shun;
Still fleeth all deathly tumult;

Still bloometh here the golden age:
So praise then God on high for his good will!

(Divine Providence)
The Highest's fame is to the magnet like,
When from above more strength to it it draweth.
For this must all wise princes flourish
To make a land in fortune blest.
Thee hath, O Time, for more prosperity
Unto this house the Lord of ages chos'n.

(Time)
What do I lack in gifts of favor?

(Divine Providence)
Still greater ones have I to offer.

(Time)
My fame is now already rare.

(Divine Providence)
To God's renown will it yet greater be.

4. Aria (A, T) Divine Providence, Time

(Divine Providence, Time)

<pre>
                  triumph   soon coming
Now quarrel, now {   } the {   } ages
                  glory   earlier
</pre>

With blessing for this most illustrious house.
This friendly contention all hearts now bestirreth

(Time)
To strike up the lyres,

(Divine Providence)
to combat,

(Time)
to jesting,

(Both)
And strive to the glory of Almighty God.

5. Recit. (A, T) Divine Providence, Time

(Divine Providence)
Consider, though, O happy land,
How much I thee in this own age have given.
In Leopold thou hast a bond of grace.
Behold his Lady's wisdom bright,
Behold the Prince's life so noble,
Behold his daughter's crown of grace,
All that his house no splendor lack
And thou no timely good should need.
If I thy future strength must ready,
Then gain thou from the starry pole
By thine appeal their lofty princely weal!
Come, Anhalt, pray for greater years and ages!

(Time)
Ah! Pray for this great bliss;
For lacking God and them
I would not for a moment's time
For thee contented be.
Yes, Anhalt, yes, thou bendest now the knee,
Thine ardent wishes join the plea.
But yet, O kindly destiny!
God tends himself to these illustrious spirits,

And to this realm's most virtuous candles,[3]
Which burn for him in ardent worship fair.
Because God doth so love their warmth,
There comes to them a priceless store of wealth,
And to this land much temporal success.

6. Aria (A) Divine Providence

The ages' Lord such store of happy moments,
Thou godly house, to thee so long hath dealt.

> For in that harmony of spirits
> Who God their shield and strength have chosen,
> Is heaven's bliss so glad to join its voice.

7. Recit. (T, A) Time, Divine Providence

(Time)
Help, Master, help that now all mortals praise me
And promise this world-famous house
No evil, only golden ages.
Come, pour o'er them the streams of blessedness!
Yea, through my aid may dearest Leopold,
To many thousands' health and joy,
Who here beneath his grace are dwelling,
Until grey age thy favor hold!
Enliven this his godly breast!
Let to these most illustrious persons,
Whom thou to thine own praise didst choose,
On whom till now thy gracious light shone brightly,
In nought but full prosperity
This fairest age yet many years do service!
Renew, O Lord, with every season's change
Upon them thy good faith and love!

(Divine Providence)
The Master's grace is every morning new.
Now shall his care, his Spirit's special grace,
Around such princes hover
Who in the Prince of Life are living.

8. Chorus [Aria] (T, A, and S, A, T, B) Time, Divine Providence

(Time)
Give pleasure terrestrial,

> (Divine Providence)
> give gladness celestial,

(Tutti)
O fortunate ages, bring joy to this house!

(Divine Providence, Time)
'Tis right that with these most illustrious spirits
  The mercy
{   } of heaven should choose to find dwelling;
  The blessing

(Tutti)
Their fortune, their long life, let ev'ryone cry!

[1.] This title is found in the PT.

[2.] Twice in this cantata, here and in movement 7, *hold* is rhymed with *Leopold*. *Hold* 'gracious, favoring' is cognate with *Huld* 'grace, favor.' Perhaps the rhyme calls attention to the etymology of Leopold 'bold for the people.' The rhyme would also have suited the name of Hunold himself, whose pseudonym Menantes looks as though it were from Greek *meinein* 'to wait, abide, stand firm.'

[3.] The 'candles of virtue' are the members of the noble house.

BWV 135 **Ach Herr, mich armen Sünder**

Third Sunday after Trinity.

Poet unknown.

1. Cyriakus Schneegass, verse 1 of the hymn, 1597; the cantus firmus in the bass is the melody of "Herzlich thut mir verlangen" (cf. BWV 161/1); 2-5. based freely on verse 2-5, respectively; 6. verse 6 of the hymn.

25 June 1724, Leipzig.

BG 28; NBA I/16.

1. Chorus [Verse 1] (S, A, T, B)

Ah Lord, me a poor sinner
Blame not within thy wrath;
Thy solemn rage yet soften,
Else is my hope forlorn.
Ah Lord, may'st thou forgive me
My sin and mercy send,
That I have life eternal
And flee the pain of hell.

2. Recit. (T)

Ah, heal me now, thou soul's physician,
I am so ill and weak;
One could in truth my bones all number,
So grievously have this my toil and woe,
My cross and sorrow dealt with me;

My countenance
Is full of tears and now all swollen;
Like rapid streams they are, which down my cheeks are rolling.
My soul is now with terror torn and anxious;
Ah, thou Lord, why this waiting?[1]

3. Aria (T)

Comfort me, Jesus, in my spirit,
Or I'll sink now into death;
Lift me, lift me through thy dear kindness
From my spirit's great distress.
For in death is nought but stillness,
Where for thee no thought is given.[2]
Dearest Jesus, if it please thee,
Fill with joy my countenance!

4. Recit. (A)

I am from sighing weary,[3]
My soul hath neither strength nor might,
For I the whole night through,
Oft lacking peace of mind and calmness,
In copious sweat and tears am lying.
I fear nigh unto death and am with mourning old,
For my great fear is manifold.

5. Aria (B)

Yield, all ye evildoers,[4]
My Jesus comforts me!

He brings, when past are tears and weeping,
The sun of joy once more its radiance;
The storms of sadness are transformed,

The enemy must sudden perish
And their own darts recoil against them.

6. Chorale [Verse 6] (S, A, T, B)

In heaven's throne be glory
With lofty fame and praise
To Son and to the Father
As well in equal wise
To Holy Ghost with honor
For all eternity,
Who shall us all let share in
Eternal blessedness

---

1. This line is verbatim from verse 2 of the hymn.
2. Cf. *Ps.* 6:6. This line is verbatim from verse 3 of the hymn.
3. This line is verbatim from verse 4 of the hymn.
4. This line is verbatim from verse 5 of the hymn.

BWV 136 **Erforsche mich, Gott, und erfahre mein Herz**

Eighth Sunday after Trinity.

Poet unknown.

1. *Ps.* 139:23; 6. Johann Heermann, verse 9 of "Wo soll ich fliehen hin," 1630 (Fischer-Tümpel, I, #322).

18 July 1723, Leipzig.

BG 28; NBA I/18.

---

1. Chorus [Dictum] (S, A, T, B)

Examine me, God, and discover my heart; prove thou me and discover what my thoughts are.

2. Recit. (T)

Ah, that the curse which then the earth did strike[1]
As well mankind to heart hath stricken!
Who can for righteous fruit be hopeful
While this foul curse into the soul so pierceth,
That it the thorns of sin now yieldeth
And wicked thistles bears?
But often themselves are wont hell's very children
As angels of light to put forward;
As though in this corrupted nature
From thorns like these one grapes could harvest.
A wolf would make the purest wool his cover,
But once the day breaks forth,
He'll be, ye feigners, a terror,
Yea, not to be endured.

3. Aria (A)

There comes the day
To bring concealment judgment,
At which hypocrisy may quake with fear.

For then his zealous wrath will ruin
What strategem and lies have woven.

4. Recit. (B)

The heavens are themselves not pure,[2]
How shall then now a man before this judge e'er stand?
But he whom Jesus' blood hath cleansèd,

Who is through faith to him united,
Knows that o'er him he'll no harsh judgment pass.
If he's by sin still vexed,
By weakness of his efforts,
He hath in Christ, no less,
Both righteousness and power.

5. Aria (T, B)

We feel in truth the marks of error
Which Adam's fall on us have placed.

> But yet, who hath in Jesus' wounding,
> That mighty stream of blood, found refuge,
> Is by it purified anew.

6. Chorale (S, A, T, B)

Thy blood, that liquid rich,
Hath such great force and strength
That e'en the merest trickle
Can all the world deliver,
Yea, from the jaws of Satan,
Set free and disencumber.

---

[1] Cf. *Gen.* 3:17-18.
[2] Cf. *Job* 15:15.

BWV 137 **Lobe den Herren, den mächtigen König der Ehren**

Twelfth Sunday after Trinity.

Joachim Neander, the five verses of the hymn, 1680.

19 August 1725, Leipzig.

BG 28; NBA I/20.

---

1. Chorus [Verse 1] (S, A, T, B)

Praise the Almighty, the powerful king of all honor,
O thou my spirit belovéd, that is my desire.
Come ye in throngs,
Psalt'ry and lyre, awake!
Let now the music be sounding.

2. Aria [Verse 2] (A)

Praise the Almighty, who all things so gloriously ruleth,
Who upon pinions of eagles to safety doth lead thee;
He thee protects
As even thee it will please;
Hast thou of this no perception?

3. Aria [Verse 3] (S, B)

Praise the Almighty, who doth with his splendor adorn thee,
Who hath thy health given to thee, and kindly doth guide thee;
In what great need
Hath not the merciful God
Over thee his wings extended?

4. Aria [Verse 4] (T) with Instrum. Chorale

Praise the Almighty, who thine estate clearly hath favored,
Who doth from heaven with streams of his love blessing shower;
Think now on this,
What the Almighty can do,
Who with his love now hath met thee.

5. Chorale [Verse 5] (S, A, T, B)

Praise the Almighty, all that's in me, give his name honor.
All things that breath possess, praise him with Abraham's children!
He is thy light,
Spirit, yea, this forget not;
Praising him, close thou with amen!

BWV 138 **Warum betrübst du dich, mein Herz?**

Fifteenth Sunday after Trinity.

Poet unknown.

1. Verse 1 of the hymn, Nürnberg, 1561,[1] with interpolated recitative;
3. verse 2 with interpolated recitative; 7. verse 3 of the hymn.

5 September 1723, Leipzig.

BG 28; NBA I/22.

1. Chorus [Verse 1] (S, A, T, B) and Recit. (A)

(S, A, T, B)
Why art thou troubled, O my heart?
Art anxious and bowed down with grief
For merely temporal worth?

(A)
Ah, I am poor,
Bowed down with heavy sorrow.
From evening until morning
Endures my wonted need.

May God forgive!
Who will me yet deliver
From out the belly of this
Malignant world?[2]
How wretchedly am I disposed!
Ah! Were I only dead!

(S, A, T, B)
Put trust in this thy Lord and God,
Who ev'rything created hath.

2. Recit. (B)

I am despised,
The Lord hath made me suffer
Upon the day of his great wrath.
Provisions for my keeping
Are rather small;
They pour for me as wine of gladness
The bitter chalice filled with tears.
How can I now my post maintain in calmness
When sighing is my portion and tears are all I have to drink?[3]

3. Chorale [Verse 2] (S, A, T, B) and Recit. (S, A)

(S, A, T, B)
He can and would thee not forsake,
He knows full well what thou dost lack;
Heaven and earth are his.

(S)
Ah! What?
God clearly careth for the kine,
He gives the birds their proper nurture,
He filleth the fledgling ravens.[4]
But I, I know not in what manner

I, wretched child,
My bit of bread shall garner;
Where is the man who will for my deliv'rance strive?

(S, A, T, B)
Thy Father and the Lord thy God,
Who stands by thee in every need.

(A)
I am forsaken,
It seems
As if e'en God himself in my poor state would hate me.
Though he hath ever meant the best for me.
Ah sorrows,
Will ye then be every morning
And every day again made new?
I cry continually ;
Ah! Poorness, cruel word!
Who will stand by me then in my distress?

(S, A, T, B)
Thy Father and the Lord thy God,
Who stands by thee in every need.

4. Recit. (T)

Ah, comfort sweet! If God will not forsake me,
And not abandon me,[5]
Then can I in repose
And patience find courage.
The world may just the same despise me,
But I will cast my sorrows
With joy upon the Lord,
If he helps not today,
He'll help me yet tomorrow.
Now I'll most gladly lay

My cares beneath my pillow
And want to know no more than this for my true comfort:

5. Aria (B)

With God stands all my confidence,
My faith shall let him govern.

> Now can no apprehension nag me,
> Nor can now any want yet plague me.
> For e'en amidst the greatest sadness
> Bides he my Father, my true gladness,
> He shall in wond'rous wise protect me.

6. Recit. (A)

Well then!
Thus I'll as well find soft repose.
My sorrows, your divorcement[6] bill receive now!
Now I can live as though in heaven.

7. Chorale [Verse 3] (S, A, T, B)

Since thou my God and Father art,
Thy child wilt thou abandon not,
A father's heart thou hast!
I am a wretched clump of earth,
On earth I know not any hope.

---

[1] This hymn is sometimes attributed to Hans Sachs.

[2] Cf. *Rom.* 7:24.

[3] Cf. *Ps.* 42:3.

[4] Cf. *Ps.* 147:9.

[5] Cf. *Heb.* 13:5.

[6] The metaphorical *Scheidebrief* is probably inspired by *Mt.* 5:31, a passage near the Gospel lection appointed for this day.

BWV 139 **Wohl dem, der sich auf seinen Gott**

Twenty-third Sunday after Trinity.

Poet unknown.

1. Johann Christoph Rube, verse 1 of the hymn, 1692; the cantus firmus in the soprano is the melody of "Mach's mit mir, Gott, nach deiner Güt" (cf. BWV 156/1); 2. based freely on verse 2; 3. based freely on *Mt.* 22:15-22; 4-5. based freely on verses 3 and 4; 6. verse 5 of the hymn (same melody as in 1).

12 November 1724, Leipzig; again after 1744 (Neumann Hb). BG 28; NBA I/26.

1. Chorus [Verse 1] (S, A, T, B)

Blest he who self can to his God
With childlike trust abandon!
For though now sin and word and death
And every demon hate him,
Yet he'll be ever confident,
If he but God his friend doth make.

2. Aria (T)

God is my friend; what use that raging
Which now the foe hath raised against me!
I am consoled midst spite and hate.

> Yea, though ye tell the truth but rarely,
> Be ever false, what's that to me?
> Ye scorners are to me no danger.

3. Recit. (A)

The Savior sends, indeed, his people
Directly midst the angry wolves.[1]
About him have the lowly[2] rabble
Themselves, to harm and mock him,
With cunning ranged.
But since his mouth such wise response doth make,
He shields me also from the world.

4. Aria (B)

Misfortune wraps from all directions
Round me an hundredweight of chain.
Yet sudden appeareth the help of his hand.

> I see the light of hope from far off;
> I've learned at last that God alone
> To men the best of friends must be.[3]

5. Recit. (S)

Yea, though I bear my greatest foe within,
The heavy weight of error,
My Savior lets me find a solace.
I give to God what God doth own,[4]
My inmost heart and spirit.
If he will now accept them,
My debt of sin shall pass, and fall shall Satan's craft.

6. Chorale (S, A, T, B)

I therefore scorn the host of hell!
Scorn also death's jaws yawning!
Scorn all the world! No more can me
Its pounding fill with mourning!

God is my shield, my store and help;
Blest he who God as friend hath found!

---

1. Cf. *Mt.* 10:16.
2. For *Bösen* 'wicked' in a rather social sense, cf. Latin *mali* 'the lower classes.'
3. This and the preceding line are verbatim from the hymn.
4. Cf. *Mt.* 22:21.

BWV 140 **Wachet auf, ruft uns die Stimme**

Twenty-seventh Sunday after Trinity.

Poet unknown.

1, 4, and 7. Philipp Nicolai, verses 1-3 respectively of the hymn, 1599.

25 November 1731 and perhaps 1742, Leipzig.

BG 28; NBA I/27.

---

1. Chorus [Verse 1] (S, A, T, B)

Wake, arise, the voices call us
Of watchmen from the lofty tower;
Arise, thou town Jerusalem!
Midnight's hour doth give its summons;
They call to us with ringing voices;
Where are ye prudent virgins now?
Make haste, the bridegroom comes;
Rise up and take your lamps!
Alleluia!

Prepare to join
The wedding feast,
Go forth to meet him as he comes!

2. Recit. (T)

He comes, he comes,
The bridegroom comes![1]
O Zion's daughters, come ye forth,[2]
His journey hieth from the heavens[3]
Into your mother's house.[4]
The bridegroom comes, who to a roebuck
And youthful stag is like,[5]
Which on the hills doth leap;[6]
To you the marriage meal he brings.
Rise up, be lively now
The bridegroom here to welcome!
There, look now, thence he comes to meet you.

3. Aria (S, B) Soul, Jesus

(Soul)
When com'st thou, my Savior?[7]

(Jesus)
I'm coming, thy share.

(Soul)
I'm waiting with my burning oil.[8]

     (Soul, Jesus)
      Now open
     {   } the hall
      I open
     For heaven's rich meal.

(Soul)
Come, Jesus!

(Jesus)
Come, O lovely soul!

4. Chorale [Verse 2] (T)

Zion hears the watchmen singing,
Her heart within for joy is dancing,
She watches and makes haste to rise.
Her friend comes from heaven glorious,
In mercy strong, in truth most mighty,
Her light is bright, her star doth rise.
Now come, thou precious crown,
Lord Jesus, God's own Son!
Hosannah pray!
We follow all
To joy's glad hall
And join therein the evening meal.

5. Recit. (B)

So come within to me,
Thou mine elected bride!
I have myself to thee
Eternally betrothed.[9]
I will upon my heart,
Upon my arm like as a seal engrave thee[10]
And to thy troubled eye bring pleasure.
Forget, O spirit, now
The fear, the pain
Which thou hast had to suffer;
Upon my left hand shalt thou rest,
And this my right hand shall embrace thee.[11]

6. Aria (S, B)

(Soul)
My friend is mine,

> (Jesus)
> And I am thine,[12]

(Both)
Let love bring no division.

> (Soul, Jesus)
>   I will   thee
> {   } with {   } on heaven's roses pasture,[13]
>   Thou shalt   me
> Where pleasure in fullness, where joy will abound.[14]

7. Chorale [Verse 3] (S, A, T, B)

Gloria to thee be sung now
With mortal and angelic voices,
With harps and with the cymbals, too.
Of twelve pearls are made the portals;
Amidst thy city we are consorts
Of angels high around thy throne.
No eye hath yet perceived,
No ear hath e'er yet heard
Such great gladness.
Thus we find joy,
Io, io,
Ever in dulci jubilo!

---

1.   *Mt.* 25:6.

2.   S. of S. 3:11.

3.   *Lk.* 1:78.

4.   *S. of S.* 3:4; 8:2. Note the matriarchal marriage system.

5.   *S. of S.* 2:9 and 17; 8:14.

6. *S. of S.* 2:8.
7. *Is.* 62:11.
8. *Mt.* 25:4.
9. *Hos.* 2:20.
10. *S. of S.* 8:6.
11. *S. of S.* 2:6. The Biblical text suggests "embrace" rather than "kiss."
12. S.of S. 2:16; 6:3. The Biblical *sein* 'his' is altered to *dein* in BG to suit the sense of the dialogue. It allows the rhyme in the translation.
13. *S. of S.* 6:3.
14. *Ps.* 16:11.

BWV 143 **Lobe den Herrn, meine Seele II**

New Year's Day (Feast of the Circumcision).

Poet unknown.

1. *Ps.* 146:1; 2. Jakob Ebert, verse 1 of "Du Friedefürst, Herr Jesu Christ," 1601; 3. *Ps.* 146:5; 5. *Ps.* 146:10; 7. Ebert, verse 3 of the hymn.

Date uncertain.

BG 30; NBA I/4.

1. Chorus [Dictum] (S, A, T, B)

Praise thou the Lord, O my spirit.

2. Chorale [Verse 1] (S)

Thou prince of peace, Lord Jesus Christ,
True man and very God,
A helper strong in need thou art

In life as well as death.
So we alone
In thy dear name
Are to thy Father crying.

3. Recit. [Dictum] (T)

Blest he who hath for his help Jacob's God, whose hope upon the
Lord, on his God, resteth.

4. Aria (T)

Thousandfold misfortune, terror,
Sadness, fear and sudden death,
Heathen who the land have covered,
Sorrows and still greater need,
These may other nations see,
We, instead, a year of grace.

5. Aria [Dictum] (B)

The Lord is king now evermore, thy God, Zion, evermore.

6. Aria (T) with instr. chorale

Jesus, of thy flock the Savior,
In the future bide our shield;
That this year bring us good fortune
Keep thy watch in every place.
Lead, O Jesus, this thy throng
Even to the next new year.

7. Chorus [Verse 3] (S, A, T, B)

Hallelujah![1]
Give thought, Lord, now unto thy work:
Thou art a Prince of peace;

So help us, every one, with grace
At this appointed time;
Let us henceforth
Thy godly word
In peace make ring still longer.

---

1. *Halleluja* is apparently from *Ps.* 146:10.

BWV 144 **Nimm, was dein ist, und gehe hin**

Septuagesima Sunday.

Poet unknown (Picander?); PT (Leipzig, 1724); Facs: Neumann T, p. 426.

1. *Mt.* 20:14; 3. Samuel Rodigast, verse 1 of the hymn, 1674 (Fischer-Tümpel, IV, #167); 6. Markgraf Allbrecht von Brandenburg, verse 1 of "Was mein Gott will, das g'scheh allzeit," 1574 (Wackernagel, III, #1240ff.).

6 February 1724, Leipzig.

BG 30; NBA I/7.

---

1. Chorus [Dictum] (S, A, T, B)

Take what is thine and go away.

2. Aria (A)

Murmur not,
Man of Christ,

When thy wish is not fulfilled;
Rather be with that contented

Which thee thy God hath apportioned;
He knows what will help thee.

3. Chorale (S, A, T, B)

What God doth, that is rightly done,
His will is just forever;
Whatever course he sets my life,
I will trust him with calmness.
He is my God,
Who in distress
Knows well how to support me;
So I yield him all power.

4. Recit. (T)

Wherever moderation rules
And ev'rywhere the helm doth tend,
There is mankind content
With that which God ordains.
However, where immoderation doth its judgment speak,
There shall both grief and woe ensue,
The heart shall not
Be satisfied,
And unremembered shall be this:
What God doth, that is rightly done.

5. Aria (S)

Contentedness,
In this life it is a treasure
Which is able to bring pleasure
In the greatest time of grief,
Contentedness.
For it findeth in whatever
God ordaineth satisfaction,
Contentedness.

6. Chorale (S, A, T, B)

What my God will, let be alway,
His will, it is the best will.
To help all those he is prepared
Who in him faith keep steadfast.
He frees from want, this faithful God,
And punisheth with measure.
Who God doth trust, firm on him builds,
Him shall he not abandon.

BWV 145 Ich lebe, mein Herze, zu deinem Ergötzen
Auf, mein Herz, des Herren Tag
So du mit deinem Munde bekennest Jesum

Third Day of Easter (revised version: Easter Day).

Christian Friedrich Henrici (Picander), *Ernst-Schertzhaffte und Satyrische Gedichte, Teil III* (Leipzig, 1732); Facs: Neumann T, p. 341.

A. added later for a performance on Easter Day; Caspar Neumann, verse 1 of the hymn, ca. 1700, to the melody of Johann Crüger's "Jesus, meine Zuversicht"; B. added later from the cantata of the same name by Georg Philipp Telemann for a performance on Easter Day; *Rom.* 10:9; 5. Nikolaus Herman, verse 14 of "Erschienen ist der herrlich Tag," 1560 (Wackernagel, III, #1374).

Perhaps 19 April 1729, Leipzig; Parody: 1 and 3 ← ? a work from the Cöthen period.

BG 30; NBA I/10.

A. Chorale (S, A, T, B)

Rise, my heart, the Lord's own day
Hath the night of fear now banished:
Christ, who in the tomb did lie,
Doth in death no longer tarry.
Henceforth am I full of hope,
Jesus hath the world redeemed.

B. Chorus [Dictum] (S, A, T, B)

If thou with thine own mouth dost acknowledge Jesus, that he the
Lord is, and dost in thy heart believe this, that he by God from the
dead hath been lifted up, thou shalt be blessed.

1. Aria (T, S) Jesus, Soul

(Jesus, Soul)
  I live now, my spirit,   thy
{   } to {   } purest pleasure,
  Thou livest, my Jesus,   my

  My   thy
{   } life is exalting {   } life to the stars.
  Thy   my

(Both)
The bond which indicts thee is broken asunder,[1]
And peace hath provided a conscience of quiet
And opened to sinners the heavenly gate.

2. Recit. (T)

Now order, Moses, as thou wilt,
That we the threat'ning law should practise;
For I have my release here now
With Jesus' blood and wounding signed in writing.

And it holds force,
I am redeemed, I am set free
And live life now with God in peace and unity,
The plaintiff has no case against me,
For God is now arisen.
My heart, remember this!

3. Aria (B)

Mark thou, my heart now, forever just this,
When thou all else dost forget,
That thy Savior is alive;
See that this be to thy doctrine
A foundation firm forever,
For on this it shall stand secure.
Mark thou, my heart now, just this.

4. Recit. (S)

My Jesus lives,
From me shall no one take this,
I'll die, then, with no grieving.
I am assured
And am of this most certain
That me the darkness of the grave
To heaven's majesty shall raise.
My Jesus lives,
I have in this enough;
My heart and mind
Would this day yet to heaven tend,
To see the face of my redeemer.

5. Chorale (S, A, T, B)

Thus we are also rightly glad,
Singing our Hallelujah fair
And praising thee, Lord Jesus Christ;

To comfort us thou art aris'n.
Hallelujah!

[1.]   Cf. *Col.* 2:14.

BWV 146 **Wir müssen durch viel Trübsal in das Reich Gottes eingehen**

Jubilate (Third Sunday after Easter).

Poet unknown.

1. *Acts* 14:22 (slightly altered); 8. transmitted without text; Neumann T suggests using Johann Rosenmüller or Johann Georg Albinus, verse 7 of "Alle Menschen müssen sterben," 1652 (Fischer-Tümpel, IV, #311); Wustmann supplies Gregorius Richter, verse 9 of "Lasset ab von euren Tränen," 1658 (Fischer-Tümpel, I, #309).

12 May 1726 or 1728 (Dürr), or ca. 1737 (Neumann T).

BG 30; NBA I/11.

---

1. Sinfonia

2. Chorus [Dictum] (S, A, T, B)

We must pass through great sadness that we God's kingdom may enter.

3. Aria (A)

I would unto heaven go,
Wicked Sodom, I and thou
Are henceforth divided.

My abiding is not here,
For I'll live, indeed, with thee
Nevermore at peace now.

4. Recit. (S)

Ah! Were I but in heaven now!
What threatens me not the evil world!
With weeping do I rise,
With weeping in my bed I lay me,
How treacherous do they lie in wait!
Lord! Mark it, look at this,
They hate me so, and with no fault,
As though the world had power
As well to slay me fully;
And though I live with sighing and forbear,
Forsaken and despised,
Yet doth it take in my sorrow
The greatest pleasure.
My God, this weighs me down.
Ah! Would that I,
My Jesus, e'en today
With thee in heaven were!

5. Aria (S)

I shall my tears of sorrow
With anxious bosom sow.
And still my heart's distress
To me will splendidness[1]
Upon the day of the glad harvest deliver.[2]

6. Recit. (T)

I am prepared
My cross with patience e'er to carry;

I know that all of these my torments
Won't match the splendidness
Which God unto his chosen masses
And also me will make apparent.[3]
I weep now, for the world's great tumult
At all my mourning seemeth glad.
Soon comes the time
When my heart shall rejoice;
Then shall the world without a savior weep.
Who with the foe doth strive and fight
Will have his crown then on him laid;
For God lifts no one without labor into heaven.

7. Aria (T, B)

How will I be joyful, how will I take comfort,
When all of this transient sadness is past!

> I'll gleam like the heavens, and shine like the sunlight,
> When vex shall my heavenly bliss
> No grieving, weeping, and lament.

8. Chorale (S, A, T, B)

[Ah, I have already witnessed
This enormous majesty;
Now shall I have fine adornment
In the shining robe of heaven;
With the golden crown of honor
I shall stand before God's throne then,
And shall such great gladness see,
Which can never have an end.][4]
[For who blessed passeth thither,
Where no death will knock again,
He shall all those things obtain then
That he ever could desire.

He'll be in that stronghold sure
Where God his own dwelling hath,
He'll have in that mansion lodging
Which no misery afflicteth.][5]

---

1. The theme of metamorphosis from bad to good is found in each of Bach's three cantatas for Jubilate Sunday (BWV 12, 103, and 146), a theme appropriate to *Acts* 14:22: "Through many tribulations we must enter the kingdom of God." In BWV 12/6 *Regen* is changed to *Segen*; in BWV 103/1 *Traurigkeit* to *Freude*; in the present passage *Herzeleid* 'heart's distress' is transformed with a play on words to *Herrlichkeit* 'splendidness.' Paul Gerhardt offers a pattern for this kind of word-play in the final chorale of BWV 103: *Leid* 'pain' is to be transformed into *Freud*, with *ei* and *eu* pronounced almost alike in Bach's time and region.

2. A paraphrase of *Ps.* 126:6.

3. Cf. *Rom.* 8:18.

4. The text supplied by Neumann T.

5. The text supplied by Wustmann.

BWV 147 **Herz und Mund und Tat und Leben**

The Visitation of the Blessed Virgin Mary.

Poet unknown; Movements 1, 3, 5, 7: Salomo Franck, *Evangelische Sonn-und Fest-Tages-Andachten* (Weimar and Jena, 1717); Facs: Neumann T, p. 291.

6. Martin Jahn, verse 6 of "Jesu, meiner Seelen Wonne," 1661 (Fischer-Tümpel, V, #497); 10. Jahn, verse 16 or 17 of the same hymn.

2 July 1723, Leipzig; 1, 3, 5, 7 ← BWV 147a/1, 3, 7, 5.

BG 30; NBA I/28.

First Part

1. Chorus (S, A, T, B)

Heart and mouth and deed and living
Must for Christ their witness offer
Without fear and falsity
That he God and Savior is.

2. Recit. (T)

O thou most blessed voice!
Now Mary makes her spirit's deepest feelings
Through thanks and praising known;
She undertakes alone
To tell the wonders of the Savior,
All he in her, his virgin maid, hath wrought.
O mortal race of men,
Of Satan and of sin the thrall,
Thou art set free
Through Christ's most comforting appearance
From all this weight and slavery!
But yet thy voice and thine own stubborn spirit
Grow still, denying all such kindness;
Remember that the Scripture saith
An awesome judgment shall thee strike!

3. Aria (A)

Be ashamed, O spirit, not,
This thy Savior to acknowledge,[1]
Should he as his own e'er name thee[2]
'Fore his Father's countenance.
For he who him on earth now
To deny is not afraid

Is by him to be deniéd
When he comes in majesty.

4. Recit. (B)

The mighty can by stubbornness be blinded
Till them the Highest's arm thrust from their throne;
But this arm doth exalt,
E'en though 'fore it the earthly ball doth quake,
In turn the meek and humble,
Whom he shall save.
O highly favored Christians,
Rise, get yourselves prepared,
Now is the time of joy at hand,
Now is the day of grace:[3] the Savior bids
You arm both soul and body with faith's blessings;
Rise, call to him with fervor and with yearning,
That ye in faith may now receive him.

5. Aria (S)

Make ready, O Jesus, to thee now the way;
My Savior, elect now
My soul ever faithful
And look down with eyes full of grace now on me!

6. Chorale (S, A, T, B)

Blest am I that I have Jesus,
Oh, how firmly I hold him,
That he bring my soul refreshment
When I'm ill and filled with grief.
I have Jesus, who doth love me
And himself to me entrusteth;
Ah, I'll hence leave Jesus not,
Even though my heart should break.

Second Part

7. Aria (T)

Help, Jesus, help both that I may confess thee
In health and woe, joy and grief,
And that I may my Savior call thee
In steadfast faith and confidence,
That e'er thy love within my heart be burning.

8. Recit. (A)

The wondrous hand of might sublime
Doth work in earth's unseen recesses;
Since John now must be made full of the Spirit,
The bond of love tugs him
Already in his mother's body;
That he the Savior know,
Although he not at once
Him with his mouth address,
He is stirred up, he leaps and springeth,
So that Elizabeth the marvel doth proclaim,
So that Maria's mouth the gift of lips doth offer.
If ye, O ye of faith, the flesh's weakness see,
And if your heart with love is burning,
But still your mouth thy Savior not acknowledge,
God is it who gives you great strength;
He shall in you the spirit's power awaken,
Yea, thanks and praise upon your tongue shall lay then.

9. Aria (B)

Of Jesus' wonders[4] I'll be singing
And bring to him my lips' glad off'ring;
He will by bond of his own love
My feeble flesh, my mundane voice
Through holy fire overpower.

10. Chorale (S, A, T, B)

Jesus shall remain my gladness,
Essence of my heart, its hope;
Jesus from all grief protecteth,
He is of my life its strength,
Of mine eyes the sun and pleasure,
Of my soul the joy and treasure;
Therefore I will Jesus not
From my heart and sight allow.

---

1.   Cf. *Mt.* 10:32.
2.   The PT: *Soll er seine Braut dich nennen* "Should he as his bride e'er name thee."
3.   Cf. 2 *Cor.* 6:2.
4.   OSt and BG have *Wunden* "wounding."

BWV 147a **Herz und Mund und Tat und Leben**

Fourth Sunday in Advent.

Salomo Franck, *Evangelische Sonn-und Fest-Tages-Andachten* (Weimar and Jean, 1717); Facs: Neumann T, p. 291.

6. "Dein Wort laß mich bekennen," not identified.

22 December 1716, Weimar (if ever finished and performed); 1, 2, 4, 3 → BWV 147/1, 3, 5, 7.

NBA I/1, Krit. Bericht.

---

1. Chorus (= BWV 147/1)

2. Aria (= BWV 147/3)

3. Aria (= BWV 147/7)

4. Aria (= BWV 147/5)

5. Aria

Let me the criers' voices hear now,
Which now with John in faith are teaching,
For I shall in this time of grace
From dreariness and darkness deep
To that true light become converted.

6. Chorale

Thy word let me confess now, etc.

BWV 148 **Bringet dem Herrn Ehre seines Namens**

Seventeenth Sunday after Trinity.

Probably Picander; Movements 2-5, similar to a poem of six verses in Christian Friedrich Henrici (Picander), *Sammlung Erbaulicher Gedancken* (Leipzig, 1724/1725); Facs: Neumann T, p. 307.

1. *Ps.* 96:8-9 or 29:2; 6. melody without text of "Auf meinen lieben Gott"; Neumann T supplies Erk's suggestion of verse 6 of this hymn (Lübeck, before 1603); BG supplies Spitta's suggestion of the eleventh

and final verse of "Wo soll ich fliehen hin," Johann Heermann, 1630 (Fischer-Tümpel, I, #322).

Perhaps 19 September 1723, Leipzig.

BG 30; NBA I/23.

---

1. Chorus [Dictum] (S, A, T, B)

Bring to the Lord honor for his name's sake, worship ye the Lord with holy display.

2. Aria (T)

I hasten to hear now
The lessons for living
And seek out with gladness that holiest house.

> How lovely a summons
> Of sounds of glad music
> To praise the Almighty the sanctified make!

3. Recit. (A)

Like as the hart for cooling waters cries,
So I cry, God, to thee.[1]
For as my only rest
There is no one but thee.
How holy and how precious
Is, Master, this thy sabbath feast day!
I'll praise here all thy might
Within the confines of the righteous.
Oh, would the children only this

Night's loveliness consider,
For God doth dwell in me.

4. Aria (A)

Voice and heart to thee are open,
Master, merge thyself with them!

> I in thee, and thou in me;
> Faith and love and trust and patience
> Shall my bed of rest now be.

5. Recit. (T)

And bide, my God, in me
And me thy Spirit give;
May it within thy word so rule me
That I may act in all my dealings
As thou dost seek of me,
So that I may in time
Within thy majesty,
My dearest God, with thee
That mighty Sabbath feast then honor.

6. Chorale (S, A, T, B)

[Amen at every hour
I'll say with deepest faith;
Be willing thou to guide us,
Lord Christ, at every moment,
So that we for thy name's sake
Forever praise thee.[2] Amen.]
[Lead both my heart and will
Through thine own Spirit hence,
That I may shun all perils
Which me from thee could sever,

And I within thy body
A member bide forever.]³

---

1.   Cf. *Ps*. 42:2.

2.   The text supplied by Neumann T.

3.   The texts supplied by BG.

BWV 149 **Man singet mit Freuden vom Sieg in den Hütten der Gerechten**

St. Michael and All Angels.

Christian Friedrich Henrici (Picander). *Ernst-Schertzhaffte und Satyrische Gedichte, Teil III* (Leipzig, 1732); Facs: Neumann T, p. 342.

1. *Ps*. 118:15-16; 7. Martin Schalling, verse 3 of "Herzlich lieb hab ich dich, O Herr," 1571 (Wackernagel, IV, #1174).

29 September 1728 or 1729, Leipzig; Parody: 1 ← BWV 208/15.

BG 30; NBA I/30.

---

1. Chorus [Dictum] (S, A, T, B)

They sing now of triumph with joy in the tents of all the righteous:
The right hand of God the triumph wins, the right hand of God is
exalted, the right hand of God the triumph wins.

2. Aria (B)

Might and power be now sung to
God, the victim¹ which is slaughtered
And hath Satan now made flee,

Who us day and night accused.
Triumph's praise is to the godly
Through the lamb's own blood forthcoming.

3. Recit. (A)

I have no fear
Before a thousand foes,
For God's own angels are encamped
Round me on every side;
Though all should fall, though all collapse,
I'll be ne'erless untroubled.
How could I ever lose my courage?
God shall send me more horse and chariots
And brimming hosts of angels here.[2]

4. Aria (S)

God's own angels never yield,
They are present all about me.

>At my sleeping, they keep watch,
>At my going,
>At my rising,
>In their hands do thy support me.

5. Recit. (T)

I give thee thanks,
O my dear God, for this;
And grant to me as well
That I for all my sins feel sorrow,
For which my angel know such gladness
That he shall upon my day to perish
Into thy heav'nly bosom carry.

6. Aria (A, T)

Be watchful, O ye holy watchmen,
The night is nearly spent.[3]

> My yearning shall no rest give me
> Till I 'fore the countenance
> Of my loving Father stand.

7. Chorale (S, A, T, B)

Ah Lord, let this thine angel dear
At my last hour this soul of mine
To Abraham's lap carry,
My body in its resting place
In quiet, free of woe and pain,
Sleep till the day of judgment!
And then from death awaken me,
That with mine eyes I may see thee
In total joy, O Son of God,
My Savior and my throne of grace!
Lord Jesus Christ, O hear me now, o hear me now,
I will thee praise eternally!

[1.] Cf. *Rev.* 5:12. "Lamb" is not allowed by the meter.
[2.] Cf. *Ps.* 3:7 and 34:7.
[3.] Cf. *Is.* 21:11.

BWV 150 **Nach dir, Herr, verlanget mich**

Unspecified Occasion.

Poet unknown.

2. *Ps.* 25:1-2; 4. *Ps.* 25:4; 6. *Ps.* 25.14.

Date uncertain, perhaps early Weimar period, 1708-1709 (cf. Dürr, p. 628).

BG 30; NBA I/41.

---

1. Sinfonia

2. Chorus [Dictum] (S, A, T, B)

For thee, Lord, is my desire. My God, my hope is in thee. Let me not confounded be now, so that all my foes may not triumph over me.

3. Aria (S)

I am and shall be e'er content,
Though here in time may bluster
Cross, storm and other trials,
Death, hell, and what must be.
Though mishap strike thy faithful liege,
Right is and shall be ever right.

4. Chorus [Dictum] (S, A, T, B)

Lead thou me in thy true pathways and teach thou me; for thou art the God who saves me; daily I await thee.

5. Aria (A, T, B)

Cedars must before the tempest
Oft much stress and torment suffer,
Often are they e'en laid low.
Thought and deed to God entrust ye,
Heeding not what howls against you,
For his word tells otherwise.

6. Chorus [Dictum] (S, A, T, B)

These mine eyes are looking e'er to the Lord, for he shall pluck my
foot from the net's confinement.

7. Chorus (S, A, T, B)

All my days which pass in sadness
Endeth God at last in gladness;
Christians on the thorny pathways
Follow heaven's power and blessing.
May God bide my faithful shield,
May I heed not mankind's spite;
Christ, he who now stands beside us,
Helps me daily win the battle.

BWV 151 Süßer Trost, mein Jesus kömmt

Third Day of Christmas (St. John, Apostle and Evangelist).

Georg Christian Lehms, *Gottgefälliges Kirchen-Opffer* (Darmstadt, 1711);
Facs: Neumann T, p. 257.

5. Nikolaus Herman, verse 8 of "Lobt Gott, ihr Christen allzugleich,"
1560 (Wackernagel, III, #1365).

27 December 1725, Leipzig; again after 1728 (Neumann Hb).

BG 32; NBA I/3.

1. Aria (S)

Comfort sweet, my Jesus comes,
Jesus now is born amongst us!

Heart and soul with joy are filled,
For my dearest God hath me
Now for heaven's prize elected.

2. Recit. (B)

Rejoice then, O my heart,
For now shall yield the pain
Which hath so long a time oppressed thee.
God hath his precious Son,
Whom he so high and dear doth hold,
Into this world committed.
He leaves the heavenly throne
And would now all the world
From its own chains of slav'ry
And its own servitude deliver.
O deed most wonderful!
God is made man and on earth desires
E'en lowlier than we to live and much more humbly.

3. Aria (A)

In Jesus' meekness can I strength,
Within his poverty find riches.

To me doth this his poor estate
Nought but pure health and wealth reveal,
Yea, his own wonder-working hand
Shall nought but wreathes of blessing make me.

4. Recit. (T)

Thou precious Son of God,
Thou hast for me now heaven opened wide

And through thy humble life
The light of blessedness o'er us now brought.
Since thou now, thou alone,
The Father's keep and throne,
Because thou didst love us, relinquished,
We would in turn as well
For this within our hearts now hold thee.

5. Chorale (S, A, T, B)

Today he opens new the door
To that fair paradise;
The cherub stands no more in front,
God be laud, grace and praise.

BWV 152 **Tritt auf die Glaubensbahn**

The Sunday after Christmas.

Salomo Franck, *Evangelisches Andachts-Opffer . . . in geistlichen Cantaten* (Weimar, 1715); Facs: Neumann T, p. 275.

30 December 1714, Weimar.

BG 32; NBG *Jg.* 48-50,1; NBA I/3.

---

1. Sinfonia

2. Aria (B)

Walk on the road of faith,
God hath the stone established

Which holds and bears up Zion;
Man, stumble not thereon!
Walk on the road of faith!

3. Recit. (B)

The Savior is in charge
In Israel o'er fall and resurrection.
The noble stone doth bear no fault
Whene'er the wicked world
So hard on it is dashed,
Yea, over it to hell doth fall,
For it with spite into it runneth
And God's own grace
And mercy won't acknowledge!
But blessed is
The chosen man of Christ,
Who on this cornerstone his faith's foundation layeth,
For he thereby health and redemption findeth.

4. Aria (S)

Stone surpassing every treasure,
Help that I may for all time,
Through my faith, upon thee stablish
My foundation for true grace
And may not on thee be wounded,
Stone surpassing every treasure!

5. Recit. (B)

Now angry is the clever world
That God's own Son
Hath left his lofty throne of praise,
Hath self in flesh and blood appareled,
And as a mortal suffers.

The greatest wisdom of this earth must
Before the will of God
The greatest folly seem now.[1]
For what God hath decreed
Can merest reason never fathom;
That blind seductress misleads the blind in spirit.[2]

6. Aria (S, B) Soul, Jesus

(Soul)
How shall I, O lover of souls, now embrace thee?

(Jesus)
Thou must all abandon and thyself deny thee!

(Soul)
How shall I perceive then the eternal light?

(Jesus)
Perceive me with faith and yield not unto spite!

(Soul)
Come, teach me, O Savior, of earth to be scornful!

(Jesus)
Come, spirit, through sadness to gladness walk joyful!

(Soul)
Ah, draw me, Beloved, I'll follow thee hence!

(Jesus)
I'll give thee the crown midst grief and offense!

---

[1]   Cf. 1 *Cor.* 1:18-19.

[2]   Cf. *Mt.* 15:14.

BWV 153 **Schau, lieber Gott, wie meine Feind**

The Sunday after New Year's Day.

Poet unknown.

1. David Denicke, verse 1 of the hymn, 1646 (Fischer-Tümpel, II, #383); 3. *Is.* 41:10; 5. Paul Gerhardt, verse 5 of "Befiehl du deine Wege," 1653 (Fischer-Tümpel, III, #435); 9. Martin Moller, verses 16-18 of "Ach Gott, wie manches Herzeleid," 1587, after Bernard of Clairvaux, "Jesu dulcis memoria" (Wackernagel, I, #38).

2 January 1724, Leipzig.

BG 32; NBA I/4.

1. Chorale (S, A, T, B)

Behold, dear God, how all my foes,
With whom I e'er must battle,
So cunning and so mighty are
That they with ease subdue me!
Lord, if thy grace sustain me not,
Then can the devil, flesh and world
With ease to ruin bring me.

2. Recit. (A)

My dearest God, ah, grant me yet thy mercy,
Ah, help me, help this wretch now!
I dwell here now midst very lions and midst serpents,

And they desire for me through rage and cruelty
With no delay
My finish to accomplish.

3. Aria [Dictum] (B)

Fear have thou none, I am with thee. Waver not, I am thy God; I
strengthen thee, I also help thee through this the right hand of mine
own righteousness.

4. Recit. (T)

Thou dost assure, O God, unto my soul's repose,
Encouragement when I in sorrow lie.
Ah, yet is all my torment
From day to day now ever larger,
For of my foes the toll is great,
My life is now their aim,
Their bows are now for me strung tight,
They aim now all their shafts for my destruction,
I shall at their own hands soon perish;
God! My distress is known to thee,
And all the world is now my den of torture;
Help, Helper, help! Deliver now my spirit!

5. Chorale

And though now all the devils
Desire to stand against thee,
Yet shall there be no question
That God would e'er retreat;
What he hath undertaken
And whate'er he desires,
This must at length be finished
To his intent and aim.

6. Aria (T)

Storm then, storm, afflictions' tempests,
Rush, ye waters, down on me!
Strike, misfortune's fires,
Fall on me together;
Foes, disturb ye my repose,
If to me God this assure:
I am thy shield and Redeemer.

7. Recit. (B)

Bear up, my heart,
Endure yet all thy pain,
And let thy cross not ever crush thee!
God will full soon
In his good time refresh thee;
Remember how his Son,
Thy Jesus, while his years were tender,
Much greater woe did suffer,
When him the raging tyrant Herod
The gravest state of deathly peril
With murder-dealing fists did cause!
He scarce was come to earth then
When he was forced to flee for safety!
So come, with Jesus comfort take
And hold to this with faith:
To ev'ryone who here with Christ shall suffer
Shall he his paradise apportion.

8. Aria (A)

Though I must my life's full course
Run neath cross and sorrow's burden,
Yet it shall in heaven end.
There is nought but jubilation,

And there, too, shall Jesus transform all my sadness
To happiest pleasure, to unceasing gladness.

9. Chorale (S, A, T, B)

Thus will I, while I yet have life,
The cross with gladness bear to thee;
My God, make me for it prepared,
The cross will serve me all my years!

Help me my life to meet forthright,
That I my course may run complete,
Help me to master flesh and blood,
From sin and scandal keep me free!

If thou my heart in faith keep pure,
I'll live and die in thee alone;
Jesus, my hope, hear my desire,
O Savior mine, bring me to thee!

BWV 154 **Mein liebster Jesus ist verloren**

First Sunday after Epiphany.

Poet unknown.

3. Martin Jahn, verse 2 of "Jesu, meiner Seelen Wonne," 1661 (Fischer-Tümpel, V, #497); 5. *Lk.* 2:49; 8. Christian Keymann, verse 6 of "Meinen Jesus laß ich nicht," (Fischer-Tümpel, IV, #13).

9 January 1724, Leipzig; perhaps first in Weimar; again after 1735.

BG 32; NBA I/5.

1. Aria (T)

My precious Jesus now hath vanished:

> O word which me despair doth bring,
> O sword which through my soul doth drive,
> O thund'rous word, when mine for hearing.[1]

2. Recit. (T)

Where shall I, then, my Jesus meet,
Who will show me the way
Whereon my soul's most fervent desiring,
My Savior, hath now journeyed?
No sorrow could me ever touch so deeply
Than if I were to lose my Jesus.

3. Chorale (S, A, T, B)

Jesus, my shield and Redeemer,
Jesus, my true confidence,
Jesus, mighty serpent-slayer,
Jesus, of my life the light!
How my heart now thee desireth,
Little Jesus, for thee acheth!
Come, ah come, I wait for thee,
Come, O little Jesus dear!

4. Aria (A)

Jesus, let me find thee,
Let now my transgressions
Not the swelling clouds become
Where thou, to my terror,
Wouldst from me lie hidden;
Soon thyself again reveal!

5. Arioso [Dictum] (B)[2]

Know ye then not that I must be there where my Father's business is?

6. Recit. (T)

This is the voice of my beloved,[3]
God praise and thanks!
My Jesus, my devoted shield,
Makes through his word
Himself heard for new comfort;
I was with grieving sick,
My sorrow sought the very quick,
My bones were nearly wasted;
But now, though, will my faith again be strong,
Now I am filled with joy;
For I behold the glory of my spirit,
My Savior, my true sunlight,
Who after mourning's night of grief
Through his bright light doth make my heart rejoice.
Rise, spirit, get thyself prepared!
Thou must to him
Into his Father's house, into his temple draw;
There he himself within his word revealeth,
There would he in the sacrament restore thee;
But if thou worthily his flesh and blood would taste now,
Then thou must Jesus kiss in faith and firm repentance.

7. Aria (A, T)

What bliss, I have now found Jesus,
Now am I no more distressed.
He whom this my soul doth love
Comes to me for joyous hours.
I will, O my Jesus, now nevermore leave thee,
I will now in faith ever steadfast embrace thee.

8. Chorale (S, A, T, B)

This my Jesus I'll not leave,
I'll forever walk beside him;
Christ shall let me more and more
To the springs of life be guided.
Blessed those who say with me:
This my Jesus I'll not leave.

---

1. Cf. Johann Rist, "O Ewigkeit, du Donnerwort," and *Lk*. 2:35.
2. Representing the *Vox Christi*.
3. *S. of S*. 2:8.

BWV 155 **Mein Gott, wie lang, ach lange?**

Second Sunday after Epiphany.

Salomo Franck, *Evangelisches Andachts-Opffer . . . in geistlichen Cantaten* (Weimar, 1715); Facs: Neumann T, p. 276; PT (Leipzig, 1724); Facs: Neumann T, p. 423.

5. Paul Speratus, verse 12 of "Es ist das Heil uns kommen her," 1524 (Wackernagel, III, #55).

19 January 1716, Weimar; again 16 January 1724, Leipzig?

BG 32: NBA I/5.

---

1. Recit. (S)

My God, how long, how long then?
Of grief there is too much,

I see no end at all
Of yearning and of sorrow!
Thy soothing face of grace
Beneath the night and clouds itself hath hidden;
Thy hand of love, is now, ah, quite withdrawn;
For comfort I'm most anxious.
I find now, to this wretch's daily anguish,
My cup of tears is ever full replenished,
The joyful wine doth fail;
And falls nigh all my confidence!

2. Aria (A, T)

Thou must trust now, thou must hope now,
Thou must rest assured in God!
Jesus knows the proper hour,
Thee with help to fill with joy.
When this troubled time is over,
All his heart shall thee lie open.

3. Recit. (B)

So be, O spirit, be contented!
If it should to thine eyes appear
As if thy dearest friend
Were e'er from thee now parted,
When he a short time thee hath left,
Heart, keep thy faith:
A short time will it be,[1]
When he for bitter weeping
The wine of hope and gladness,
And honey sweet for bitter gall will grant thee![2]
Ah, do not think
That he delights to bring thee sadness;
He only tests through sorrow thine affection;

He maketh now thy heart to weep through cheerless hours,
So that his gracious light
To thee appear e'en still more lovely;
He hath reserved thy joy
For last,
To thy delight and consolation;
So yield to him, O heart, in all things power![3]

4. Aria (S)

Cast, my heart now, cast thyself
In the Highest's loving bosom,
That he grant to thee his mercy.
Lay now all thy sorrows' yoke,
All that thee till now hath burdened,
On the shoulders of his mercy.

5. Chorale (S, A, T, B)

Though it should seem he were opposed,
Be thou by this not frightened,
For where he is at best with thee,
His wont is not to show it.
His word take thou more certain still,
And though thy heart say only "No,"
Yet let thyself not shudder.

---

[1].   Cf. BWV 12/6: *Herz! glaube fest, alle Pein/ Wird doch nur ein Kleines sein.*

[2].   Cf. the punning metamorphosis from bad to good in BWV 12/10: *Verwandle dich, Weinen, in lauteren Wein,/ Es wird nun mein Ächzen ein Jauchzen mir sein!*

[3].   Cf. Samuel Rodigast, the final line of "Was Gott tut, das ist wohlgetan."

BWV 156 **Ich steh mit einem Fuß im Grabe**

Third Sunday after Epiphany.

Christian Friedrich Henrici (Picander), *Ernst-Schertzhaffte und Satyrische Gedichte, Teil III,* (Leipzig, 1732); Facs: Neumann T, p. 337.

2. Johann Hermann Schein, verse 1 of "Mach's mit mir, Gott, nach deiner Güt,", 1628 (Fischer-Tümpel, I, #478) with interpolated aria; 6. Kaspar Bienemann, verse 1 of the hymn, 1582 (Wackernagel, IV, #1046).

Probably 23 January 1729, Leipzig.

BG 18; NBA I/6.

---

1. Sinfonia

2. Aria (T) and Chorale (S)

(T)
I stand with one foot in the grave now,

(S)
Deal with me, God, of thy good will,

(T)
Soon shall my ailing corpse fall in,

(S)
Help me in all my suff'ring,

(I)
Come, O my God, whene'er thou wilt,

(S)
What now I ask, deny me not.

(I)
I have e'en now my house prepared,

(S)
Whene'er my soul's departure,
Receive it, Lord, into thy hand.

(I)
Just let my end with blessing come!

(S)
For all is good, if good the end.

3. Recit. (B)

My fear and need,
My living and my death
Stand, dearest God, within thy power;
Thus shalt thou turn as well
Thy gracious eye upon me.
But if for all my sins thou seekest
In ill health's bed to lay me,
My God, I beg of thee,
Let thy dear kindness greater be than justice rightly bids;
Yet if thou dost for me intend
That now my suff'ring should consume me,
I am prepared;
Thy will should in me be fulfilled,
So spare me not and have thy way,

Let my distress not long continue;
The longer here, the later there.

4. Aria (A)

Lord, what thou wilt shall be my pleasure,
Forsooth thy word is strongest yet.

> In my gladness,
> In my sadness,
> In dying, in weeping and prayer,
> Unto me alway fulfill,
> Lord, what thou wilt.

5. Recit. (B)

And if thou wish me not to suffer,
To thee I'll be sincerely thankful;
However, grant to me as well
That also in my lively body
My soul may free from sickness be
And evermore in health continue.
Tend it with Holy Ghost and word,
For this is my true health,
And if my soul and body fail,
Yet thou art, God, my strength, the portion of my heart!

6. Chorale (S, A, T, B)

Lord, as thou wilt, so deal with me
In living and in dying!
Alone for thee is my desire,
Lord, leave me not to perish!
Support me only in thy grace,
But as thou wilt, let me forbear,
For thy will has no equal.

BWV 157 Ich lasse dich nicht, du segnest mich denn!

The Purification of the Blessed Virgin Mary (The Presentation of Christ in the Temple); originally for a funeral?

Christian Friedrich Henrici (Picander), *Ernst-Schertzhaffte und Satyrische Gedichte, Teil I* (Leipzig, 1729; 2nd ed., 1732, 3rd ed., 1736); Facs: Neumann T, p. 316; PT (1727); Facs: Neumann T, p. 390

1. *Gen.* 32:27; 5. Christian Keymann, verse 6 of "Meinen Jesum laß ich nicht," 1658 (Fischer-Tümpel, IV, #13).

6 February 1727, Pomßen, for the funeral of Johann Christoph von Ponickau?

BG 32; NBA I/32.

1. Duetto [Dictum] (T, B)

I'll not let thee go, thou must bless me first.

2. Aria (T)

I shall hold to my Jesus firmly,
I'll let him never from me go.
He is alone my sure abode,
Thus is my faith now fixed with might
Upon his saving countenance;
For this support shall have no equal.

3. Recit. (T)

My dearest Jesus thou,
When I must stress and trouble suffer,

Then art thou my true pleasure,
In unrest my true rest,
When I'm afraid, my bed of comfort.
The fickle world is never true,
E'en heaven age must suffer,
The world's delights are lost like chaff;
If I did not, my Jesus, have thee,
To whom could I besides thee hold to?
Thus I shall never let thee go,
Thy blessing, then, shall bide with me.

4. Aria, Recit., and Arioso (B)

Yes, yes, I hold to Jesus firmly,
Thus shall I e'en to heaven go,
Where God and his own lamb's invited
In crowns are at the wedding feast.
There I'll not leave, my Savior, thee
Where bides thy blessing, too, with me.
Ah, what delight
To me is my death's casket,
For Jesus in my arms doth lie!
Then can my soul with joy rest fully!
Yes, yes, I'll hold to Jesus firmly,
Thus shall I e'en to heaven go!
O land so fair!
Come, gentle death, and lead me hence,
Where God and his own lamb's invited
In crowns are at the wedding feast.
I am so glad
The suff'ring of this time
From me today to put aside now;
For Jesus waits for me in heaven with his blessing.
There I'll not leave, my Savior, thee
Where bides thy blessing, too, with me.

5. Chorale (S, A, T, B)

This my Jesus I'll not leave,
I'll forever walk beside him;
Christ shall let me more and more
To the springs of life be guided.
Blessed those who say with me:
This my Jesus I'll not leave.

BWV 158 **Der Friede sei mit dir**

Third Day of Easter (Easter Tuesday).

Poet unknown; Salomo Franck?

2. Johann Georg Albinus, verse 1 of the hymn, 1649 (Fischer—Tümpel, IV, #312), with interpolated aria; 4. Martin Luther, verse 5 of "Christ lag in Todesbanden," 1524 (Wackernagel, III, #15).

Date uncertain.

BG 32; NBA I/10.

---

1. Recit. (B)

May peace now be with thee,
O thou most anxious conscience!
Thine intercessor's here,
Who hath thy book of debts
And the Law's dread curse

Now settled and destroyed.[1]
May peace now be with thee,
The prince of all this world,
Who for thy soul hath lain in wait,
Is through the lamb's own blood now conquered and laid low.
My heart, why art thou so downcast,
When thou by God through Christ art loved?
He saith himself to me:
May peace now be with thee!

2. Aria (B) and Chorale (S)

(B)
World, farewell, of thee I'm weary,
Salem's shelter I prefer,

(S)
World, farewell, of thee I'm weary,
I would now to heaven go,

(B)
Where I God in peace and quiet
Ever blessed can behold.

(S)
Where will be a peace most tranquil
And eternal grand repose.

(B)
I'll bide there where I shall be dwelling contented

(S)
World, with thee is war and strife,
Nought but merest vanity;

(B)
And crowned in the glory of heavenly splendor.

(S)
But in heaven evermore
Peace and joy and happiness.

3. Recit. and Arioso (B)

O Lord, now govern all my thoughts,
That I, while in the world
As long as thou dost please to let me here remain,
A child of peace may be,
And let me to thee from my affliction
Like Simeon in peace depart now![2]
I'll bide there where I shall be dwelling contented
And crowned in the glory of heavenly splendor.[3]

4. Chorale (S, A, T, B)

Here is the proper Easter lamb,
Whereof God hath commanded;
It is high on the cross's trunk
In ardent love now burning.
His blood signeth now our door,
Our faith doth it to death display;
The strangler cannot now touch us.
Alleluia!

[1.]   Banking metaphors are characteristic of Salomo Franck.

[2.]   An allusion to the "Nunc dimittis" or "Song of Simeon."

[3.]   Such words as *Zierde* and *Krone* abound in Salomo Franck.

BWV 159 **Sehet! Wir gehn hinauf gen Jerusalem**

Estomihi (Quinquagesima Sunday).

Christian Friedrich Henrici (Picander), *Ernst-Schertzhaffte und Satyrische Gedichte, Teil III* (Leipzig, 1732); Facs: Neumann T, p. 339.

1. *Lk.* 18:31; 3. Paul Gerhardt, verse 6 of "O Haupt voll Blut und Wunden," 1656 (Fischer-Tümpel, III, #467) with interpolated aria; 5. Paul Stockmann, penultimate and 33rd verse of "Jesu Leiden, Pein und Tod," 1633 (Fischer-Tümpel, II, #37).

Date unknown, perhaps 27 February 1729, Leipzig (Dürr).

BG 32; NBA I/8.

---

1. Arioso [Dictum] (B)[1] and Recit. (A)

(B)
See now!

(A)
Come, ponder well, my mind,
Where doth thy Jesus go?

(B)
We're going up

(A)
O cruel path! That way?
O uninviting hill, of all my sins the token!
How sorely wilt thou have to climb it!

(B)
To Jerusalem.

(A)
Ah, do not go!
Thy cross for thee is now prepared,
Where thou thy bloody death must suffer;
Here do they scourges seek, there, bind the switches;
The bonds now wait for thee;
Ah, take thyself not them to meet!
If thou couldst hold in check thy journey,
I would myself not to Jerusalem,
Ah, sadly down to hell then venture.

2. Aria (A) and Chorale (S)

(A)
I follow thy path

(S)
I will here by thee tarry,

(A)
Through spitting and scorn;

(S)
Do not treat me with scorn![2]

(A)
On cross will I once more embrace thee,

(S)
From thee I will not venture
As now thy heart doth break.

(A)
I will not let thee from my breast,

(S)
And when thy head grows pallid
Upon death's final stroke,

(A)
And if thou in the end must part,

(S)
E'en then will I enfold thee

(A)
Thou shalt thy tomb in me discover.

(S)
Within my arm's embrace.

3. Recit. (T)

So now I will,
My Jesus, for thy sake
In my own corner sorrow;
The world may ever still
On venom of desire be nurtured,
But I'll restore myself with weeping
And will not sooner yearn
For any joy or pleasure
Ere thee my countenance
Have in thy majesty regarded;
Ere I through thee have been redeemed;
Where I will find with thee refreshment.

4. Aria (B)

It is complete,
The pain is over,
We are from all our sinful ruin
In God restored to right.

Now will I hasten
And to my Jesus make thanksgiving;
World, fare thee well,
It is complete!

5. Chorale (S, A, T, B)

Jesus, this thy passion
Is my purest pleasure,
All thy wounds, thy crown and scorn,
Are my heart's true pasture;
This my soul is all in bloom
Once I have considered
That in heaven is a home
To me by this offered.

[1.]   Representing the *Vox Christi*.

[2.]   Lines 3-4 are transposed in the PT.

BWV 161 **Komm, du süße Todesstunde**

Sixteenth Sunday after Trinity; also for the Purification.

Salomo Franck, *Evangelisches Andachts-Opffer . . . in geistlichen Cantaten* (Weimar, 1715); Facs: Neumann T, p. 283.

1. Christoph Knoll, verse 1 of the hymn, 1611 (see Fischer-Tümpel, I, p. 101); this chorale is interpolated vocally into the aria only in the later Leipzig version; 6. verse 4 of the same hymn.

6 October 1715, Weimar.

BG 33; NBA I/23.

---

1. Aria (A) and Chorale (S)

Come, O death, thou sweetest hour,
When my soul
Honey takes
From the mouth of lions;[1]
Heartfelt is now my yearning
To have a blessed end,
For I am here surrounded
With sadness and distress.
Make sweet now my departure,
Tarry not,
Final light,
That I may embrace[2] my Savior.
I wish to take departure
From this most wicked world,
I yearn for heaven's pleasure,
O Jesus, come then soon!

2. Recit. (T)

World, thy delights are weights,
Thy sweetness is to me as poison loathed,
Thy joyful light
Is my dire omen,[3]
And where one once did roses pick
Are thorns of countless toll
To torment this my soul.
Now pallid death's become my rosy morning,
With it doth rise for me the sunlight
Of splendor and of heav'nly pleasure.[4]
I sigh then from my heart's foundation
But for my final hour of dying.
It is my wish with Christ now soon to pasture,
It is my wish to leave this world behind me.[5]

3. Aria (T)

My desire
Is my Savior to embrace now
And with Christ full soon to be.

> Though as mortal earth and ashes
> I by death be ground to ruin,
> Will my soul's pure luster shine
> Even like the angels' glory.

4. Recit. (A)

Now firm is my resolve,
World, fare thee well!
And I have only this for comfort,
To die within the arms of Jesus:
He is my gentle sleep.[6]
The cooling grave will cover me with roses
Till Jesus shall me re-awaken,
Till he his sheep
Shall lead forth to life's sweetest pasture,[7]
That there e'en death from him not keep me.
So now break forth, thou happy day of death,
So strike then thou, the final hour's stroke![8]

5. Chorus (S, A, T, B)

If it is my God's intention,
I wish that my body's weight
Might today the earth make fuller,
And my ghost, my body's guest,
Life immortal take for raiment
In the sweet delight of heaven.
Jesus, come and take me hence!
May this be my final word.

6. Chorale (S, A, T, B)

The flesh in earth now lying
By worms will be consumed,
Yet shall it be awakened,
Through Christ be glorified,
And shine bright as the sunlight
And live without distress
In heav'nly joy and pleasure.
What harm to me, then, death?

---

1. Cf. *Jg.* 14:8.
2. It is difficult to judge whether Salomo Franck's use of *küssen* is to be taken literally or more with the connotations of the French *embrasser*.
3. Literally, 'comet.'
4. The theme of metamorphosis in Salomo Franck is more commonly ameliorative (cf. BWV 12/6; 21/10). Here the series of transformations is strikingly negative.
5. Cf. *Phil.* 1:23.
6. P has also *sanfter Tod* "gentle death."
7. P and BG have *Himmelsweide.* Translate: "Lead forth to heaven's own sweet pasture."
8. The text and composition, with the death knell represented as a ticking clock, is found in another cantata for the Sixteenth Sunday after Trinity, BWV 95/5, and elsewhere.

BWV 162 Ach! ich sehe, itzt, da ich zur Hochzeit gehe

Twentieth Sunday after Trinity.

Salomo Franck, *Evangelisches Andachts-Opffer* . . . *in geistlichen Cantaten* (Weimar, 1715); Facs: Neumann T, p. 285.

6. Johann Rosenmüller or Johann Georg Albinus, verse 7 of "Alle Menschen müssen sterben," 1652 (Fischer-Tümpel, IV, #311).

3 November 1715, Weimar; revised, 10 October 1723, Leipzig.

BG 33; NBA I/25.

---

1. Aria (B)

Ah! I see now,
As I go to join the marriage,
Bliss and mis'ry.
Spirit's bane and bread of life,
Heaven, hell, and life and death,
Heaven's rays and hellfire's burning[1]
Are together.
Jesus, help me to survive now!

2. Recit. (T)

O awesome marriage feast,
To which the king of heaven
To man his summons sends!
Is then the wretched bride,
The nature of mankind, not much too poor and worthless,
That God Almighty's Son to her be wed?
O awesome marriage feast,
How is our flesh come into such great honor,
That God's own Son
Hath it for evermore accepted?
Though heaven is his throne
And earth doth offer to his feet a footstool,[2]
Yet would he kiss the world,
His bride and most beloved!
The marriage supper is prepared,

The fatted calf is slaughtered.
How glorious is ev'rything made ready!
How happy he whom faith now leadeth hither,
And how accursed is yet he who this feast disdaineth!

3. Aria (S)

Jesus, fountain of all mercy,
Quicken me, thy wretched guest,
For thou hast invited me!
I am faint, weak and sore laden,
Ah, enliven now my spirit,
Ah, how starved I am for thee!
Bread of life, which I have chosen,
Come, unite thyself to me!

4. Recit. (A)

My Jesus, let me not
Without a robe approach the marriage,
That on me fall thy judgment not;
With horror have I been a witness
As once the wanton wedding guest,
Without a robe appearing,
Rejected and condemned thou hast!
I know mine own unworthiness:
Ah! Give to me the marriage robe of faith;
Let thine own merits serve as mine adornment!
Give as my wedding garment
Salvation's cloak, the candid silk of chasteness!
Ah! Let thy blood, that noble purple, cover
The ancient cloak of Adam and all its sinful patches,
And I'll be fair and pure
And thee most welcome be,
And I'll right worthily the lamb's high feast be tasting[3]

5. Aria (A, T)

Now in my God am I made glad!
The power of love so much hath stirred him,
That he hath in this time of grace
With simple favor put around me
The raiment of his righteousness.[4]
I know he'll give, when life is over,
His glory's shining robe
To me in heaven also.

6. Chorale (S, A, T, B)

Ah, I have already witnessed
This his awesome majesty.
Soon now shall I be made lovely
In the shining heav'nly robe;
In a golden crown of glory
Shall I stand before God's throne there,
Gazing at that state of joy
Which no end can ever know.

[1.] This series of nouns and compound nouns with both asyndeton and polysyndeton is a special feature of the style of Salomo Franck.

[2.] Cf. *Is.* 66:1.

[3.] Cf. *Rev.* 19:9. Salomo Franck's most prominent theme is the preference of heavenly over worldly glory.

[4.] Cf. *Is.* 61:10.

BWV 163 **Nur jedem das Seine!**

Twenty-third Sunday after Trinity.

Salomo Franck, *Evangelisches Andachts-Opffer . . . in geistlichen Cantaten* (Weimar, 1715); Facs: Neumann T, p. 287.

5. Instrumental citation of "Meinen Jesum laß ich nicht" (cf. BWV 157/5); 6. Johann Heermann, final verse of "Wo soll ich fliehen hin," 1630 (Fischer-Tümpel, I, #322).

24 November 1715, Weimar.

BG 33; NBA I/26.

---

1. Aria (T)

To each but what's due him!

> If rulers must gather
> Toll, taxes, and tribute,
> Let no one refuse
> The debt that he owes!
> Yet bound is the heart but to God the Almighty.

2. Recit. (B)

Thou art, my God, of every gift the giver;
We have all that we have now
Alone from thine own hand.
Thou, thou hast to us given
Soul, spirit, life and body
And wealth and goods and rank and class!
What ought we then
To thee
In gratitude for these deposit,
When all of our possessions
Just thee and not to us belong?
But there's one thing, which thee, O God, doth please:
The heart shall all alone,
Lord, thy true tribute money be.
Ah! Oh alas! Is that not worthless coin?

For Satan hath thy form on it disfigured,
This counterfeit has lost all value.

3. Aria (B)

Let my heart the coinage be
Which I thee, my Jesus, pay now!
If it be not fully pure,
Ah, then come forth and renew it,
Lord, the lovely shine in it!
Come and work it, melt and stamp it,
That thine image then in me
Fully new may be reflected.[1]

4. Arioso (S, A)

I would to thee,
O God, my heart have gladly given;
The will indeed I have,
But flesh and blood would ever strive against me;
And now the world
This heart doth captive hold
And will not let the spoils be taken from her.
In truth I must despise her,
If I am thee to love.
So make then now my heart with all thy blessings full;
Remove from it all worldly longings
And make of me thereby a proper Christian.

5. Aria (S, A) with instr. chorale

From me take me, make me thine!
From me take me and my purpose,
That thy purpose be accomplished;
Make thee mine of thy dear kindness,
That my heart and this my spirit

In thee bide for evermore;
From me take me, make me thine!²

6. Chorale (S, A, T, B)

Lead both my heart and mind
Through thine own Spirit hence,
That I may all things shun now
Which me from thee could sever,
And I within thy body
A member bide forever.

---

1. The coinage metaphor in this text springs not only from the Gospel lection in which the Pharisees test Jesus with a coin bearing Caesar's likeness; it reflects Salomo Franck's own interest in numismatics. The concept of the coin's image as an object of imitation is not found in the Gospel reading, but it does occur in a poem Franck wrote on the coin collection of Duke Wilhelm Ernst.

2. The text of this aria is a bold experiment in jingle. The sound "i" is used in 28 words. One may compare BWV 12/6 for this Franckian characteristic.

BWV 164 Ihr, die ihr euch von Christo nennet

Thirteenth Sunday after Trinity.

Salomo Franck, *Evangelisches Andachts-Opffer . . . in geistlichen Cantaten* (Weimar, 1715); Facs: Neumann T, p. 282.

6. Elisabeth Kreuziger, verse 5 of "Herr Christ, der einig Gotts Sohn," 1524 (Wackernagel, I, #236).

26 August 1725, Leipzig.

BG 33; NBA I/21.

---

1. Aria (T)

Ye who the name of Christ have taken,
Where bideth now your sense of mercy,
Whereby one Christ's true members knoweth?
It is from you, ah, all too far.
Your hearts should be with kindness filled,
And yet they're harder than a stone.

2. Recit. (B)

We've heard, indeed, what love itself doth say:
All those with mercy who have here received their neighbor,
These shall before the court
Have mercy for their judgment.[1]
And yet we give no heed to this!
We listen to our neighbor's sighs unmoved!
He knocks upon our heart; but opened is it not![2]
We see him wring his hands despairing,
His eye, too, which with tears o'erflows;
But still the heart will not to love be prompted.
The Levite and the priest
Who here now step aside
The image make of loveless Christians;
They act as if they knew of others' suffering nothing,
And they pour neither oil nor wine
Into their neighbor's wounds.[3]

3. Aria (A)

Just through love and through compassion
Will we be like God himself.
Hearts Samaritan in kindness
Find the stranger's pain as painful
And are in compassion rich.

4. Recit. (T)

Ah, melt indeed with thine own radiant love
This frigid heart of steel,
That I the true love of the Christian,
My Savior, daily practise;
And that my neighbor's mis'ry,
No matter who he is,
Friend or a foe, heath'n or Christian,
E'er strike me to the heart as much as mine own suffering!
My heart, be loving, soft and mild,
Then will in me thine image be revealed.[4]

5. Aria (S, B)

To hands which are ever open
Heaven's doors will open wide.
Eyes which flow with tears' compassion
By the Savior's grace are seen.
To hearts which for love are striving
God himself his heart will offer.

6. Chorale (S, A, T, B)

Now slay us through thy kindness,
Arouse us through thy grace;
The former man now weaken,
So that the new may live
And, here on earth now dwelling,
His mind and every yearning
And thought may raise to thee.

[1.] Cf. *Mt.* 5:7.

[2.] Cf. *Mt.* 7:7.

[3.] Cf. *Lk.* 10:34.

[4.] Cf. BWV 163/3.

BWV 165 **O heilges Geist—und Wasserbad**

Trinity.

Salomo Franck, *Evangelisches Andachts-Opffer . . . in geistlichen Cantaten* (Weimar, 1715); Facs: Neumann T, p. 279.

6. Ludwig Helmbold, verse 5 of "Nun laßt uns Gott, dem Herren," 1575 (Wackernagel, IV, #932).

16 June 1715, Weimar; again 4 June 1724?, Leipzig.

BG 33; NBA I/15.

---

1. Aria (S)

O Holy Spirit's water bath,[1]
Which to God's kingdom doth admit us
And in the book of life inscribe us!
O stream, which every evil deed
Through its most wond'rous power drowneth
And new life unto us bestoweth!
O Holy Spirit's water bath!

2. Recit. (B)

The sin-begotten birth of Adam's curséd offspring
Hath spawned the wrath of God, both death and utter ruin.
For that which of the flesh is born
Is nought but flesh, by sin contaminated,
Polluted and infected.
The Christian, though, how blest!
Within the Spirit's bathing water
He's made a child of grace and blessing.
He clads himself in Christ

And in his guiltless silken whiteness;
He is in Christ's own blood, the purple robe of glory,
Within baptism dressed.[2]

3. Aria (A)

Jesus, who for love most mighty
In baptism hath assured me
Life, salvation, and true bliss,
Help me for this to be joyful
And renew this bond of mercy
In the whole of my life's span.

4. Recit. (B)

I have, in truth, O bridegroom of my soul,
For thou new birth didst give me,
To thee sworn ever to be faithful,
O holy lamb of God;
Yet I've, alas, baptism's bond oft broken
And not fulfilled what I did promise;
Have mercy, Jesus, now,
Be gracious unto me!
Forgive me all the sins committed,
Thou know'st, my God, how painfully I suffer
The ancient serpent's sting,
Whose sinful bane corrupts my soul and body;
Help that I, faithful ever, choose thee,
O blood-red serpent's form,
Now on the cross exalted,
Which every pain doth still
And me restore when all my strength hath vanished.

5. Aria (T)

Jesus, death of mine own death,
Let this through my lifetime

514 CANTATAS

And in my last hour's need
'For mine eyes to hover:
Thou my healing serpent art
For the sinful poison.
Jesus, heal my soul and spirit,
Let me life discover!

6. Chorale (S, A, T, B)

His word, baptism, supper all
Help counter every evil;
In faith the Holy Spirit
In this to trust doth teach us.

[1.] The sense of this line is that the sacred bath consists of Spirit and of water. It is most awkward to translate within its metrical limitations.

[2.] Cf. *Gal.* 3:27.

BWV 166 **Wo gehest du hin?**

Cantate (Fourth Sunday after Easter).

Poet unknown.

1. *Jn.* 16:5; 3. Bartholomäus Ringwaldt, verse 3 of "Herr Jesu Christ, ich weiß gar wohl," 1582 (Wackernagel, IV, #1473); 6. Ämilie Juliane von Schwarzburg-Rudolstadt, verse 1 of the hymn, 1686 (Fischer-Tümpel, V, #631).

7 May 1724, Leipzig.

BG 33; NBA I/12.

---

1. Aria [Dictum] (B)

Where to dost thou go?

2. Aria (T)

I'll be unto heaven mindful,
Nor the world my heart surrender.

> For in leaving or in staying
> I'll keep e'er that question near:
> Man, ah man, where dost thou go?

3. Chorale (S)

I pray to thee, Lord Jesus Christ,
Hold me to these reflections
And let me never any time
From this resolve to waver,
Instead to it be ever true
Until my soul shall leave its nest
And into heaven journey.

4. Recit. (B)

Like as the rain-sent water soon subsideth
And many hues are quickly faded,
So is it, too, with pleasures of the world,
For which so many men such admiration hold;
For though one now and then may see
That his most hoped-for fortune blooms,
Yet can still in the best conditions
Quite unannounced the final hour strike him.

5. Aria (A)

Let ev'ryone beware
When his good fortune laughs.

On earth it is so easy
That evening be quite other
Than in the morning had been thought.[1]

6. Chorale (S, A, T, B)

Who knows how near to me mine end is?
Hence fleeth time, here cometh death;
Ah, with what promptness and what quickness
Can come to me my trial of death.
My God, I pray through Christ's own blood:
Allow but that my end be good!

---

[1]   Cf. *Ecclus.* 18:26.

BWV 167 **Ihr Menschen, rühmet Gottes Liebe**

St. John the Baptist.

Poet unknown.

5. Johann Gramann, verse 5 of "Nun lob, mein Seel, den Herren,"
Königsberg, 1548 (Wackernagel, I, #455).

24 June 1723, Leipzig.

BG 33; NBA I/29.

---

1. Aria (T)

Ye mortals, tell of God's devotion
And glorify his graciousness!

> Praise him with purest heart's emotion,
> That he to us within our time
> The horn that saves, and life's true pathway[1]
> In Jesus, his own Son, hath given.

2. Recit. (A)

Now blessed be the Lord God of Israel,[2]
Who doth in his mercy come unto us
And his own Son
From heaven's lofty throne
To save the world hath sent us.
First at that time did John appear
And must the way and path
Make ready for the Savior;
And then did Jesus come himself,
That wretched mankind's children
And all the fallen sinners
With grace and love might be made glad
And unto paradise in true repentance guided.

3. Aria (S, A)

God's true word deceiveth not;
All comes true as he doth pledge.

> What he in that paradise[3]
> Many hundred years ago now
> To our fathers hath assured
> Have we here, praise God, experienced.

4. Recit. (T)

The woman's seed did come
When once the time was ready;
The blessing which God Abraham,
The faith's great man, had promised
Is like a beam of sunlight on us broken,
And all our sorrow is grown silent.
A dumb man, Zacharias, cries
Aloud his praise to God for this his wondrous deed,
Which he the folk[4] made manifest.
And think, ye Christians, too, what God for you hath done,
And raise to him a song of praise!

5. Chorale (S, A, T, B)

Now laud and praise with honor
God Father, Son, and Holy Ghost!
May he in us add measure
To what he us in mercy pledged,
That we may firmly trust him,
Entirely rest on him;
Sincere on him depending
May our heart, mind and will
Steadfast to him be cleaving;
To this now let us sing:
Amen, we shall achieve it,
This is our heart's firm faith.

[1.]   Cf. *Lk.* 1:69.

[2.]   Cf. *Lk.* 1:68.

[3.]   I.e., in the Garden of Eden.

[4.]   I.e., the Jews.

BWV 168 **Tue Rechnung! Donnerwort**

Ninth Sunday after Trinity.

Salomo Franck, *Evangelisches Andachts-Opffer* . . . *in geistlichen Cantaten* (Weimar, 1715); Facs: Neumann T, p. 281.

6. Bartholomäus Ringwaldt, verse 8 of "Herr Jesu Christ, du höchstes Gut," 1588 (Wackernagel, IV, #1523).

29 July 1725, Leipzig?

BG 33; NBA I/19.

1. Aria (B)

Make a reck'ning![1] Thundrous word,
Which e'en rocky cliffs split open,
Word by which my blood grows frigid!
Day of reck'ning! Soul, go forth!
Ah, thou must God make repayment
Of his blessings, life and body.
Make a reck'ning! Thund'rous word!

2. Recit. (T)

All is but borrowed wealth
That I through out my life am holding;
Soul, being, will and blood
And post and rank, all by my God are given;
They are mine to care for
And ever faithfully to manage,

From lofty hands received in trust.
Ah! Oh alas! I shake
Whenever I my conscience enter
And then in my accounts so many errors witness!
I have both day and night
The many things which God hath lent me
Indifferently consumed!
How can I thee, O God of right, escape then?
I cry aloud and weep:
Ye mountains, fall! Ye hills, conceal me now[2]
From God's own wrathful judgment
And from the flash of his own countenance!

3. Aria (T)

Principal and interest also,
These my debts, both large and small,
Must one day be reckoned all.
All for which I'm yet indebted
Is in God's own book now written
As in steel and adamant.

4. Recit. (B)

But yet, O frightened heart, live and despair thou not!
Step gladly 'fore the court!
And if thy conscience should convict thee,
Thou must be here constrained to silence;
Behold thy guarantor,
He hath all debts for thee released!
It is repaid and fully wiped away
What thou, O man, thy reck'ning art still owing;
The lamb's own blood, O love most mighty!,
Hath all thy debt now canceled

And thee with God hath settled.
It is repaid, thy balance cleared!
And meanwhile,
Since thou know'st
That thou a steward art,
Thus be concerned and ever mindful
That thou make prudent use of Mammon
To benefit the poor;
Thus shalt thou, when both time and life have ended,
In heaven's shelter rest secure.

5. Aria (S, A)

Heart, break free of Mammon's fetters,
Hands now, scatter good abroad!
Make ye soft my dying pallet,
Build for me a solid house,
Which in heaven ever bideth
When earth's wealth to dust is scattered.

6. Chorale (S, A, T, B)

Make me strong with thy Spirit's joy,
Heal me with thine own wounding,
Wash me with thine own dying sweat
In mine own final hours;
And take me then, whene're thou wilt,
In true believing from the world
To thine own chosen people.

---

1.   Cf. *Lk.* 16:2. It is characteristic of Salomo Franck that the imagery of the
     cantata is drawn from the language of finance.

2.   Cf. *Lk.* 23:30.

BWV 169 **Gott soll allein mein Herze haben**

Eighteenth Sunday after Trinity.

Poet unknown.

7. Martin Luther, verse 3 of "Nun bitten wir den Heiligen Geist," 1524 (Wackernagel, I, #208).

20 October 1726, Leipzig; Parody: 1, 5 & ← *Harpsichord Concerto in E Major*, BWV 1053.

BG 33; NBA I/24.

1. Sinfonia

2. Arioso and Recit. (A)

God all alone my heart shall master.
I see, though, that the world,
Which doth its rot as priceless hold,
While it doth me so fondly court,
Would gladly all alone
Beloved be of this my soul.
But no; God all alone my heart shall master:
I find in him the highest worth.
We see, indeed,
On earth, now here, now there,
A rivulet of joy sublime
Which from the Highest's kindness welleth;
God is, indeed, the source, whose streams he ever filleth,
Where I'll draw that which for all time
Shall fill me and bring true refreshment:
God all alone my heart shall master.

3. Aria (A)

God all alone my heart shall master,
I find in him the highest worth.

> He loves me in the worst of times
> And shall, when I have come to bliss,
> With treasures of his house refresh me.

4. Recit. (A)

What is the love of God, then?
The spirit's rest,
The heart's desire and joy,
The soul's true paradise.
It shuts the gates of hell
And heaven opens wide;
It is Elijah's chariot,
Which shall lift us to heaven above
To Abraham's own bosom.[1]

5. Aria (A)

Die in me,
World and all of thine affections,
That my breast,
While on earth yet, more and more
Here the love of God may practise;
Die in me,
Pomp and wealth and outward show,
Ye corrupted carnal motives!

6. Recit. (A)

This means that ye must too
Be to your neighbor true!

For so it stands in Scripture written:
Thou shalt love God and also neighbor.

7. Chorale (S, A, T, B)

Thou love so tender, give to us thy grace,
Let us perceive now the fire of love,
That we may sincerely love one another
And in peace and of one mind be ever.
Kyrie eleis.

[1.]   Cf. 2 *Kg.* 2:11 and *Lk.* 16:22.

BWV 170 **Vergnügte Ruh, beliebte Seelenlust**

Sixth Sunday after Trinity.

Georg Christian Lehms, *Gottgefälliges Kirchen-Opffer* (Darmstadt, 1711);
Facs: Neumann T, p. 260.

28 July 1726, Leipzig.

BG 33; NBA I/17.

---

1. Aria (A)

Contented rest, belovéd inner joy,

> We cannot find thee midst hell's mischief,
> But rather in the heavenly concord;
> Thou only mak'st the weak breast strong.
> Thus I'll let only virtue's talents
> Within my heart maintain their dwelling.

2. Recit. (A)

The world, that house of sin,
Brings nought but hellish lyrics forth
And seeks through hate and spite
The devil's image e'er to cherish.
Her mouth is filled with viper's bane,
Which oft the guiltless strikes with death,
And would alone her "Raca!"[1] utter.
O righteous God, how far
In truth is man from thee divided;
Thou lov'st, but yet his mouth
Cries curse and hate abroad
And would his neighbor under foot e'er trample.
Ah, this great sin defies propitiation!

3. Aria (A)

What sorrow fills me for these wayward spirits,
Who have, my God, so much offended thee;
I tremble, yea, and feel a thousand torments,
When they in nought but harm and hate find joy.
O righteous God, what may'st thou then consider,
When they who deal alone with Satan's plotters
Thy judgment's stern command so bold do flout.
Ah, I've no doubt but that thou then hast thought:
What sorrow fills me for these wayward spirits!

4. Recit. (A)

Who shall, therefore, desire
To live in this existence,
When nought but hate and misery
Before his love are seen?
But, since I e'en my foe
As though my closest friend

By God's commandment am to love,
Thus flees
My heart all wrath and hate
And seeks alone with God its dwelling,
Who is himself called love.
Alas, O peaceful soul,
When will he thee indeed bring to his heav'nly Zion?

5. Aria (A)

I'm sick to death of living,
So take me, Jesus, hence!

> I fear for mine offenses,
> Let me find there that dwelling
> Wherein I may have rest.

[1.] Hebrew *Raca* 'thou fool!' Cf. *Mt.* 5:22.

BWV 171 **Gott, wie dein Name, so ist auch dein Ruhm**

New Year's Day (Feast of the Circumcision).

Christian Friedrich Henrici (Picander), *Ernst-Schertzhaffte und Satyrische Gedichte, Teil III* (Leipzig, 1732); Facs: Neumann T, p. 336.

1. *Ps.* 48:11; 6. final chorale without text; BG supplies Johannes Herman, verse 3 of "Jesu, nun sei gepreiset," 1593; PT supplies verse 2 of this hymn.

1 January 1729?, Leipzig. Parody: 1 → *Mass in B Minor,* BWV 232/ 13; 4 ← BWV 205/9.

BG 35; NBA I/4, 133.

1. Chorus [Dictum] (S, A, T, B)

God, as thy name is, so is, too, thy fame to the ends of the earth.

2. Aria (T)

Lord, as far as clouds are stretching,
Stretcheth thine own name's great fame.
Ev'rything which stirs the lips,
Ev'rything which draweth breath,
Will now in thy might exalt thee.

3. Recit. (A)

Thou sweetest name[1] of Jesus thou,
In thee is my repose;
Thou art my earthly comfort,
How can I then
Midst cross be ever anxious?
Thou art my sure defense and my great sign,
To which I run
Whene'er I am oppressed.
Thou art my being and my light,
My glory, my true confidence,
My helper in distress,
And my reward for the new year.

4. Aria (S)

Jesus shall my first word be
In the new year to be spoken.
On and on
Laughs his name within my mouth now,
And within my final moments
Is Jesus, too, my final word.

5. Recit. (B)

And since thou, Lord, hath said:
If ye pray in my name's honor,[2]
Ev'rything is "Yes!" and "Amen!"
Thus do we cry,
Thou Savior of the world, to thee:
Reject us now no more,
Protect us through this year
From fire, plague and risk of war!
Leave us thy word, that brilliant light,
Still pure and clearly burning;
Give our authorities
And unto all the nation
Thy healing blessing to acknowledge;
Give evermore
Joy and health to every station.
We pray this, Lord, in thy name's honor;
Say "Yes!" to this say "Amen, amen!"

6. Chorale (S, A, T, B)

[Let us this year complete then
To bring praise to thy name
And sing to it our praises
Within the Christian fold.
If thou our life wouldst limit
Through thine almighty hand,
Support these thy dear Christians
And this our fatherland!
Thy blessing turn upon us,
Give peace in every region,
Make undisguised in this land
Thy joy-inspiring word;

To devils bring destruction
Here and in all the world!]³

---

1. Cf. *Lk.* 2:21.
2. Cf. *Jn.* 14:13.
3. This is the verse of the hymn in Picander's text.

BWV 172 **Erschallet, ihr Lieder, erklinget ihr Saiten!**

Pentecost (Whitsunday).

Probably Salomo Franck; PT (Leipzig, 1731); Facs: Neumann T, p. 444.

2. *Jn.* 14:23; 5. instrumental chorale: "Komm, Heiliger Geist, Herre Gott" (cf. BWV 59/3); 6. Philipp Nicolai, verse 4 of "Wie schön leuchtet der Morgenstern," 1599.

20 May 1714, Weimar; revised and performed several times, Leipzig.

BG 35; NBA I/13, and 35.

---

1. Chorus (S, A, T, B)

Resound now, ye lyrics, ring out now, ye lyres!
O happiest hours!
God shall all the souls to his temples now gather.

2. Recit. [Dictum] (B)

He who loves me will keep my commandments, and my Father will then love him, and we unto him will journey and with him make our dwelling.

3. Aria (B)

O most Holy Trinity,
Mighty God of honor,

> Come still in this time of grace,
> Make with us thy sojourn,
> Come still unto our heart's shelters,
> Be they e'er so poor and small,
> Come and yield to our entreaty,
> Come and sojourn with us here!

4. Aria (T)

O paradise of souls,
Through which God's Spirit wafteth,

> Who at Creation blew,
> The Spirit ever present;
> Rise, rise, prepare thyself,
> Thy Comforter is near.

5. Aria (S, A) Soul, Holy Ghost, with instr. chorale

(Soul)
Come, make me no longer tarry,
Come, thou gentle heav'nly wind,
Waft now through the spirit's garden![1]

(Holy Ghost)
I'll enliven thee, my child.

(Soul)
Dearest love, thou so charming,
Of all joy abundant store,
I shall die if I not have thee.

(Holy Ghost)
Take from me the kiss of grace.

(Soul)
Come to me in faith most welcome,
Love most precious, come to me!
Thou from me my heart hast stolen.

(Holy Ghost)
I am thine, and thou art mine!

6. Chorale (S, A, T, B)

From God to me comes joyful light,
When thou with thine own precious eye
With kindness dost regard me.
O Lord Jesus, my trusted good,
Thy word, thy soul, thy flesh and blood
Me inwardly enliven.
Take me
Kindly
In thine arms now, make me warm now with thy favor:
To thy word I come invited.

7. First Movement Repeated

---

1. *Herzensgarten* is an etymology of the *Seelenparadies* in Movement 4: 'paradise' is derived from the Persian for 'garden.'

BWV 173 **Erhöhtes Fleisch und Blut**

Second Day of Pentecost.

Poet unknown; PT (Leipzig, 1731); Facs: Neumann T, p. 445.

29 May 1724, Leipzig; Parody ← BWV 173a/1-5, 8.

BG 35; NBA I/14.

---

1. Recit. (T)

Exalted flesh and blood,
Which God himself accepts,
Which he on earth already
Assigns a heav'nly bliss,
As God's own child transformed now,
Exalted flesh and blood!

2. Aria (T)

A redeemed and hallowed spirit
Sees and savors God's own kindness.
Praising, singing, tune your lyres,
God's devotion tell the nations!

3. Aria (A)

God shall, O ye mortal children,
For you mighty things achieve.

> Mouth and spirit, ear and vision
> Cannot now amidst such fortune
> And such holy joy keep still.

4. Aria (B, S)

(B)
For hath God the world so loved,[1]
So his mercy
Helps us poor ones,
That he gives to us his Son,

Gracious blessings for our pleasure,
Which like fertile streams are flowing.

(S)
His New Testament of grace
Is effective
And has power
In the human heart and voice,
That his Spirit for his honor
Teach them faithfully to call him.

(Both)
Now we'll let our duty bound
Bring its off'ring,
Grateful singing;
For his light, made manifest,
Now is to his children bending
And to them appeareth clearly.

5. Recit. (S, T)

O infinite, whom yet we Father call,
We would in turn our hearts as off'rings bring thee;
From these our breasts, which full with worship burn,
Shall rise our sighing's fire, to heaven soaring.

6. Chorus (S, A, T, B)

Stir, Almighty, now our souls,
That the Holy Spirit's blessings
Their effect within us work now!
As thy Son did bid us pray,
Will it through the clouds come bursting
And give ear to our petition.

[1.] Cf. *Jn.* 3:16.

BWV 173a **Durchlauchster Leopold**

Birthday of Prince Leopold of Anhalt-Cöthen (10 December).

Poet unknown.

10 December 1717-1722?, Cöthen; Parody: 1-5, 8 → BWV 173; 7 → BWV 175/4.

BG 34; NBA I/35.

1. Recit. (S)

Illustrious Leopold,
Now singeth Anhalt's world
Again with glad contentment,
Thy Cöthen comes to thee
To bow the knee before thee,
Illustrious Leopold!

2. Aria (S)

Golden sunlight's happy hours,
Those which very heaven gathers,
Make again now their appearance;
Praising, singing, tune the lyres,
That his fame may be extended!

3. Aria (B)

Leopold's most splendid virtues
Give to us now much to do.

Mouth and spirit, ear and vision
Cannot now midst his good fortune,
Which doth gladly tend him, rest

4. Aria (B, S)

(B)
Here beneath his purple hem
Is great gladness
Born of sadness;
Each one gives he ample room
Blessing's riches to enjoy here,
Which like fertile streams are flowing.

(S)
And as a country's father should,
He sustaineth,
Harm averteth;
Therefore now the hope is born
That he shall soon Anhalt's country
Bring into good fortune's station.

(Both)
Yet we'll let our duty not
In our pleasure
Now escape us,
This day, when e'en heaven's light
Doth its servant fill with gladness
And upon his scepter smileth.

5. Recit. (S, B)

Illustrious one, whom Anhalt "Father" calls,
We will in turn our hearts to thee now offer;
From these our breasts, which full with worship burn,
Shall rise our sighing's fire to heaven soaring.

6. Aria (S)

Behold this lovely day's bright light
Still many, many times yet.

And just as now attend it
High well-being and good fortune,
So may it know, when it breaks forth
In future years no trouble here.

7. Aria (B)

Thy name shall like the sun go forth,
E're whiling midst the stars shall stand!
Leopold in Anhalt's borders
Shall in princely fame be glorious.

8. Chorus (S, B)

Lift us, O great Prince, as well,
And all those who for thine honor
Here most humbly raise their voices!
Happy be thy life's full course,
May thy people have such blessing
As upon thine head we're laying!

BWV 174 Ich liebe den Höchsten von ganzem Gemüte

Second Day of Pentecost.

Christian Friedrich Henrici (Picander), *Ernst-Schertzhaffte und Satyrische Gedichte, Teil III.* (Leipzig, 1732); Facs: Neumann T, p. 341.

5. Martin Schalling, verse 1 of the hymn, 1571 (Wackernagel, IV, #1174.

6 June 1729, Leipzig; Parody: 1 ← Brandenburg Concerto III, BWV 1048/1.

BG 35; NA I/14.

---

1. Sinfonia

2. Aria (A)

I love the Almighty with all of my spirit,
He holds me, too, exceeding dear.

> God alone
> Shall all souls' true treasure be,
> Where I have forever a wellspring of kindness.

3. Recit. (T)

What love this, which to none is like!
O what a priceless ransom this!
The Father hath his child's own life now
For sinners up to death delivered
And all those who did paradise
Make light of and then lost it
To blessedness elected.
For so hath God the world now loved![1]
My heart, remember this
And in these words receive thy comfort;
Before this mighty banner's sign
Now tremble even hell's own portals.

4. Aria (B)

Take it now,
Clasp your hope, ye hands which trust him!

Jesus gives his paradise
And requires but this of you:
Keep your faith until the finish!

5. Chorale (S, A, T, B)

My heart doth love thee so, O Lord.
I pray, stand not from me afar
With thy support and mercy.
The whole world gives not joy to me,
For sky and earth my quest is not,
If I can only have thee.
And even if my heart should break,
Yet thou art still my confidence,
My Savior and my heart's true hope,
Who me through his blood hath redeemed.
Lord Jesus Christ,
My God and Lord, my God and Lord,
To scorn now put me nevermore!

[1.] *Jn.* 3:16.

BWV 175 **Er rufet seinen Schafen mit Namen**

Third Day of Pentecost.

Christiane Mariane von Ziegler, *Versuch in Gebundener Schreibart, Teil I* (Leipzig, 1728), with many changes; Facs: Neumann T, p. 364.

1. *Jn.* 10:3; 5a. *Jn.* 10:6; 7. Johann Rist, verse 9 of "O Gottes Geist, mein Trost und Rat," 1651 (Fischer-Tümpel, II, #247), with an added *Alleluia.*

22 May 1725, Leipzig; Parody: 4 ← BWV 173a/7.

BG 35; NBA I/14.

---

1. Recit. [Dictum] (T)

He calleth his own sheep by name then and leadeth them outside!

2. Aria (A)

Come, lead me out,
With longing doth
My soul desire green pasture!

> My heart doth yearn,
> Sigh day and night,
> My shepherd, thou my pleasure.

3. Recit. (T)

Where art thou then?
Ah, where art thou now hidden?
Oh! To me soon appear!
I long for thee.
Break forth, O welcome morning!

4. Aria (T)

It seems to me, I see thee coming,
Thou com'st through the proper door.
Thou art by faith received amongst us
And must then our true shepherd be.
I recognize thy voice so graceful,
So full of love and gentleness,
That in my soul I'm moved to anger

At doubters that thou Savior art.[1]
5a. Recit. [Dictum] (A)
They, however, did not see what it was that he with this had been saying to them.

5b. Recit. (B)

Ah, yes! We mortals are often to deaf men to be likened:
Whenever blinded Reason fails to grasp what he hath spoken to it.
Oh! Folly, mark it well when Jesus to thee speaks,
It is for thy salvation done.

6. Aria (B)

Open ye both ears and listen,
Jesus' oath is your assurance
That he devil, death hath slain.

> Blessing, plenty, life abundant
> Shall he give to every Christian
> Who obeys, his cross doth bear.

7. Chorale (S, A, T, B)

Now, spirit dear, I'll follow thee;
Help me to seek out more and more
At thine own word a new existence,
One thou wouldst give me of thy mercy.
Thy word is, yea, the morning star,
Whose glory shineth near and far.
And I'll to those who would deceive me
Eternally, my God, not listen.
Alleluia, alleluia!

---

[1]   The Ziegler PT and Bach's texts often differ. The differences in this case are typical. Perhaps there was a theological basis (the doctrine of

justification by faith, n.b. line 3) for some of the changes. Here is the
PT version of 4:

[4.] ARIA
Mir ist, als säh ich dich schon kommen,
Du gehst zur rechten Thür hinein,
Ich werd im Glauben aufgenommen,
Du wirst der wahre Hirte seyn.
Wer wolte nicht die Stimme kennen,
Die voller Huld und Sanfftmuth ist
Und nicht so gleich vor Sehnsucht brennen,
Weil du der treuste Hirte bist.

Me thinks I see thee e'en now coming,
Thou com'st through the proper door.
I shall in faith by him be welcomed,
Thou wilt in truth the shepherd be.
Who would not recognize thy voice now,
So full of grace and gentleness,
And not at once with yearning burn then,
For thou the faithful shepherd art?

2.   In 5 Bach's text makes a change which personifies Reason as Folly, a
change consistent with the attention to the nature of Faith in 4.

BWV 176 **Es ist ein trotzig und verzagt Ding**

Trinity.

Christiane Mariane von Ziegler, *Versuch in Gebundener Schreibart, Teil I*
(Leipzig, 1728), with many changes; Facs: Neumann T, p. 365.

1. After *Jer.* 17:9; 6. Paul Gerhardt, verse 8 of "Was alle Weisheit in
der Welt," 1653 (Fischer-Tümpel, III, #415).

27 May 1725, Leipzig.

BG 35; NBA I/15.

---

1. Chorus [Dictum] (S, A, T, B)

There is both daring and deception within all human spirits.[1]

2. Recit. (A)

I say it was deceit
That Nicodemus dares by day come not,
To Jesus, but by night.
The sun was forced one day for Joshua so long to stand in place,
Until at last the victory was fully won;
Here, though, does Nicodemus wish: O would the sun now go to rest!

3. Aria (A)

Thy dear light, before so bright,
Must for me the clouds obscure,
While I go to seek the master,
For by day I am too fearful.
No man can these wonders do,
For his nature and vast power
Seem to be divinely chosen;
God's own Spirit on him rests.

4. Recit. (B)

So marvel then, O Master, not,
That I should thee at night be seeking!
I'm fearful, lest by daylight

My weakness could not stand the test.
And yet I hope thou shalt my heart and soul
To life exalt and take.
For all who have faith in thee only shall not be forsaken.[2]

5. Aria (A)

Have courage now, fearful and timorous spirits,
Recover now, hear ye what Jesus doth pledge:
That I through believing shall heaven inherit.
When this great promise fulfillment achieves,
Shall I in heaven
With thanks and with praises
Father, Son and Holy Ghost
Honor, the Three-in-One named.

6. Chorale (S, A, T, B)

Rise, that we may now all as one
To heaven's portals hasten;
And when at last within thy realm
May we forever sing there
That thou alone art truly king,
All other gods excelling,
God Father, Son and Holy Ghost,
Of good men shield and Savior,
One being, but three persons.

[1.] Luther's text: "Es ist das Herz ein trotzig und verzagt Ding." RSV: "The heart is deceitful above all things, and desperately corrupt." The *Septuagint* says that the heart is "deep" and that man is difficult to fathom. The Lord alone understands him. *Trotzig* and *verzagt* apparently encompass the daring and the timidity of this "deep" creature.

[2.] This line is not in Ziegler's PT. Cf. *Jn.* 3:15.

BWV 177 Ich ruf, zu dir, Herr Jesu Christ

Fourth Sunday after Trinity.

Johann Agricola, the five verses of the hymn, 1529?/31 (Wackernagel, III, #78 ff.); PT (Leipzig, 1725); Facs: Neumann T, p. 433.

6 July 1732, Leipzig (so Dürr).

BG 35; NBA I/17.

1. Chorus [Verse 1] (S, A, T, B)

I call to thee, Lord Jesus Christ,
I pray thee, hear my crying;
Both lend me grace within this life
And let me not lose courage;
The proper path, O Lord, I seek,
Which thou didst wish to give me:
For thee living,
My neighbor serving well,
Thy word upholding justly.

2. Aria [Verse 2] (A)

I pray still more, O Lord my God,
Thou canst on me bestow this:
That I be never brought to scorn,
Give hope as my companion,
And then, when I must hence depart,
That I may ever trust thee,
Not relying
On my works only,
Else shall I e'er regret it.

3. Aria [Verse 3] (S)

Now grant that I with heart sincere
Be to my foes forgiving;
Forgive me also at this hour,
For me my life renewing;
Thy word my food let always be
With which my soul to nurture,
Me defending,
When sorrow draweth nigh
And threatens to distract me.

4. Aria [Verse 4] (T)

Now let no joy nor fear from thee
Within this world divert me.
Make me steadfast until the end,
Thou hast alone the power;
Who has thy gifts has them for free;
For no man can inherit
Nor acquire yet
Through his works thy dear grace
Which us redeems from dying.

5. Chorale [Verse 5] (S, A, T, B)

I lie midst strife and now resist,
Help, O Lord Christ, my weakness!
Unto thy grace alone I cling,
For thou canst make me stronger.
Come now temptation, Lord, defend,
Let it not overthrow me.
Thou canst check it
Lest it bring me to harm;
I know thou shalt not let it.

BWV 178 **Wo Gott der Herr nicht bei uns hält**

Eighth Sunday after Trinity.

Poet unknown.

1. Justus Jonas, verse 1 of the hymn, based on *Ps.* 124, 1524 (Wackernagel, III, #62); 2. verse 2 with interpolated recitative; 3. based on verse 3; 4. verse 4; 5. verse 5 with interpolated recitative; 6. based on verse 6; 7. verses 7 and 8 of the hymn.

30 July 1724, Leipzig.

BG 35; NBA I/18.

1. Chorus [Verse 1] (S, A, T, B)

Where God the Lord stands with us not,
Whene'er our foes are raging,
And he doth not our cause support
In heaven high above us,
Where he Israel's shield is not
Nor breaks himself the foe's deceit,
Then is our cause defeated.

2. Chorale [Verse 2] and Recit. (A)

What human power and wit contrive
Shall us in no wise frighten;
For God Almighty stands with us
And shall set us from their devices free.
He sitteth in the highest seat,

He shall expose their counsels.
Who God in faith embrace securely
Shall he abandon never, nor forsake them;
He foils the will of wicked men
And hinders all their evil deeds.
When they most cunningly attack,
With serpent's guile their artful plots conceiving,
Their wicked purpose for achieving,
God doth pursue another path:
He leads his people with his mighty hand,
Through ocean-cross into the promised land,
When he will all misfortune banish.
It stands in his hands' power.

3. Aria (B)

Like as the savage ocean waters
Midst raging storm a ship will shatter,
So rageth, too, the foe's deep wrath
To steal the soul's most precious wealth;
They seek now Satan's realm to broaden,
And Christ's own little ship should founder.

4. Chorale [Verse 4] (T)

They lie in wait like heretics,
And for our blood are thirsting;
They claim that they are Christians, too,
Who God alone give worship.
Ah God, that precious name of thine
Must serve as capstone to their crime;
Thou shalt one day awaken.

5. Chorale [Verse 5] (S, A, T, B) and Recit. (B, T, A)

(S, A, T, B)
They open wide their hungry jaws,

(B)
As lions do, with roaring rage resounding;
They bare at us the fangs of killers,

(S, A, T, B)
Intending to devour us.

(T)
And yet,

(S, A, T, B)
Praise and thanks to God evermore

(T)
Shall Judah's hero shield us still,

(S, A, T, B)
Their aim they'll not accomplish!

(A)
They shall like unto chaff subside,
When once his faithful people like green trees shall stand.

(S, A, T, B)
He shall their snares asunder break
And their false doctrine bring to nought.

(B)
God will all vain and foolish prophets
With fire of his anger slay then
And bring their heresies to ruin.

(S, A, T, B)
From God they'll not defend it.

6. Aria (T)

Hush, hush then, giddy intellect!

> Say not, "The pious are now lost!"
> The cross did them but bring new birth.
> To all who put their trust in Jesus
> Stands e'er the door of blessing open;
> And when by cross and sadness pressed,
> They shall with comfort be refreshed.

7. Chorale [Verses 7 and 8] (S, A, T, B)

The foe are all within thine hand,
With them all their conceptions;
Their onslaughts are to thee, Lord, known,
But help us not to waver.
If mind opposing faith assail,
Henceforth shall its assurance fail,
For thou thyself shalt help us.
Both heaven and the earth as well
Hast thou, Lord God, established;
Thy light for us let brightly shine,
Our hearts shall be enkindled
With proper love for thy great faith,
Until the end steadfastly thine.
The world let ever murmur.

BWV 179 Siehe zu, daß deine Gottesfurcht nicht Heuchelei sei

Eleventh Sunday after Trinity.

Poet unknown.

1. *Ecclus.* 1:34; 6. Christoph Tietze, verse 1 of the hymn, 1663 (Fischer-Tümpel, IV, #349).

8. August 1723, Leipzig; Parody: 1 and 3 → *Mass in G*, BWV 236/1 and 5.

BG 34; NBA I/20.

1. Chorus [Dictum] (S, A, T, B)

Watch with care lest all thy piety hypocrisy be, and serve thy God not with feigning spirit!

2. Recit. (T)

Today's Christianity,
Alas, is ill-disposed:
Most Christian people in the world
Are lukewarm like Laodicaeans,[1]
And like the puffed up Pharisaeans,
Who outwardly appear so pious
And like the reeds their heads to earth bend humbly,
Though in their hearts there lurks a pompous vanity;
They go, indeed, into God's house
And there perform their superficial duties,
But does all this in truth a Christian make?
No, hypocrites themselves can do this.

3. Aria (T)

Likeness of false hypocrites,
We could Sodom's apples[2] call them,
Who, with rot though they be filled,
On the outside brightly glisten.
Hypocrites, though outward fair,
Cannot stand before God's throne.

4. Recit. (B)

Who is both inward and without the same
Is a true Christian called.
Such was the publican in temple,
Who beat in great remorse his breast,
Ascribing to himself no pious character;
So this one call to mind,
O man, a laudable example
For thine own penitence.
Art thou no robber, marriage wrecker,
No unjust bearer of false witness,
Ah, do thou not in fact presume
That thou art therefore angel-pure!
Confess to God most humbly thy transgressions,
And thou shalt find both help and mercy!

5. Aria (S)

Dearest God, have mercy now,
Let thy help and grace be present!

    Mine offenses vex me so,
    Like an abscess in my body;[3]
    Help me, Jesus, lamb of God,
    For I sink now deep in mire![4]

3. Aria (T)

Likeness of false hypocrites,
We could Sodom's apples[2] call them,
Who, with rot though they be filled,
On the outside brightly glisten.
Hypocrites, though outward fair,
Cannot stand before God's throne.

4. Recit. (B)

Who is both inward and without the same
Is a true Christian called.
Such was the publican in temple,
Who beat in great remorse his breast,
Ascribing to himself no pious character;
So this one call to mind,
O man, a laudable example
For thine own penitence.
Art thou no robber, marriage wrecker,
No unjust bearer of false witness,
Ah, do thou not in fact presume
That thou art therefore angel-pure!
Confess to God most humbly thy transgressions,
And thou shalt find both help and mercy!

5. Aria (S)

Dearest God, have mercy now,
Let thy help and grace be present!

Mine offenses vex me so,
Like an abscess in my body;[3]
Help me, Jesus, lamb of God,
For I sink now deep in mire![4]

1. Chorus (S, A, T, B)

Deck thyself, O soul beloved,
Leave sin's dark and murky hollows,
Come, the brilliant light approaching,
Now begin to shine with glory;
For the Lord with health and blessing
Hath thee as his guest invited.
He, of heaven now the master,
Seeks his lodging here within thee.

2. Aria (T)

Be lively now: thy Savior knocks,
Ah, open soon thy spirit's portals!

> Although thou in enchanted joy
> But partly broken words of gladness
> Must to thy Jesus utter now.

3. Recit. and Chorale [Verse 4] (S)

How costly are the holy banquet's off'rings!
None other like them can be found.
All else the world
Doth precious think
Is trash and idle nothing;
A child of God would seek to have this treasure
And say:
Ah, how hungry is my spirit,
Friend of man, to have thy kindness
Ah, how oft I am with weeping
For this treasure filled with yearning!
Ah, how often am I thirsting

For the drink from life's true sovereign,
Hoping ever that my body
Be through God with God united.

4. Recit. (A)

My heart within feels fear and gladness;
It is with fear inspired
When it that majesty doth weigh,
When it no way into the secret findeth
Nor with the mind this lofty work can fathom.
God's Spirit, though, can through his word instruct us
How here all spirits shall be nurtured
Which have themselves in faith arrayed.
Our gladness, though, is ever strengthened
When we the Savior's heart behold
And of his love the greatness witness.

5. Aria (S)

Life's true sunlight, light of feeling,
Lord, thou who art all to me!

> Thou wilt see that I am loyal
> And my faith wilt not disparage,
> Which is weak and fearful yet.

6. Recit. (B)

Lord, let in me thy faithful loving,
Which out of heaven thee hath driven,
Yea, not in vain have been.
Enkindle thou my spirit with thy love,
That it may only things of heav'nly worth
In faith be seeking
And of thy love be ever mindful.

7. Chorale [Verse 9] (S, A, T, B)

Jesus, bread of life most truly,
Help that I may never vainly,
Nor perhaps e'en to my sorrow,
Be invited to thy table.
Grant that through this food of spirits
I thy love may rightly measure,
That I too, as here on earth now,
May become a guest in heaven.

[1.] Dürr, p. 485, gives the date of the hymn as 1649; Neumann T, p. 143, gives 1653; Fischer-Tümpel, IV, p. 66, reports that in Johann Franckens *Hundert-Thönige Vater-Unsers-Harffe* (Wittenbergk, 1646), the first lines of a large number of Franck's hymns were mentioned which had by that date already been composed, but not yet published, among them this hymn.

BWV 181 **Leichtgesinnte Flattergeister**

Sexagesima Sunday.

Poet unknown; PT (Leipzig, 1724); Facs: Neumann T, p. 426.

13 February 1724, Leipzig.

BG 37; NBA I/7.

---

1. Aria (B)

Insincere and fickle spirits
Sap the word of all its strength.
Belial[1] with all his children

Seeketh also to obstruct it,
That it may no use afford.

2. Recit. (A)

O most unhappy band of wayward spirits,
Who stand as though beside the path;[2]
And who shall then of Satan's guile be telling,
If from the heart the word he steals,
Which, in good judgment blind,
The harm doth not believe or grasp?
One day those hearts, so stony,
Which wickedly resist
Will their salvation forfeit
And meet at last their doom.
So strong, indeed, was Christ's last word
That very cliffs did crumble;
The angel's hand did move the tomb's own stone,
Yea, Moses' staff could once
Bring from a mountain flowing water.
Wouldst thou, O heart, still harder be?

3. Aria (T)

Injurious thorns in their infinite toll,
The worry of pleasure to increase its treasure,
These shall both the flames and the torment of hell
Eternally nourish.

4. Recit. (S)

By these will all our strength be choked,
The noble seed will lie unfruitful,
If we not well our souls obey,
And hearts in season
For fertile land do not make ready,

So that our hearts those sweet rewards may savor
To us this word revealeth:
The powers of this life and of life hereafter.

5. Aria (S, A, T, B)

O Master, give us every season
Our heart's repose, thy holy word.

> Thou canst through thine almighty hand
> Alone a fair and fruitful land
> Within these hearts of ours make ready.

---

1. In Hebrew *Belial* means 'wickedness' and in the New Testament is used for Satan.
2. Cf. *Lk.* 8:11-12, in the Gospel for Sexagesima: "Now the parable is this: The seed is the word of God. The ones along the path are those who have heard; then the devil comes and takes away the word from their hearts, that they may not believe and be saved." This passage inspired the imagery of planting in the cantata.

BWV 182 Himmelskönig, sei willkommen

Palm Sunday or the Annunciation.

Probably Salomo Franck.

1. *Ps.* 40:8-9; 7. Paul Stockmann, 33rd verse of "Jesu Leiden, Pein und Tod," 1633 (Fischer-Tümpel, II, #37).

25 March 1714, Weimar; again 25 March 1724, Leipzig.

BG 37; NBA I/8.

---

1. Sonata

2. Chorus (S, A, T, B)

King of heaven, thou art welcome,
Let e'en us thy Zion be!

> Come inside,
> Thou hast won our hearts completely.

3. Recit. [Dictum] (B)[1]

Lo now, I'm coming. Of me in the book is written: What thy will is,
my God, I do gladly.

4. Aria (B)

Strong compassion,
Which, O mighty Son of God,
From the throne
Of thy majesty did drive thee!
Strong compassion,
That thou didst to heal the world
As a victim give thyself,
That thyself with blood didst sentence.

5. Aria (A)

Lie before your Savior prostrate,
Hearts of all who Christian are!

> Don ye now a spotless robe
> Of your faith in which to meet him;

Life and body and possessions
To the king now consecrate.

6. Aria (T)

Jesus, let through weal and woe
Me go also with thee!

> Though the world shout "Crucify!"
> Let me not abandon,
> Lord, the banner of thy cross;
> Crown and palm shall I find here.

7. Chorus [Chorale] (S, A, T, B)

Jesus, this thy passion
Brings me purest pleasure;
All thy wounds, thy crown and scorn,
Are my heart's true pasture;
This my soul is all in bloom
Once I have considered:
In yon heaven is a home
To us[2] by this offered.

8. Chorus (S, A, T, B)

So let us go forth to that Salem of gladness,
Attend ye the King both in love and in sorrow.

> He leadeth the way
> And opens the path.

[1.] Representing the vox Christi.

[2.] *Mir* 'to me' in contemporary hymnbooks, changed in Bach to *uns*.

BWV 183 Sie werden euch in den Bann tun II

Exaudi (The Sunday after Ascension).

Christiane Mariane von Ziegler, *Versuch in Gebundener Schreibart, Teil I* (Leipzig, 1728), with several changes; Facs: Neumann T, p. 361.

1. *Jn.* 16:2; 5. Paul Gerhardt, verse 5 of "Zeuch ein zu deinen Toren," 1653 (Fischer-Tümpel, III, #413).

13 May 1725, Leipzig.

BG 37; NBA I/12.

1. Recit. [Dictum] (B)[1]

In banishment they will cast you,[2] there cometh, yea, the time when he who slays you will think that he doeth God a good deed in this.

2. Aria (T)

I have no fear of death's dread terror,
I shudder not at misery.

> Since Jesus' arm will guard me safely
> I'll follow glad and willingly;
> Would ye deny my life protection
> And think God thus your service do,
> He shall himself at last reward you,
> So good, with this I'll be content.

3. Recit. (A)

I am prepared my blood and poor existence
For thee, my Savior, to surrender;
My whole humanity I'll give to thee.
My strength is that thy Spirit will stand by me,
E'en though there be for me perhaps too much to suffer.

4. Aria (S)

Highest helper, Holy Ghost,
Thou who me the path dost show
On which my course should be,
Relieve my weakness as my pleader,
For of mine own strength / of myself / my pleading faileth;
I know thou carest for my good.

5. Chorale (S, A, T, B)

Thy Spirit is a teacher,
Which tells us how to pray:
Thy praying is attended,
Thy singing soundeth well.
It riseth heavenward,
It riseth, never ceasing,
Until he help hath given
Who only help can give.

[1.] Representing the *vox Christi*.

[2.] I.e., "they will excommunicate you." Cf. *Jn.* 16:2.

BWV 184 **Erwünschtes Freudenlicht**

Third Day of Pentecost.

Poet unknown; PT (Leipzig, 1731); Facs: Neumann T, p. 446.

5. Anarg von Wildenfels, verse 8 of "O Herre Gott, dein göttlich Wort," 1526.

30 May 1724, Leipzig; Parody: 1-4, 6 ← BWV 184a; 6 → BWV 213/13.

BG 37; NBA I/14.

---

1. Recit. (T)

O welcome light of joy,
Which with the new law forth doth break
Through Jesus, our good shepherd!
We, who were wont in death's deep vales to wander,
Perceive so fully now
How God to us that long expected shepherd sendeth,
Who shall our souls now feed
And with his word and spirit turn
Our steps to righteous pathways.
We, his elected folk, are conscious of his might;
Within his hand alone is that which us restores
And doth our hearts with vigor strengthen.
Us in his flock he loveth
Who his support and help remember.
He draweth us from idle things terrestrial
To gaze upon him

And evermore rely upon his favor.
O shepherd, for the flock who gives himself,
And till the grave and till his death them loves!
His arm against our foes is mighty,
His caring can us sheep in spirit nurture,
Yea, come the time to walk through death's dark valley,
Our help and strength shall be his gentle staff.[1]
We'll follow, then, with gladness till the grave.
Rise! Haste to him, in bliss to stand before him.

2. Aria (S, A)

O fortunate Christians, O flock filled with rapture,
Come, draw now to Jesus with gratitude nigh!

> Despise the attraction of worldly deceptions,
> That your satisfaction then perfect may be!

3. Recit. (T)

Be joyful then, all ye elected spirits!
Your joy is based secure in Jesus' heart.
This comfort could no mortal tell of.
This joy doth reach e'en down below
To those who in the bonds of sin were lying,
Which hath now Judah's hero burst asunder.
A David stands with us.
A hero's arm doth free us from the foe.
When God with might the flock doth shield,
When he in wrath hurls at their foe his bolt,
When he the bitter cross's death
For them doth shun not,
Then strike them shall no further woe,
Then live they shall within their God rejoicing.

Here taste they now the noble pasture
And hope for there the perfect joy of heaven.

4. Aria (T)

Joy and blessing are prepared
The devoted throng to crown now.

> Jesus brings the golden age
> To those who come to know him.

5. Chorale (S, A, T, B)

Lord, I hope e'er thou wilt all those
In no distress abandon,
Who thy word well as servants true
In heart and faith consider;
Thou givest them thy bliss e'en now
And keepest them from ruin.
O Lord, through thee I pray, let me
Both glad and willing die now.

6. Chorus (S, A, T, B)

O good shepherd, help thy people,[2]
Leave us still thy holy word!

> Let thy gracious face shine brightly,
> Ever bide our God and shield,
> Who with hands which have all power
> Shall turn now to life our footsteps!

[1.] Cf. *Ps.* 23:4.

[2.] *Trost der Deinen* literally means "Help or Comfort of thy people."

BWV 184a Glückwunschkantate zum Neujahrstag

New Year's Day Congratulations, probably for the Princely House of Anhalt-Cöthen.

Poet and Text unknown.

1 January 1723?, Cöthen; Parody: → BWV 184.

NBA I/14 and I/35, Krit. Bericht.

BWV 185 Barmherziges Herze der ewigen Liebe

Fourth Sunday after Trinity.

Salomo Franck, *Evangelisches Andachts-Opffer* (Weimar, 1715); Facs: Neumann T, p. 280

1. Johann Agricola, the melody of the hymn, 1522?/31 (Wackernagel, III, #78); 6. verse 1 of the hymn.

14 July 1715, Weimar; again 20 June 1723, Leipzig.

BG 37; NBA I/17.

1. Aria (S, T) with instrum. Chorale

O heart filled with mercy and love everlasting,
Stir up and arouse now my spirit with thine;
So that I may practise both goodness and mercy,
O thou, flame of loving, come soften my heart.

2. Recit. (A)

Ye hearts which have yourselves
To stony cliffs perverted,
Now melt to softness mild;
Now weigh what you the Savior teacheth,
Act, act with charity
And strive while yet on earth now
To be just like the Father!
Ah! Summon not through that forbidden judgment
Almighty God to judgment's seat,
Else will his zealous wrath destroy you.
Forgive and ye will be forgiven;
Give, give within this lifetime;
Store up a principal
Which there one day
God will repay with ample store of interest.[1]
For as ye judge, so will ye be judged also.

3. Aria (A)

Be concerned within this life,
Spirit, ample seed to scatter,
So the harvest thee may gladden
In the rich eternity
Where those who good things here have planted
Gladly there the sheaves shall gather.

4. Recit. (B)

How selfishness deceives itself!
Concern thyself
First from thine eye the beam to loosen,
Then may'st thou for the mote be also troubled
Which in thy neighbor's eye is found.[2]
If now thy neighbor be not fully pure,

Remember, thou art, too, no angel;
Amend, then, thine own failings!
How can one blind man with another
Still walk the straight and narrow?
What, will they not to their great sorrow
Fall in the pit now both together?

5. Aria (B)

This is the Christian art:
But God and self discerning,
With true affection burning,
Not, when forbidden, judging,
Nor stranger's work destroying,
One's neighbor not forgetting.
With gen'rous measure measuring:
This makes with God and men goodwill,
This is the Christian art.

6. Chorale (S, A, T, B)

I call to thee, Lord Jesus Christ,
I pray thee, hear my crying;
Both lend me grace within this life
And let me not lose courage;
The proper path, O Lord, I seek,
Which thou didst wish to give me:
For thee living,
My neighbor serving well,
Thy word upholding justly.

---

[1] Cf. BWV 168/3.

[2] Cf. Lk. 6:41.

BWV 186 **Ärgre dich, o Seele, nicht**

Seventh Sunday after Trinity.

Poet unknown; movements 1, 3, 5, 8, 10 based on Salomo Franck, *Evangelische Sonn-und Fest-Tages-Andachten* (Weimar and Jena, 1717); Cf. Facs. to BWV 186a: Neumann T, p. 291.

6. Paul Speratus, verse 12 of "Es ist das Heil uns kommen her," 1524 (Wackernagel, III, #55); 11. verse 11 of the hymn.

11 July 1723, Leipzig; 1, 3, 5, 8, 10 ← BWV 186a.

BG 37; NBA I/18.

First Part

1. Chorus (S, A, T, B)

Vex thyself, O spirit, not,
That the all-surpassing light,
God's true image shining bright,
Self in servant's form doth veil;
Vex thyself, O spirit, not![1]

2. Recit. (B)

The servant form, the need, the wanting
Strike Christ's own members not alone,
For he, your head, himself seeks poor to be.
And is not plenty, is not surplus wealth
The barb[2] of Satan,
Which we with scruple must avoid?
In contrast, when for thee

The burden grows too heavy,
When poverty grieves thee,
When hunger thee doth waste,
And thou wouldst soon surrender,
Thou dost not think of Jesus, of thy health.
If thou just like that crowd[3] art not fed quickly,
Then sighest thou: Ah, Lord, for how long wouldst thou then forget me?

3. Aria (B)

If thou art to bring me help,
Haste thou not to stand beside me?
Now my heart is full of doubt,
Thou dost spurn perhaps my weeping;
But, O soul, thou shouldst not doubt,
Let mere reason not ensnare thee.
Thy true helper, Jacob's light,
Thou canst in the Scripture witness.

4. Recit. (T)

Ah, that a Christian so
Should for his body care!
Which is it more?
An earthly structure
Which must again to earth be changéd,
A cloak which is but lent.
He could, indeed, the finest share have chosen,
Which would his hope not e'er betray:
The soul's salvation
Which in Jesus lies.
O blessed he who him in Scripture sees,
How he through all this teaching
On all those who shall hear him
The spirit's manna sends!

Thus, when your sorrow doth your heart both gnaw and eat,
Then taste and witness yet, how kind your Jesus is.

5. Aria (T)

My Savior now appeareth
In all his works of blessing.
Since he with strength appears
To give weak souls instruction,
The weary bodies nurture,
This sates both flesh and soul.

6. Chorale (S, A, T, B)

Though it should seem he were opposed,
Be thou by this not frightened,
For where he is at best with thee,
His wont is not to show it.
His word take thou more certain still,
And though thy heart say only "No,"
Yet let thyself not shudder.

Second Part

7. Recit. (B)

The world is but a mighty wilderness,
The heavens will be stone, the earth will change to iron,
When Christians through their faith give witness
That Christ's own word is their most precious wealth;
The gift of sustenance
Almost appears to flee them,
A constant dearth gives rise to tears,
So that they but the world may all the more forsake now;
Then shall at last the Savior's word,
That greatest wealth,

Find in their hearts its place:
Yea, if he mourned his people there,
So must e'en here his heart be breaking
And over them his blessing telling.

8. Aria (S)

God's outstretched arms would clasp the wretched[4]
With mercy here and there;[5]
He gives to them of his great mercy
The greatest wealth, the word of life.

9. Recit. (A)

Now may the world with all its pleasure vanish,
And dearth straightway begin,
Yet shall the soul with joy be full.
If through this vale of tears the path's
Too hard, too long,
In Jesus' word lies health and blessing.
It is for its[6] feet a lantern and a light upon its pathways.[7]
Who faithfully through desert rides
Shall in this word find drink and food;
The Savior shall one day, the word assureth,
Him open paradise's portals,
And when their course is run,
He shall upon the faithful set their crown.

10. Aria (S, A)

O soul, let no sadness
From Jesus divide thee,
O soul, be thou true!
The crown doth await thee,
Reward of his mercy,
When thou the bonds of the body art free.

11. Chorale (S, A, T, B)

Our hope awaits the fitting time
Which God's own word hath promised.
When that shall be to give us joy
Hath God no day appointed.
He knows well when the day is best
And treats us not with cruel guile,
For this we ought to trust him.

[1.]   Cf. *Mt.* 11:5.

[2.]   *Des Satans Angel* 'the barb (fishhook) of Satan' is a fishing metaphor appropriate to the Gospel story, the feeding of the four thousand, *Mk.* 8:1-9.

[3.]   I.e., the four thousand.

[4.]   Note the false etymology: *Armen . . . umarmen.*

[5.]   I.e., both here in this world and there in the Biblical world.

[6.]   I.e., the soul's feet.

[7.]   Cf. *Ps.* 119:105.

BWV 186a **Ärgre dich, o Seele, nicht**

Third Sunday in Advent.

Salomo Franck, *Evangelische Sonn-und Fest-Tages-Andachten* (Weimar and Jena, 1717); Facs: Neumann T, p. 291.

6. Ludwig Helmbold, verse 8 of "Von Gott will ich nicht lassen," 1563 (Wackernagel, IV, #904).

13 December 1716, Weimar; 1-5 → BWV 186/1, 3, 5, 8, 10.

Reconstruction by Diethard Hellmann, Hänssler Verlag (Stuttgart, 1963).

---

1. Chorus (See BWV 186/1.)

2. Aria 1

Art thou he who shall come here,
Friend of souls, in church's garden?
Now my heart is full of doubt,
Shall I for another wait, then?[1]
But, O soul, thou shouldst not doubt,
Let mere reason not ensnare thee.
Thy true Shiloh,[2] Jacob's light,
Thou canst in the scripture witness.

3. Aria 2

Messiah now appeareth
From all his works of blessing.
Unclean will be made clean:
The lame in spirit walking,
The blind in spirit seeing[3]
The shining light of grace.

4. Aria 3 (See BWV 186/8.)

5. Aria 4 (See BWV 186/10.)

6. Chorale

For this though I e'en suffer
Here opposition's force etc.

---

[1] Cf. *Mt.* 11:3.

[2] *Shiloh* is a word of uncertain meaning used by Jacob in his deathbed speech, *Gen.* 49:10. In BWV 186/5 it seems to have been glossed with *Helfer* 'Savior,' since 'Messiah' is one of its several suggested meanings.

[3] Cf. *Mt.* 11:5.

BWV 187 **Es wartet alles auf dich**

Seventh Sunday after Trinity.

Poet unknown (Christoph Helm?);[1] PT (Rudolstadt, 1726).

1. *Ps.* 104:27-28; 4. *Mt.* 6:31-32; 7. Hans Vogel, verses 4 and 5 of "Singen wir aus Herzensgrund," 1563.

4 August 1726, Leipzig; Parody: 1, 2, 3, 5 → *Mass in G Minor*, BWV 235/6, 4, 3.

BG 37; NBA I/18.

First Part

1. Chorus [Dictum] (S, A, T, B)

Here look now all men to thee, that thou givest to them food at the proper time. When thou to them givest, they gather it; when thou openest thine hand, then are they with thy kindness well satisfied.

2. Recit. (B)

What creatures are contained
By this world's orb so vast!
Regard the mountains, then, how they are ranged in thousands;
What doth the sea not bear? The streams and seas are teeming.
The birds' expansive host
Glides through the air to plain.
Who feedeth such a toll,
And who can then supply them with the needs of nature?
Can any monarch set his sights upon such honor?

Could all the gold of earth
Buy them a single meal?[2]

3. Aria (A)

Thou Lord, thou dost alone the year crown with thy wealth.

> Distilled are oil and blessing
> Upon thy foot's own traces,
> And it is thine own grace
> Which every good thing doth.

Second Part

4. Aria [Dictum] (B)

Therefore do not be anxious and saying: "What will, then, our food be, what will, then, our drink be, what will we have, then, for clothing?" For after such things hanker the gentiles. For your own heavenly Father knows that by you all these are needed.

5. Aria (S)

God supplieth every being
Which here below breath doth keep.
Would he me alone not furnish
What to all he hath assured?
Yield, ye sorrows, his allegiance
Doth for me as well provide
And is for me daily proven
Through that Father's loving gifts.

6. Recit. (S)

If I can only cleave to him with childlike trusting
And take with gratitude what he for me hath planned,

Then I shall see myself unaided never
And how he e'en for me the debt hath paid in full.
All fretting is in vain, and wasted is the trouble
Which the despondent heart for its requirements makes;
Since God, forever rich, upon himself these cares hath taken,
I know that he for me as well my share hath fixed.

7. Chorale (S, A, T, B)

God hath the earth in fullness set,
And for its food lets it not lack;
Hill and vale he moisture gives
That the kine the grass may grow;
From the earth both wine and bread
God creates and gives our fill,
So that man his life may have.

We give great thanks and pray of him
That he give us the Spirit's will,
That we it well understand,
E'er in his commandments walk,
His name's honor magnify
In Christ and may never cease:
And we'll sing rightly "Gratias!"

[1.] Helm is suggested by W. Blankenburg, BJ (1977).

[2.] *Mal* is here translated as *Mahl* 'meal.' It might be simply the word *Mal* 'time,' in which case translate "buy this a single time."

BWV 188 **Ich habe meine Zuversicht**

Twenty-first Sunday after Trinity.

Christian Friedrich Henrici (Picander), *Ernst-Schertzhaffte und Satyrische Gedichte, Teil III* (Leipzig, 1732); Facs: Neumann T, p. 343.

6. First verse of the hymn, Lübeck, before 1603 (cf. Fischer-Tümpel, IV, #575).

1728 or soon thereafter, Leipzig.

BG 37; NBA I/25.

---

1. Sinfonia

2. Aria (T)

I have now all my confidence
To the faithful God assigned
Where rests my expectation firmly.

> When all shall break, when all shall fail,
> When no one faith and word shall keep,
> E'en so is God surpassing gracious.

3. Recit. (B)

God meaneth well for ev'ryone,
E'en midst the very worst of trouble.
Though he awhile his love concealeth,
His heart for us in secret cares,
This can he nevermore withdraw;
And even if the Lord would slay me,
My hope shall rest in him,
Because his angered countenance
Is nothing but
A cloud which casts a shadow;
It only holds the sunlight back,
So that with help of gentle showers
The heav'nly blessing
Then that much richer might become.

The Lord transforms himself into a wrathful God
To make his comfort seem that stronger;
He would, he could not wish us evil.
I'll not let him go, until he me bless.[1]

4. Aria (A)

Not to fathom is the manner
In which God his people leads.

> Even our own cross and pain
> Must to our advantage be
> And to bring his name great honor.

5. Recit. (S)

The world's great might shall disappear.
Who can depend on rank and honor?
But God abideth evermore;
Blest all those who in him are trusting!

6. Chorale (S, A, T, B)

In my beloved God
I trust in fear and need;
He can me e'er deliver
From sadness, fear and trouble.
My sorrow can he alter,
For all rests in his hands now.

---

[1]   Cf. *Gen.* 32:36 and BWV 157/1.

BWV 189 **Meine Seele rühmt und preist**

The Visitation of the Blessed Virgin Mary (July 2)

Poet unknown.

Not by Bach, probably by Georg Melchior Hoffmann (see BJ 1956, p. 155 and Dürr, p. 1003).

Not in Neumann; text from Wustmann, p. 287.

1. Aria (T)

Meine Seele rühmt und preist
Gottes Huld und reiche Güte.

> Und mein Geist,
> Herz und Sinn und ganz Gemüte
> Ist in meinem Gott erfreut,
> Der mein Heil und Helfer heißt.

2. Recit. (T)

Denn seh ich mich und auch mein Leben an,
So muß mein Mund in diese Worte brechen:
Gott, Gott! was hast du doch an mir getan!
Es ist mit tausend Zungen
Nicht einmal auszusprechen,
Wie gut du bist, wie freundlich deine Treu,
Wie reich dein Liebe sei.
So sei dir denn Lob, Ehr und Preis gesungen.

3. Aria (T)

Gott hat sich hoch gesetzet
Und sieht auf das, was niedrig ist.

> Gesetzt, daß mich die Welt
> Gering und elend hält,
> Doch bin ich hoch geschätzet,
> Weil Gott mich nicht vergißt.

4. Recit. (T)

O was für große Dinge
Treff ich an allen Orten an,
Die Gott mir getan,
Wofür ich ihm mein Herz zum Opfer bringe;
Er tut es dessen Macht
Den Himmel kann umschränken,
An dessen Namens Pracht die Seraphim in Demut nur gedenken.
Er hat mir Leib und Leben,
Er hat mir auch das Recht zur Seeligkeit,
Und was mich hier und dort erfreut,
Aus lauter Huld gegeben.

5. Aria (T)

Deine Güte, dein Erbarmen
Währet, Gott, zu aller Zeit.

> Du erzeigst Barmherzigkeit
> Denen dir ergebnen Armen.

1. Aria (T)

This my soul extols with praise
God's dear grace and generous kindness.

And my soul,
Heart and mind and all my spirit
Are in this my God well pleased,
Who my health and helper is.

2. Recit (T)

When I behold myself and how I live,
Then must my mouth with words like these be opened:
God, God! What hast thou then for me here done!
Not e'en with tongues in thousands
Could ever one declare it,
How good thou art, how faithful is thy word,
How rich thy charity.
So be to thee praise, laud, and honor sung then.

3. Aria (T)

God sitteth high above us
observing all in low estate.

'Tis true that to the world
I but low and poor do seem,
Yet I am highly treasured
Since God forgets me not.

4. Recit (T)

Behold, what might wonders
I meet in every place and clime,
That God for me hath done;
So I to him my heart an offering render;
His is the deed whose might
Can heaven itself encompass,
The glory of whose name the Seraphim are humbly every mindful.
He gave me life and body,

He gave me too the right to be redeemed,
And—what me here and there doth please—,
With love alone he gave it.

5. Aria (T)

All thy kindness, all thy mercy
Lasteth, God, as long as time.

> Thou dost show thy graciousness
> To thy poor devoted creatures.

BWV 190 Singet dem Herrn ein neues Lied

New Year's Day (Feast of the Circumcision and the Naming of Christ).

Perhaps Picander (See BWV 190a).

1. *Ps.* 149:1, 150:6, 150:4; Martin Luther, beginning of the German Te Deum, 1529 (Wackernagel, III, 31); 2. Martin Luther, same text with interpolated recitative; 7. Johannes Herman, verse 2 of "Jesu, nun sei gepreiset," 1593.

1 January 1724, Leipzig; Parody: 1, 2, 3, 5 → BWV 190/1, 2, 3, 5.

BG 37; NBA I/4.

1. Chorus [Dictum] and Chorale (S, A, T, B)

Sing ye the Lord a new refrain! The assembly of saints should sing to
    him praises!
Honor him with timbrels and dancing, honor him with strings and
    with piping!

Lord God, we give thee praise!
All that which breath doth own, honor the Lord!
Lord God, we give thee thanks!
Alleluia!

2. Chorale (S, A, T, B) and Recit. (B, T, A)

(S, A, T, B)
Lord God, we give thee praise,

(B)
That thou with this the newborn year
Us newfound joy and newborn blessing grantest
And still with favor on us thinkest.

(S, A, T, B)
Lord God, we give thee thanks,

(T)
That thy great kindness
Throughout the time now past
Both all our land and our own city fair
From famine, pestilence and war protected hath.

(S, A, T, B)
Lord God, we give thee praise,

(A)
For thy paternal faith
Hath yet no limits,
Amidst us is it every morn renewed.[1]
Thus do we fold,
O merciful God, for this
In humbleness our hands now
And say throughout our lives
With mouth and heart our praise and thanks.

(S, A, T, B)
Lord God, we give thee thanks!

3. Aria (A)

Honor, Zion, this thy God,
Honor this thy God with gladness,
Rise! And speak now of his fame,
Who within his holy shrine
As thy shepherd evermore
Shall to verdant pastures lead thee.[2]

4. Recit. (B)

Now let the world desire
What flesh and blood with pleasure fills;
Just this, this ask I of the Lord,[3]
Just this one thing I seek,
That Jesus, my true pleasure,[4]
My shepherd true, my strength and health,
And of my soul the fairest part,
Should as a lamb of his own pasture
Again this year within his care embrace me
And nevermore from his dear arms release me.
His kindly will,
Which me the way to life doth show,
Now rule and lead me on an even course,
And I shall this new year in Jesus' name begin.

5. Aria (T, B)

Jesus shall be all to me,
Jesus shall be my beginning,
Jesus is my sign of joy.
Jesus' care I would commit me.
Jesus helps me through his blood,
Jesus makes my ending good.

6. Recit. (T)

Now, Jesus grant me
That with the newborn year, e'en his anointed flourish;
May he bless both the trunk and branches,
So that their fortune to the clouds be rising.
May Jesus bless both church and school,
May he bless every faithful teacher,
May he bless those who hear their teaching;
May he bless council and the court;
May he pour, too, o'er every house
Within our town the springs of blessing forth;
May he grant that again
Both peace and trust
Within our borders kiss each other.[5]
Thus live we shall throughout the year in blessing.

7. Chorale (S, A, T, B)

Let us the year accomplish
For glory to thy name,
That we to it be singing
In Christian company;
Wouldst thou our life be sparing
Through thine almighty hand,
Keep, then, thy beloved Christians
And our own fatherland.
Thy blessing to us send now,
Give peace in every quarter;
Give unalloyed this country
Thy grace-inspiring word.
To hypocrites bring ruin
Both here and ev'rywhere!

---

1. Cf. *Lam.* 3:23.

2. Cf. *Ps.* 23:2.

3. Cf. *Ps.* 27:4.

4.   A citation of the hymn of Johann Franck.

5.   Cf. *Ps.* 85:11.

BWV 190a **Singet dem Herrn ein neues Lied!**

The Bicentennial of the Augsburg Confession.

Christian Friedrich Henrici (Picander), *Ernst-Schertzhaffte und Satyrische Gedichte, Teil III* (Leipzig, 1732); Facs: Neumann T, p. 333; Reprint: *Sicul, Annales Lipsienses, Sectio XXXVII* (1731) and *Das Jubilierende Leipzig* (1731).

1. *Ps.* 149:1, 150:4 and 6; Martin Luther, beginning of the German Te Deum, 1529 (Wackernagel, III, #31); 2. Martin Luther, the same text with interpolated recitative; 7. Martin Luther, verse 3 of "Es woll uns Gott genädig sein," 1524 (Wackernagel, I, #189).

25 June 1730, Leipzig; Parody: 1, 2, 3, 5 ← BWV 190.

1. Chorus (= BWV 190/1.)

2. Chorale and Recit.

Lord God, we give thee praise,
God, that thou both our shield
And our redeemer art.
Lord God, we give thee thanks.
Triumphant shall we go forth
And seek now, Lord, thy countenance,
For thy dear grace extends
As far as heaven's breadth,
And thine own truth sheds light
As far as clouds are ranging.

Lord God, we give thee praise
That still thy brilliant light
Within our land doth shine.
O God, how great is this thy kindness,
Which doth such faith to all thy children show!
Forget that loving disposition,
My Zion, yea, forget it not!
Lord God, we give thee praise.

3. Aria

Honor, Zion, this thy God,
Praise him greatly for his name's sake.
Rise! Proclaim it, ponder well
What the Lord for us hath done;
Therefore pray before him now,
Glorify his teaching's harvest.

4. Recit.

Lord, if thine Evangel's word,
That heav'nly teaching,
Had not supplied our consolation,
We had by woe and death
Been leveled to the ground.
That is our bread of life,
That is our spirit's strength,
That doth our soul refreshment bring,
And it with blessedness restore.
Here is true righteousness, the shield of faith,
Which but 'fore God in heaven has weight.

5. Aria

Blessed are we through the word,
Blessed are we through the doctrine,

Blessed are we here and there,[1]
Blessed, if our faith be steadfast.
Blessed, if we not alone
Hearers, rather, doers be.

6. Recit.

Now God, we offer thee
Our lips' reward for this,
We, all we who by thine own names have named us,[2]
And Christ, who is thy Son, acknowledge.
Take henceforth in thy care thy church,
That it as on that rock
Be more and more established firmly.
Make larger this thy flock so tiny,
Within thy hand stand power and might.

7. Chorale

Now thank, O God, and give thee praise,
The people in their good works.
The land bears fruit and mends its ways,
Thy word is made to prosper.
Us bless the Father and the Son,
And bless us God the Holy Ghost,
Whom all the world doth glorify,
To him pay rev'rence unexcelled;
Now say sincerely "Amen."

---

[1] "Here and there" probably refers to the contemporary and original adherents to the Augsburg Confession.

[2] It may well be that *deinen* is a misprint for *deinem*, in which case translate "by thine own name."

BWV 191 **Gloria in excelsis Deo**

First Day of Christmas.

1. *Lk.* 2:14 (beginning of the Gloria of the Mass; 2 and 3. the shorter Doxology.

After 1740; Parody: ← *Mass in B Minor,* BWV 232/4, 7, 11.

BG 41; NBA I/2.

First Part[1]

1. Chorus (S, A, T, B)

Glory be to God on high, and on earth peace, good will towards men.

Second Part

2. Aria (S, T)

Glory be to the Father, and to the Son, and to the Holy Ghost.

3. Chorus (S, A, T, B)

As it was in the beginning, is now, and ever shall be, world without end. Amen.

[1.] This translation is from the *1928 Book of Common Prayer.*

BWV 192 **Nun danket alle Gott**

Unspecified occasion (perhaps Reformation).

Martin Rinckart, the three verses of the hymn, 1636 (Fischer-Tümpel, I, #526).

Ca. 1730.

BG 41; NBA I/34.

---

1. Chorus [Verse 1] (S, A, T, B)

Now thank ye all our God
With heart and voice and labor,
Who mighty things doth work
For us in every quarter,
Who us from mother's womb
And toddler's paces on
A countless toll of good
And still e'en now hath done.

2. Aria [Verse 2] (S, B)

The ever bounteous God
Through all our life be willing
An always joyful heart
And noble peace to give us,
And us within his grace
Maintain for evermore,
And us from every want
Deliver here and there.[1]

3. Chorus [Verse 3] (S, A, T, B)

Laud, honor, praise to God,
The Father and the Son now
And him alike to both
On the high throne of heaven,
To God the Three-in-One,
As he was at the first
And is and e'er shall be,
Both now and evermore.

---

1. I.e., both on earth and in heaven.

BWV 193 **Ihr Tore /Pforten/ zu Zion**

Inauguration of the New Town Council.

Poet unknown.

25 August ?1727, Leipzig; Parody: 1, 3, 5 ← BWV 193a/ 1, 7, 9.

BG 41; NBA I/32.

---

1. Aria (S, A, T, B)

Ye gateways /portals/ to Zion, ye dwellings of Jacob, be ye glad![1]

> God is of our hearts' the pleasure,
> We're the people of his pasture,
> Ever is his kingdom's realm.

2. Recit. (S)

The guard of Israel doth sleep and slumber not;[2]
For thus far is his countenance
The shadow over our right hand;[3]
And therefore all the land
Hath given forth its harvest with abundance.
Who can, O Lord, enough for this exalt thee?

3. Aria (S)

God, we thank thee for thy kindness,
For thy fatherly devotion
Shall endure for evermore.

> Thou forgivest our transgressions,
> Thou attendest our petitions,
> Thus shall come all flesh to thee.[4]

4. Recit. (A)

O Leipzig, New Jerusalem, content be thou in this thy feast day!
For peace is still within thy towers,
Secure stand yet for judgment here the seats,[5]
And in the palaces hath justice found a dwelling.
Ah, grant that thy great fame and light
Be thus steadfast and last forever!

5. Aria (A)

Send down, Lord, thy blessing here,
Let them increase and find favor
Who for thee now justice steward
And who guard thy humble folk!
Send down, Lord, thy blessing here![6]

6. Recit. (Lost?)

7. (Repetition of the First Movement)

[1.] Cf. *Ps.* 87:2.

[2.] *Ps.* 121:4.

[3.] *Ps.* 121:5. The *1928 Book of Common Prayer* has "defense" instead of "shadow."

[4.] *Ps.* 65:3.

[5.] Cf. Ps. 9:8.

[6.] After this follows the notation: *Recit tacet/ Chorus ab initio repetatur.*

BWV 193a Ihr Häuser des Himmels, ihr scheinenden Lichter

Nameday of August II.

Christian Friedrich Henrici (Picander), *Ernst-Schertzhaffte und Satyrische Gedichte, Teil II* (Leipzig, 1729; 2nd. ed. 1734); also PT (Leipzig, 1727); Facs: Neumann T, p. 394.

3 August 1727, Leipzig; Parody: 1, 7, 9 → BWV 193/1, 3, 9.

NBA I/36, Krit. Bericht.

The English translation is found below after this transcription (in the original spelling, which means spellings like "solte" for "sollte," "kan" for "kann," "Greiße," for "Greise" and superimposed "e" instead of umlaut, here rendered as adscript "e") of the facsimile of the in Neumann, pp. 394-95:

Bey der
Hohen Nahmens-Feyer

Ihro
Koenigl. Maj. in Pohlen und Churfl. Durchl. zu Sachsen etc. bezeigte
In einer geringen MUSIC
Seinen allerunterthaenligsten Glueckwunsch
Christian Friedrich Henrici
Leipzig den 3. Aug. 1727

Dramma per Musica

Providentia, Fama, Salus, Pietas

(1.) Aria (Der Rath der Goetter)

Ihr Haeuser des Himmels, ihr scheinenden Lichter
Seyd gebueckt.
Denn AUGUSTUS Nahmens-Glaentzen
Wird in eure helle Grentzen
Heute heilig eingerueckt.

>   Da Capo.

(2.) [Recit.] (Providentia)

Preißwuerdigster August,
du Schmuck der Welt, Du auch des Himmels Lust,
Nun schreib ich Deines Nahmens Ruhm
Als ein der Ewigkeit
Schon laengst geweihtes Eigenthum,
Zum Wunder der noch spaeten Zeit
Und als ein Licht der Nachwelt ein.
Ihr Sterne machet Platz, AUGUSTUS soll hinein.

(3.) Aria (Providentia)

Nenne deinen August: Gott!
Prange, Rom, mit Spiel und Feste,
Sachsens August ist der Groeste,

Weil Sein eigne Lorbern bluehn;
Sachfens August ist der Beste,
Denn Sanfftmuth und Liebe verewigen Ihn.

Da Capo.

(4.) [Recit.] (Fama)

O! schoener Tag, o! schoene Blicke,
AUGUST lebt; Er blueht im Gluecke!
Was aber hat allhier
Das Goettliche Verhaengniß fuer.
Soll ich von Englands Pein
Von Moscau Plagen
Noch ferner sagen?
Nein! Nein!
Der Tag soll heute freudig seyn;
AUGUSTUS lebt; Er blueht im Gluecke.

(5.) Aria a duetto (Fama und Providentia)

(Fama und Providentia)
{Ich will/Du solt} ruehmen, {ich will/du solt} sagen

(a 2)
Von den angenehmen Tagen,
Wie sich Reich und Land erfreut;

(Providentia)
Aber von der Seltenheit
Deines Koenigs Herrlichkeit

(Fama und Providentia)
{Will ich/Solst du} selbst die Sterne fragen.

Da Capo.

(6.) [Recit.] (Providentia, Fama, Salus)

(Providentia)
So AUGUSTUS nicht
An Ruhm und Thatten Seines gleichen,
So soll auch Seiner Jahre Lauff
Ein unerhoertes Ziel erreichen.

(Fama)
So recht! Und ob ich zwar
Bey nahe gantz und gar
Durch Seines Lobes Wunder-Dinge
Mich heiser oder muede singe,
So kan mir doch
Nichts suesser fallen,
Als lange lange noch
Von Seinem Ruhm zu schallen.

(Providentia)
Sein Bild, Sein hheilig Angesicht
Haeng ich im Saal der Goetter auf,
Damit Sein Leben auf der Erden
Von dem Verfall der Zeit
Kan desto mehr geschuetzet werden.

(Salus)
So soll die Grenzens Muedigkeit
Noch taeglich frischer Quellen haben,
Mit unerschoepfften Heyl und Lust,
Die Koenigliche Brust,
Das edelste der Welt, zu laben.

(7.) Aria (Salus)

Herr! so gross als Dein Erhoehen
Pflantz ich auch Dein Wohlergehen

Ewigem Gedeyen ein.
Deine Krafft will ich erhalten,
Wie die Alder nicht veralten,
Wie die Felsen feste seyn.

Da Capo.

(8.) [Recit.] (Pietas)

Wie bin ich doch ergoetzt,
Daß Sachfens Wunsch und Pflicht
Nun der Erhoerung werth geschaetzt.
Das uns erfreute Licht
Erregt im Lande Jubel-Lieder,
Der Koenig lebt. Er staerckt Sich wieder!
Der Himmel will, Er soll unsterblich seyn.
Wohlan! so bauet Freuden-Sauelen,
Und weyhet Andachts-Tempel ein,
Dem Koenige die Ehre der Vergoetterung
Noch lebend zu ertheilen.

(9.) Aria (Pietas)

Sachsen, komm zum Opffer-Heerd,
Laß den Weyrauch lieblich brenne,
Daß Sein Hertze moeg erkennen,
Daß du Seines Glantzes werth.

Da Capo.

(10.) [Recit.] (Pietas)

Doch worzu wollen wir viel Tempel bauen?
So viel Dir, Mildester August,
An Unterthanen ist bewust,
So viel wirst Du auch Hertzen schauen,

Die Tempel und Altaere sind,
Von Lieb und Demuth angezuendt,
Die heute vor Dein Heyl und Leben
Den Wunsch durch mich an statt des Opffers geben:

(11.) Aria (Pietas und Chor)

(Pietas)
Himmel, erhoere das bethende Land,
Schuetze den Koenig mit maechtiger Hand,
Segne des Besalbten Nahmen!

(Chor)
Amen! Amen! Amen!

(Pietas)
Langes Leben, Fried und Ruh
Setze Seinen Jahren zu;
Und pflege von oben den Fuerstlichen Saamen!

(Chor)
Amen! Amen! Amen!

(Tutti)
So haben wir goeldene Zeiten zu erben,
So scheuen sich selber die Greiße zu sterben.

Horat.
Praesenti Tibi maturos largimur honores.

A Drama in Music

Providence, Fame, Health, Piety

1. Aria (The Council of the Gods)

Ye houses of heaven, ye radiant torches, bow ye low.
For Augustus' name's great luster
Shall within your radiant borders
This day solemnly be brought.

> Da Capo.

2. [Recit.] (Providence)

Most laudable August,[1]
Thou worldly gem, thou even heaven's joy,
I now inscribe thy name's great fame
To be eternity's
Now long established property,
The marvel of all recent time
And as a light for future years.
Ye stars must now make room, Augustus shall come in.

3. Aria (Providence)

Call, then, this thine August god!
Boast, then, Rome, in games and feasting,
Saxon August is the greatest,
For this his own laurels bloom;
Saxon August is unequaled,
For kindness and love have immortalized him.

> Da Capo.

4. [Recit.] (Fame)

Oh, lovely day, oh, lovely vision,
Augustus lives, he blooms with fortune!
However, what hath here
Yon Providence divine in store?
Shall I of England's woe,
Of Moscow's terrors
Make further mention?
No, no!
Today shall this day gladsome be;
Augustus lives, he blooms with fortune!

5. Aria a duetto (Fame and Providence)

(Fame and Providence)
{I will/Thou shalt} boast now, {I will/thou shalt} speak now

(Both)
Of these days so full of pleasure,
How the realm and land are glad:

(Providence)
But of this great rarity,
This thy king's great majesty,

(Fame and Providence)
{Will I/Shalt thou} ask the very heavens.

        Da Capo.

6. [Recit.] (Providence, Fame, and Health)

(Providence)
Just as Augustus hath
In fame and deeds not found his equal,

So shall as well his years' own course
A toll unheard of yet accomplish.

(Fame)
Well done! And though I may
Myself nigh totally
In praise of all his deeds of wonder
Make hoarse and even worn by singing,
Yet can I have
No sweeter duty
Than long, so long still yet,
All his great fame to echo.

(Providence)
His form, his holy countenance
I'll hang within the god's own halls,
So that his earthly life's achievements
From the decay of time
Be all the more protection given.

(Health)
So shall good fortune's gentleness
Each day have freshened new resources
From which with endless health and joy
It may the royal breast,
The noblest in the world, give comfort.

7. Aria (Health)

Sire, though high be thy position,
Graft I will e'en thy well-being
Onto everlasting growth.
I will keep now thy great power,
Like the eagles never aging,
Like the cliffs which firmly stand.

Da Capo.

8. [Recit.] (Piety)

I am, indeed, so pleased
That Saxon hope and due
Now of thine ear are worthy thought.
The light which makes us glad
Bestirs the land to jubilation.
The king doth live. His strength returneth!
'Tis heaven's wish that he immortal be.
Rejoice and raise triumphant columns!
And worship's temples consecrate,
That to the king the honor of a deity
While living be allotted.

9. Aria (Piety)

Saxons, come to sacrifice,
Let the incense sweetly burn now,
That his heart may here acknowledge
That ye are his glory worth.

> Da Capo.

10. [Recit.] (Piety)

But wherefore would we many temples build thee?
The number, O most kind August,
Of loyal subjects thou dost know,
This number thou of hearts will witness
Which temples are, and altars, too,
With humble love here inflamed,
Which this day for thy life and safety
Their wish through me in place of off'rings gives thee:

11. Aria (Piety, Chorus)

(Piety)
Heaven, give ear to the prayers of this land,
Shield thou the king with powerful hand,
Bless the name of thine anointed!

(Chorus)
Amen! Amen! Amen!

(Piety)
Lengthy lifetime, peace and calm
Add thou unto all his years;
And tend from above all the princely descendants!

(Chorus)
Amen! Amen! Amen!

(Tutti)
Thus shall we have ages of gold to inherit,
When hesitate even the aged to perish.[2]

[1.] In order to keep the name of the king in its original position, it is necessary to stress its second syllable, as in German.

[2.] The cantata closes with a quotation from Horace, *Epistles* 2.1.15: *Praesenti Tibi (sic) maturos largimur honores* (To Thee in our presence we pour out early honors).

BWV 194 **Höchsterwünschtes Freudenfest**

Dedication of an Organ; also Trinity.

Poet unknown; PT (Leipzig, 1723); Facs: Neumann T, p. 387 (only title page preserved); PT of First Part (Leipzig, 1731); Facs: Neumann T, p. 446.

6. Johann Heermann, verses 6 and 7 of "Treuer Gott, ich muß dir klagen," 1630 (Fischer-Tümpel, I, #347); 12. Paul Gerhardt, verses 9 and 10 of "Wach auf, mein Herz, und singe," 1647 (Fischer-Tümpel, III, #380), to the melody of "Nun laßt uns Gott dem Herren," 1587.

2 November 1723, Störmtal near Leipzig; 4 June 1724, ?16 June 1726 and 20 May 1731, Leipzig (First Part only); Parody: ← BWV 194a.

BG 29; NBA I/31.

First Part

1. Chorus (S, A, T, B)

O most lovely feast of joy,
Which the Lord for his great glory
In constructed sanctuaries
Lets us gladly celebrate.
O most lovely feast of joy!

2. Recit. (B)

Unending mighty God, ah, turn thyself
To us, to thine elected, to thy people,
And to the prayers of thy servants!
Ah, let us thee
Through our most fervent singing
Our lips' oblation offer!
We dedicate our sincere hearts to thee,
Our altar's thanks.
Thou, whom no house, no temple keeps,
For thou no end or limit hast,
May thou this house thy favor give, and make thy countenance
A faithful throne of grace, a light of joy.

3. Aria (B)

What the Highest's light hath filled
Never shall in night be veiled,
What the Highest's holy nature
For his dwelling shall have chosen
Never shall in night be veiled,
What the Highest's light hath filled.

4. Recit. (S)

How could from thee, thou highest countenance,
When thine unending brilliant light
Into the dark foundations seeth,
A house thy favor find?
For creeping vanity doth here from every side come in.
Where're thy majesty doth enter,
There must the house be pure
And of this guest be worthy found.
Here human skill is vain,
So let thine eye stand ever open[1]
And fall with grace upon us;
And we will then with holy joy to thee
Our bullocks and our sacrifice of singing,
Before thy throne be laying
And lift to thee our hopes devotedly.

5. Aria (S)

Help, God, that we this achieve,
And thy fire into us come,
That it also at this moment,
As in Isaiah's mouth then,[2]
Its effective power receive
And us hallowed to thee bring.

6. Chorale (S, A, T, B)

Holy Ghost enthroned in heaven,
Equal God eternally
With the Father and the Son both,
Of the troubled hope and joy!
All the faith which I possess
Hast thou in me set aflame;
Over me with mercy govern,
Never let thy mercy falter.
Send thy help now down upon me,
O thou noble bosom guest!
And the good work bring completion
Where thou its beginning hast.
Blow in me the spark alive
Till, when once my course is run,
I the chosen may resemble
And the goal of faith accomplish.

Second Part

7. Recit. (T)

Ye holy ones, be joyful now,
Haste, hasten, this your God to honor:
Your hearts be now exalted
To God's own glorious realm,
From where he now o'er thee,
Thou holy dwelling, watcheth
And to himself the heart made pure
From this earth's vanity he draweth.
A rank which truly blest is named
Beholds here Father, Son, and Ghost.
Come forth, ye souls which God inspireth!
Ye will now choose the finest portion;

The world can give you no refreshment,
Ye can in God alone live blest and in contentment.

8. Aria (T)

The Highest's presence here alone
Can of our joy the fountain be.
Now vanish, world and all thy pomp,
In God is our contentment found!

9. Recit. (B, S)

(B)
In truth can man to God ascend in heaven?

(S)
One's faith can the creator's ear draw to him.

(B)
It often is too weak a bond.

(S)
God leads himself and firms the hand of faith,
Its purpose to accomplish.

(B)
But how, then, when the flesh's weakness would lose courage?

(S)
The Highest's power proves mighty in the feeble.

(B)
The world will surely scorn them.

(S)
Who doth God's grace possess despiseth all such scorn.

(B)
Besides this what could they be lacking!

(S)
Their only wish, their all is found in God.

(B)
God is invisible and distant:

(S)
'Tis good that this our faith doth teach us
To see one's God within the spirit.

(B)
Their flesh doth hold them captive.

(S)
The Highest's grace increaseth all their longing,
For he doth build the place where they his glory see.

(Both)
Because he faith doth now reward
And with us dwell,
With us his very children,
Thus shall the world and mortal state our gladness not diminish.

10. Aria (S, B)

Oh, how good for us it is
That now God a house hath chos'n!

>   Taste and witness now as well,
>   God is gracious unto you.[3]
>   Pour out all your hearts to him,
>   Here before God's throne and house!

11. Recit. (B)

And so come forth, thou holy congregation,
Prepare thyself for holy joy!
God dwells not only in each human breast,
He buildeth here his house.
Come forth and arm yourselves with spirit and with gifts,
That he in both thine heart and in this house take pleasure!

12. Chorale (S, A, T, B)

Say "yes" to my endeavors,
And help me best to counsel;
To outset, midst and finish,
Ah Lord, dispense thy favor!
Thy blessing pour upon me,
My heart be now thy shelter,
Thy word be now my portion,
Till I to heaven journey!

---

1. Cf. 1 *Kg.* 8:29.
2. Cf. *Is.* 6:6-7.
3. Cf. *Ps.* 34:9.

BWV 194a **Glückwunschkantate**

Congratulations, probably for the Princely House of Anhalt-Cöthen.

Poet and text unknown.

Before 1723, probably Cöthen; Parody: ? → BWV 194.

NBA I/35.

BWV 195 **Dem Gerechten muß das Licht immer wieder aufgehen**

Wedding.

Poet unknown.

1. *Ps.* 97:11-12; 6. Paul Gerhardt, verse 1 of the hymn, 1647 (Fischer-Tümpel, III, #391) to the melody of "Lobt Gott, ihr Christen alle gleich"; this chorale takes the place of three movements in an earlier version, in which the cantata was divided into two parts.

After 1737; Parody: 6 and 8 → BWV 30a/5 and 1(13).

BG 13, 1: NBA I/33.

First Part (Before the Marriage Vows)

1. Chorus [Dictum]

For the righteous must the light ever new be arising, and gladness for upright spirits.
O ye righteous, glad be in the Lord, and thanks give him and praise him for his holiness / for his name's sake.

2. Recit. (B)

This joyous light's upright admirers
Must ever constant increase follow,
Which their good fortune shall make grow.
And for these newly weds,[1]
In whom we so much righteousness
And virtue praise,
Today a joyous light doth wait,

Which offers them new blessing still.
Oh, what a happy union!
Thus shall this pair good luck, each in the other find now.

3. Aria (B)

Praise ye God's good will and trust,
Praise ye him with lively gladness,
Praise ye God, soon-wedded couple!

>   For your present marriage union
>   Lets you nought but bliss discover,
>   Light and gladness ever new.

4. Recit. (S)

Rejoice, for joined is here a bond
Which so much blessing prophesieth.
The priest's own hand
Will now his blessing
Upon your married state,
Upon your heads be laying.
And when this blessing's power henceforth in you hath
flourished,
Then praise your God's paternal hand.
He joined himself your bond of love
And granted that his new beginning
As well a happy end accomplish.

5. Chorus (S, A, T, B)

We come here, thy great holiness,
O God of endless might, to honor.
What thine own hands are here beginning
Thy mighty power can bring fulfillment
And to thy blessing clearly witness.

Second Part (After the Marriage Vows)

6. Chorale (S, A, T, B)

Now thank ye all and bring your praise,
Ye mortals in the world,
To him whose praise the angel hosts
In heaven always tell.

[6. Aria]²

Rise and praise the Highest's kindness
With your grateful hearts and spirits,
O delightful wedded pair.
For your wishing, for your hoping,
Hath now fully found fulfillment
And your fortune is made clear.

> Da Capo.

[7. Recit.]

Most noble pair, thou art from henceforth wedded,
Already wait now blessing's perfect hours
For thee and thine illustrious house.
The Highest spake through his own servant's mouth
Now over thee his blessing's word.
It shall in sooth stay with thee
And noble fruit encourage.
So go ye hence in peace now,
To you is a great good,
A lasting good, alloted,
That even time shall not reduce.
But thou, O Lord, let now their supplications,
Which once again before thy throne ascend,
Now thine attendance witness;
That thy dear favor doth upon this couple fall.

[8. Chorus]

Highest, grant thou to this pair
Gladness which thy blessing giveth;
Grant that thine own gracious hand
Ever in their married state
Luck and health to them be guiding.

[1.] MS: *Auch Dir, Hochedles Paar* "E'en thee, most noble pair."

[2.] In brackets follow the texts of three movements found in a manuscript added to the OP.

BWV 196 **Der Herr denket an uns**

Perhaps the wedding for the pastor Johann Lorenz Stauber and Regina Wedemann, an aunt of Maria Barbara Bach (so Spitta, but cf. Dürr, p. 601).

Poet unknown.

2-5. *Ps.* 115:12-15.

?5 June 1708, Arnstadt.

BG 13, 1; NBA I/33.

---

1. Sinfonia

2. Chorus [Dictum] (S, A, T, B)

The Lord careth for us and blesseth us. He blesseth the house Israel, he blesseth the house Aaron.

3. Aria [Dictum] (S)

He blesseth those the Lord fearing, both the humble and mighty.

4. Aria [Dictum] (T, B)

The Lord bless you all now more and more, you and all your children.

5. Chorus [Dictum] (S, A, T, B)

Ye are the anointed ones of God, who heaven and earth hath created. Amen.[1]

[1.] Bach adds the Amen to the Psalm's text.

BWV 197 **Gott ist unsre Zuversicht**

A Wedding.

Poet unknown.

5. Martin Luther, verse 3 of "Nun bitten wir den Heiligen Geist," 1524 (Wackernagel, I, #208); 10. adaptation of Georg Neumark, verse 7 of "Wer nur den lieben Gott läßt walten," (Fischer-Tümpel, IV, #365).

After 1735 (so Dürr), ca. 1742 (so Neumann), Leipzig; Parody: 6, 8 ← BWV 197a/4, 6.

BG 13, 1; NBA I/33.

First Part

1. Chorus

God is our true confidence,
We rely upon his hands now.

> When he doth our pathways lead,
> When he doth our heart command,
> There is blessing never ceasing.

2. Recit. (B)

God is and bides the best provider,
He orders best the house.
He guideth all our deeds, sometimes with wonders rare,
Each to a happy end,
To where our purpose had not thought.
What reason thinks impossible,
That comes to pass.
He hath his children's fortune, those who love him,
From infancy upon his hand long written.

3. Aria (A)

Lull to sleep all care and sorrow,
To the slumber
Which a child's deep trust doth bring.

> God's own eyes, forever waking,
> Serving as our guiding star,
> Will then all, themselves, provide us.

4. Recit. (B)

So follow God and his persuasion.
That is the proper course.

It leads through danger's path
E'en finally to Canaan
And through the love which he hath tested
E'en to his holy altar, too,
And bindeth heart and heart together;
Lord, be thyself in these flames present!

5. Chorale (S, A, T, B)

Thou love so sweet, give us now thy grace,
Let us feel deeply the fire of love,
So that we sincerely may love each other
And in peace be of one mind forever.
Kyrie eleis!

Second Part

6. Aria (B)

O thou charming bridal pair,
Thee shalt only health encounter,
For God shall from Zion bless thee[1]
And shall guide thee evermore,
O thou charming bridal pair!

7. Recit. (S)

Just as God hath towards thee
With faith and father's love from thy first steps intended well,
So would he evermore
Thy first and truest friend
Until the end continue.
And therefore canst thou trust securely,
He shall thee ne'er

Amidst thy hands' great sweat and toil
Let no good thing be lacking.
Rejoice, thy joys cannot be numbered.

8. Aria (S)

Amusement and mirth,
Success and good health
Shall increase and strengthen and comfort.

The vision, the breast
Shall ever its share
Of sweet satisfaction be given.

9. Recit. (B)

And this thy happy course of life
Shall till thy latter years continue.
For God's great kindness hath no end;
It gives thee much,
Yea, more than e'en the heart itself could hope for.
Thou ought on this now rest assured.

10. Chorale (S, A, T, B)

So journey glad on God's true pathways,
And what ye do, that do in faith!
Now earn ye well your God's great blessing,
For it is every morning new:
For he who doth his confidence
In God place, him he'll not forsake.

---

[1] Cf. *Ps.* 128:5.

BWV 197a **Ehre sei Gott in der Höhe**

First Day of Christmas.

Christian Friedrich Henrici (Picander), *Ernst-Schertzhaffte und Satyrische Gedichte, Teil III* (Leipzig, 1732); Facs: Neumann T, p. 335; The music for Movements 1-3 and the beginning of 4 is missing.

1. *Lk. ;*2:14; 7. Kaspar Ziegler, verse 4 of "Ich freue mich in dir," 1697 (Fischer-Tümpel, I, #567).

25 December ?1728, Leipzig; Parody: 4, 6 → BWV 197/6, 8.

BG 41; NBA I/2.

1. Chorus[1] [Dictum]

Glory to God in the highest, peace be on earth and unto men a sign of good favor.

2. Aria

Be telling, ye heavens, of God's great glory,
Ye feast days, make manifest now his might.

> But forget not, all the while,
> His affection, his great faith,
> Which he to them who are fallen extends.

3. Recit.[1]

Oh, love to which no love is like:
The high-exalted Son of God

Forsakes his heav'nly realm;
A prince forsakes the royal throne
And, here to serve,
Is born a wretched man amongst us,
So that the mortal race of man
Might not be lost forever;
What is thy due,
My faithful Jesus, now in turn?

4. Aria (A)

O thou lovely treasure dear,

> Raise thyself from this thy manger,
> Find instead upon my lips now
> And in this my heart thy place.

5. Recit. (B)

The child is mine,
And I am his,
Thou art the sum of all my substance;
Besides thee shall
With me
No wealth, no jewel find good favor.
In want I'll have abundant store,
In sadness
I'll have gladness,[2]
When I'm sick, he healeth me,
When I'm weak, he lifteth me,
When I'm astray, he seeketh me,
And when I falter, he holds me,
Yea, when I at the last must die,
He bringeth me to life in heaven;
Beloved store, through thee
To me yet in the world shall heaven itself be given.

6. Aria (B)

I'll not let thee go,
I'll close thee within
My heart now through faith and affection.

And thee, O my light,
No torment, no pain,
Yea, not even hell shall steal from me.

7. Chorale (S, A, T, B)

Lead on, 'tis my desire
To cleave to thee, O Jesus,
E'en though the world should break
Into a thousand pieces.
O Jesus, thou, just thou,
Thou art my life alone;
In thee, alone in thee,
My Jesus, will I sleep.

---

1. This title, lacking in the PT, is added by Neumann T.
2. *Leide/Freude* rhymes.

BWV 198 Laß, Fürstin, laß noch einen Strahl (Trauerode)

Funeral of Queen Christiane Eberhardine of Saxony, wife of the Elector Augustus II.

Johann Christoph Gottsched; PT (Leipzig, 1727); Facs: Neumann T, p. 396; Reprint (Leipzig, 1728); also in Sicul, *Das Thränende Leipzig*, (Leipzig, 1727); *Annales Lipsienses, Sectio XXXI* (1730); *Oden der Deutschen Gesellschafft* (new ed. 1728); Facs: Neumann T, p. 366.

17 October 1727, Leipzig; Parody: 1, 3, 5, 8, 10 → *St. Mark
Passion*, BWV 247/1, 49, 27, 59, 131; 1, 10 →   BWV 244a/1, 7.
BG 13, 3: NBA I/38.

Funeral Ode

First Part

1. Chorus (S, A, T, B)

Let, Princess, let still one more glance
Shoot forth from Salem's starry heavens.
And see how many tearful offerings
We pour around thy monument.

2. Recit. (S)

Thy Saxons, like thy saddened Meissen,[1]
Stand numb beside thy royal tomb;
The eye doth weep, the tongue cries out:
My pain must be without description!
Here mourn August[2] and Prince and land,
The nobles moan, the commons sorrow,
How much for thee thy folk lamented
As soon as it thy fall perceived!

3. Aria (S)

Be mute, be mute, ye lovely lyres!

> No sound could to the nations' woe
> At their dear cherished mother's death,
> O painful word!, give meet expression.

4. Recit. (A)

The tolling of the trembling bells
Shall our lamenting souls' great terror
Through their rebounding bronze awaken
And pierce us to the very core.
Oh, would that now this anxious peeling,
Which on our ears each day doth shrill,
To all the European world
A witness of our grief might render!

5. Aria (A)

How died our Lady so content!

>   How valiantly her spirit struggled,
>   For her the arm of death did vanquish
>   Before it did her breast subdue.

6. Recit. (T)

Her living let the art of dying
With ever steadfast skill be seen;
It would have been impossible
Before her death that she grow pallid.
Ah, blessed he whose noble soul
Doth raise itself above our nature,
At crypt and coffin doth not tremble,
When him his maker calls to part.

7. Chorus (S, A, T, B)

In thee, thou model of great women,
In thee, illustrious royal queen,
In thee, thou keeper of the faith,
The form of kindness was to witness.

Second Part

8. Aria (T)

Eternity's sapphiric house,
O Princess, these thy cheerful glances
From our own low estate now draweth
And blots out earth's corrupted form.
A brilliant light a hundred suns make,
Which doth our day to mid of night
And doth our sun to darkness turn,
Hath thy transfigured head surrounded.

9. Recit.—Arioso—Recit. (B)

What wonder this? This thou hast earned,
Thou model of all queens forever!
For thou wast meant to win the glory
Which hath transfigured now thy head.
Before the lamb's own throne thou wearest
Instead of purple's vanity
A pearl-white robe of purity
And scornest now the crown forsaken.
As far the brimming Vistula,
The Dniester and the Warth are flowing,
As far the Elb' and Muld' are streaming,
Extol thee / both the / town and land.
Thy Torgau[3] walketh now in mourning,
Thy Pretzsch[4] is weary, pale and weak;
For with the loss it hath in thee,
It loseth all it vision's rapture.

10. Chorus ultimus (S, A, T, B)

No, royal queen! Thou shalt not die;
We see in thee our great possession;

Posterity shall not forget thee,
Till all this universe shall fall.
Ye poets, write! For we would read it:
She hath been virtue's property
Her loyal subjects' joy and fame,
Of royal queens the crown and glory.

---

1.   The southernmost of three towns on the Elbe mentioned in the poem.

2.   Pronounce with the accent on the second syllable, as in German.

3.   A town of Saxony on the Elbe.

4.   Another town on the Elbe, down river from Torgau, halfway to Wittenberg.

BWV 199 **Mein Herze schwimmt im Blut**

Eleventh Sunday after Trinity.

Georg Christian Lehms, *Gottgefälliges Kirchen-Opffer* (Darmstadt, 1711); Facs: Neumann T, p. 260.

6. Johann Heermann, verse 3 of "Wo soll ich fliehen hin," 1630 (Fischer-Tümpel, I, #322).

12 August 1714, Weimar; several performances after 1714.

NBG XIII, 2; NBA I/20.

1. Recit. (S)

My heart is bathed in blood,
For now my sins' great brood
Within God's holy vision

A monster makes of me.
And now my conscience feels the pain:
For me my sins can nought
But hell's own hangmen be.
O hated night of sin!
Thou, thou alone
Hast brought me into such distress;
And thou, thou wicked seed of Adam,
Dost rob my soul of all its peace
And shuts to it the heav'nly gate!
Ah! What unheard-of pain!
My dried and wasted heart
Will after this no comfort moisten,[1]
And I must hide myself before him
Before whom very angels must conceal their faces.

2. Aria and Recitative (S)

Silent sighing, quiet mourning,
Ye may all my pains be telling,
For my mouth is tightly closed.

> And ye humid springs of weeping
> Could a certain witness offer
> To my sinful heart's remorse.

My heart is now a well of tears,
My eyes are heated sources.
Ah God! Who will give thee then satisfaction?

3. Recit. (S)

But God to me shall gracious be,
For I my head with ashes,
My countenance with tears am bathing,
My heart in grief and pain am beating

And filled with sadness say now:
God be this sinner gracious!
Ah yes! His heart shall break
And my own soul shall say:

4. Aria (S)

Deeply bowed and filled with sorrow
I lie, dearest God, 'fore thee.

> I acknowledge all my guilt,
> But have patience still with me,
> Have thou patience still with me!

5. Recit. (S)

Amidst these pains of grief
To me comes now this hopeful word:

6. Chorale (S)

I, thy sore-troubled child,
Cast every sin of mine,
All ye which hide within me
And me so fiercely frighten,
Into thine own deep wounds now,
Where I've e'er found salvation.

7. Recit. (S)

I lay myself into these wounds now
As though upon a very crag;
They shall be now my resting place.
Upon them will I firm in faith be soaring,
In them content and happy singing:

8. Aria (S)

How joyful is my heart,
For God is reconciled
And for my grief and pain
No more shall me from bliss
Nor from his heart exclude.

---

1. Instead of *befeuchten* "moisten,'" NBG XIII, 2 reads *befruchten* "fertile"

BWV 200 **Bekennen will ich seinen Namen**

The Purification of the Blessed Virgin Mary (The Presentation of Christ in the Temple).

Poet unknown (fragmentary).

After 1735, perhaps in the 1740's (so Dürr, p. 545).

C. F. Peters (1935); NBA I/28.

---

1. Aria (A)

Acknowledge will I his name's honor,
He is the Lord, he is the Christ,
In whom the seed of every nation
Salvation and redemption hath.
No death robs me of confidence:
The Lord is of my life the light.[1]

---

1. This text is an adaptation of the "Song of Simeon" (the "Nunc dimittis"),
   Lk. 2:29-32.

CPSIA information can be obtained
at www.ICGtesting.com
Printed in the USA
LVHW041204020820
662185LV00001B/15